BESTSELLING BOOK SERIES

Working After Retirement For Dummies®

P9-EMN-903

Questions to Ask a Career Counselor

Career counselors can steer you into the right kind of job that you'll enjoy in retirement, but you have to see one and ask the right questions to get the right direction. Use this list as a guide when you visit a career counselor:

- How do I decide what type of work I want to do now that I'm retired?
- How do I write a resumé and how much of my work history should I include?
- How do I know what to write in a cover letter?
- How do I manage the interview process?
- How should I prepare for an interview?
- How can I network with people in fields in which I am interested?
- Should I think about going back to school to retrain?
- How do I find out which organizations are hiring retirees in my area?

Questions to Ask a Financial Advisor?

Your portfolio management and withdrawal strategies can be much different in retirement. Visit a reputable financial advisor and get his or her take on the following:

- How do you set your fees?
- Do you get commissions from the products you recommend?
- To which professional association do you belong?
- Have you ever been disciplined by the SEC, the NASD, or other regulator?
- What type of clients do you normally work with?
- What is your investment philosophy?
- What kind of performance can I expect on my portfolio?
- How will you achieve that performance?
- What type of investments do you prefer?
- How do you minimize risk?
- Will you rebalance my portfolio regularly?
- What types of reports will I get about my portfolio and how often will I get them?
- Will you be available if I were to call about a tax or risk question?
- Will we sit down regularly to review my portfolio or do I need to call for an appointment when I want one?
- Can you tell me why the last two clients who you lost decided to switch their portfolio manager to someone else?
- Have you asked a client to seek services from someone else? And why?

For Dummies: Bestselling Book Series for Beginners

Working After Retirement For Dummies®

Cheat Sheet

Designing Your Resumé

Use a resumé that features a functional description of your job history, as well as gives a chronological history. That way you can focus on your skills directly related to the type of position you want. Here are the key parts of that type of resumé (aside from "Contact info," you can actually name these parts as I've labeled them below: Summary, Experience, and so on):

- **Contact info:** Centered at the top you should include your name, address, telephone number, and email address.
- **Highlights or Summary:** Summarize the highlights of your career. Include key words found in the employer's position description as you describe your knowledge and skills. Revise this section as needed for each job application.
- **Experience:** Don't list your job history in this section. Instead prepare a series of paragraphs that talk about your skills and prove that you have the skills needed for the job advertised.
- **Work History:** Use this section to provide a list of your previous jobs in chronological order. Each job can be just one line that includes your job title, your company, and your dates of employment. You don't have to go back more than 10 years, but if the jobs most related to what you want to do now were positions you held earlier in life then include them. Also include volunteer work related to the type of job you now want.
- **Education:** List your degrees and the schools you attended with any related information about your course emphasis.
- **Certifications or Technical Skills:** If you have related certifications or technical skills that are relevant to the type of job you seek, include them in this section.

Finding Job Listings

You may find barriers to your job search because of your age. Here are web resources that provide information and job listings specifically for people aged 50 and older:

- **AARP (www.aarp.org):** This site finds the best employers to work for through its, "Best Employers for Workers Over 50 Program." Find out more about this program at www.aarp.org/money/careers/employerresourcecenter/bestemployers/.
- **Experience Works (www.experienceworks.org):** Experience Works provides low income seniors with training and job placement. If you qualify you can even earn while you train by working in community service positions.
- **Maturity Works (www.maturityworks.org):** On this site, you can find a database of job postings for the senior network run by the National Council on Aging.
- **Senior Job Bank (www.seniorjobbank.org):** This job bank lists hundreds of jobs available for seniors each day. Access to the site is free for seniors. You'll find a wide variety of jobs are available, from entry level to senior executive.
- **Seniors4Hire (www.seniors4hire.org):** Seniors4Hire provides access to job listings for free as long as you are at least 50 years old.
- **Your Encore (www.yourencore.com):** This site lists short-term projects for scientists and engineers who are retired. Projects usually involve solving a specific problem.
- **Employment Network for Retired Government Experts (www.enrge.us):** This site helps former U.S. government workers find work after retirement in the private sector. You must be a retired federal, state, or local government employee or a government employee within 12 months of a scheduled retirement, to use this free service.

For Dummies: Bestselling Book Series for Beginners

Working After Retirement

FOR

DUMMIES®

by Lita Epstein

BICENTENNIAL
1807
WILEY
2007
BICENTENNIAL

Wiley Publishing, Inc.

Working After Retirement For Dummies®

Published by
Wiley Publishing, Inc.
111 River St.
Hoboken, NJ 07030-5774
www.wiley.com

WILEY

About the Author

Lita Epstein, MBA, excels at translating complex financial topics critical to people's everyday life. She enjoys helping people develop good financial, investing, and tax-planning skills. She designs and teaches online courses on topics such as investing for retirement, getting ready for tax time, and finance and investing for women.

Lita lives in a 55-plus community in Florida and works (and plays) with many people who moved there after retirement, but for various reasons have gone back to work. Some because they were bored, but many because their money just isn't going as far as they thought. Others have gone back to work to get access to group health insurance, because it is just too expensive to buy on an individual basis.

Lita has over a dozen books on the market, including *Streetwise Crash Course MBA, Streetwise Retirement Planning,* and *Alpha Teach Yourself Retirement Planning in 24 Hours,* as well as books on Social Security and Medicare. Lita also is a faculty member in the College of Graduate Business and Management at the University of Phoenix.

She was the content director for the financial services Web site, MostChoice.com, and managed the Web site Investing for Women. She also wrote TipWorld's Mutual Fund Tip of the Day in addition to columns about mutual fund trends for numerous Web sites.

Author's Acknowledgments

Many people were involved in making this book a reality. First, a special thank you to Tracy Boggier, my acquisitions editor at Wiley, who successfully championed this book through the editorial board process. Also at Wiley, a special thanks to Jennifer Connolly, my project editor, whose helpful and insightful comments, as well as her expert editing, helped make this book the best it could be. In addition, I want to thank my agent, Jessica Faust, who helps me regularly with all my book projects. And finally, last but not least, my husband, H.G. Wolpin, who puts up with all my craziness as I try to meet deadlines.

Publisher's Acknowledgments

We're proud of this book; please send us your comments through our Dummies online registration form located at www.dummies.com/register/.

Some of the people who helped bring this book to market include the following:

Acquisitions, Editorial, and Media Development

Project Editor: Jennifer Connolly

Acquisitions Editor: Tracy Boggier

Copy Editor: Jennifer Connolly

Technical Editor: Rob Moritz

Editorial Manager: Michelle Hacker

Editorial Supervisor: Carmen Krikorian

Editorial Assistant: Erin Calligan, Joe Niesen, David Lutton, and Leann Harney

Cover Photos: © Comstock Images

Cartoons: Rich Tennant (www.the5thwave.com)

Composition Services

Project Coordinator: Erin Smith

Layout and Graphics: Carl Byers, Joyce Haughey, Shane Johnson, Stephanie D. Jumper, Barry Offringa, Laura Pence

Anniversary Logo Design: Richard Pacifico

Proofreaders: Melanie Hoffman, Charles Spencer, Techbooks

Indexer: Techbooks

Publishing and Editorial for Consumer Dummies

Diane Graves Steele, Vice President and Publisher, Consumer Dummies

Joyce Pepple, Acquisitions Director, Consumer Dummies

Kristin A. Cocks, Product Development Director, Consumer Dummies

Michael Spring, Vice President and Publisher, Travel

Kelly Regan, Editorial Director, Travel

Publishing for Technology Dummies

Andy Cummings, Vice President and Publisher, Dummies Technology/General User

Composition Services

Gerry Fahey, Vice President of Production Services

Debbie Stailey, Director of Composition Services

Contents at a Glance

Introduction 1

Part 1: Getting Ready to Retire . . . Not! 7
Chapter 1: The World of Work After Retirement 9
Chapter 2: Why You May Need or Want to Go Back to Work 19
Chapter 3: Assessing Your Talents for Your Next Job 31
Chapter 4: Seeking Help to Determine What You'd Like to Do Next 41

Part 11: Your Wallet to Your Health: The 411
When You Re-Enter the Workforce 55
Chapter 5: Getting a Grasp on Managing What You Saved for Retirement 57
Chapter 6: Managing Your Money So It Doesn't Run Out 77
Chapter 7: Collecting Social Security and Going Back to Work 93
Chapter 8: Delaying Social Security and Working 109
Chapter 9: Trying to Stay Healthy — Before Age 65 125
Chapter 10: Exploring Medicare's Maze of Benefits 139

Part 111: Finding Your Next Job 163
Chapter 11: Rebuilding Your Job Search Skills 165
Chapter 12: Surviving the Interview — Especially Those Tough Questions 179
Chapter 13: Overcoming Myths About Older Workers During Your Job Search 193
Chapter 14: Working 9 to 5 or Not! Exploring Your Hourly Options 201

Part 1V: Revisiting Your Former Career
or Starting Your Own Business 217
Chapter 15: Staying on the Job Part-Time 219
Chapter 16: Consulting for Your Former Company 233
Chapter 17: Consulting in Your Former Industry 245
Chapter 18: Buying or Starting Your Own Business or Franchise 261

Part V: Knowledge to Philanthropy: Opportunities
to Broaden the Mind and More 287
Chapter 19: Going Back to College: Expanding Your Knowledge and Skills 289
Chapter 20: Volunteering in the Business and Community World 303

Part VI: The Part of Tens 323

Chapter 21: Top Ten Companies to Work for in Retirement 325

Chapter 22: Top Ten Skills for Running Your Own Business 331

Chapter 23: Ten (Almost) Great Volunteering Experiences
to Take Advantage Of 337

Index 341

Table of Contents

Introduction *1*

About This Book..2
Foolish Assumptions 2
What You're Not to Read 3
How This Book Is Organized..3
    Part I: Getting Ready to Retire . . . Not!.......................3
    Part II: Your Wallet to Your Health: The 411
       When You Re-Enter the Workforce 3
    Part III: Finding Your Next Job 4
    Part IV: Revisiting Your Former Career
       or Starting Your Own Business 4
    Part V: Knowledge to Philanthropy: Opportunities
       to Broaden the Mind and More 4
    Part VI: The Part of Tens 4
Icons Used in This Book..5
Where to Go from Here...5

Part I: Getting Ready to Retire . . . Not! *7*

Chapter 1: The World of Work After Retirement **9**

Making that Critical Decision — Stay Retired or Go Back to Work 9
    Needing or wanting to work...10
    Assessing your talents..11
    Figuring out what you want to do 11
Managing Your Money and Your Health.................................12
    Taking inventory on what you have.................................12
    Keeping yourself solvent 12
    Sorting out the rules of Social Security and work...........13
    Staying healthy with and without Medicare 14
Going Job Hunting...14
Working Less Than Full Time 15
Revisiting Your Past or Starting Your Own Business...............15
    Working for your company — again 16
    Following your dream of owning your own business.........16
Expanding Your Horizons...17

Chapter 2: Why You May Need or Want to Go Back to Work 19

Facing the Financial Facts 19
Lost nest egg 20
Reduced pension payments...23
Didn't save enough..24
Maintaining Your Lifestyle in Retirement....................................25
Budgeting for specific phases of retirement.....................25
Knowing what to budget for 26
Losing Professional Contact . . . or Just Getting Bored 28
Keeping your professional network alive..........................28
Finding a new network of retired professionals 29
Going back to school 29
Teaching others in your field..30

Chapter 3: Assessing Your Talents for Your Next Job 31

Determining Your Strengths and Weaknesses...........................31
Assessing Your Last Job 32
Uncovering Your Worker Type 33
Determining your working type...33
Understanding your worker type 35
Using How You Like to Work to Find the Ideal Job 38
Working autonomously..38
Needing direction 38
Working in teams 39
Applying Your Skill Sets..39
Carving Out Your Creative Talents 40

Chapter 4: Seeking Help to Determine
What You'd Like to Do Next 41

Talking with Someone One on One..41
Seeing the need for a career counselor 41
Finding a career counselor...42
Determining what to talk about...44
Testing Your Values, Interests, Personality, and Skills 45
Exploring your values 45
Determining your interests 46
Taking personality tests 47
Taking skills assessments...48
Networking with others 48
How to build your network 49
Online job networks for seniors 50
Joining a Support Group 52
Uncovering how support groups work...............................52
Finding support groups near you..54

Part II: Your Wallet to Your Health: The 411 When You Re-Enter the Workforce 55

Chapter 5: Getting a Grasp on Managing What You Saved for Retirement 57

Exploring Your Retirement Accounts 57
    Defined contributions versus defined benefits 58
    Pensions (defined-benefit plan) 58
    Employer savings plans (defined-contribution plans) 62
    IRAs 64
Taking Out Your Money — the Official Rules 66
    When you must start to draw money 66
    How much you must withdraw 68
Investing the Money You Have 71
    Avoiding common mistakes 71
    Allocating your investments 72
    Changing your strategies as you age 75

Chapter 6: Managing Your Money So It Doesn't Run Out 77

Determining Your Budget 77
    Budgeting for each phase of retirement 78
    Accounting for everything 78
    Developing a retirement budget 82
Planning Your Withdrawal Strategies 82
    Tracking everything 83
    Exploring what you have 84
Allocating Your Assets and Withdrawing Safely 87
    Checking out the chart 87
    Following an example 89
Calculating Whether Your Income Is Enough 90
Dealing with Taxes 91
    Taxation of your pensions 91
    Taxation of your retirement savings 92

Chapter 7: Collecting Social Security and Going Back to Work 93

Working and Collecting 93
    Following the rules 93
    Figuring benefits if you retire early 94
Impacting Your Current Benefits by Going Back to Work 96
    Understanding the Retired Earnings Test (RET) basics 96
    Reviewing the rules 97
    Calculating how much you can lose 98
    Getting special treatment in your first year of retirement 99

Increasing Benefits When You Go Back to Work 100
Starting Your Own Business and Social Security Benefits 101
Complicating Your Taxes...102
How Social Security benefits are taxed 102
Calculating your income...103
Taxes on pensions and retirement savings when collecting 106
What isn't taxed?...107

Chapter 8: Delaying Social Security and Working **109**
Taking a Look at Pension Legislation 109
Checking out the past on pensions...110
Looking to the future 111
Going the way of dinosaurs..112
Understanding the fate of your funds..113
Retiring Early — Not Eligible to Collect Social Security 115
Taking pensions while still working for your company................115
Withdrawing employer retirement savings.....................................117
Continuing to save 117
Delaying Benefits — Deciding Not to Collect 119
Improving future Social Security benefits 119
Understanding the benefit of delaying benefits 120
Calculating your best time to start collecting Social Security 122
Deciding not to wait any longer..123

Chapter 9: Trying to Stay Healthy — Before Age 65 ....**125**
Exploring Health Insurance Types...125
Group health plans..126
Losing a Group Plan..129
COBRA 131
Association health plans 132
AARP 132
Individual health plans 133
State guaranteed issue health insurance pools..............................133
Finding and Paying for Health Insurance . . .
After You Retire but Before Medicare 134
Researching coverage exclusions 134
Finding insurance coverage 135
Uncovering hidden costs..136
Figuring Out When Your Health Coverage Will End...............................137

Chapter 10: Exploring Medicare's Maze of Benefits **139**
Getting Started with Medicare..139
Starting coverage...140
Missing Medicare deadlines...140
Facing penalties 141
Delaying coverage because you're covered at work 141

Traditional Medicare — Parts A and B 142
    Part A 142
    Part B 145
Medicare Advantage Plans — Part C 148
    Examining the plans 148
    Figuring out which plan is best for you 150
Prescription Coverage — Part D 150
    Demystifying the basic drug benefit 151
    Obtaining Plan D prescription coverage 152
    Knowing what to do if you have drug coverage
       from another source 153
    Ensuring the drugs you take are covered 155
    Finding the right plan for you — it can happen! 156
    Adding up the costs 156
    Paying for Part D coverage 157
Paying for Things Medicare Doesn't Cover 158
    Medicare Advantage Plans 158
    Medigap 158
    Long-term healthcare 160
Getting Medicare Coverage, If You Don't Qualify 161

Part III: Finding Your Next Job **163**

Chapter 11: Rebuilding Your Job Search Skills **165**
Building Your Resumé 165
    Keeping up with change 166
    Preparing your resumé 167
    Using the employer's needs 168
    Emphasizing accomplishments 170
    Avoiding dating yourself 170
    Taking advantage of writing tips 171
Formatting Your Resumé 171
Using Your Network 173
Tapping the Internet 174
    Scouring job-listing sites 174
    Checking in on company Web sites 175
Looking through the Classifieds 176
    Newspapers 176
    Grocery stores 177
    Senior centers 177
    Churches or synagogues 177
Counting on Your Support Groups 177
    Senior centers 178
    Health centers 178
    Churches or synagogues 178

Chapter 12: Surviving the Interview —
Especially Those Tough Questions 179

Getting Ready for the Interview Mentally 179
    Understanding the need to stay calm..............................180
    Reducing stress before an interview 180
Reviewing the Basics for Answering Interview Questions 182
Answering Basic Questions 183
    Getting to know you..184
    Testing your knowledge of the company 184
    Sizing up your longevity 184
Dealing with the Tough Questions....................................185
    How to deal with qualification questions, like 186
    How to deal with longevity questions, like 188
Preparing an Interview Checklist.....................................190

Chapter 13: Overcoming Myths About Older Workers
During Your Job Search 193

Going Toe to Toe with Training Myths 193
    Emphasizing your ability to learn 194
    Leveraging your longevity......................................194
Poking Holes in Productivity Myths 195
    Pointing out your increased productivity........................195
    Advertising your adaptability...................................196
    Capitalizing on your creativity 197
Coping with Cost Myths 198
    Keeping reality in check when it comes to your paycheck 198
    Telling the truth about benefit costs 199
    Accident costs are higher for older workers 200

Chapter 14: Working 9 to 5 or Not! Exploring
Your Hourly Options 201

Seeking Part-Time Work 201
    Considering your needs and wants...............................202
    Finding the best of the best for part-time work
    and flexible schedules...203
Finding Temporary Agencies that Specialize in 50+ workers.................206
    Working with the nation's largest senior placement
    and training service...207
    Using online resources 208
    Finding work if you're a scientist or engineer 210
    Searching for jobs if you're a retired government expert 210
Telecommuting — Not Telemarketing!..................................210
    Understanding telecommuting 211
    Finding a telecommuting job 211

Most Popular Part-Time Jobs for Older Workers 212
    Bank teller 212
    Customer greeters 212
    English instructor 213
    College or university faculty member 213
    Floral assistant 214
    Home care aides 214
    Mystery shopping 215
    Teacher's assistant 215
    Tour guide 216

Part IV: Revisiting Your Former Career or Starting Your Own Business 217

Chapter 15: Staying on the Job Part-Time 219

Switching to Part-Time 219
    Developing a restructuring plan 220
    Proposing the change 221
Sharing Your Job 221
    Finding the right fit 222
    Creating a winning job-sharing team 223
Telecommuting from Home 224
Convincing Your Boss 225
    Taking steps in the right direction 225
    Finding help online 226
Proposing an Independent Contractor Arrangement 226
Going Back to Work as a Temporary Worker 229
Using a Phased Retirement Arrangement 230

Chapter 16: Consulting for Your Former Company 233

Understanding Consulting 233
    Checking out the advantages 234
    Reviewing the required skills 234
    Seeing how consultants work 235
    Learning how to listen 236
Starting to Talk with Your Employer About Consulting 237
Researching Compensation Issues 237
    Researching fee structures 237
    Setting your fees 238
Negotiating Contracts 240
    Confidentiality 240
    Expenses 243
    Deadlines 243
Getting Paid 244
    Activity log 244
    Invoices 244

Chapter 17: Consulting in Your Former Industry **245**

Being Your Own Boss After Retiring — Try Consulting 245
Assessing Your Skills to Be a Consultant in Your Industry 246
Picking Your Niche 247
Building and Using Your Network 247
    Finding contacts for your network 247
    Getting to know your contacts 248
    Becoming a known entity 248
    Becoming someone to recommend 249
Understanding Your Non-Compete Clauses 249
Pricing Your Services 250
    Networking with others to gather pricing details 250
    Setting your price 250
Writing Your Contracts 251
    Finding an attorney 251
    Understanding contract parts 252
    Designing your contracts 255
Writing Proposals 256
Setting Up a Successful Consulting Business 257
    Developing a business plan 257
    Networking effectively 257
    Following-up regularly 258

**Chapter 18: Buying or Starting Your
Own Business or Franchise** **261**

Starting Your Own Business 261
    Supplementing your retirement 262
    Funding your retirement 263
    Getting started — developing a business plan 265
    Marketing your business 266
    Funding your business 267
    Deciding your business location 269
Buying an Existing Business 269
    Deciding what type of business to buy 270
    Finding businesses for sale 271
    Assessing the value of a business 272
    Intending to buy, but 278
    Funding the purchase of a business 278
Finding a Franchise 279
    What is franchising? 279
    Finding franchise opportunities 282
    Key things to consider before signing a contract 283
    Funding requirements 285

Part V: Knowledge to Philanthropy: Opportunities to Broaden the Mind and More 287

Chapter 19: Going Back to College: Expanding Your Knowledge and Skills 289
Popular Senior Learning Opportunities 290
    Elderhostel 290
    TraveLearn 291
    Osher Lifelong Learning Institute (OLLI) 292
    SeniorNet 293
    Local community colleges 294
    Learning online 294
Learning Abroad 295
    University of Strathclyde's Senior Studies Institute 295
    Adult Residential Colleges Association (ARCA) 296
    Archaeology Abroad 296
    Adult cultural program — France 297
    Taking art in Italy 298
    Learning a language 298
Becoming a Teacher Yourself 298
Starting Your Own Learning Group 300
    Forming a book club 300
    Putting together a travel group 301
    Starting an investment club 301

Chapter 20: Volunteering in the Business and Community World 303
Understanding That You Have Something to Offer 303
Being a Volunteer in the Business World 304
    SCORE 304
    Volunteers in Medicine clinics 305
    Small-business incubators 305
Helping Out in Your Community 306
    Executive Service Corps Affiliate Network 306
    AARP 307
    Environmental Alliance for Senior Involvement 310
    Experience Corps 311
    Generations United 311
    North Carolina Center for Creative Retirement 312
    OASIS 313
    Senior Corps 314
Volunteering Internationally 315
    Earthwatch Institute 315
    Global Citizens Network 316
    Global Volunteers 317

Globe Aware 318
Landscope Expeditions 318
LiFeline..319
Orphanage Outreach...321
Volunteering Virtually...321

Part VI: The Part of Tens 323

Chapter 21: Top Ten Companies to Work for in Retirement 325

Business Services...325
Cars 325
Consulting Services 326
Education 326
Entertainment..327
Financial Services 328
Healthcare..328
Industrial Equipment 329
Pharmaceuticals...329
Retailing/Direct Selling 330

Chapter 22: Top Ten Skills for Running Your Own Business 331

Administrative Skills..331
Decision Making 332
Financial Skills 332
Industry-Specific Skills 332
People Management..333
Physical and Emotional Stamina.......................333
Problem Solving 333
Self-Motivation..334
Sales and Marketing..334
Time Management...335

Chapter 23: Ten (Almost) Great Volunteering Experiences to Take Advantage Of 337

Advocate 337
Business Executive 338
Caregiver 338
Environmentalist 339
Home-Based 339
Internationalist 339
Medical Professional..340
Park Enthusiast 340

Index 341

Introduction

. . . .

Can you imagine yourself sunning by the pool, playing cards, or golfing with friends and then eating out — all day, everyday for the rest of your life? That might sound great when you first start doing it, but few people find they want to keep doing it for the 20 to 30 years they will likely live in retirement.

More and more of today's retirees are choosing to go back to work, whether it's because they need the money, they need access to healthcare insurance, or they just want to do something more productive. Many are choosing to start their own business from their homes just to avoid getting back into the day-to-day grind — and the politics — of working in a traditional job.

Others are going back to work part-time in a totally new field to try something new or just to bring in some extra cash. Still others are going back to work full time, many in service environments where they don't make much more than minimum wage but need to get access to group health insurance.

I fit into the category of someone who was downsized just before the age of 50 and had to decide what to do next. I decided I wanted to work from home and started my own writing business. As you can see, I'm still at it.

Actually I started to work on building that business even before being laid off because it was a direction that I'd hoped to take at some point in the future. That point of decision came sooner than expected when I was laid off after the dot.com I was working for imploded, but I've never regretted it. I love being my own boss and deciding what I want to do next and when I want to do it.

That's true for many people once they reach the age of 50. I live and work in a 55-plus active-adult community with neighbors all around me that chose to work again. Some work from home as consultants for their former company or for others in their former industry; others choose to start their own home-based businesses.

Many work for Disney World, who has been so successful recruiting from my community that they set up shop here one day a month to recruit both full- and part-time workers. My neighbors enjoy the ticket and merchandise benefits, which they use when their families visit. Most work part-time, but those who need access to healthcare insurance often choose to work full-time. The money may not be great, just barely over minimum wage, but the benefits make up for it.

Scenarios like this one repeat themselves in communities all over the country as baby boomers reach retirement age. You've probably seen many articles written about how baby boomers are changing the meaning of the word retirement. It's true, and companies are changing the way they think of retirement as well.

About This Book

In *Working After Retirement For Dummies,* I introduce you to alternative ways to work after retirement, as well as talk about things you must consider to live in retirement — how to manage your finances, your retirement portfolio, and your healthcare.

More and more companies are creating alternatives to traditional retirement, making it possible for people to work part-time and collect partial retirement benefits. Others find they need the brain power of all the baby boomers whose decisions to retire are draining these companies of years of needed experience, so they are finding creative ways to keep them involved after retirement through mentor programs, consulting, part-time work, or other innovative programs.

Throughout this book, I explore the various work alternatives and give you the ammunition you need to look for a new job or run your own business. Most people over the age of 50 face some job discrimination and must respond to the myths about our age group, so I help you deal with those challenges as well.

Although I'd love for you to read this book from cover to cover, you don't have to. Because this is a reference book, you can pick and choose what you want or need to read. Throughout *Working After Retirement For Dummies,* I've included information that might be of interest to only some readers depending on their individual choices. For example, if you want to start your own business, you won't need to read about how to write a resume or deal with tough interview questions. You can easily pick and choose the topics that are most relevant to you and skip chapters that don't match your particular situation. Of course, you won't be penalized for reading everything!

Foolish Assumptions

While writing this book, I made some key assumptions about who you are and why you've picked up this book to plan your work life after retirement:

✔ You're a retiree who just found out that their pension will be much less than expected and now must consider going back to work.

✔ You're a retiree who just can't afford to pay for healthcare insurance or can't get access to it at all, so you must find a way back into a group health insurance package by going back to work.

✔ You're a retiree who wants to do more than just play cards, golf, or swim and is looking for more intellectual stimulation either by working, volunteering, or maybe going back to school.

What You're Not to Read

You don't have to read the paragraphs marked tech stuff or those gray-shaded boxes. That's extra information you might find interesting, but isn't required for you to understand the points I'm making.

How This Book Is Organized

Working After Retirement For Dummies is divided into six parts, which I outline in the sections that follow.

Part 1: Getting Ready to Retire . . . Not!

In Part I, I discuss the reasons people are going back to work, offer you tools for how to assess your own skills and interests, and then talk about how to figure out what you want to do next.

Part II: Your Wallet to Your Health: The 411 When You Re-Enter the Workforce

In Part II, I focus on your pocketbook and your healthcare. I help you sort out how much money you do have available in retirement and figure out how to be sure you don't run out of money during retirement. I also introduce you to the maze of healthcare and insurance issues that you'll face in retirement. I do split that into two discussions — one for people who retired early and don't have Medicare and a second for people who do have Medicare. In addition, I introduce you to the Social Security maze and discuss tax impacts for retirees.

Part III: Finding Your Next Job

In Part III, I talk about all the basics you need to find your next job. I start with ideas for rebuilding your job search and interviewing skills. Then I talk about the myths you'll need to combat when looking for a job when you're over the age of 50 and give you ideas for how to fight back. Finally, I explore options to full-time work.

Part IV: Revisiting Your Former Career or Starting Your Own Business

In Part IV, I explore various ways to stay in your field or think about starting your own business. First I talk about alternatives to working full-time within your own company. Then I explore consulting for your former company or within your former industry. Finally, I talk about starting your own business, buying an existing business, or buying a franchise.

Part V: Knowledge to Philanthropy: Opportunities to Broaden the Mind and More

In Part V, I explore options for you to consider if you don't need the money, but want to go back to work to expand your knowledge or travel. First I explore various learning opportunities, then I talk about volunteering both in the United States and globally.

Part VI: The Part of Tens

The Part of Tens is the hallmark of the *For Dummies* series. In this part, I highlight the top ten companies to work for in retirement, the top ten business skills in retirement, and ten great volunteering experiences you may want to try.

Icons Used in This Book

For Dummies books use little pictures, called *icons,* to flag certain chunks of text that either you don't want to miss or you're free to skip. The icons in *Working After Retirement For Dummies* are

Look to this icon for ideas on how to improve your life in retirement, whether you are working, volunteering, or looking for ways to expand your knowledge and horizons.

This icon marks anything I want you to recall about working after retirement after you're finished reading this book.

This icon points out any aspect of working after retirement that comes with dangers or perils that could hurt the future of your retirement, whether it's financial, related to your healthcare, or related to your work choices.

The Technical Stuff icon points out material that generally can be as, well, technical. Although I think that the information is interesting, it's not vital to your understanding of the issue. You can skip it if you want to.

This icon alerts you to stories from retirees who started their own business after retirement with some quotes about their experiences while running their own business.

Where to Go from Here

Ready to start the rest of your life? It can be both exciting and nerve racking.

If you want to explore the basics of why you need to work and what you want to do next, then start with Part I. However, if you already know what you want to do, you may want to just jump into Part II and start with learning the tools to manage your money and healthcare.

You could just start with any chapter whose topic interests you the most. You don't have to read this book in order. You can start anywhere that you'd like. If, as you are reading a chapter, you find a brief discussion about a topic you don't know, you'll probably find a reference to another chapter that explores the topic more deeply.

Part I

Getting Ready to Retire . . . Not!

"Oh, we're doing just great. Philip and I are selling decorative jelly jars on the Web. I run the Web site and Philip sort of controls the inventory."

In this part . . .

Not quite ready to retire yet? Well, you're not alone. Many retirees need or want to go back to work. In this part, I review the reasons people are choosing to go back to work. I help you find tools to assess your strengths and weaknesses and then help you find resources that will aide you in figuring out what you want to do next.

Chapter 1

The World of Work After Retirement

In This Chapter

▶ Retiring or working

▶ Managing money and health

▶ Exploring work alternatives

▶ Running a business

▶ Expanding your knowledge

▶ Giving back to your community

As you face the fact that you'll probably be living 20 to 30 or more years in retirement and begin to realize that it's a long time to just play in retirement, you may start wondering whether that's really what you want to do for the rest of your life.

You also may wonder if you truly have the financial resources in place to fund that long of a period without working. Even if you do, you may wonder if you'll need more intellectual stimulation than you currently have planned.

In this chapter, I introduce you to all the challenges you face as you plan your retirement years. You may decide retirement isn't all it's cracked up to be and consider the possibility of returning to work — whether it's because you need the money, you want to do something to give back to your community, or you want to explore options for stimulating yourself intellectually.

Making that Critical Decision — Stay Retired or Go Back to Work

After you get home from your final retirement party and you face a life without having to go into work every day, the initial sense of relief is wonderful.

But, when you continue to do that for weeks or months on end, you may end up deciding this is not how you want to spend the rest of your life.

While you may not want to go back to the daily grind of working 40 to 60 hours a week or more, you may find that you don't have enough money to maintain the lifestyle you've come to know and enjoy. You're now at cross-roads to decide whether or not to go back to work, how to go about doing that, and what you want to do.

Needing or wanting to work

Many newly retired people find they must face a difficult truth — their retirement nest egg just won't go as far as they thought it would, especially with healthcare costs rising twice as fast as incomes. That makes things even more difficult when you're on a fixed-income retirement budget with no chance for raises to cover those ever increasing costs. Here are some scenarios of why people need or want to go back to work:

✔ Without going back to work at least part-time to supplement your retirement income, you could quickly find that your spending money you thought would be available for entertainment and travel quickly disappears. As healthcare and other costs of living continue to rise during retirement, you could find that you don't even have enough money for the day-to-day basics you need.

✔ You've probably read stories in your local paper about seniors eating pet food in order to be able to afford their medicines. While Medicare prescription drug coverage helps to some extent, the infamous Medicare Part D *donut hole,* where all of a sudden seniors find they have no coverage for awhile, is still creating financial crises for many people dependent on a fixed income who can't afford monthly financial surprises.

✔ While healthcare expenses can be the biggest problem, people who worked for companies that were sold or went bankrupt can be hard hit too. Many of these people who expected a certain guaranteed pension find they're earning about half what they expected when the company switched to another type of employer-retirement plan, such as a cash-balance plan. Suddenly they find out that they have no choice but to go back to work to pay the bills.

✔ Others just have to admit they didn't save enough to keep up the lifestyle they've become accustomed to and want to continue to enjoy. Still others who thought they had equity of $500,000 to a million dollars in the home they bought 20 to 30 years ago and planned to use that for their retirement portfolio, found it's worth half what they expected as the housing bubble burst around the U.S. in 2006. I talk more about managing your retirement assets in Chapters 5 and 6.

✔ Money is not the only reason people choose to go back to work. Some find they miss the professional camaraderie they enjoyed in the workplace and want to return there to reconnect with their professional network.

✔ Some retirees decide they want to go back to school or teach to get the intellectual juices going. Throughout this book you'll find many alternatives you can consider to the traditional retirement of golfing, swimming, card playing, and periodic travel. You can either go back to work, volunteer, or go back to school and still be among the ranks of today's retirees.

Assessing your talents

Suppose you do make the choice that you want to earn some money, but you just can't face going back to the same old grind. You're ready for a complete job change doing anything but what you did before.

Or, you may just want to step out of your comfort zone and look for new and different ways to use your talents, but you've got to figure out what it is you want to do next. In Chapter 3, I introduce you to the resources you can access to assess your talents and determine your next steps.

You can use these tools to gauge your strengths and weaknesses and figure out what you truly enjoy doing and what you hate to do. You can also figure out how you like to work, whether it's alone or in teams and whether you like to work under the direction of someone else or if you prefer to be autonomous.

Figuring out what you want to do

After you've assessed yourself, you then need to figure out the type of job you want to do. In Chapter 4, you can find information about whether or not to seek a job counselor and how to find one.

I also give you pointers about how to set up an effective network to improve your professional contacts and tap into possible work opportunities. If you find you need the support of others, I introduce you to how support groups work and how to find them.

Managing Your Money and Your Health

Managing your retirement savings and pensions, especially after paying the ever-increasing costs of healthcare, can require a difficult balancing act. You certainly don't want to run out of money during retirement, so you want to be sure that the amount you take out each year leaves you with enough in your portfolio for your future needs as well.

If you've never managed a large investment portfolio before retirement, when you get a sizeable lump sum from rolling out your employer-sponsored retirement savings, you'll be faced with a daunting task of what to do with all that money.

You also could be faced with decisions about how to get and pay for health insurance, if you retire before you're eligible for Medicare.

Taking inventory on what you have

Your first step should be to take an inventory of what you do own in retirement savings and what cash flow you can expect from pensions. Then you need to learn rules that govern how and when you can start to use that money.

You also need to learn how to invest those assets wisely, so they'll continue to grow at an appropriate rate and help you to extend the life of your portfolio throughout your retirement years. I discuss how to do all that in Chapter 5. You'll find that your strategies for managing your portfolio will change as you age.

Keeping yourself solvent

Once you understand how to manage the funds, you then will need to develop withdrawal strategies for each type of retirement asset you have, whether it's an annuity, IRA, or traditional pension. You find the key things you need to consider in Chapter 6.

Another new set of rules you need to learn in retirement are the tax rules for your pension funds and retirement savings. I give you an overview of these critical rules and how to deal with them in Chapter 6.

Sorting out the rules of Social Security and work

If you do go back to work and have already started to collect from Social Security, the rules governing that can be a maze of confusion. You can work and collect your Social Security benefits after you've reached your full retirement age (which was 65 but is gradually increasing to 67) without facing a reduction in your benefits.

But, if you started collecting Social Security early before you reached full retirement age and then decide to go back to work, you will face a partial reduction in your Social Security benefits. I talk about all this and what you need to do in Chapter 7.

Completing your tax returns when you work and collect Social Security can be a bit more complicated. In some cases, your Social Security benefits may be taxed and in other situations they may not be, it all depends on how much income you have and how that income is derived. You can find more information on these tax issues in Chapter 7.

All the news is not bad though; you can improve your Social Security benefits for the rest of your life if you go back to work and replace some low-dollar earning years with years that you earn more money. That's because Social Security calculates benefits based on your highest 35 years of earnings. So, for example, if you stopped working for 10 to 20 years to raise a family, all those zero-dollar-earning years can get replaced with higher earnings as you work after retirement.

You can decide not to collect Social Security at all when you first retire even if you're eligible. If you're too young, you may not yet be eligible to apply for Social Security. Most people must wait at least until the age of 62. There are some exceptions to the rule, but that impacts very few and I won't go into those details here.

You do get a benefit for waiting though. If you delay collecting Social Security past full retirement age, your lifetime monthly benefit will go up every month until age 70. So if you plan to work until 70 and you'd like to increase your potential Social Security payment, you may want to delay collecting benefits until age 70, but don't wait any longer.

Your benefits won't increase any higher after age 70, except for cost of living adjustments. I discuss all these rules about delaying Social Security in Chapter 8.

Staying healthy with and without Medicare

Your health insurance will vary dramatically depending on whether or not you qualify for Medicare and have retiree health coverage through your former employer. If you're not eligible for Medicare, individual health insurance for many people age 50 or older will likely be more than $600 to $700. You can double those estimates if you and your spouse both need individual plans.

Many people 50 years and older have difficulty even getting individual health coverage because of their preexisting conditions. Even arthritis, which afflicts more than 50 percent of people over age 50, can result in a denial of coverage or a rider that won't cover anything the insurance deems related to arthritis. You can forget any coverage for joint-related medical needs.

Access to affordable group health insurance sends more people back to work after retirement than any other single issue. Some people I know who even have retiree group health coverage from their former employer find premiums and other out-of-pocket expenses they must pay skyrocketing, driving them back to work. Those who do not have access to group healthcare tend to look for a job that includes health insurance benefits.

Even friends who do have Medicare are finding that the premiums for Part B and D plus the required out-of-pocket expenses that are still required are eroding their monthly retirement income. They, too, have sought either part-time jobs or started a small home-based business to supplement their income primarily to pay medical-related expenses.

I talk about healthcare issues for people under age 65 in Chapter 9 and focus on Medicare and related issues for people 65 and older in Chapter 10.

Going Job Hunting

If you're going back to work after a long stint at the some company for most of your life, you probably haven't had to build a resume and look for a job in a very long time. The job market definitely changed dramatically and job-seeking skills are very different than ones you used many years ago.

As you look for a job today, you'll find that most companies prefer contact electronically, either by e-mail or by filling out an application online or both. You won't find many situations where telephone contact is encouraged early in the application process unless you find the opening through a friend who can give you contact information for the hiring manager.

Yes, it's true, networking is still the best way to get a job, but you'll still need to conform to the new resume rules and deal with what can sometimes be tough interview questions directed primarily at older workers. I talk about rebuilding your job search skills in Chapter 11.

I talk about difficult interview questions you may be asked and how to answer them in Chapter 12. Finally, in Chapter 13 you can read a discussion of the myths you'll need to combat during your job search. I give you some ammunition for detecting and responding to them as well, if they crop up during your job search.

Working Less Than Full Time

You don't have to go back to work full-time after retirement. More and more companies are adopting flexible hiring policies. You can usually find what you'd probably think of as traditional part-time work, but you may find the hours more flexible. You also could search for telecommuting jobs that will let you work primarily from your home.

If you don't want to guarantee your time year-round to a company, you will find temporary agencies that focus on serving the 50-plus age group. They can find you assignments that range from a few weeks to a few months.

You can find more details about flexible work alternatives in Chapter 14. You may also want to review the top ten companies to work for in Chapter 21, to get an idea of what some of the top companies offer older workers in benefits and flexibility to keep them happy and working.

In the 1980s and early 1990s many companies downsized and laid off older workers offering sizeable retirement packages to lure them to leave, you won't find that as common today. Many companies face a different problem — brain drain. They don't know how they'll be able to find enough qualified workers to replace those Baby Boomers who will be retiring.

Revisiting Your Past or Starting Your Own Business

Often after retiring, people realize they want to work for their company again or maybe even start their own business. In either case, you can find several opportunities to fit the bill.

Working for your company — again

Even if you've left your company, you may want to revisit working for them again either in a part-time position, as an independent contractor, or as a consultant. More and more companies are starting to offer phased retirement programs that let you cut back your hours and collect a partial retirement pension.

Others are allowing their workers to leave and roll out their 401(k) or other employer-based retirement savings. Once they've formally left and gotten their money, companies rehire them when they are ready to come back to work. This helps the worker, who can afford to cut back hours because he can then supplement his part-time income by withdrawing funds from the rolled-out pension plan. I talk about going back to work for your old company in Chapter 15.

If you were a high-level executive with a unique set of skills, you may be able to set up a consulting contract with a guaranteed income in exchange for a minimum number of work hours. I discuss various consulting arrangements you may want to consider with your former employer in Chapter 16.

If you can't work something out with your former employer, or you just don't want to go back there, you can also consider consulting in your former industry. I talk more about how to do that in Chapter 17.

Following your dream of owning your own business

Another option you have may be to take this time to follow a life-long dream of being your own boss and running your own company. You can do that in three different ways — start a business from scratch, buy an existing business, or buy a franchise (a business in a box). I discuss the pros and cons of each of these options in Chapter 18. In Chapter 22, I review the top ten skills you need to run a business.

Many retirees I know have chosen to run a one- or two-person (usually husband and wife) business from their home. Others have turned a hobby into a business.

For example, some who enjoy painting, now work as painting contractors in the area. A former business owner who ran a new-home construction company, now runs a new-home construction inspection company from his home. He gets most of his clients through referrals of other people who bought homes in the area.

Many of my friends who run home-based businesses are not looking to earn big bucks. They just want to supplement their income, primarily to pay healthcare premiums and out-of-pocket expenses and to have some additional money for more entertainment and travel expenses. They don't want to work the hours or endure the stresses of managing a larger company.

Expanding Your Horizons

If you don't need to make money, but want to do something more stimulating than the traditional retirement activities of playing golf, cards, or mahjong or going swimming, you may want to consider going back to school. Some retirees decide they want to complete a traditional degree program, but others just take courses for the joy of learning.

In Chapter 19, I explore all the educational options people aged 50 and older can consider, both in this country and globally. You'll find you can often combine an educational program with an enjoyable vacation trip.

If you don't need the money, but would like to work and help others, you can consider volunteering your time. Myriad volunteer options are available for seniors right in their own community, or they can travel and volunteer around the world. In Chapter 20, I explore some excellent volunteer opportunities both in the U.S. and around the globe.

Now for the best stuff: In the Part of Tens section you can find the best companies to work for, key skills you'll need if you want to start your own business, and the top ten volunteer opportunities you may want to explore. Whatever you decide to do in retirement, always remember that it should be something you enjoy doing!

Chapter 2

Why You May Need or Want to Go Back to Work

In This Chapter

▶ Needing the money to live

▶ Paying for doing the things you enjoy

▶ Staying in touch professionally

▶ Getting bored

*U*nfortunately, you may have discovered that your retirement nest egg will not go as far as you planned. Or your company may have defaulted on its pension plan and you are receiving much less per month than expected. Many of you found that your 401(k) became a 201(k) after the stock market crash of 2001. Perhaps healthcare costs have sent you back to work. For whatever reason, if you run short on funds in retirement, you have to go back to work.

Even if you don't need the money, you may be thinking of going back to work because you're bored or want more professional contact. The fact is, if you're heading back to work, you're not alone. In this chapter, I explore the reasons many people are going back to work after retirement; I give you ideas of what you can do to minimize your risk of being forced back to work and yet maintain your lifestyle; and I share ideas of how you can avoid becoming bored in retirement.

Facing the Financial Facts

Your dream retirement may include traveling to all the spots you never had time to visit, spending time with friends and family, working on your favorite hobby, learning new crafts, or whatever else fits your idea of the perfect retirement.

Now that you've made it to the other side, you find that your finances just aren't enough. People find there are three key reasons they just don't have enough in retirement — their planned nest egg was lost because investments went sour, their pension payments are not as high as expected, or they just didn't save enough. I keep you up-to-date on what is happening to retirement and people's finances on my Web site "Working After Retirement" (www. workingafterretirement.info).

Lost nest egg

Millions of Americans lost their retirement nest eggs in the stock market as it crashed between 2000 and 2002. Most had funds invested through their employers' retirement savings programs, such as a 401(k). Others had their own retirement savings in Individual Retirement Accounts (IRAs).

Just to give you an idea of how people's retirement savings in 401(k)s turned into 201(k)s, here's what happened to the two key stock indexes:

> The Dow Industrial Average dropped from 11,497 to 8,341. That's a 25 percent drop in 30 of what many think are the most solid companies.

> Nasdaq dropped from 4,069 to 1,336. That's a 67 percent drop in what were primarily high-growth technology stocks, which were all the rage in the late 1990s and early 2000s. Many people thought the bubble would never burst and kept pouring more and more of their hard-earned savings into these growth stocks.

Unfortunately, too many people forgot the basics of asset allocation, or chose to believe the tech-stock hype that asset allocation was dead. Asset allocation is a means to invest your portfolio in a number of asset classes, such as stocks, bonds, and cash. A smart investor keeps a well-balanced portfolio that mixes stocks, bonds, and cash, as well as assets that meet various investment strategies, such as growth, value, or balanced. How much you allocate to each type of asset in this mix is called the *allocation*. A conservative allocation could be 20 percent in stock and 80 percent in bonds and/or cash. An aggressive portfolio could be the opposite — 80 percent in stocks and 20 percent in cash and/or bonds. Many different types of asset allocations fit between these two scenarios. I talk more about asset allocation and managing your portfolio in Chapter 5.

Asset allocation also looks at the individual assets you hold. Many portfolio managers will tell you never to hold more than 4 percent of your portfolio in the stock of one company. That's for your safety. If the company goes bust (and we've seen how even multi-billion-dollar companies such as Enron can go bust), you still have other assets (such as real estate, mutual funds, or bonds) to prevent a dramatic drop in your retirement savings portfolio.

Employer-based retirement savings programs vary greatly

While I focus in this chapter on the 401(k), which is the most common form of an employer-sponsored retirement savings fund, you may have a different kind of employer-sponsored fund. People working for nonprofit entities have 403(b)s, which are similar to 401(k)s. If you work in a small company, you may not have a 401(k), instead your plan may be called a Simplified Employee Pension (SEP) IRA, a Savings Incentive Match Plan for Employees (SIMPLE) IRA, or a Keogh Plan (these are very rare today). Deferred profit-sharing plans may also be offered by your employer.

If you work in a company that made its contribution to your 401(k) in stock, you can quickly end up with more than 4 percent of that company's stock in your portfolio. Take a look at what's in your 401(k) and be sure it's not over-loaded with your company's stock. That can be an even greater risk for someone still working at the company. Not only is their retirement fund tied to the company, but their employment is as well. That's definitely putting too many eggs in the same basket and is a recipe for disaster.

Dependence on stock in even great companies that look very safe can be a big mistake as well. For example, when I was living in Atlanta, I met many people who worked at Coca-Cola and filled their retirement portfolios with its stock, watching their portfolios grow gleefully as the stock climbed. In June 1995, Coca Cola reached the highest high that it was going to reach for ten years — $63.75. At the end of June 2006 it was trading in the low 40s. That's more than a 35 percent loss to people who held on hoping for recovery.

The drop from the $60 range to the $40 range was a fast one. It happened between December 2000 and March of 2001. A few times since then, Coca Cola reached into the $50 range. Hopefully some of the folks whose portfolios were heavy in Coca-Cola stock wised up and shifted assets during these times before the stock dropped back into the $40 range. Even if they did, they're still looking at significant losses because they held too many eggs in the same basket.

Stock losses are not the only reason nest eggs are lost

While poor choices in managing one's retirement portfolio is the primary reason people lose their nest eggs, other things can happen as well:

✔ Your company closes or goes bankrupt and the 401(k) assets cannot be found. I talk more below about what types of protections are in place and how you might be able to find the assets.

- You leave your job and take your 401(k) assets with you and then spend them. That's a big no-no if you want money in retirement, but more than 45 percent of employees that take out their 401(k) when they switch jobs spend at least part of it before putting the money into an individual retirement plan.

- You borrow against your 401(k) and are not able to pay it back fully in the designated time or before you're retired, so you lose the assets.

- You divorce and don't protect your rights to your spouse's retirement savings at his or her place of employment and then can't find the money.

Finding a lost retirement account

If you worked for a company that went bankrupt, merged, was acquired by another, or for any other reason closed, your retirement savings may not be lost. The U.S. Department of Labor has an Abandoned Plan Coordinator that may be able to help you locate your missing nest egg. For information about the Abandoned Plan Program, call 1-866-444-3772 or you can write the coordinator at:

Abandoned Plan Coordinator

U.S. Department of Labor

Employee Benefits Security Administration

Office of Enforcement

2000 Constitution Avenue, NW, Suite 600

Washington, DC 20210

Protecting your retirement savings in divorce

Many people do not think of retirement when divorcing, but this can be the only time you will be able to guarantee your rights to your spouse's employer-based retirement plans. If you've stayed at home and taken care of the children while your spouse was working, you probably didn't save for retirement or, at the very least, you didn't save an equivalent amount to what your spouse's retirement plan offered at work. You do have the right to get part of that employer-based retirement plan, but you must protect that right with a Qualified Domestic Order signed by the court at the time of your divorce. The order is then filed with the company that manages the retirement plan.

Reduced pension payments

Not all people's retirement income comes from retirement savings plans. In fact, up until about the 1980s, most people retiring could count on what is called a defined-benefit plan or pension plan. In that type of plan, your employer contributes a certain amount of your income into a retirement portfolio managed by the company, and you get a monthly benefit for the rest of your life when you retire based on the income you earned and your years of service.

This type of retirement plan is rapidly disappearing today. In 2003, only 15.5 percent of people working for private companies were covered by a defined-benefit plan and another 16.6 percent had some combination of a defined-benefit plan and a defined-contribution plan (those are 401(k)-type plans where you and the employer contribute to the plan, but you manage how the money will be taken out).

Getting your pension paid by PBGC

If you were expecting a pension from a company that went bankrupt, you may still have a chance to collect the funds. Most pension plans are protected by the Pension Benefit Guaranty Corporation (PBGC), which protects the retirement incomes of 44.1 million American workers in 30,330 private-sector defined-benefit pension plans. The PBGC was created by the Employee Retirement Income Security Act of 1974 (ERISA). ERISA protects other forms of employer-based retirement programs also.

Companies that offer pension plans guaranteed by PBGC pay insurance premiums for that guaranty. If the company at some time in the future cannot fund its pension benefits, the PBGC takes over and pays those benefits out of its insurance fund. If you worked for a company that offered you a pension and it no longer exists, you may find that you can still collect on the pension through PBGC. On its Web site, PBGC provides a tool that you can use to search for pensions that may be available to you. To find out if there are pension funds waiting for you, a family member, or a friend:

1. Go to www.pbgc.gov.

2. Look for the section called, "Workers and Retirees."

3. Then click on "Pension Search: Help Us Find Missing Participants."

4. Search by name to find out if a pension is available for you.

I know people who needed to leave the 55-plus community I'm living in now because they found that their pensions were cut dramatically when PBGC took over. PBGC by law guarantees a maximum monthly payout of up to $3,971.59 for a single straight-life annuity, if you retire at age 65, but it drops to just $1,787 if you retire early at age 55. These amounts are even lower if you chose an annuity that protects your spouse as well. To find out more about how PBGC works, go to www.pbgc.com.

Losing pension benefits and getting cash

Many employers are terminating their defined-benefit plans. Between 1975 and 2004, more than 165,000 pension plans were terminated. Most of these terminated plans involved small businesses. For more information about changes in pension law, read Chapter 8.

Others were converted to a new type of retirement plan called a cash-balance plan, which is a hybrid between the traditional defined-benefit plan and the defined-contribution plan.

Over 350 large corporations switched to cash-balance plans, including American Airlines, American Express, AT&T, BP, CBS, Chase Manhattan, Citigroup, Duke Energy, GE, Hallmark, IBM, JP Morgan, Wells Fargo, and Xerox, and many more are considering doing so. If you want to follow the trend to cash-balance plans, there is an excellent Web site that monitors them called Cash Pensions (www.cashpensions.com). If your company is considering the conversion, you may find there are employee groups organizing to influence the decision.

Employees converted to a cash-balance plan may find that they will have a lot less money each month in retirement. While they will get a lump sum cash payout when they retire, whether or not they have enough money throughout retirement will depend on how well they manage these funds.

Didn't save enough

Even if you receive a retirement pension or lump-sum payment from your employer's retirement plan, you may find you still haven't saved enough to pay for all the things you need and want during retirement. In fact, fewer than 50 percent of workers today calculate how much they will need to retire and develop a specific plan specifying how much they need to save to make that goal.

More than half of the workers saving for retirement have less than $50,000 saved. How long do you think that would last? Not long if you plan an income of $30,000 per year. How much do you need to save? That depends on so many different factors, but the best way to figure that out is to prepare a budget for retirement and estimate your monthly cash needs. In the next section, "Maintaining Your Lifestyle in Retirement," I talk about the items you need to consider when planning your retirement budget.

Generally, you can expect to safely draw between 4 and 5 percent out of your retirement nest egg each year, if you want to be certain that you don't outlive your assets. For example, if you have $300,000 in retirement savings, then at 4 percent you could draw $12,000 per year and at 5 percent you could draw $15,000 per year. If you get a $1,000 per month check from Social Security, then your total income in retirement would be between $24,000 and $27,000.

Maintaining Your Lifestyle in Retirement

The primary reason most people go back to work after retiring is the need for additional money. While the reasons most often heard are to remain active and to learn new things, when people who go back to work are asked to name one reason, money is the reason for working after retirement. So if your dream retirement does not involve working, then you need to be sure you are saving enough money for your expected life span.

One of the best interactive tools on the Internet for calculating how much money you need in retirement is the Ballpark E$timate (`www.choosetosave.org/ballpark/`). The interactive worksheet collects information about your current age, retirement age, salary when working, expected age at death, inflation assumption, wage growth assumption, rate of return on your investments, pension benefits, retirement income, and retirement savings.

Budgeting for specific phases of retirement

When planning your budget and income needs during retirement, you need to consider several different budgets depending on the phase of retirement you are in. You may think now that you can supplement any needed funds by working, but at some point you may not be able to work, so you need to plan for that contingency as well.

Most people actually need to think of retirement in at least three different phases, and if you retired before you could collect Social Security, then you would need to think about budgets for four distinct phases. So review the four phases below and calculate your budget needs for the ones you still expect are relevant based on your age and health.

Phase 1

If you retired early before you could collect Social Security, you're included in Phase 1. You need to calculate financial needs without Social Security benefits, plus you need to figure out how to get and pay for healthcare until you can qualify for Medicare. In many cases, you need even more cash than you did while working to pay for your health insurance and medical care. Health costs drive most of the retirees in Phase 1 back to work for more money to pay for healthcare and, in some cases, to get access to a group health plan. I know retirees who would not need the money from working if they could get reasonable health insurance. I talk more about health insurance in the section, "Paying for healthcare," below.

Phase 2

Count yourself a member of Phase 2 once you're retired, collecting Social Security, eligible for Medicare, but still very active. You may also be getting funds from an employer pension or drawing down funds from a retirement portfolio. Your financial needs will be a bit less than when you were working because you don't need to spend as much money on clothes, travel, work and other work expenses. Usually you can plan for a budget that is about 90 percent of the budget you had while working. Since many people end up with a monthly income that is less than that, they go back to work to supplement that income.

Phase 3

If you're retired, collecting Social Security, getting medical coverage through Medicare, but are not as active in your community, you've reached Phase 3. In this phase of retirement, you don't spend money on travel and entertainment and can usually live on about 70 percent of the income you earned while working.

Phase 4

Phase 4 includes the oldest group of retirees: you're collecting Social Security, are on Medicare, and likely are receiving funds from a pension or from your retirement portfolio, but your medical costs are on the rise as you age. Once you've reached this phase, you probably need about 85 percent of the income you needed while working to cover your daily needs as well as your increased medical expenses.

Knowing what to budget for

After you identify your phases of retirement (see the section, "Budgeting for specific phases of retirement" earlier in this chapter), you then need to guesstimate a budget for each one. Yes it will be a guess. No one can be absolutely positive of what will be needed and what the future costs will be for anything. But, you can get pretty close with some careful budgeting. Here are some tips for what items to consider when budgeting.

Funding travel and entertainment

Travel and entertainment ends up on the list of most people's dream retirement. Whether or not they'll be able to take those trips or participate in entertainment activities depends upon how much cash they have each month.

Working at least part time helps many people pay for the travel and entertainment they want as part of their retirement. Many people's retirement income includes enough for the basics of life, but not enough for any extras. In order to take those trips, dine out regularly with friends, or buy tickets for entertainment, many seniors go back to work.

Maintaining your home

Ideally, by the time you enter retirement, your mortgage should be paid off. Carrying a mortgage on a fixed retirement income can be a big drain on your budget and may be the primary reason you are forced back into the workforce. Yet 40 percent of retirees today do still have a mortgage to pay.

In addition to the mortgage, you will need to pay for insurance, property taxes, maintenance, and utilities. On a fixed retirement income, as these costs rise each year they can put a greater and greater strain on your fixed income. Many states do give seniors a reduction in property taxes, so be sure to check with your property tax collector regarding tax benefits for seniors.

Keeping food on the table

How much money you'll need for the food portion of your budget will depend entirely on how you plan to make your meals. Many seniors go out to eat regularly with friends, others live by making their meals as cheaply as possible at home. Those who do have expensive dining out habits are more likely to work part-time to make a little extra money to pay for their dining out fun.

As you prepare your food budget, think about whether you believe you'll eat frugally at home or want to spend more as part of your social life and eating out with friends. Estimating this carefully can help you determine how much money you will have for other things on your fixed budget — like travel and entertainment.

Remember, in retirement your income is fixed and you can't expect to get raises like you did while you were working. As your expenses increase, you'll either need to cut back on other things in your budget, you'll need to draw down more funds from your retirement savings, or you'll need to go back to work to make some extra money.

Paying for healthcare

Too often I see stories in the paper that indicate seniors are having to make the choice between keeping food on their table and staying healthy. Once you are old enough to get Medicare, healthcare costs will drop, but if you retired before being eligible for Medicare, those few years may be very expensive. Even if you are on Medicare, out-of-pocket costs can still be high because Medicare doesn't pay all your costs.

I know couples who do not yet qualify for Medicare and are paying over $20,000 per year just for their medical insurance. I know others who can't qualify for medical insurance because of their preexisting conditions. Millions of people who retired early in their 50s or were laid off and couldn't find other work are left without health coverage.

If you have recently left your place of employment and health insurance is not one of your retiree benefits, which is more and more common today, be sure to hold on to your COBRA benefits until you can find an individual health policy. COBRA is short for Consolidated Omnibus Budget Reconciliation Act, which protects your right to continuing health coverage after you leave a job. While you must pay for the full costs for COBRA benefits, and they can be very expensive, I can guarantee you that an individual health policy will be more expensive than your group plan.

I talk more about the types of individual health plans available to seniors, as well as alternatives under Medicare in Chapter 10. But, don't forget to consider healthcare costs when planning your retirement budget. Needing to pay the ever rising costs of healthcare drives more seniors back to work than any other expense factor.

Losing Professional Contact . . . or Just Getting Bored

After years of getting up, rushing to work, and filling your day solving problems in your workplace, you may be finding it hard to just get up and have no where to go. If you didn't take the time to plan your retirement, you're probably finding it even harder to transition from work to retirement.

You can always go back to work — many people do — but, the good news is that if you're bored, it's not hard to find alternatives to work for your time, especially if you treat looking for alternatives the same way you looked for a solution in your workplace. Start by researching alternatives for volunteer opportunities that need your involvement either in your neighborhood or around your city or town. What those opportunities might be will depend on what you enjoy doing. I talk more about volunteer opportunities in Chapter 20.

Keeping your professional network alive

For many people who have worked their entire lives, their professional lives are dependent on the people with whom they work. Once you stop working, you may find that while you don't miss the daily grind, you do desperately miss the professional contracts you had each day.

You don't have to stop making contact with the people you worked with professionally, but you do have to change how you see them. If you haven't left your workplace yet, be sure to get contact information for all the people you'd like to stay in touch with. If you have already retired, set up a lunch date or meet people for drinks after their work and get the contact information you need.

Take your newfound time and organize some fun social activities that can include you and other professionals you worked with, whether they are still working or not. This will help you stay in touch with your work life as you transition to your new life outside of work.

Finding a new network of retired professionals

You will find it hard to fill your days with people who are still committed to the workplace, so you also may need to find networks of retired professionals in your area. There are a number of ways you can find new professional friends:

✔ Build a strong social network by volunteering to work at your favorite nonprofit organization. Help others or work toward solving a problem that you care about.

✔ Join a club with people who enjoy doing the same activities that you enjoy doing. Your local newspaper probably has a long list of clubs. You can also find ideas through your church or synagogue. Another good source for a professional club near you could be the national professional organization you participated in while working. It's possible that there are local groups not connected to your old workplace through which like-minded professionals meet.

✔ Get involved in community service. You can remain connected with all types of professionals doing work to help your community.

✔ Make your hobby your profession. Join a group that also enjoys doing the same hobby you enjoy. It's a great way to meet new people and build a new social network.

✔ Don't forget to rebuild your relationships with your spouse and other family members. If you've been working full-time and now finally have the time you want in retirement, take the time to renew your relationship with your family.

I talk more about volunteer opportunities for retirees in Chapter 20.

Going back to school

Another way to keep your mind active and remain involved professionally is to go back to school. You can do this to further your professional knowledge or to learn something entirely new.

Many seniors have decided to go back to school to avoid getting bored, so you won't be the only older person in the classroom. In fact, in Chapter 19, I discuss opportunities around the world for retirees who want to continue to learn.

Teaching others in your field

Some of you might enjoy teaching, and many retirees do teach. Cities and counties around the country are begging for teachers. Many have certification programs that they sponsor for people who don't have a teaching certification, but want to teach.

There is a shortage of teachers in most fields, and you will probably find it relatively easy to find openings if teaching is how you want to fill your day. You can teach children in public school settings or you can teach classes through your professional organization. Many technical schools and community colleges also are constantly looking for professionals who can teach courses.

While committing to a full-time, public-school teaching job may not be what you're looking for in retirement, teaching periodic courses through a private school, community college, a technical college, or your professional organization might be just what you need.

Chapter 3

Assessing Your Talents
for Your Next Job

In This Chapter

▶ Exploring strengths and weaknesses

▶ Finding your likes and dislikes

▶ Discovering your worker type

▶ Gauging your interests

▶ Cornering your creativity

So what do you want to do next? After retiring, most people are ready for a complete job change — doing anything but what they did before. Others don't want to step out of their comfort zone.

Before you can decide what to do next, you must take stock on what you like and don't like to do, as well as assess your talents, to help figure out what your next job should be. In this chapter, I discuss the types of self-exploration you can do to help you determine what your next job might be.

Determining Your Strengths and Weaknesses

One of the hardest things for most people is to admit that they have some weaknesses. Well get over it. If you have a hard time admitting to weaknesses now is not the time for pride. You certainly don't want to pick a job after retirement at which you'll constantly be struggling to keep up.

You don't have anything to prove. You've already had one successful career. Most likely if you're going back to work now you're doing it to help make financial ends meet or to get in on a group health insurance plan. You're not at the beginning of your career when you needed to prove yourself.

Take some time to think about your strengths and weaknesses — write them down if you want to. What is it that you are really good at doing? If you enjoy doing that, it's even better. In retirement, you certainly don't want to be doing something that makes it hard to get up in the morning and get out of the house. Your aches and pains will already be making it hard to get out of bed.

If you can find a job that builds on your strengths and doesn't depend on things at which you feel you are weak, it will be much easier to show up at the workplace every day. So make a list of all your strengths and weaknesses and seek work that helps you build on your strengths.

Assessing Your Last Job

One of the best ways to figure out what you want to do next is to look at what you liked best at your previous job or jobs. Also, consider what you liked to do least. For example, I'm sure most of you hated filing (I know that's my least favorite thing to do), but some of you might really enjoy getting things organized for someone else. Boy — if that's the case — I could sure use a volunteer.

Make a list of all the things that you really enjoyed doing at work. It doesn't have to be things that were even part of your job. For example, if you really enjoyed helping others work out their personal finances, then a good job after retirement might be something in the financial industry. Or if you enjoyed helping people decide on decorations for their homes, maybe you would enjoy working as an interior decorator. Or maybe you'd like to work for a new homes builder in his decorator department helping people who just purchased a new home make color choices or pick other items for their new home's interior.

You need to take stock of what you enjoyed doing through most of your career and what you really hated doing. Definitely avoid taking a job in retirement that will require you to do most of the things you hated doing. I can guarantee that it will be much more difficult to go to work if you hate being there. Once you've retired, other pressures, such as being with friends and family or going out to play a round of golf, will be getting in the way of going to work. So, it's best to find something that you look forward to doing each day.

Uncovering Your Worker Type

One helpful tool to assist you with deciding what to do next is to discover your worker type. In Chapter 4, I introduce you to some formal self-assessment tests you can take on the Internet or through a professional counselor to assist you with self-assessment.

In this section, I introduce you to a quick quiz to help you sort out the type of worker and work that might fit you the best. Hopefully this will help you identify your strengths and lead you to a job that you truly will enjoy doing.

Determining your working type

Quickly circle eight words or phrases in the list in Table 3-1 that best fit your image of yourself. Don't spend a lot of time choosing. This works best when you pick the words quickly. If you want this to mean something, don't cheat by looking at the explanations of the values below.

Table 3-1		Worker-Type Worksheet	
Word	*Value*	*Word*	*Value*
Adventurous	E	Mechanically inclined	R
Analytical	I	Methodical	C
Assertive	E	Nature Lover	R
Athletic	R	Numerically inclined	C
Broad-minded	I	Obedient	C
Concrete	R	Observant	I
Conforming	C	Open	A
Conscientious	C	Optimistic	E
Cooperative	S	Orderly	C
Creative	A	Outgoing	S
Efficient	C	Patient	S

(continued)

Table 3-1 *(continued)*

Word	Value	Word	Value
Empathetic	S	Precise	I
Energetic	E	Scholarly	I
Expressive	A	Scientific	I
Extroverted	E	Self-confident	E
Forgiving	S	Self-controlled	R
Friendly	S	Sensitive	S
Generous	S	Spontaneous	E
Helpful	S	Stable	R
Imaginative	A	Straightforward/ frank	R
Innovative	S	Structured	C
Intellectually self-confident	I	Talkative	E
Intuitive	S	Unconventional	A
Logical	I	Well-organized	C

After you've finished circling the words or phrases, add up how many of each letter value you have:

A _____

C _____

E _____

I _____

R _____

S _____

You will most likely have one dominant value of three or more and several of one or two. The dominant value matches your strongest worker type, but the other values also influence what you like to do — the next section, "Understanding your worker type," explains how your specific worker types can influence the kind of job you may enjoy.

Understanding your worker type

So, what do the values in Table 3-1 mean? First let me tell you what the values stand for:

- A = Artistic (also known as Creators)
- C = Conventional (also known as Organizers)
- E = Enterprising (also known as Persuaders)
- I = Investigative (also known as Thinkers)
- R = Realistic (also known as Doers)
- S = Social (also known as Helpers)

In the following sections, I discuss each worker type individually, exploring each type's strengths and what each type likes to do including favorite hobbies. Then I give you some examples of possible job choices that fit each type to get you to starting thinking about what type of job you might like to do.

Use this information to help you sort out the type of job you want to do next. You probably found that you actually fit into several worker type categories, but one more strongly than others. You certainly can mix and match the skill sets to discover what you might look for and enjoy if you go back to work.

Artistic (creators)

The skills in which Artistic people excel include drawing; painting; playing a musical instrument; writing stories, poetry, or music; singing; acting; dancing; or fashion or interior designing. For fun they most enjoy attending concerts; going to the theater; visiting art exhibits; reading fiction, plays, or poetry; working on crafts; taking photographs; and expressing themselves in other creative ways. They also excel at dealing with ambiguous ideas.

If your worker type is Artistic, your might be able to turn your hobbies into your own business for profit. The type of Artistic hobbies that have successfully been turned into small businesses include photography, writing, desktop publishing, sewing, homemade crafts, painting, designing sets for plays, or speaking a foreign language. Other hobbies you might enjoy but probably won't help you make any extra money include taking dance lessons, playing a musical instrument, or traveling.

With these skills, you may be able to find paying jobs as a copywriter, drama or English teacher, graphic or interior designer, writer, photographer, or editor.

Conventional (organizers)

Conventional worker types work well within a system and can do a lot of paperwork in a short time. If you're a Conventional worker type, you also probably excel at keeping accurate records, using a computer terminal, and writing effective business letters. You probably prefer following clearly defined processes, enjoy using data-processing equipment, like working with numbers, excel at keeping track of details, and enjoy collecting or organizing.

Your hobbies might include collecting memorabilia, playing computer or card games, keeping club or family records and files, reading home magazines, and writing your family history. None of these translate easily into a small business, but your organizational skills can certainly be used to start one that assists other small businesses with record keeping, bookkeeping, or other organizational needs.

With these skills (and possibly a few courses in accounting) you could get work as an accountant or bookkeeper. You may also enjoy working as a cashier, librarian, bank teller, clerk, or data-processing worker.

Enterprising (persuaders)

Enterprising worker types like to initiate projects and convince people to do things their way. If this is your worker type, you likely enjoy selling things or promoting ideas. You also enjoy giving speeches or leading a group. You probably like to organize activities amongst your friends and persuade others to join you.

You particularly enjoy wining a leadership or sales award, being elected to office, or having power or status. You would likely enjoy starting your own business or campaigning for someone else in a political campaign. Your hobbies might include discussing politics, reading business journals, watching the stock market, attending meetings and conferences, and leading community organizations.

With these skills you might want to consider looking for work as a financial planner, bartender, interpreter, manufacturer's representative, salesperson, public relations representative, real estate agent, or travel agent.

Investigative (thinkers)

Investigative worker types excel at thinking abstractly, solving mathematical problems, or understanding scientific theories. If this is your worker type, you probably enjoy doing complex calculations, using a microscope or computer, and interpreting formulas. You like to work independently, using computers or working in a lab doing experiments.

You probably like to read scientific or technical journals, analyze data, and do research to challenge your intellect. Your hobbies might include joining a book club, studying astronomy, doing crossword puzzles, and collecting things (such as rocks, stamps, or coins). You may enjoy operating an amateur radio or flying recreationally. You also might enjoy getting involved in conservation efforts or working to save an endangered species.

With these skills the types of work you might want to consider include technical writer, science teacher, management consultant, medical lab technologist, or research analyst. If your computer skills are strong, you may also want to look for work in this area.

Realistic (doers)

Realistic worker types like to fix things. If this is your worker type, you probably enjoy solving electrical problems, reading a blueprint, or operating tools and machinery. For fun you might like to go camping and pitch a tent or you might like to play sports games or maybe even plant a garden.

Realistic worker types usually like to work outdoors and work with their hands. They enjoy being physically active and building things.

Hobbies for Realistic worker types might include refinishing furniture, growing plants and flowers, hunting and fishing, playing sports, woodworking, coaching team sports, building models, repairing cars or other equipment, target shooting, and landscaping. Most of these hobbies could be a good way to make a little extra money doing things for others who are not as good with their hands.

In retirement, depending on what you enjoy doing most, you may want to take a job or start your own business as an automobile mechanic, groundskeeper, painter, carpenter, electrician, or plumber.

Social (helpers)

Social worker types enjoy teaching or training others. If you are a Social worker type, you likely can express yourself clearly and break things down into smaller pieces to make it easier for other people to learn. You usually enjoy leading a group discussion and possibly even mediating a dispute. You work well with others and enjoy planning or supervising activities.

You like to help people solve their problems, participate in meetings, or do volunteer work. You like to work with young people and help others. Your hobbies likely include volunteering in social action groups, joining community organizations, and helping others with personal concerns. You also probably enjoy caring for children. You like to meet new friends, go to parties, and play team sports or attend sporting events. You're also likely to be active in a religious organization.

In retirement, you may want to consider jobs as a teacher, retirement counselor, school counselor, librarian, real estate appraiser, social worker, or mediator.

Using How You Like to Work to Find the Ideal Job

Some people enjoy working totally by themselves while others prefer working within teams. Also, some people need a lot of direction, while others prefer to work without a supervisor looking over them all the time. How you like to work also influences what kind of job you may enjoy most. In the next sections, I explore different ways people work and the types of jobs that best fit those working ways.

Working autonomously

If your preference is to work autonomously, you need to find a job that will allow you to work by yourself without much supervision. Otherwise you will be spending most of your day resenting your supervisor.

You likely won't last long at a job that requires you be supervised regularly, either you'll quit or get fired, so avoid accepting that type of job. Be sure to talk about your preference to work autonomously during your interview.

If this creates a problem during the interview, it's best that you don't get the job. You would probably butt heads with someone who prefers to keep a tight reign on his or her staff. Your best bet is to move on and look for something else.

Needing direction

If you like the type of job where you're given lots of direction and don't need to make decisions, then you should look for a job in which the supervisor prefers to be in control and give you direction.

Many people in retirement actually prefer not having the responsibilities of being the boss, but instead just enjoy being out among people. You might enjoy taking direction and not having to make decisions. This might be just the right match for you in retirement, especially if you've been making decisions all your work life and are burned out.

You may find that when you get into your job you don't enjoy taking direction. Often, retirees take a job that requires them to accept direction, and they find that the younger people giving the directions keep making the wrong decisions. It can be frustrating. If that happens to you, you might have to rethink your job choice and find something else.

Working in teams

Some people really enjoy working in teams rather than alone. If that is your preference, you need to find a job that encourages teamwork. In today's world that is probably the most common theme for most businesses, so you shouldn't have a hard time finding a job where teamwork is the norm.

Applying Your Skill Sets

You may be wondering if you have all the skills for a particular kind of job — or perhaps you're wondering what skills are even needed for a particular job. In the next sections I give you a couple of options for figuring out your skill sets and applying them to your job search.

One of the best ways to research skill sets is to use a tool online at America's Career InfoNet. You may also pass this information on to your grandchildren if any of them are having a hard time figuring out what they want to do. If you're not Internet savvy, ask a friend or family member to help you explore this site. It's well worth the time if you're not sure what you want to do next.

To use the career skills profiler, go to `www.acinet.org/acinet/skills`. Using the tool, you can get a comprehensive list of the skills you need for just about any job. You can start the search in one of three ways — by browsing job families, searching by keyword, or searching by skills you have. The type of search you do depends if you:

- ✔ **Know that you want to work in a particular field, but aren't sure exactly what you want to do in that field:** You can find a job type by searching job families. For example, if you know you'd like to work in healthcare, but are not sure what type of job you want, then you would start the Skills Profiler by selecting the "Menu Search" button.

- ✔ **Know exactly what you want to do, but want to know more details about the skills needed or the work activities involved in a particular job choice:** You can start the process by doing a "Keyword Search" for the job or jobs that interest you. As you start typing the job, choices will pop up on the screen. Pick the one that comes closest to the type of job you want to consider. You will then get a comprehensive list of the skills you need. The rest of the process is similar to the one discussed above for the search by job families.

> ✔ **Have absolutely no idea what you want to do, but instead prefer to start out by doing a skills inventory:** You should choose the "Search without an Occupation" option. After you get to the skills profile and you see the list of occupations that match your profile, you will then be able to click on any occupation listed to find a comprehensive overview of the particular occupation on a state by state basis. This overview will include wages that can be expected, job trends nationwide and in your state, a list of the most important knowledge, skills and abilities for the occupation you've chosen, the education and training you need, and any related occupation profiles.

Carving Out Your Creative Talents

If you want to go back to work after retirement, the most important thing to help you get out of the house each day is trying to find a job that lets you do something you truly enjoy. Working in a job that allows you to draw on your creative talents might be the best answer for finding a job that you love.

So what are your creative talents? Do you like to write, paint, draw, do photography, work with plants, do home crafts, or anything else that sparks your creative bug?

If so, you may be wondering how you can turn your creative ideas into a way to make the extra money you need. One of the best ways to get started is by networking (I discuss networking in-depth in Chapter 4). You can network at art fairs, by introducing yourself to others who own businesses with a creative element similar to your talent, or by joining an online community. Through networking, you can find people with the same creative talents who have found a way to make money with their craft. They may give you tips and suggestions and may even let you help out with their current business. You just never know until you ask!

Chapter 4

Seeking Help to Determine What You'd Like to Do Next

In This Chapter

▶ Talking with a counselor

▶ Testing yourself

▶ Building a network

▶ Seeking support

*Y*ou're finally free from the rat race. You know you'd like to do something else, but aren't sure what that is. You don't have to figure that out alone. There are numerous services out there you can tap into — counseling, testing, networks, and support groups. This chapter will review the resources available for helping you to decide what to do next.

Talking with Someone One on One

You may have discussed your retirement plans with your family and friends numerous times, but can't seem to decide what to do next. Sometimes you need to find a dispassionate third party that can help you sort out your choices and dig into your psyche to help you find what's best for you.

Seeing the need for a career counselor

You might think that you are a little too old to work with a career counselor, but you're not. People are living 20 years or more in retirement. You've got lots of time, and you need to figure out something that best suits you at this point in your life. Today, career counseling involves much more than just figuring out what you want to do when you get out of school. Career counselors frequently work with older adults to sort out career- and life-planning issues.

Don't be concerned if you seem as undecided as you were when you first graduated high school or entered college. You are entering an entirely new phase of life and it's not unusual to need a little help.

You're facing an entirely new path:

- ✔ When you were younger you were on a career path. Now you need to take the time to plan a path that fits your personal values, interests, likes, dislikes, and skill levels at this phase of your life. I'm sure you're finding that these values, interests, likes, and dislikes are much different than they were when you were 20.

- ✔ If you worked all your life, you probably clocked in at work at least 2,100 hours annually (and with overtime even more). Now you have all that extra time you need to fill and you probably don't want to fill it with another highly stressful and demanding job, but you do want to work whether for money, health insurance, or just to stay intellectually active.

- ✔ You had a set daily routine while you were working. Now you've got to figure out an entirely new routine.

- ✔ You always had to meet deadlines while working. Now you only need to meet them if you set them yourself.

- ✔ Your schedule was set by your job requirements. Now you get to set your own schedule.

- ✔ You had to be accountable to your boss, and even if you were a boss, you had to be accountable to your business. Now you're only accountable to yourself.

- ✔ Your social circle was likely dominated by your colleagues. Now you need to find an entirely new social circle.

These changes are huge for anyone, and getting help from a professional can make this transition much easier for you, as well as help you make the right choices that will lead to an enjoyable retirement with work you enjoy that fits your personality.

Finding a career counselor

So, how do you go about looking for a career counselor? One of the best ways to find a good counselor is to seek references from friends, associates, or possibly the human resources staff at your company. If you don't know anyone who can recommend someone, a good place to start is the National Board of Certified Counselors (www.nbcc.org/counselorfind2). There you can find counselors with a specialty in aging.

Retirees redefining space

"As people approach retirement, they must redefine their space," says Martha Russell of Russell Career Services and former president of the National Career Development Association. She says this redefinition affects three key areas — your role, your physical space, and the impact caregiving has on your life.

✔ Your role as a person is changing, especially the role you may play as a parent and grandparent. When you stop working full-time, you will have more time for your role as a parent and grandparent. Many people, especially men who've had demanding jobs, want to be there for their grandchildren in a way they couldn't be available for their kids.

✔ Your physical space will change — even more dramatically if you plan to relocate to a retirement community. You must decide how to redefine the people around you and build a new social network — choosing new friends and changing how you interact with the family.

✔ Caregiving can have a major impact on careers and retirement plans — especially caring for elderly family members. This becomes a value issue — balancing around family, work, and social obligations.

After you do find a number of counselors, choose the one that is right for you by:

✔ Examining the counselors' backgrounds

✔ Making sure you connect with the counselor

✔ Requesting referrals

✔ Asking the counselors about:

- **Credentials:** Career counselors don't have to be licensed in most states, so anyone who is self-trained can hang out a shingle. Ask where the counselor trained, whether he has an advanced degree in psychology or social work, and whether he's sought certification from a professional group, such as the National Board of Certified Counselors or the National Career Development Association.

- **Clientele:** Ask the counselor what type of clients he specializes in, such as those beginning careers or transitioning to retirement. You definitely want to find a counselor who works with clientele near your age group.

- **Testing:** Ask what type of testing is used as part of the process. Does he assess career change and transferable skills? Does he provide an interpretation of test results?

- **Scope:** Ask about the scope of your counselor. Can he help you not only with decisions related to your job choice, but also how that choice impacts this period of change, such as any personal barriers, family roles, and changing values? For example, in the past, career advancement may have been your priority, but now your role as grandparent and the time you can spend with family may be more important.

- **Outcomes:** Ask how the counselor can help you discover your next steps. What can you expect will be the outcome of your work with the counselor?

Be sure you ask the counselors you are considering for a detailed explanation of their services. Make sure you understand the services being offered, their expectations about your degree of involvement, and your financial commitment.

When you choose a professional, be sure to pick one that understands your career is a part of your life, so he will carefully consider your values as you start your next life adventure as you enter your retirement years. You want a counselor that can help put your decision-making process in perspective — considering all your life choices, not just those related to work.

Determining what to talk about

After you've found the right person, you're probably wondering what you should talk about and how the process works. Many counselors start by giving you a series of assessment tests, while others prefer to talk with you once or twice to get to know you before testing.

Your career counselor likely will do one or more of the following:

- ✔ Invite you to participate in individual and group counseling sessions to help you clarify your life and career goals.

- ✔ Help you identify your options by administering and interpreting tests and inventories to assess your abilities, interests, values, and personality.

- ✔ Encourage you to explore your options through activities and planning experiences.

- ✔ Help you improve your decision-making skills.

- ✔ Assist you in developing your career plans while in retirement.

- ✔ Help you relearn job-hunting strategies (you probably haven't looked for a job in a long time) and assist with the development of a resume.

- ✔ Help you understand how to integrate whatever type of work you choose with your other changing life roles.

- ✔ Provide support as you experience the stress of transitioning from your previous work to what you will do for the rest of your life in retirement.

Before your appointment with a counselor, think about what types of help you want so you'll be able to work with your counselor effectively to find out what's best for you.

Testing Your Values, Interests, Personality, and Skills

You probably have taken career tests before when you were trying to figure out what you wanted to do for the rest of your life, while you were in high school or college. You're also probably wondering why you should take any more now. You will find you answer the questions on these tests differently at different points of your life, depending on the type of decisions you are trying to make and how these decisions will impact your life planning.

First, let me say that you shouldn't think of these as tests, but more as tools for helping you to make a decision. Don't expect these tests to find the perfect job for you or to map out your next steps. These tools will help you explore yourself. They will give you an opportunity to look at yourself in a type of intellectual mirror and help you determine what you might want to do next.

You will find tests that focus on several specific areas — your values, your interests, your personality, and your skills. I explore tests you can take for free or for a small fee on the Internet in each of these areas. If you do seek professional counseling, your counselor may give you similar tests as part of the counseling process. You can find the most current set of links for tests on the Internet on my Web site, "Working After Retirement" (www. workingafterretirement.info).

Exploring your values

You explore your values by taking value inventories that measure what motivates you and how important different values are to you. These can include autonomy, flexible work schedule, helping others, interpersonal relations, leisure time, outdoor work, prestige, salary, and security. You may find it hard to make a list of what you like and don't like from past work experiences. Value inventories can help you determine that. Here are three good ones available on the Internet:

> ✔ **The Value Questionnaire**
> (www.mrs.umn.edu/services/career/career_planning/
> valquestion.php): This questionnaire from the University of
> Minnesota helps you explore the things most important to you
> right now.

✔ **Prioritizing Work Values Exercise**
(www.mrs.umn.edu/services/career/career_planning/
workvalues2.php): Also from the University of Minnesota, this exercise, like the Value Questionnaire (see bullet above) assists you with
exploring the things most important to you at this point of your life.

✔ **Soul Survival** (www.career-intelligence.com/assessment/
career_values.html): From the Career-Intelligence Web site, this
assessment first explains the importance of determining your values and
then includes an accompanying exercise to help you do just that. You do
have to join the Web site to use its tools, but there is no fee to join. You'll
find lots of useful resources on this site.

✔ **Work Related Values Assessment** (www.nwc.edu/career/planning/
phase1/workvalues.htm): Developed by the U.S. Department of
Labor and found online at Northwestern College Career Development
Center, this worksheet defines each of the core work values. Armed with
this information, you are then asked to pick your three most important
values.

Determining your interests

Narrowing down your interests can be a hard thing to do, or you may even
find it difficult to list your interests. Interest inventories help you figure out
your interests by asking questions regarding what activities you like to do
and what activities you don't like to do. By determining these likes and dislikes, you can get some help in finding work that you might enjoy doing.

Career interest inventories are not free on the Internet. If you're sure you
know what you like and don't like to do, you probably don't need to take
them at this point. But, if you are curious to explore your interests, here
are three good interest inventories that you can use for a small fee on the
Internet:

✔ **The Campbell Interest and Skill Survey** used to be available only to
career counselors, but is now available on the Internet for an $18 fee.
It was developed by internationally recognized career expert, David
Campbell and is published by NCS Pearson. This is a 320-question
survey and your results will be compared to people who are successfully employed in the fields you're interested in. You can access the test
online at U.S. News and World Report (www.usnews.com/usnews/
edu/careers/ccciss.htm).

✔ **The Career Key** (www.careerkey.org) helps you match your interests
and skills. You can take the test for a fee of $7.95. In addition to learning
more about yourself, you'll get information about jobs that match your
personality.

✔ **Self-Directed Search** (`www.self-directed-search.com`) is an interest and skills assessment that is popular among career counselors. You can take this 15-minute test on the Internet for $9.95. Your report will appear on the screen once you've paid for the assessment. Before taking the test, you can quickly review the format online, including questions about your likes and dislikes of various activities, your competencies, your occupations, as well as a self-assessment of your abilities.

Taking personality tests

You'll find that many personality inventories are based on the theories of psychologist Carl Jung. He believed there were eight personality types — extroverts, introverts, thinking, feeling, sensing, intuitive, judging, and perceptive. Basically what these inventories do is sort out the ways people prefer to take in information and make decisions. These assessments also look at how you get your energy — from the outside world or your inner self. Finally, these inventories assess whether you are the type of person who likes to find closure or a person who prefers to keep options open.

You won't be able to find these tests for free either. In fact, the most respected personality test — the Myers-Briggs Type Indicator (MBTI) requires that you pay for the interpretive assistance of a certified MBTI practitioner. How much you pay will be determined by the type of test you take (online or on paper) and the amount of counseling time involved. You can find sources for the test online at Career-Intelligence.com.

I don't recommend you seek to take the MBTI on the Internet. If you do think you need this extensive personality profiler, then your best bet is to work with a professional counselor, since you'll need to have the results interpreted by a professional, and the results are more meaningful if done by someone who knows you.

But, if you are thinking of opening your own business, Career Intelligence offers a good package that includes the MBTI and the Strong Interest Inventory with a focus on whether you would do well opening your own business. This assessment package will help you determine whether your personality and your interests fit the role of a small business owner. Interpretive counseling is also included in this package, which is called "Strong and MBTI Entrepreneur Report" (`www.career-intelligence.com/assessment/Entrepreneur.asp`). The fee for the package is $149.

One test you can take on the Internet that is similar to the MBTI, but much cheaper, is the Keirsey Temperament Sorter (`www.advisorteam.com/temperament_sorter`), which is used by corporations, professional counselors, and major universities. It's a simple test to take and you can complete it quickly online. After answering the 70 questions in this test, you'll get insights into your temperament, personality types, and motivations. You can get an initial temperament analysis for free and a more detailed analysis of your personality types and motivations for $14.95.

Taking skills assessments

You may have a hard time listing all your skills. Many people overlook all the things they've learned over a lifetime of work. Don't despair, there are a number of skill profilers that can help you put together a list of your skills. Here are three good Web sites you can use for free to construct your skill profile:

- ✔ **Career InfoNet Skills Profiler** (www.acinet.org/acinet/skills) is an excellent tool that helps you not only to get a comprehensive list of your skills, but also helps you find career options that match those skills. I talk more about how to use this tool in Chapter 3.

- ✔ **Career-Intelligence.com** offers an excellent article about how to develop your career skill set and a worksheet to help you do just that. You can access the article at www.career-intelligence.com/assessment/career_skillset.asp and the worksheet at www.career-intelligence.com/assessment/career_skillset_worksheet.asp. You will have to register for the site, but registration is free.

- ✔ **Lifework Transitions.com** (www.lifeworktransitions.com/exercises/exercs.html) provides a series of exercises to help you sort out your skills. You'll find several different skill surveys you can complete.

Networking with others

I'm sure you've heard the phrase, "It's not what you know, but who you know." That's so true, and it becomes even more important when you're trying to get around the hidden myths that make it difficult for you to get a job as you get older. I talk more about these myths in Chapter 13.

Building a strong network can be your best defense at any time of your career, but even more critical when trying to go back to work after retirement. A network helps people to share information about openings not necessarily advertised on the job market. Your network may also help introduce you to the person who is doing the hiring. In addition to building a core group of people who can assist you in finding a job, you're also building a group of people who can support you emotionally as well.

In order to build an effective network, you should use both formal and informal networks you already have in place. Formal networks include those you actually join and pay dues to, such as professional associations, alumni groups, or clubs such as the Lion's Club. Informal networks include people you think of as friends from work, your religious organization, or other social situations.

How to build your network

You can build an effective network if you follow these six steps:

1. **Plan your network.** First you must write out your goals for your network. Think about what you want to achieve by forming this network. Do you want to learn information about potential jobs, get ideas for how to improve yourself, learn about new developments in your field, discover training opportunities, or seek emotional support? Most likely you want to do a combination of these options. You also want to think about how you might help the people in your network. Networks are about sharing. So you should think about what you have to offer to the members of your potential network as well.

2. **Build your contacts.** Start by writing down the types of people you want in your network. This can include their background, position, personality traits, leisure interests, and values. Then make a list of people who you already know that you want in your network. Next make a list of people you'd like to have in your network, but don't know yet. Decide how you will contact your potential network members — by phone, e-mail, chat rooms, online discussion groups, or meeting them in person. You probably will use a mix of these options.

3. **Conduct information interviews.** This is a great way to find out about types of jobs, as well as make contact with people who you would like in your network but don't know well. Before even going on the interview, learn all you can about the type of work you are considering. Develop a list of people you do know who might help you make the contacts you want to make. If you don't know the person, the best way to contact them first is with a brief personal note that talks about what you want to learn and asks for an appointment. Tell them you'll follow up by telephone in a few days. Then call to set the appointment. Make it clear that you're not seeking a specific job, but want to learn more information about the job opportunities in their industry. People do enjoy talking about themselves and their work. Be sure to ask open-ended questions and listen carefully. Don't overstay your welcome. As you finish the interview, ask for recommendations of others you can talk to for more information. Be sure you write a thank you note and mention a key piece of information you learned from the interview.

4. **Organize your network.** Once you've pulled together all your names, you need to organize them. Figure out how the information you've collected will be helpful to you. One good tool to use is Microsoft Outlook. There you can put each person's contact information and any specific notes you may have about their background and your contact with them. You can use the Outlook calendar to set up contact reminders you may want to track. You can set up category lists and periodically plan to send out e-mails to members in your network based on the categories you've developed. You can then keep track of your individual contacts with each of them in their individual contact record in Outlook.

5. **Take action.** Set up a plan for contacting your network. For example, you can plan to make one cold call (a call to someone you'd like in your network but don't know — possibly to set up an information interview), meet someone for lunch, and reconnect with two others in your network each week. Make notes in the individual records for each person you contact, including the key information you discussed during the contact, so you'll have the information for follow-up contact later.

6. **Continue to build your network.** Your network is something that will never be complete. You should always be looking for people to add to your network and expand your horizons.

You'll be surprised how quickly you can build an effective network that will help you not only find a job after retirement, but will also help build an active social network outside of work. One of the hardest things for most retirees is the loss of professional contacts. You can avoid this feeling of loss by proactively building your network even before you retire.

Online job networks for seniors

You'll find online networks for people over 55 that are looking for jobs popping up all over the Internet. Seniors can log onto these sites and find work, primarily consulting work but also some salaried jobs. Most of these sites focus on specific areas, such as finance, engineering, or biotechnology and some of them were even started by companies seeking to reconnect with retired workers. Here are four of the top sites you can find on the Internet:

✔ **YourEncore.com** (www.yourencore.com): Eli Lilly and Company and Proctor & Gamble started this site in 2003 to reconnect with retirees from these two companies. By 2006, the site is flourishing and assists older job seekers with positions in member and nonmember companies. The members seek older professionals who were scientists, engineers, or product developers during their careers before retirement. The jobs posted are primarily short-term projects designed to solve specific problems. Boeing, National Starch, 3M Co., and Ethicon Endo-Surgery joined the founders as member companies. YourEncore.com hires the job seekers as contractors because many corporations have pensions that are set up that do not legally allow the corporation to hire someone already drawing a pension from that company, even on a contract basis.

✔ **Seniors4Hire** (`www.seniors4hire.org`): Seniors4Hire started by accident in 2003. Forward Group actually intended to start a site for teens looking for jobs called Teens4Hire, which does still exist on the Internet, but found that many employers were interested in hiring older adults. They didn't believe teens had the right attitude. Three companies that are now members of the site urged the Forward Group to develop Seniors4Hire — Bank of America, RadioShack Corp., and Regal Entertainment Group. You can join the site for free as long as you are at least 50 years old. In 2006, the site had over 200,000 job seekers age 50 or older and more than 550 employers that post jobs. Industry groups that post on the site include financial services, retail, telecommunications, and healthcare.

✔ **Employment Network for Retired Government Experts** (`www.enrge.us`): This site focuses on building a job network for former U.S. government workers who want to try working in the private sector. The founder Jay Zavala is a Vietnam-era veteran and retired government professional. In addition to running this site, he owns his own business consulting firm, Zavala, Inc., based in Massachusetts. He created this network for men and women who dedicated their careers to government service and want to remain productive in their professions or fields of expertise after retirement. Only retired federal, state, or local government employees or government employees within 12 months of a scheduled retirement can use this free service. Government contractors, entrepreneurs, venture capitalists, human resource managers, investors, inventors, industrialists, small, large, and emerging business owners, and other employers use this site's database of candidates. Jobs offered through this site tend to be contract-based, but some are full- or part-time. Employers pay $1,000 to access the database for an 18-month period.

✔ **SeniorJobBank** (`www.seniorjobbank.org`): This is the older of the senior job-networking sites on the Internet. It was started in 1999, but didn't really take off until the NHC Group of Massachusetts relaunched it in 2005. You'll find about 200 jobs available each day and listings are on a state-by-state basis. Anyone over the age of 50 can use the site for free. Employers pay $89 per job posting. You'll find jobs ranging from entry level to senior executive.

Joining a Support Group

As you sort out all the changes you're facing moving from a full-time career to retirement, you may find that you need support from others who face similar challenges. While your family and friends may be there for support, sometimes only someone else experiencing the same life changes can really offer the type of support you need.

Support groups provide mutual aid and support for people who share the same quandary. A good support group can be a place where you can find accurate and current information to help you make informed choices, as well as provide emotional support for the changes you are going through.

Support group successes have been shown over and over again in the medical field. People who participate in support groups for a particular disease from which they are recovering usually show faster improvement than those who do not participate.

Support groups can communicate through newsletters, meetings, or discussion forums on the Internet. Moral support from a group can be very helpful when struggling with a lifestyle change. They can help you improve and promote coping skills and reduce the stress associated with the change. Change isn't easy, and knowing there are others out there struggling with the same life stresses makes it easier to cope. You won't feel so alone trying to handle the stresses that come with this major life change. I can guarantee that moving from full-time work to retirement is a major life change, probably one of the most major changes you still have to face.

Uncovering how support groups work

Support groups work a bit differently depending on the method of communication chosen for the group. I participated in or ran groups using each of the three common methods — newsletters, meetings, and discussion forums.

Newsletter support groups

Newsletter support groups are primarily for information sharing. You won't get much individual support from this type of support group. But, if you are the type of person who just wants a place to share information and aren't comfortable talking with a group of strangers, this might be your best choice. You also may find that the newsletter support group provides information you can share with another type of support group — meetings or discussion forums.

Meeting support groups

Meeting support groups set a specific meeting time — usually once a week, once every two weeks, or once a month. People share issues related to the topic of the group and help each other sort through the issues. It's important to have some strict rules in this type of support group. In ones that I've run in the past, I've always insisted that people agree to these rules before participating:

- ✔ **Anything said in the room stays in the room.** People must feel secure that they can open up regarding private issues and that these private issues will not be discussed outside the room.

- ✔ **People should not respond by telling someone they are wrong, but instead discuss how they might handle a situation in a better way.** If people are critical of each other, groups will tend to break down as people become more and more afraid to speak up and clam up to avoid criticism. The environment must be supportive and helpful, not destructive and critical.

- ✔ **Set a time limit for each person to speak initially, so everyone gets a chance to participate.** You don't want someone dominating the group and not giving others time to discuss issues critical for them.

The leader of the group should maintain the rules set by the group, but should not impose so much structure that the group becomes stifled. The leader usually gathers information about issues discussed that can be shared in the next meeting or asks someone else to do the research on a particular issue.

Discussion forum support groups

These forums usually are managed by professional associations for their members, but you can also find them on the Internet in places like Delphi Forums (`www.delphiforums.com`), which are member-managed communities. Delphi Forums started in 1983 and is a thriving group of communities on just about any topic you might want.

Usually a discussion forum will have a series of discussion threads, initially created by the forum manager. The organization of the threads helps people to find the information they are seeking. Also the threads help participants to carry on discussions about specific topics. You'll be amazed by how much support you can receive through these types of support groups, but you also must be careful. Even though most of these groups require password access, they still are not as private as those small face-to-face meetings where you know and can see who is participating.

What type works best for you will depend on the type of person you are. Meetings work the best if you need that personal face-to-face contact in order to open up. Discussion forums can be the best if you like to have feedback, but prefer not to talk about things in front of others. You can even create an identity in a discussion forum that is different than the name you use in the real world. That's both a blessing and a curse; while you can hide your true identity, so can anyone else who is participating. So be careful what you post on an Internet forum.

Finding support groups near you

The best place to find support groups near you is through organizations to which you belong. This can include professional organizations, business organizations, religious organizations, or social organizations to which you belong.

Many churches, synagogues, and mosques provide various types of support groups for their members and don't necessarily advertise them. The best way to find out about them is to talk with your religious leader. Often the support groups based within a religious community are kept secret to provide support in a confidential way to the people participating.

Other good places to start when looking for support groups are community centers, especially ones that provide senior activities. Many community centers host support groups of all types.

If you're having no luck finding groups in your area on your own, you can try searching for one through the American Self-Help Clearinghouse (`mentalhelp.net/selfhelp`). Search for a topic of your choice at this site and you'll get a list of groups that may be near you. The clearinghouse maintains a database of over 1,100 national, international, model, and online self-help support groups for addictions, bereavement, health, mental health, disabilities, abuse, parenting, caregiver concerns, and other stressful life situations. You can also find lists of local self-help clearinghouses worldwide, information on starting face-to-face and online groups, and a registry for persons interested in starting national or international self-help groups.

Part II
Your Wallet to Your Health: The 411 When You Re-Enter the Workforce

In this part . . .

You may find it difficult to manage your retirement savings and pensions, as well as figure out how to preserve them while paying the mounting costs of health care. In this part I help you get a grip on what you have saved and provide you with strategies so you can develop a plan that will help you avoid running out of money during retirement. You also find information that will help you traverse the bureaucratic maze of Social Security and Medicare benefits. In addition, I give you ideas on how to get the health care you need and coverage for it, whether you qualify for Medicare or you don't.

Chapter 5

Getting a Grasp on Managing What You Saved for Retirement

....

In This Chapter

▶ Exploring what you own

▶ Following the distribution rules

▶ Investing wisely

....

*Y*ou likely own a large portfolio of investments to manage from your employer-based retirement savings plans (401(k)s, cash benefit plans, profit-sharing plans, and others. In addition, you may also have IRAs or other retirement savings. Each type of plan has a different set of rules for how you can manage the money and how you can withdraw the money.

In this chapter, I review the many different types of retirement accounts you may hold and the rules for each. I also talk about investing strategies to help you continue to grow your portfolio in retirement.

Exploring Your Retirement Accounts

Hopefully, you've been saving all your life for retirement through various types of employer-based retirement savings plans or individual retirement accounts. Most likely your contribution was automatically taken out of your paycheck, and if you had retirement benefits, your employer contributed to your retirement savings account as well.

But do you understand what you have? The language of retirement savings is unique. Many people paid into a retirement account their entire working life, but have no idea how to manage the nest egg they now own.

Before we discuss management strategies, I first want to explore exactly what you might have. I also want to introduce you to the language of retirement savings.

Defined contributions versus defined benefits

Every retirement account is either a defined-contribution or defined-benefit account. They differ greatly regarding who manages them and how much freedom you have to get your money.

- ✔ **Defined-benefit plans** are traditional pension plans. In these types of plans, the rules specify what your benefit will be no matter how much you or your employer put into the plan. The benefit usually is determined by your last three or last five years of wages or salary. Another key factor that is used to determine your benefit is the number of years you worked for the company or government entity. Once determined, your defined benefit will be the same for the rest of your life and will never run out. Your employer continues to manage the money to be sure you won't run out.

- ✔ **Defined-contribution plans** include various types of retirement plans that you can contribute to while working, such as a 401(k) or 403(b). Many times the employer matches at least part of your contribution. When you are ready to retire, the nest egg you've saved will have to last you for the rest of your life. You will decide how and when to take the money out of the account. It's your responsibility to manage the way the funds are invested. You also must be sure you don't run out of money in retirement.

If you're already collecting your retirement benefits, this chapter will help you understand what you have. If you haven't started to collect benefits and are just beginning your pre-retirement planning, this chapter will help you with your decision making about how to handle your employer-sponsored retirement savings.

Pensions (defined-benefit plan)

Traditional pensions gradually are becoming extinct (read Chapter 8 for more information about why). If you do have one, consider yourself lucky. Most companies are shifting their pension plans to cash-balance plans (a hybrid between a defined-contribution and defined-benefit plan) or changing the rules for new hires so they don't qualify for them. Instead, new hires only get access to a defined-contribution plan.

Pensions were started in the workplace to reward employees for loyalty and long-term service to a company. The benefits are considered "backloaded," because you have to be with a company a long time to see any value in a defined-benefit plan.

Calculating payout

The money you'll actually receive at retirement is based on your age, your earnings, and your years of service. Some companies calculate their benefits as a percentage of your salary and years of service. For example, 1 percent of final pay times the number of years of service. Other plans calculate the benefit by a specific dollar amount. For example, $25 per month for every year that you worked for the company. Other companies promise an exact dollar amount per month, such as $100 per month. All companies set a minimum age before you can qualify for benefits.

Most pension benefits are calculated using this common formula:

$$\text{Pay} \times \text{Years of Service} \times \text{Benefit Factor} = \text{Pension Payment}$$

Here's what each element refers to:

- ✔ **Pay:** The figure to be used for pay varies greatly from company to company. Some use the highest three to ten years, others use the most recent three to ten years. In some companies, bonuses and incentives are included in the calculation, while others don't include those extras. You'll need to read the fine print in your pension plan documentation to find out how the pay level to be used in the formula is determined.

- ✔ **Years of Service:** If you worked steadily for a company without taking any extended breaks, then this is an easy number to calculate. But, if you took an extended break, such as time off under the Family Medical Leave Act, then the way these breaks are handled can impact your years of service. In some companies or government entities, you can buy back the years of service lost during breaks.

- ✔ **Benefit Factor:** All pensions have a benefit factor that will be stated in your documents. The factor usually ranges between 1 and 2 percent of your pay. This is usually set to give the highest benefit to a long-term employee who has worked the ideal maximum number of years for the company. For example, if a company wants to reward a 40-year employee with a guarantee of 50 percent of his salary at retirement, the factor would be 1.25 percent ($40 \times .0125 = 50$ percent).

Using this formula, I can show you how a company backloads a pension plan. I will look at three employees. Larry who worked 40 years for the company, Sandy who worked 20 years for the company, and Kathy who worked 10 years for the company. All three ended their careers with their highest five years averaging $50,000. Check out what their individual formulas look like:

Kathy's pension benefit: $50,000 \times 10 \times .0125 = \$6,250$

Sandy's pension benefit: $50,000 \times 20 \times .0125 = \$12,500$

Larry's pension benefit: $50,000 \times 40 \times .0125 = \$25,000$

You can see that Larry's pension is four times Kathy's and twice Sandy's. The employer in this example wanted people to stay around for a long time and rewarded them with a good pension to encourage that longevity. That type of reward is rare in today's global economy. If your grandchildren are just entering the job market today, they will have a hard time finding a company that still offers pensions to their newly hired employees.

Deciding payout method

The key decision you have to make when filling out the paperwork to start collecting your pension benefits is how you want to receive them. Most companies offer you a number of different payout options. Here are the three most common:

- **Single life allowance:** You will get the biggest monthly check if you choose this option, but all payments stop upon your death. If your spouse does not have a pension plan, that means he or she would have to live on savings and Social Security benefits.

- **Joint allowance:** You will get a reduced monthly check for your lifetime, but if you die first, your spouse (or other named beneficiary) will continue to get the check. Many companies offer a variation on this and you can set it up so your beneficiary gets 25, 50, or 75 percent of your benefit. If you choose the reduced beneficiary benefit, your check will be higher, but be careful. Often the costs of living in retirement are not much different for the sole remaining person and can sometimes be higher if medical costs are high. So think twice before agreeing to a reduced benefit for your beneficiary.

- **Pop-up joint allowance:** You will get a lower monthly check than the standard joint allowance, but the big advantage of this option is that if your beneficiary dies first, your check will pop back up to the single life allowance. This option also provides for a 25, 50, or 75 percent benefit for your beneficiary rather than the full benefit.

Before you decide how you want to take your retirement benefits, you also might want to think about whether you want to work for the company again as a consultant or part-time after you retire. Most companies don't allow you to earn money directly from the company once you're collecting a retirement check. So, if you do think you'd like to go back to work after you officially retire, check the rules before starting your pension payout.

You might find that your company offers other options as well. In making your decision about which one to choose, take a look at what you will receive monthly and add in whatever your spouse will receive. Also compare what the benefits will be after one of you dies and determine what will give both of you the best benefit through both of your lifetimes.

WARNING!

You may want to consult a financial advisor before making a choice about your pension options. You will have to live with your choice for the rest of your life. You can't change the decision you make at retirement three years into retirement.

Changing the pension rules

Companies made these pension plan promises, but now most don't want to keep them. Their retirement benefits are a heavy burden, especially because so many companies underfunded their retirement portfolios and don't have the cash they need to pay all their retirees. So instead, many large companies converted to a hybrid called the cash-balance plan, which is somewhere between a defined-benefit and defined-contribution plan, but much closer to a defined-contribution plan.

If your traditional defined-benefit plan was converted to a cash-balance plan, then a formula was used at the time of conversion to determine a cash value for the traditional defined-benefit plan based on your years of service and your salary. After conversion, your employer will continue to contribute to this plan. When you retire, your payout will be based on the cash value at retirement.

Your employer manages the money in your cash-balance plan. Each year you are still working, your employer contributes a portion of your pay plus an interest credit (which can be a fixed amount or a variable amount set to an index, such as the one-year U.S. Treasury bill interest rate).

If your company converted to a cash-balance plan, then at retirement you will be offered one of two ways to get your money:

✔ **Annuity:** An annuity guarantees you a set amount each month for the rest of your life. Your company or a company they designate (usually an insurance company or financial institution) continues to manage the money.

> ✔ **Lump-sum cash payout:** The lump-sum cash payout should be rolled into an individual retirement account (IRA) or you'll be hit with a huge tax bill. You'll be responsible for managing the money.

Employer savings plans (defined-contribution plans)

In today's world, few people stay with a company long enough to earn a pension. Many people move around to get promotions and pay increases. Others find they are laid off before they have enough time with the company for the pension to be worth anything.

In answer to this changing world, many companies have changed their retirement benefits to something more portable called a 401(k). If you work for a nonprofit entity, you have a similar type of plan called a 403(b). Both of these plan names are parts of the tax code.

They are called defined-contribution plans because it is defined upfront how much the company will contribute to the plan rather than how much the company will give you as a retirement benefit. Most companies structure their defined-contribution plans based on a matching system. You decide to put in a certain percentage of your salary and the company will match it dollar for dollar up to a certain percentage or dollar amount. For example, a common match companies offer is that for the first 5 percent you contribute to your 401(k), your company will contribute 5 percent.

You should contribute at least as much as the company will match. If you don't contribute an amount equal to the match the company offers, it's like giving up free money.

The biggest benefit defined-contribution plans offer over defined-benefit plans is that you can take your contributions with you when you change jobs. How much you will be able to take with you depends on how long you work with the company.

Vesting (getting ownership rights)

Everything you contribute to the 401(k) or 403(b) is yours to take whenever you leave. But, contributions your employer made must become *vested* (get ownership rights) before you can take the money with you. Be sure you understand the vesting rules before deciding to change jobs. If you're a year or less away from being fully vested, you may want to hold on and be sure to get your employer's contributions.

Employers have two ways they can set up vesting rules — three-year cliff vesting and six-year graded vesting. Here's how they work:

- ✔ **Three-year cliff vesting:** You will become fully vested and be able to take all your employer's contributions to your retirement plan with you once you've worked for a company for at least three years. If you leave before that time, you lose all your employer's matching contributions, but you can take your contributions with you.

- ✔ **Six-year graded vesting:** You start building your rights to your employer's contributions after you have worked for the company for one year. Beginning with year two, you become 20 percent vested each year. After you've worked six years for the company, you are 100 percent vested and can take all your employer's contributions to your retirement plan with you.

If you change jobs and are 100 percent vested, you can roll out the funds in your employer's retirement account to an individual retirement account IRA or you can roll the funds into your new employer's 401(k). I've always rolled them into my personal IRA so I could pick my own investments and not be limited to those chosen by my employer as part of the 401(k) plan.

Don't ever take the money and spend it. Unfortunately, 40 percent of the people who roll out their 401(k)s spend at least part of the money rather than roll it over into another retirement savings account. If you do that, you'll be living on a very limited income in retirement or you'll be working until you die. Not only do you extend your working years, you also get a lot less of the money.

There are stiff penalties and taxes on the money when you withdraw it early. You pay a 10 percent penalty, plus it's taxed at your regular income tax rate. Many people give up as much as 40 percent of their lump sum to taxes if they decide to use it right away.

While the portability is an important benefit of 401(k)s and 403(b)s, the big thing you lose is the portfolio management skills of a professional pension plan manager. You make the investment choices for your defined-contribution plan. You are responsible to be sure you'll have enough money to make it through retirement.

Types of defined-contribution plans

The 401(k) and 403(b) are the most common types of defined-contribution plans if you worked for a major corporation, but if you worked for a small business, you may have a different type of plan from your current or former workplace:

✔ **SEP-IRA:** The Simplified Employee Pension (SEP-IRA) is actually a type of IRA your employer sets up for you. Your employer makes all contributions to your SEP-IRA. Your employer can contribute as much as 25 percent of your compensation (but most do contribute much less) up to a max of $44,000. You are immediately fully vested in this type of plan and can take it all with you when you leave.

✔ **SIMPLE IRA:** The Savings Incentive Match Plan for Employees (SIMPLE IRA) allows contributions from the employer and employee. In a SIMPLE IRA, the employer can contribute up to 3 percent of your salary. Employees can contribute up to $10,000. If you are 50 or older, you can contribute up to $12,500 beginning January 1, 2007. You are immediately fully vested in this type of plan.

✔ **Profit-sharing plans:** Some small businesses set up profit-sharing plans rather than defined-contribution plans. These allow you to share a slice of your company's profits. Annual contributions to these types of plans are based on the company's performance and are likely to vary each year. Your employer can contribute as much as 25 percent of your salary up to a maximum of $44,000. Vesting rules vary from company to company. You'll have to check with your company to find out when you become fully vested and can take the money with you when you leave.

✔ **Keoghs:** These are the granddaddy of small-business retirement plans, which were established in 1962. You won't find many of these around today. Some are structured similarly to a traditional pension plan while others are closer to a defined-contribution plan. It all depends on how your employer set it up. If you are part of a Keogh plan, you will need to ask the person responsible for benefits to explain how the plan works and what your benefits will be when you leave.

IRAs

In addition to employer-sponsored retirement savings, you can also open individual retirement accounts. Individual retirement accounts come in three different options — traditional tax-deductible, non-tax-deductible, and ROTH.

Traditional tax-deductible IRA

This type of IRA is primarily for someone who does not have a retirement savings plan or pension through their employer. If you have a traditional IRA, you can contribute up to $4,000 per year and it's fully tax deductible. If you are 50 years old or older, you can add $1,000 and contribute up to $5,000. In 2008, the base amount per year will go up to $5,000 and anyone 50-plus will be able to contribute $6,000 toward the traditional IRA.

What is MAGI?

Many people wonder how modified adjusted growth income differs from adjusted growth income. The MAGI is only used when calculating IRA contributions. Your adjusted growth income is modified by adding back in certain items, such as foreign income, foreign-housing deductions, student-loan deductions, IRA-contribution deductions, and deductions for higher-education costs. If you are near the qualifying income of $100,000 for a Roth IRA, these additions can make you ineligible.

The amount you contribute is tax deductible provided you are not covered by an employer-sponsored retirement plan. If you are covered, you can't fund a traditional IRA once you make more than $60,000 if single and $85,000 if married. Your IRA grows tax-deferred until you start taking the money out at retirement. I talk about withdrawal rules in the section "Taking Out Your Money — the Official Rules," later in this chapter.

Traditional non-tax-deductible IRA

This type of IRA is primarily for someone who wants to sock away a bit more money tax-deferred, but already has an employer-sponsored retirement savings plan or pension at work. The amount you can contribute to a traditional non-tax-deductible IRA are the same as the tax-deductible type, but you won't be able to write your contributions to the IRA off on your taxes.

The traditional non-tax-deductible IRA doesn't make much sense today because there is a better option. Since you can't write off your contributions, you're much better off with a Roth IRA.

Roth IRA

Roth IRAs are an excellent way to save extra money for retirement completely tax free. You can't deduct the amount you contribute, but all the money you withdraw in retirement after the age of 59½ can be withdrawn without having to worry about taxes. That means your money can grow inside an IRA and you won't pay taxes on any of the earnings from interest, dividends, or capital gains.

The amount you can contribute to a Roth IRA is the same as the traditional tax-deductible IRA. You can contribute to a Roth IRA even if you have an employer-sponsored retirement plan. Your modified adjusted gross income (MAGI) must be less than $110,000 if you are single and less than $160,000 if you are married to be eligible to contribute to a Roth IRA.

If you have a traditional tax-deductible IRA or other retirement funds to which you contributed tax-deferred (such as a 401(k) that you take out when you leave a job), you can roll these funds into a Roth IRA, but you will have to pay income taxes on the money. If your MAGI exceeds $100,000, you can't contribute to a Roth IRA by rolling over funds from tax-deferred accounts. The rules for withdrawing the funds are more flexible than traditional IRAs. I talk more about that in the next section "Taking Out Your Money — the Official Rules."

Taking Out Your Money — the Official Rules

Every one of these retirement savings plans has slightly different rules regarding when you may start to draw the money and how much you must withdraw. Some have rules that require you start to withdraw the money by a particular date, while others leave the decision about when you want to start taking out the money completely in your hands.

I talk more about how to actually manage your withdrawals to make sure you don't run out of money during retirement in Chapter 6. That's actually a very different topic than the official withdrawal rules.

When you must start to draw money

When you can start taking out the money will depend on the type of retirement account you have. Each type has its own set of rules. All but the Roth IRA require that you pay income tax on the money as it is withdrawn. The amount of tax you will pay will depend on your income-tax bracket.

401(k)s and 403(b)s

You must make a decision about how you want your money distributed when you leave the company that provided you with a 401(k) or 403(b). If you're not near retirement age when you leave, you're best bet is to roll it out into an IRA and take control of the money. You may be able to roll the funds into your new employer's retirement savings plan, but check out the investment options before you do. Usually you can find better options in your own IRA.

If you don't roll out your account balance into an IRA, you may be able to leave the money in your employer's care and choose an annuity when you reach retirement age. If offered, the annuity options will be similar to those mentioned above in the "Pensions (defined-benefit plan)" section — single-life allowance and joint allowance. There will also likely be a cash certain option, where you can decide how many years you want to receive a payment, such as 5-year certain, 10-year certain, or 20-year certain. If you die before the end of the period chosen, your beneficiary will receive the remaining payments. If you choose an annuity, you will have payments for life (or the time period chosen), but your beneficiary will only get additional money if you choose a joint allowance.

You can leave your money in the account if you go back to work after retirement, but no matter what you do, when you reach age 70½ you will have to start taking out your money. You can't delay it longer than that.

Traditional IRAs

If you have a traditional IRA, you can't start withdrawing your funds without penalty until the age of 59½. You also must start taking the funds, even if you don't need them because you are working, once you reach age 70½.

If you retire early and want to draw the funds sooner or you decide you need the money before age 59½, you will likely face a penalty of 10 percent when withdrawing the funds. You also will have to pay taxes due on the amount of money you withdraw. You can avoid the penalty but not the income taxes if you take the money out for higher education, first-time home purchase, or death or disability.

Whenever you take funds out of a traditional IRA, you will have to pay income taxes on the money withdrawn. The one exception to this rule is that if you put money into a non-tax-deductible traditional IRA, your contributions to the fund are not taxable because you paid taxes on them before depositing the money in the IRA, but you do pay taxes on any gains made with the money contributed.

Be sure you keep your non-taxable traditional IRA separate from all other IRAs. If you co-mingle the funds of a tax-deductible IRA and a non-tax-deductible IRA, you will need to pay income taxes on all the money.

SIMPLE or SEP-IRAs

If your employer sponsored a SIMPLE or SEP-IRA for you, the rules for withdrawal are the same as they are for a traditional IRA. You own the account from the day your company opens it for you and you will be able to withdraw the money the same way you would with a traditional IRA. If you keep the money in your SIMPLE IRA for less than two years, you will have to pay a 25 percent penalty rather than just a 10 percent penalty.

Profit-sharing plan

If your company offered a profit-sharing plan, its withdrawal rules will be the same as those for a 401(k). You will have a 10 percent penalty if you withdraw the funds before age 59½ and you will have to pay income tax on the funds as you withdraw them.

Roth IRA

The Roth IRA is the only type of retirement savings you have that is not taxed as you withdraw the money as long as you wait until age 59½. If you need to withdraw the money before that age, you can withdraw your annual contributions tax-free.

If you need to withdraw the money for the purpose of buying a house for the first time, you can withdraw the money from your Roth IRA tax-free provided the money was deposited in the Roth IRA for at least five years. If you withdraw the money for any other purpose, you will need to pay taxes on the earnings, but not on your initial contributions.

Exceptions for illness and unemployment

If you are younger than 59½, you may be able to avoid paying taxes and penalties on your retirement savings for certain reasons.

If your medical expenses exceed 7.5 percent of your adjusted gross income, you can withdraw funds from your tax-deductible IRA without a penalty, but you will have to pay income taxes on the money. You can also withdraw the money you contributed in a non-tax-deductible IRA without penalty, but you will have to pay taxes on the earnings. Money in a Roth IRA can be withdrawn without paying any taxes or penalties if needed for these purposes.

You can also use IRA funds for paying health insurance if you collect federal unemployment benefits for 12 consecutive weeks. The rules for withdrawals to pay health insurance benefits are the same as those for medical expenses.

How much you must withdraw

Once you reach the age of 70½, you don't have a choice. Even if you are working, you will have to start withdrawing funds from your retirement savings accounts. The only exception to this are funds in your Roth IRA. There are no mandatory withdrawal rules for the Roth IRA.

The amount you must withdraw will be lower than the amount you will likely withdraw once you start depending on your retirement savings to meet your budget. I talk more about managing your withdrawals so you don't run out of money in Chapter 6. In this section, I will just briefly discuss the official rules for how much you must withdraw to avoid taxes and penalties.

You probably won't have to worry about these rules unless you are working and not ready to start funding your retirement with your savings. Many working retirees decide to leave the money in their retirement savings accounts as long as possible, and some even add to them.

If you don't take out the minimum amount required, you will have to pay a 50 percent penalty on any shortfall. It's a hefty penalty, so don't make this mistake. The money is much better off in your pocket than the government's.

Luckily it's not too hard to figure out your required minimum each year. The IRS developed two tables. One table assumes your beneficiary is not more than 10 years younger than you. There is a separate table if your beneficiary is 10 years younger than you (see Table 5-1).

Table 5-1	IRS Mandatory Distributions for Retirement Savings
Age	*Distribution Factor*
70	:27.4
71	:26.5
72	:25.6
73	:24.7
74	:23.8
75	:22.9
76	:21.2
77	:20.3
78	:20.3
79	:19.5
80	:18.7

(continued)

Table 5-1 *(continued)*

Age	Distribution Factor
81	:17.9
82	:17.1
83	:16.3
84	:15.5
85	:14.8
86	:14.1
87	:13.4
88	:12.7
89	:12.0
90	:11.4

This table does go up to 114, but to save space I'm just including the numbers up to age 90. You can find this full table, as well as the table to use if you have a younger beneficiary, in IRS Publication 590 (traditional IRAs) online at www.irs.gov/publications/p590. By the time you reach 70½, any money you are not withdrawing is likely sitting in a Traditional or Roth IRA. If you do still have money sitting in your former employer-sponsored retirement account that you have not started to withdraw, check with your former employer about withdrawal rules.

To calculate the amount you must withdraw each year once you reach 70½, pick out the distribution factor next to your age. Then divide the amount you have in your IRA account by this distribution factor. For example, suppose a retiree who is 72 years old has $300,000 in retirement funds. Here are the steps for calculating his minimum withdrawal:

1. Find his distribution factor on the chart. It's 25.6.

2. Divide $300,000 by 25.6.

3. The amount that must be withdrawn at age 72 to avoid a 50 percent penalty is $11,718.75.

Even the most conservative financial planner will tell you that it is safe to withdraw 4 percent yearly from your retirement savings. A 4 percent withdrawal would total $12,000. So you can see the minimum withdrawals are slightly below that and shouldn't create a major burden for you even if you are working and have to pay income taxes on your salary, Social Security, and the distribution.

Yes, by age 72 you should be getting your Social Security benefits as well. While you can delay taking those benefits, there is no reason to do so after age 70. I talk more about why that is true in Chapter 8.

If you don't need the mandatory distribution funds because you are still working, you can always deposit them in a Roth IRA. There is no age limit for depositing money in that type of IRA. That way your money can grow tax free for the rest of your life. If you never need it, you can leave it to your heirs. There is never an obligation to withdraw funds from a Roth IRA.

Investing the Money You Have

Hopefully by the time you reach retirement you will have a sizeable nest egg that you can tap as you enjoy your retirement years. Most people decide to go back to work when they realize their nest egg isn't quite large enough to do the things they want to do.

Avoiding common mistakes

Investing your nest egg properly, whatever size you have, is critical to extending its life throughout your life span. Avoiding these mistakes can help you manage your nest egg better during retirement:

- **Forgetting about asset allocation:** Many people think that the most important aspect of managing a portfolio is picking the right stocks, bonds, and mutual funds. They're wrong. The individual stocks, bonds, or mutual funds account for only 5 to 10 percent of a portfolio's success. More than 90 percent of that success can be credited to the way you allocate your assets among stocks, bonds, and money market instruments.

- **Playing it too safely:** Another key mistake most people make as they prepare for retirement is to move all their assets into investment vehicles with fixed returns, such as bonds and money market funds. That's a big mistake because most people live at least 20 years in retirement. If you depend solely on interest, which usually falls below the inflation rate, your portfolio will gradually be eaten away by inflation.

> You must continue to grow your portfolio in the early years of retirement. In order to continue to grow your portfolio and beat inflation, you do need to have at least a 20 percent stock component in that portfolio. That can be either through purchasing stocks directly or by buying stock mutual funds and letting a professional money manager do the stock picking for you.

Allocating your investments

Proper asset allocation involves five key factors — investment goal, time horizon, risk tolerance, financial resources, and investment mix. You must weigh your needs, your personality, and how well you accept risk in order to best plan your asset allocation.

Your investment goal

Why are you saving? That's an easy answer for most of you at this time — to have enough money in retirement. But some of you may be thinking you want to start a business or you may have other goals.

You may want to have enough money to help grandchildren go to college. You may want to set aside money for your grandchildren's or great-grandchildren's life events — such as weddings or christenings or bar and bat mitzvahs.

Make a list of all the things you'd like to have money for in the future and tally up what you might need to figure out your investment needs. If your needs are higher than what you have in your portfolio, you must do one of two things — change your goals or go back to work to earn more money.

Your time horizon

How long will you have until you are going to need the money? When you need the money does impact how you should invest it.

If you think you will need to use the money in two to three years, that portion of your portfolio should be in cash or money market funds. Money you'll need in three to five years is best socked away in a bond fund. The rest can be put in a faster-growing stock fund or individual stocks. Each year you can reallocate your funds to keep this mix in place.

You don't want to be forced into a situation where you have to sell a losing investment, like a stock that's not performing well at the time, just to meet your bills. By giving yourself at least a five-year horizon to sell a stock asset, you can usually find a good time to sell and avoid a huge loss. Don't get me wrong: I'm not saying you can avoid selling every stock asset without accepting some possible losses (mistakes are made and economic shocks can impact the market for a long time), but if you have at least five years to sell an asset, you have a better chance of finding a good time to sell and avoid a loss.

Your risk tolerance

How much risk can you accept in your portfolio and still be able to sleep at night? You need to think about that carefully. If your portfolio allocation is so risky that you're worrying about it each day, it's not worth the risk.

If you want to try to gauge your risk tolerance, answer these four questions:

- ✔ Do fluctuations in the market keep you up all night?
- ✔ Do you have a minimal understanding about investing?
- ✔ Do you think of yourself as a saver more than an investor?
- ✔ Do you have a great fear about losing more than 25 percent of your assets in a few weeks?

If you answered yes to all four questions, you are likely a conservative investor. You should still have a stock component in your portfolio to insure that your funds continue to grow throughout your retirement, but your best bet may be to pick a balanced mutual fund or a life-cycle mutual fund that manages the risk for you without taking any great swings up or down. You won't ever have a significant growth spurt, but you also won't experience a significant loss for a short period of time.

If you think you can tolerate a bit more risk, answer these questions:

- ✔ Do you feel comfortable with the ups and downs of the market?
- ✔ Do you understand the ins and outs of investing, as well as how the securities markets work?
- ✔ Do you understand the concept of investing for the long-term and not worrying about short-term loses in a down market?
- ✔ Can you accept significant short-term loses without panicking and selling your holdings?

If you answered yes to these questions, you are likely an aggressive investor and willing to take more risk with your portfolio to grow your money.

If your answers were a mix among these sets of questions, then you are a moderate investor and fall between these two extremes.

Your financial resources

How much do you have in your portfolio? How much you have will impact how well you can diversify your portfolio. Basically, it's not wise to put more than 4 percent of your portfolio in any one investment, such as an individual stock or bond. If you don't have enough to diversify properly, use mutual funds that are already well diversified.

Your investment mix

How well is your portfolio balanced among these three key elements — cash, stocks, and bonds? The way you mix the three key elements will impact the return you can get. A portfolio invested mostly in cash vehicles (money market funds and certificates of deposit) will have the lowest return, but is the safest, if your primary concern is loss of principal and you're not worried about taxes or inflation eating away your returns. A portfolio invested only in stocks will have the highest return but is the riskiest. By properly allocating those components, you can reduce risk and still grow your money.

In Chapter 6, I discuss withdrawal strategies. Your portfolio mix also affects how much you can withdraw from your portfolio each year and not run out of money.

Your home and your retirement portfolio

Another big part of most people's holdings in retirement is their home. By the time you retire, it's best to own that home free and clear, so you don't have a mortgage payment.

That will free up a sizeable lump of cash you can use to do other things you want. It also gives you a great safety net that you can fall back on in your later retirement years if you run out of money in your retirement savings accounts.

If you do need to take the money out of your home, you can stay in the home and apply for what is called a *reverse mortgage*. These mortgages can be structured to allow you to stay in your home for life and pay you a set monthly amount rather than you paying the bank. For more information on reverse mortgages, check out *Reverse Mortgages For Dummies* (Wiley).

Be careful though if you decide to take a reverse mortgage. Make sure you involve an attorney who understands reverse mortgage contracts. You will find some crooks out there who just want your home and will not worry about your needs.

Changing your strategies as you age

When you first retire, you can have 60 to 70 percent of your portfolio in stocks, but you may want to start shifting some of that money into bonds pretty quickly as long as market conditions are good. Remember, you likely will live about 20 years in retirement, so you want that money to last you a long time.

Stock and bond markets can be erratic with lots of ups and downs. Yes, bonds do lose value. They are safer than stocks, but you may not be able to get the face value of the bond if you want to sell it before it matures.

Bonds tend to move in the opposite direction of stocks, which makes them a good choice for balancing out a portfolio. Bonds will drop in value when interest rates rise and will increase in value when interest rates fall. That's because as interest rates rise, a bond that pays a lower interest rate will be worth less because it has a lower return.

You can decide to invest directly in bonds or stocks or use a mix of mutual funds. Mutual funds do give you the advantage of professional management, but be cautious of paying any upfront commissions (front load) or back-end commissions (back load). You also need to watch the annual fee structure for every mutual fund. Look for no-load funds (commission free) and funds whose fees are under 1 percent. A great book to read more about investing through mutual funds is *Mutual Funds For Dummies* (Wiley).

Your primary goal is to have the cash you need when you need it without having to take a loss on any part of your portfolio. I can't guarantee that you will never take a loss, everyone makes a mistake in choosing investment opportunities sometimes. But following the general rule of moving money to cash one to two years before needing it minimizes your risk of taking a loss.

The key thing you want to avoid is being forced to sell a stock or bond in a losing position just because you need the cash. Carefully managing your investment mix as you age helps you avoid this type of crisis.

Follow these steps while managing your portfolio in retirement to minimize your risk of taking a loss:

1. **Shift some stocks to bonds.** It's best to shift stock holdings to bonds about three to five years before you need the money. As you age, it's good to be sure that your portfolio balance includes bonds for the money you think you will need in three to five years. That way you can count on a higher level of growth than cash accounts offer, but your principle is less likely to be at risk.

You can, of course, convert your stock immediately to cash holdings and not touch your bond holdings if the stock market is up and the bond market is down.

2. **Shift some bonds to a cash vehicle.** Convert your bond holdings from Step 1 into cash when you think you are one or two years away from needing the money. Giving yourself that much time will enable you to convert the bonds at a good time when you will get the best return on your bonds.

Your time horizon for needing the money is a critical factor in deciding where to put your funds. You don't want to be caught in a down market when you need to sell stocks or bonds. You can avoid being caught by shifting money that you know you will need in the next two years into a cash vehicle, such as a money market fund or a certificate of deposit. You won't earn much on the money, but your principle will be safe.

Chapter 6

Managing Your Money So It Doesn't Run Out

In This Chapter

▶ Developing a budget

▶ Scheduling withdrawals

▶ Getting your assets in gear

▶ Exploring tax obligations

You likely will be living 20 years or more in retirement. When you retire, you probably won't have the means to save more. Even if you do go back to work, you probably won't be earning the same amount as you did when working full-time in a high-pressure job.

You don't want to run out of money, but how do you manage a portfolio so it will last 20 years or more? You need to figure out how much money you'll use each year. Also, you want to figure out how much money you can safely withdraw from your retirement savings portfolio to avoid running out of money during your lifetime. If you do have a shortfall, you'll need to go back to work or find some other way to raise funds.

In this chapter, I discuss the basics of budgeting in retirement. Then I explore strategies for managing your portfolio and safely withdrawing funds so you don't run out. I also discuss the bite that taxes will take out of your retirement funds.

Determining Your Budget

You won't need the same amount of money throughout retirement. In fact, most people will move through at least three phases of life during retirement. You also need to budget for different types of things than you did while you were working. In this section, I review budgeting for the phases of retirement and what items you need to include in your budget.

Budgeting for each phase of retirement

Budgeting for retirement can get very complicated. You actually have to think of retirement in three phases — active, passive, and dependent:

- **Active phase:** During this phase of your life you will still be very active, whether or not you retired early or have gone back to work. You want to take time to enjoy the money you socked away while working before retirement. You also may decide to go back to work to supplement what you saved. This is especially true for retirees who are not yet old enough to collect Social Security and get the benefits of Medicare. You'll need extra money for travel and other things you dreamed of doing during retirement. Your living costs may be a bit less than they were when you were working, but not much.

- **Passive phase:** During this phase of your life you start to slow down. You are probably well enough to continue living on your own, but probably not well enough to continue traveling or doing the other activities you did during the active phase. Your living costs will actually be the cheapest during this phase, because you'll likely cut back on travel, entertainment, transportation costs, and clothing purchases.

- **Dependent phase:** Some people avoid this phase. They are the lucky few. Most of you will get to a phase in your life where you must be dependent on others for help to meet your daily needs of life, such as help with bathing, dressing, and preparing food. Your living costs could actually be the highest in this phase of life, especially if you need to enter an assisted-living or nursing home. Either way, your medical costs will likely be much higher than in the active and passive phases of retirement.

You actually need to develop three estimated budgets to calculate what you might need in retirement. No one can be sure exactly how long they will live in retirement, but by considering your family history and your current health, you can make an educated guess.

MSN Money provides you with an excellent life-expectancy calculator at `moneycentral.msn.com/investor/calcs/n_expect/main.asp`. This calculator asks some key questions about your lifestyle, your health, and your family's health history, and then it provides a guesstimate for your life expectancy.

Accounting for everything

For budget purposes, you'll probably have most of the same line items on your budget as you did while you were working full-time, but you will be able to drop costs for commuting, child care (if they hadn't already been dropped before you retired), business gifts, and professional dues. In exchange for these budget items, you'll probably add increased health insurance premiums, increased healthcare expenses, and increased travel and leisure costs. Initially, your clothing budget might shoot up as you shift from needing daily business attire to daily leisure attire.

The following sections give you some key things to consider as you develop your retirement budget.

Food and shelter costs

Your shelter costs may change depending on whether you plan to stay in your home or move to a smaller retirement home. Or you may decide to keep two homes going in the active phase of retirement — your family home where you live now (possibly in the cold north) and a retirement home (possibly in the warmer south).

Your food costs will depend on whether you want to eat out more or save money and do more cooking at home. Your budget for personal care items may drop a little bit because you're not getting ready for work each day, but probably not by much. In the last phase of retirement, the dependent phase, these costs could rise dramatically if you need assistance with the basics of daily life.

Healthcare costs

Your healthcare costs will likely take a much larger chunk out of your budget. Before you qualify for Medicare, you probably will be paying all your medical insurance and expenses out of pocket. Some employers do offer medical insurance as part of a retirement package, but those benefits can be dropped at any time. More and more employers are cutting back their retiree health insurance coverage.

Even after you do qualify for Medicare, you need to pay premiums for Medicare Part B and Part D. You also will have out-of-pocket costs for deductibles and co-pays and will likely have additional coverage to pay for things Medicare doesn't. I discuss healthcare costs in greater detail in Chapters 9 (before Medicare) and 10 (after Medicare).

Transportation costs

During the active and passive phases, you will probably be driving yourself around, so you can budget about the same as you would for the upkeep and feeding of your car. During the dependent phase, you probably won't be driving anymore and will need to plan for public transportation or taxi services, but you won't have car expenses.

Insurance costs

You probably won't see a big difference in most of your insurance costs. If you did run your own business, of course you won't have to carry business insurance any more once you're retired. Health insurance will probably increase though in retirement.

Leisure and travel costs

Leisure and travel costs will vary greatly in the three phases of retirement. Initially they will probably be higher than you now spend, but as you age they will probably drop.

Entertainment

Entertainment costs will likely go up during the active phase, but will likely drop some during the passive phase, depending on what type of entertainment you enjoy. For example, if most of your entertainment budget is for purchasing movies on DVDs and music on CDs, the budget could remain the same in the first two phases of retirement.

If you have a big family, you may need to budget for more family gatherings at your house and the additional costs for food and other expenses to host those gatherings. In the dependent phase, you probably won't need to plan for entertainment.

Hobbies

If you enjoy a hobby, this can take a much bigger chunk of your budget in retirement because you'll have much more time to spend on your hobby. You will need to try to guesstimate your increased hobby budget and may even need to hold yourself back if you don't have enough money for all you want to do.

Pets and plants

Many people will get additional pets during retirement. In fact, studies have shown over and over throughout the years that seniors are happier and healthier if they have pets. Plants can also make a room feel more alive. You should plan for these increased costs in your budget, unless you really hate both pets and taking care of plants.

Reading materials

If you are an avid reader, you'll likely read a lot more books during retirement. Plan to increase your budget in this area if reading is one of your hobbies.

Debt obligations

Hopefully, by the time you reach retirement you've gotten rid of most of your debt and don't carry over balances on your credit cards. On a fixed income, debt becomes more and more of a burden as the basics of life continue to rise, but your fixed income doesn't. Most pensions don't include cost-of-living raises. Your retirement savings likely will be going down, not up. But, if you do still have debts to pay, add them to your budget figures.

Donations

You'll probably cut back on your donations in retirement because you no longer have the extra cash. If you do still plan to keep up a certain level of donations, calculate that in your budget as well.

Professional services

Expenses for professional services will vary depending on how much you have saved. It's a good idea to work with a financial planner at least in the beginning of your retirement years to be sure your financial assumptions are correct and you have come up with a good plan for spending down your assets. Even if you were good at managing your portfolio before retirement, managing your money so you don't run out is a very different skill set. If you do choose to work with an advisor, be sure you find someone that has experience managing portfolios for retirees.

You should also review your will and be sure that everything is in order for your estate. Another thing you may want to consider is working with an attorney to prepare a living will, so your wishes regarding your medical care are carefully spelled out on paper. That makes it much easier for your family to carry out your wishes if you are not able to make decisions for yourself.

Savings and investments

Most people don't add to their savings and investments during retirement. But if you do plan to work, you may be able to budget for additional savings and investments.

Taxes

Even in retirement you do have to budget for taxes. I talk about taxes on your retirement pension and savings in "Dealing with Taxes" later in this chapter. You won't have to pay taxes to Social Security and Medicare unless you go back to work, and then you'll only have to pay taxes on the money you earn working.

Most states reduce property taxes and some reduce state income taxes once you reach retirement age, so be sure you check out tax rules in your state after you retire. The Retirement Living Information Center maintains a state-by-state breakdown on taxes at `http://www.retirementliving.com/RLtaxes.html`.

Developing a retirement budget

Now that you have a better idea of how to budget in retirement, you might like to take the time to develop a retirement budget. While no one can know what inflation will be over the next 20 years, you may want to increase your numbers by 3 or 4 percent per year to estimate a budget that shows the possible impact of inflation. Use Table 6-1 to make it easier for you.

Table 6-1	Budgeting for Retirement in Three Phases		
Budget Item	*Active Phase*	*Passive Phase*	*Dependent Phase*
Food and shelter			
Healthcare			
Transportation			
Insurance			
Leisure and travel			
Entertainment			
Hobbies			
Pets and plants			
Reading materials			
Debt obligations			
Donations			
Professional services			
Savings and investments			
Taxes			
TOTAL BUDGET			

Planning Your Withdrawal Strategies

After you get an idea of how much you'll need in retirement (if you don't know, check out the section, "Determining Your Budget," earlier in this chapter), you should figure out how much you can safely withdraw from your retirement savings portfolio without the possibility of running out of money. You may have your money sitting in several different types of retirement savings accounts — annuities, IRAs, and traditional pensions. In the following sections, I review the strategies you need to consider for each of them.

Tracking everything

First, you should set up a chart of all your retirement holdings, so that you know what you actually have and can calculate your allocation of assets. (I talk more about asset allocation in Chapter 5. I will show you how asset allocation impacts the amount you can safely withdraw in retirement in the section called "Allocating Your Assets and Withdrawing Safely" later in this chapter.)

Make a list of all the retirement savings you hold. For each type of account you have, you should list:

- **Account type:** This includes annuities, IRAs, Employee stock plans, pensions, and so on.

- **Asset name:** Use a name by which you can quickly identify the account listed.

- **Market value:** How much you can sell the asset for today. You'll find that information on your most current statement for the account.

- **Dividends/interest:** How much you get in dividends and interest yearly.

- **Yearly payout:** How much you receive yearly as a payout. This column will primarily be for pensions and annuities at this point, but as you start to take withdrawals from IRAs, you can add them here, too.

- **Costs to sell:** Estimate what your fees or commission would be if you wanted to sell it. Leave this column blank for now if you don't know. It's not critical unless it's something you do plan to sell.

- **Your cost basis:** How much you paid to get this asset and the date you purchased it. For many of your retirement accounts, you'll have made periodic contributions, so just put in the total cost to date. You should have a total of your contributions and your employer contributions on your annual statement. For date, put the date you started your retirement savings account with your employer.

- **Years held:** List the number of years you've had the asset.

If you know how to use Microsoft Excel, then it's best to set this up as a worksheet in that program. To give you an example, I set up a worksheet using Excel in Figure 6-1. The big advantage of starting with a spreadsheet is that you won't have to add all the columns, plus you'll have a working document you can easily adjust as you move your assets around in retirement. If you don't know how to use Excel, you can start a worksheet in the same format manually, or you can grab *Excel 2007 For Dummies* or *Excel For Dummies, 2nd Edition* (both published by Wiley), to help walk you through the process.

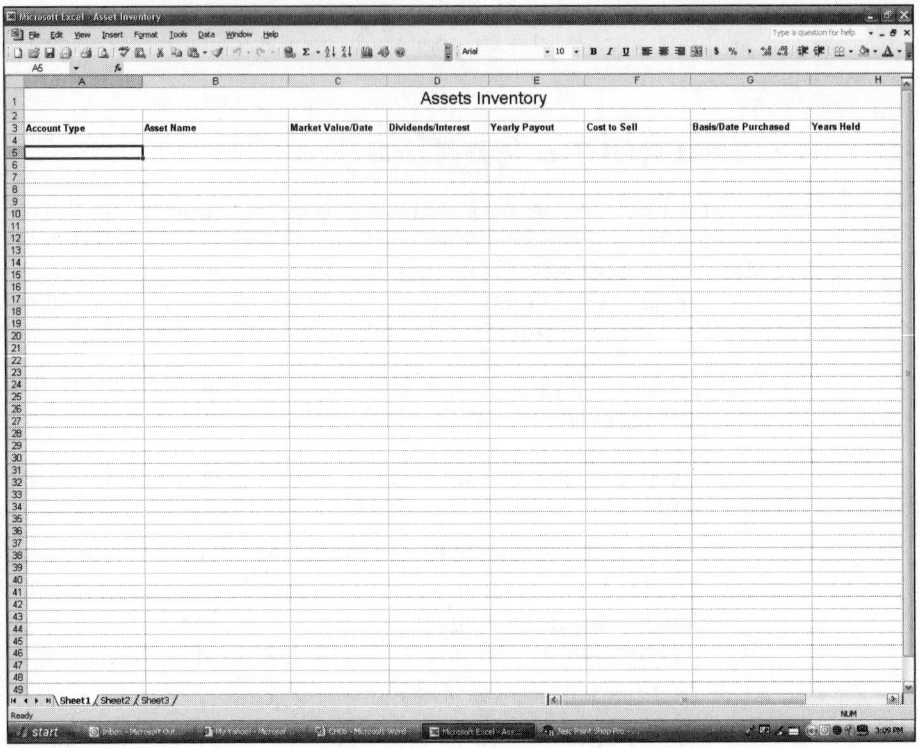

Figure 6-1:
Sample
worksheet
for tracking
your assets
in retire-
ment.

After pulling together this list, add up your total assets and your total income from dividends and interest and from yearly payouts. Total assets include all you have to work with in retirement. You want this principal to last for the rest of your life. Total dividends and interest and yearly payouts will give you an idea of how much income your portfolio is generating for you each year.

Exploring what you have

After making this list, you may know what you have, but may not be sure what these payouts all mean. I briefly review these asset types and how you receive withdrawals from each.

Annuities

If you own annuities, you can set up your withdrawal options in three differ-ent ways — single life, joint and survivor, and term certain. You may already have made this choice when you retired from your company, if your company rolled out your 401(k) into an annuity. Here's a more detailed look at the options:

✔ **Single life:** This option means that you'll be paid a certain amount for the rest of your life. This is the best choice for people who are single, divorced, or widowed and don't need to worry about income for a spouse after their death. This type of annuity does offer the highest payout, but all payouts stop when you die.

✔ **Joint and survivor:** With this option, you continue getting payouts during your life span and the life span of your beneficiary, such as your spouse. You can designate what percentage your spouse will receive, such as 50 percent, 75 percent, or 100 percent. Many people make the mistake of choosing 50 percent thinking that their spouse will only need half the money after they die. That's usually not true because living costs don't get cut in half when a spouse dies. In fact, medical costs usually increase, especially if medical bills must be paid off if the person who died was very sick at the end. Also, medical costs continue to rise as you age.

✔ **Term certain:** You decide the number of years you want an annuity to last and you'll get a guaranteed payment for that number of years. This can be risky if you outlive the term you pick. The one advantage this option has over single life and joint and survivor payouts is that the number of years for payout are guaranteed. If you die before that number has been paid out, your beneficiary gets the rest of the payments. With the other two types of payouts, once you and your beneficiary die, there is nothing left for any heirs.

Whatever payout decision you make about your annuities cannot be changed, so choose carefully. If you do consult a financial advisor to plan your retirement withdrawals, be sure to get his counseling before signing any withdrawal papers.

If you don't own an annuity, but think you'd prefer to have someone else manage your portfolio, you can consider buying a single premium annuity with your retirement savings. But, be sure you understand all the fees you'll be paying and how much you will be guaranteed to receive each month for the rest of your life. You can find out more about annuities by reading this excellent article at Kiplinger's Finance (www.kiplinger.com/personal finance/basics/archives/2002/04/story25.html).

Traditional pensions

If you are one of the lucky few that still has a traditional pension, your company will determine your payout amount. Just like with an annuity discussed above, you will need to select a payout option similar to those available for an annuity. Your employer will give you information on payout options.

Your yearly statement from your company probably doesn't give you a total value for your pension asset, so don't worry about adding that to the market value column if you don't have it.

Employee stock purchase plan

If you do hold shares of company stock in some type of stock purchase plan, you probably do want to sell it as soon as you can without taking a loss. Many times you can buy company stock at 10 to 15 percent lower than you can get it on the market, so unless your company lost value significantly, you probably won't have a loss with this stock.

You can look at your plan statement to find out how many shares of stock you hold. To find out its current market value, you'll need to look up the share price in your daily newspaper or on the Internet. One easy Web site to work with to get price quotes online for stock is Yahoo! Finance (`www.finance.yahoo.com`). At the top of the page you'll see a box called "Get Quotes." Put in the stock symbol for your company. If you don't know it, click on "Symbol Lookup" to find it.

Generally, it's not safe to hold more than 4 percent of your portfolio's assets in any one company. If you're already getting a pension from that company, you probably already depend on more than 4 percent of your retirement income from that company.

To properly allocate your assets, you should sell your company stock to reduce your holdings to the 4 percent level as soon as you can. You do want to be careful to avoid a major tax hit when you sell, so be sure to review any potential sales with your tax advisor first.

IRAs

Most of the retirement cash that you'll manage individually will be in your IRAs. These are the funds for which you'll be making your withdrawal plans and which can run out if you're not careful.

As I discuss in Chapter 5, there are numerous types of IRAs. You may even have several different IRA accounts. You will probably find it easier to roll all these accounts into one large portfolio. It will be much easier to manage if the money is all in one place.

But, be careful. If you do have both traditional tax-deductible and non-tax-deductible IRAs, keep them separate. Also if you have a Roth IRA, do not roll it into any other type of IRA, you'll lose the advantages of the Roth. You may even want to roll some of your traditional IRA money into a Roth IRA because its funds grow completely tax free. You can take money out of your Roth IRA without paying any taxes. I talk more about the tax benefits of a Roth IRA later in this chapter in "Dealing with Taxes."

If you do roll traditional IRA money into a Roth IRA, you will have to pay taxes on the rollover. You can figure out whether or not it's worth it for you to consider rolling over your traditional IRAs into a Roth IRA by reading this excellent article and using the interactive tool at Smart Money.com (`http://www.smartmoney.com/retirement/roth/index.cfm?story=convert`).

Allocating Your Assets and Withdrawing Safely

In Chapter 5, I talk about how to invest wisely using asset allocation. Now I want you to look at how to carefully withdraw these funds so you don't run out of money. Generally, the rule of thumb most financial advisors give their clients is that they can safely withdraw 4 percent of their retirement savings each year and their money will last for their lifetime.

That's a short and quick rule that does work, but if you need more income than that from your portfolio, you may want to take a bit more risk with how you allocate your asset mix. By holding a greater percentage of stocks, you may be able to withdraw more annually as long as you keep growth stocks in your portfolio. Sound scary? Well, I'll guide you through it in the sections that follow.

Checking out the chart

The chart in Figure 6-2 looks at various asset mixes between stocks and bonds. It then shows you what percentage you can withdraw based on your risk tolerance and the number of years you expect to live in retirement.

I grouped withdrawal rates into three risk levels based on your chances of having enough money throughout your retirement years — 90 to 100 percent chance that you won't run out of money, 75 to 90 percent chance, and less than 50 percent chance that your money will last throughout retirement. I also developed withdrawal rates based on the number of years you expect to live in retirement.

I developed the chart you see in Figure 6-2 using data from a study of historical stock returns over a 70-year period. Stocks historically averaged a return between 10 and 12 percent, bonds historically averaged a 4 to 6 percent return, and cash historically averaged 3 percent. I used a 3 percent inflation rate average for this chart. The withdrawal rates I show you in Figure 6-2 are adjusted for inflation.

Figure 6-2:
Use to
calculate
the amount
you can
withdraw
annually
from your
retirement
savings.

Asset Mix	Chance Your Assets Will Last Throughout Your Lifetime	Number of Years You Expect to Live in Retirement			
		15 Years	20 Years	25 Years	30 Years
100% Stocks	90% to 100%	6%	4%	4%	4%
	75% to 90%	7%	6%	5%	5%
	Less than 50%	11%	8%	7%	7%
75% Stocks and 25% Bonds	90% to 100%	6%	5%	4%	4%
	75% to 90%	7%	6%	5%	5%
	Less than 50%	10%	9%	8%	7%
50% Stocks and 50% Bonds	90% to 100%	6%	5%	4%	4%
	75% to 90%	7%	6%	5%	5%
	Less than 50%	10%	8%	7%	7%
25% Stocks and 75% Bonds	90% to 100%	5%	4%	4%	3%
	75% to 90%	6%	5%	4%	3%
	Less than 50%	9%	6%	5%	5%
100% Bonds	90% to 100%	5%	4%	3%	<3%
	75% to 90%	5%	4%	3%	3%
	Less than 50%	7%	5%	4%	4%

How Much Can You Withdraw Annually Without Outliving Your Assets?

(These withdrawal rates are inflation adjusted and based on a percentage of your initial portfolio value. If you do decide to change your withdrawal percentage be sure to recalculate your percentage based on portfolio value and the number of years left in retirement at the time you make the change.)

Keep these points in mind while using the chart:

- Use MSN Money's life-expectancy calculator (moneycentral.msn.com/investor/calcs/n_expect/main.asp) to calculate a life-expectancy guesstimate and then use that figure to determine the number of years you'll live in retirement. If you expect to live more than 30 years in retirement, you probably should choose the safe route and not increase your withdrawal rate above 4 percent. You may want to play it safe with 3 percent.

- In looking at the chart, notice that there really isn't much advantage to picking an asset mix for your portfolio riskier than 50 percent stocks and 50 percent bonds. But, you can see that if you choose a portfolio with just 25 percent stocks and 100 percent bonds, you will need to cut the percentage of your money that you can withdraw each year to 3 percent if you think you will live about 30 years in retirement. If your asset mix is 100 percent bonds, then you can only withdraw 3 percent of your portfolio if you think you will live 25 years in retirement.

⌐ As I discuss in Chapter 5, if you do want to keep growth in your portfolio, be sure to convert some of your portfolio to cash at least two years before you'll need it to be sure you're not stuck selling stocks or bonds during a downturn in the market. You should also be sure to sell stocks and use the money to invest in bonds when you are about 5 years away from needing it.

By following those two rules, your chances are very good you can avoid selling any portion of your portfolio at a loss. If five years out the stock market are down, you have the time to wait out a reversal of a down market before you'll need the money. You don't have to sell stock at exactly five years. Use the time you have before needing the money to find the best time to sell and minimize any loss.

Following an example

To show you how to use the chart, I assume a retiree, Nancy, has a retirement portfolio of $300,000 and expects to live 25 years in retirement. Looking at the chart, Nancy decides to compare three asset mixes — 50 percent stocks and 50 percent bonds, 25 percent stocks and 75 percent bonds, and 100 percent bonds.

Nancy decides to take on a bit more risk and use the rate for a 75 to 90 percent chance of not living longer than her assets in order to get a bit more cash initially. Nancy wants the extra money during the most active phase of retirement, but may decide to be more conservative as she gets older.

Using the above scenario, Nancy can use a 5 percent withdrawal rate if she allocates her portfolio with a 50/50 asset mix. She can withdraw only 4 percent of her portfolio annually if she allocates her funds using a 25/75 asset mix. She can only take out 3 percent per year if she chooses to keep all her retirement savings in bonds.

Here's how much she can take out each year using these three scenarios:

50/50 Asset Mix:	$300,000 × .05	=	$15,000
25/75 Asset Mix:	$300,000 × .04	=	$12,000
All Bonds:	$300,000 × .03	=	$9,000

If about five years into retirement, she does decide to be more conservative, she can always recalculate her withdrawal amount using the 20-year column and the remaining funds in her portfolio at that time.

If you have never managed a portfolio before, don't try to do this totally on your own at first. I highly recommend that you work with a financial planner to put together your strategy for withdrawing your funds. Even if you do have a lot of portfolio experience, it doesn't hurt to pay for a few hours of consultation time with a financial planner to be sure your assumptions are correct. A third-party view from someone who is not as personally involved in the outcome is always a good idea when you're making significant financial choices that will impact your ability to maintain your desired lifestyle in the future. When looking for a financial advisor, just keep these tips in mind:

✔ Ask for recommendations from friends.

✔ Use the resources of the Financial Planning Association to find a good advisor near your home. Check out its resources, as well as find an advisor at www.fpanet.org/public.

✔ Be sure that you understand how your financial advisor will be paid. It's best to choose someone who is paid a fee for their advice rather than someone who makes commissions on what they sell. Commission-based financial advisors do not always have your best interests in mind, because they are looking to increase their own income by making a sale.

Calculating Whether Your Income Is Enough

Now that you have developed your estimated budget, your income from your annuities and pension plans, and the amount you'll be able to withdraw from retirement savings you hold, you can calculate whether you'll have enough to live on in retirement by following these steps:

1. Calculate your annual budget needs.

2. Calculate your annual income by adding any annual annuity payouts, pension payouts, Social Security benefits (if old enough to collect — see details in Chapter 7), retirement savings withdrawals, and any other money you expect to have each year.

3. Subtract your budget from your income.

4. Find out whether you have a surplus or a shortfall. If the number is positive, you do have enough money for retirement. If the number is negative, you have a shortfall and you'll need to find some more — most likely by going out to work.

If you do have a shortfall, you're better off correcting the shortfall by taking a job as soon as possible after retirement. As you get older, it will be more and more difficult to work. By bringing in extra income, you may be able to reduce the amount you take out of your retirement savings each year and let your portfolio grow a bit more. That way you'll be able to increase your income in your later years because you'll be able to withdraw more from your portfolio.

When you do decide to quit work entirely, you can then recalculate your annual payouts by considering the number of years left at that time in retirement. Recalculate your withdrawal rate based on your asset mix and number of years in retirement when you quit.

Dealing with Taxes

Everyone hates to pay taxes. Unfortunately, you do still have to pay them in retirement. In the following sections, I review how retirement income is taxed.

Taxation of your pensions

Taxation of your pension payout is usually done for you by your company, just as taxes were taken out of your paycheck while you were working. Most pensions are taxed based on your current income tax rates. You likely will fill out a form (or may already have done so) indicating whether to take out taxes when you pick your pension payout method.

After your first year of receiving your pension payout, work with your tax advisor to be sure the proper amount is being taken out of your pension. If not, you can file a form to change the amount of tax you pay. But, you probably are better off paying any additional taxes needed by filing quarterly estimated tax forms and paying any additional taxes that way.

Paying estimated taxes quarterly gives you more control over any changes you may need as you move through the various phases of retirement and your tax deductions change. As you complete your taxes each year, do an estimation of your income for the next year and recalculate any estimated taxes you might need to pay.

Most tax advisors do this automatically as part of your income tax preparation without any additional charge. If you use a tax preparation package and prepare your own taxes, most tax preparation software for your home computer also will automatically calculate payments for the next year's quarterly estimated taxes.

Taxation of your retirement savings

Taxation of your retirement savings is much more complicated because whether you're taxed depends on the type of retirement savings account you have. Keep these factors in mind and talk to a tax professional to assess your needs:

- Most of your accounts will be taxed based on your current income tax rate. This includes money you withdraw from your traditional IRAs, your 401(k)s, your 403(b)s, and most other employer retirement savings plans. This will change each year depending on how much income you draw from your IRAs, how much you are paid through a pension or annuity, as well as any other income you receive including income you earn working full- or part-time in retirement.

- If you are old enough to collect Social Security, that adds another complication to the mix. I talk more about Social Security and taxes in Chapter 7.

- The one exception to the rule in the previous bullet is any funds you withdraw from a Roth IRA. Money you take out of a Roth IRA will not be taxed as long as you start taking it out after you reach age 59½.

  Another big advantage of the Roth IRA is that you are not forced to take your money out at any time. You can decide to leave all your money in a Roth IRA to your heirs if you so choose.

- You will have to take out mandatory distributions of all your other retirement savings. I talk more about the mandatory distribution rules in Chapter 5. If you fail to take out enough to meet the IRS mandatory distribution requirements, you will be taxed 50 percent of any shortfall.

Chapter 7

Collecting Social Security and Going Back to Work

In This Chapter

▶ Following the Social Security work rules

▶ Getting less benefits

▶ Receiving increased benefits

▶ Taxing complications

You can collect Social Security while you're working, but if you started collecting Social Security before you reached your full retirement age, your benefits may be reduced. The news is not all bad. If you go back to work, your future Social Security benefits may go up.

In this chapter, I review the Social Security rules about working and collecting. I also discuss how working affects the taxes you might have to pay on your Social Security benefits.

Working and Collecting

You can collect Social Security and work at the same time, but your Social Security benefits could be reduced. In this section, I review the rules about your benefits and work.

Following the rules

Social Security's rules about collecting and working differ depending on whether or not you've reached full retirement age. That age varies depending on the year you were born.

Full retirement age for Social Security used to be 65, but under new rules passed to improve Social Security's solvency, the age is gradually increasing to 67. You can find out what your benefits will be by calling the Social Security Administration and asking for your statement at 1-800-772-1213. (This is the same statement that is sent to you automatically each year.) You can also request a statement online at www.socialsecurity.gov. If you'd like to calculate your future benefits based on numerous earnings scenarios, you can use the Social Security Administration's calculators at www.socialsecurity.gov/planners/calculators.htm.

Table 7-1 gives you a breakdown of your full retirement age based on your year of birth.

Table 7-1	Social Security Full Retirement Age by Year of Birth
Year of Birth	**Full Retirement Age**
1937 or earlier	65
1938	65 and 2 months
1939	65 and 4 months
1940	65 and 6 months
1941	65 and 8 months
1942	65 and 10 months
1943–1954	66
1955	66 and 2 months
1956	66 and 4 months
1957	66 and 6 months
1958	66 and 8 months
1959	66 and 10 months
1960 and later	67

Figuring benefits if you retire early

As a retiree, the earliest age you can begin to collect Social Security is 62, but if you start to collect Social Security before your full retirement age, your benefit amount will be reduced for the rest of your life.

Table 7-2 shows you the factors you need to consider to calculate the percentage by which your benefits will be permanently reduced, if you start collecting benefits before full retirement age. Because full retirement age is gradually increasing to age 67, notice that the year you were born impacts the amount your Social Security benefit will be reduced.

For example, if your full retirement age is 65 and you retire at age 62, you start benefits three years early. But, if your full retirement age is 67, you'll be starting benefits five years early.

Table 7-2	Social Security Benefit Reduction If You Retire Early*		
Year of Birth	*Age 62 Reduction*	*Monthly Reduction (%)*	*Total % Reduction (In Months)*
1937	36	.555	20
1938	38	.548	20.83
1939	40	.541	21.67
1940	42	.535	22.50
1941	44	.530	23.33
1942	46	.525	24.17
1943–1954	48	.520	25.00
1955	50	.516	25.84
1956	52	.512	26.66
1957	54	.509	27.50
1958	56	.505	27.80
1959	58	.502	29.17
1960 and later	60	.500	30.00

Monthly percentage and total reductions are approximate due to rounding. The actual reductions are .555, or ⅝ of 1 percent per month for the first 36 months and .416 or ⁵⁄₁₂ of 1 percent.

The factor in the column "Monthly Reduction" gives you a way to calculate your reduction by the number of months you retire early. For example, if your full retirement age is 66 and you decide to retire at age 63, then the number of months that you will be retiring early is 36. Use the factor in the Monthly Reduction column to calculate what your permanent reduction in benefits will be.

Using this example, if your Social Security benefit at full retirement age is supposed to be $1,000 per month, here's how to do the calculation:

1. Multiply the number of months you will be retiring early by your monthly reduction factor.

   36 months × .520 = 18.72% reduction in benefits

2. Multiply the percentage reduction in benefits.

   18.72% × $1,000 = $187.20

3. Subtract the amount of the reduction in benefits from your benefit at full retirement age.

   $1,000 − $187.20 = $812.80

 So in the example above, a person whose full retirement age is 66, but who decides to retire three years early at age 63 will experience an 18.72 percent reduction in benefits for the rest of his life. If the Social Security benefit was supposed to be $1,000, instead it will be only $812.80. If you do decide to retire early, be sure you can live with that reduction in benefits before you start collecting.

Impacting Your Current Benefits by Going Back to Work

When you go back to work after you retired early and already started collecting Social Security, you could end up with reduced benefits. It all depends on whether you've reached your full retirement age.

Understanding the Retired Earnings Test (RET) basics

If you decide to go back to work before full retirement age, but have already started collecting Social Security, your benefits will be temporarily reduced by the Retirement Earnings Test (RET). The designers of Social Security made this test a requirement because they believed people who went back to back work should not collect full benefits. Congress changed this rule in 2000. Today only people who retire before their full retirement age must pass this test.

For the purposes of the RET test, only wages that you earn by working outside the home or on a part-time basis from home count as income. You don't have to include any government or military benefits, investment earnings, interest, pensions, annuities, or capital gains when calculating income for a RET test.

Once you reach full retirement age, you can work as much as you like without impacting your Social Security benefits. There are no earning limitations once you reach full retirement age.

In changing the rules to allow you to regain your benefits lost because of the RET, Congress took the position in 2000 that Social Security is something that you earn by years of work and that these benefits should not be withheld from people who choose to go back to work for whatever reason once they reach their full retirement age.

Prior to this change in rules in 2000, 960,000 Social Security beneficiaries were working and had their benefits reduced by the RET. More than 800,000 of them had already reached their full retirement age. They lost a total of $4.1 billion in benefits because of RET rules.

Reviewing the rules

If you go back to work after you start collecting Social Security but before you reach full retirement age, your Social Security benefits will be reduced under two levels of RET rules:

- ✔ People between ages 62 and the year they reach full retirement age will have $1 of benefits withheld by Social Security for every $2 earned in excess of their allowable earnings threshold. The allowable earnings threshold was $12,480 in 2006. This allowable earnings threshold is adjusted each year by Social Security based on a formula managed by Social Security called the national wage index. The new threshold information is released in the month of October, prior to the year it will be in force.

- ✔ During the year you reach your full retirement, you will only have $1 of Social Security benefits withheld for every $3 earned above the allowable earnings threshold. The allowable earnings threshold was $33,240 for 2006 and will be adjusted each year by Social Security's national wage index.

Calculating how much you can lose

Table 7-3 gives you a ballpark estimate of how your earnings will be impacted if you go back to work before you reach your full retirement age.

Table 7-3	Social Security's Ballpark Estimate of Benefit Reductions	
Monthly Social Security Benefit	**Earnings**	**Yearly Benefit**
$500	$12,480 or less	$6000 (no adjustment)
$500	$15,000	$4,740
$700	$12,480 or less	$8,400 (no adjustment)
$700	$15,000	$7,140
$700	$20,000	$4,640
$900	$12,480 or less	$10,800 (no adjustment)
$900	$15,000	$9,540
$900	$20,000	$7,040

To give you an idea of how to calculate your loss of benefits if you retire early, I created a fictitious scenario of early retiree Lucy who gets a yearly benefit of $9,600 ($800 per month) and earns $20,000 part-time. Lucy was born in 1943 and retired at age 62 in 2005. After retiring, she decided to go back to work. Her full retirement age is 66.

Here is how Lucy would calculate her reduction in benefits:

1. Subtract $12,480 from the amount of earnings above the allowable threshold.

   $20,000 − $12,480 = $7,520

2. Calculate the amount by which the Social Security benefit will be reduced. Since the benefit reduction is $1 for every $2 earned, you divide the amount of earnings over the threshold by 2.

   $7,520 ÷ 2 = $3,760

3. Subtract the amount by which Lucy's Social Security benefit will be reduced from the full benefit amount.

   $9,600 − $3,760 = $5,840

So Lucy's income for the year will be $5,840 in Social Security benefits and $20,000 from part-time work for a total of $25,840. If she didn't go out to work, her total income would have been $9,600 from Social Security.

Now take a look at what happens to Lucy during the year she reaches full retirement age, which will be in August 2009. During that year the RET rules change and she is allowed to make up to $33,240 without impacting her Social Security benefit.

So even though she hasn't yet reached full retirement age in her last year before retirement, she can continue to earn $20,000 and get her full Social Security benefit of $9,600 for a total $29,600. She can even decide to increase her earnings by as much as $13,240, for a total of $33,240, and still get all her Social Security benefits.

Getting special treatment in your first year of retirement

Many people who retire early exceed the earnings limit allowed during the first year, but there are special rules. The RET test for new retirees is based on a monthly earning amount rather than the total first year amount. That way if you continue to work at your full salary for the first half of the year and then retire six months into the year, you can earn a part-time income without losing all of your Social Security benefits.

For example, suppose Tom earns $60,000 per year and plans to retire in July. The first six months he will earn $30,000 or $5,000 per month. If he's only 63, under the regular RET rules he would have exceeded the maximum allowable income of $12,480, but luckily that doesn't apply during the first year he retires.

Instead, during your first year of retirement, you can use a special RET test based on a monthly income. For 2006, that monthly allowable income was $1,040. So as long as Tom doesn't earn more than $1,040 per month, he won't lose any Social Security benefits even though he earned $30,000 before retiring.

If he were to earn $2,000 per month, then he would exceed the allowable income by $960 per month and would lose $1 in Social Security benefits for every $2 he earns, so his monthly benefit would be reduced by $480.

If that special rule was not in place, then the $12,000 he earns in the last six months of the year plus the $30,000 that he earns in the first six months of the year would total $42,000. If you subtract $12,480 from $42,000, you find that he would exceed allowable earnings by $29,520, and $14,760 of his Social Security benefits would be lost. During a six-month period of collecting Social Security, that would be $2,460 per month, which is well above the maximum Social Security benefit.

Increasing Benefits When You Go Back to Work

If you go back to work after retirement, you may end up with an increase in your Social Security benefits. This is especially true for people who took a long break from working during their prime earning years.

For example, a women who took off 15 years to raise a family would not have earned any income to credit to her Social Security account. Those years would be counted as $0 earning years.

Social Security calculates your benefit by using your top 35 earning years. If 15 of those years are zero-dollar earning years, it can lower your benefit significantly.

For example, suppose you earned $30,000 a year for 20 years and $0 a year for 15 years. Your average earnings per year would be calculated this way:

1. 20 years × $30,000 = $600,000

2. 15 years × $0 = $0

3. 35-year earning history (total of Steps 1 and 2) = $600,000

4. Average earnings per year = $600,000 ÷ 35 = $17,143

Your Social Security benefits would be based on an earnings average of just $17,143 and result in a much lower benefit amount than you would have received if you had income of $30,000 for 35 years.

Now, suppose you went back to work for ten years part-time for $20,000 per year after you started to collect your benefits at age 62. Social Security would then automatically recalculate your benefits each year that you continued working. As you replace those $0 earnings years with $20,000 earnings years, your Social Security benefit would gradually increase.

Now, I recalculate your average earnings after five years of no earnings and ten years of part-time earnings of $20,000 in retirement:

1. 20 years × $30,000 = $600,000

2. 5 years × $0 = $0

3. 10 years × $20,000 = $200,000

4. 35-year earning history (total of Steps 1, 2, and 3) = $800,000

5. Average earnings per year = $800,000/35 = $22,857

You can see that your average earnings that Social Security now would use to calculate your benefit is $22,857, which is $5,714 higher than at age 62 when you had 15 years of no earnings.

The calculation I just showed you is a simplification of how Social Security calculates your benefits. During a 35-year work history, there are adjustments to earnings based on the national wage index. I just wanted to show you how your benefit amount could be increased by a decision to go back to work in retirement, especially if you had a lot of zero-dollar work years or very low earnings years.

Starting Your Own Business and Social Security Benefits

If you are thinking of working from home and starting your own business, that too could mean that you would be subject to the RET test, but it's different for people who are self employed. Self-employed people must include any income earned if they performed substantial services in their business.

So what does substantial really mean? Social Security measures whether or not someone has performed substantial services by the number of hours spent on one's business. If you work 45 hours or more per month on your own business, that is considered substantial and any money earned could reduce benefits.

If you work fewer than 15 hours per month, you are considered fully retired. Time spent working on your own business between 15 and 45 hours per month may or may not count depending on your occupation and size of your business.

If you do want to start your own business and work part-time before you reach full retirement age, be sure you sit down with a Social Security claims representative and review your plans to find out if you could lose benefits based on self-employed RET rules. The Social Security claims representative can let you know how your benefits might be impacted by your business plans.

When calculating how much income to claim from your business, you would use your net income figure after you subtract all your business expenses. You do not have to use your total gross sales figure, which would be the total income you take into the business from sales. Everyone who runs a business has some expenses they can use to reduce their gross sales number.

Complicating Your Taxes

If you do go back to work after retirement, you will be complicating the way you must file your income taxes. You also could end up paying more taxes on your Social Security benefits.

Your total income from earnings, Social Security, pensions, and retirement savings withdrawals could kick you up into a higher tax bracket. Here is a review of tax implications of going back to work after retirement when collecting Social Security.

How Social Security benefits are taxed

Each year that you collect Social Security, you have to determine whether your Social Security benefits are taxable. You do this by comparing your actual income to the base amount of income you can make without owing additional income taxes.

To calculate the amount you must compare to the base amount, you must include one-half of your Social Security benefits in the calculation plus all other income including pensions, interest, retirement savings withdrawals, and capital gains.

What is the base amount? That depends on how you file your taxes. Here is the base amount you are allowed without paying taxes on your Social Security:

- ✔ **$25,000** if you are single, head of household, or qualifying (widow)
- ✔ **$25,000** if you are married filing separately and living apart from your spouse during the current tax year.

> ✔ **$32,000** if you are married and filing jointly.
>
> ✔ **$0** if you are married filing separately and you lived with your spouse at any time during the current tax year.

When you compare your total income to the base amount, if the total income exceeds your base amount, your Social Security benefits will be taxed. If you file a joint return, you and your spouse must combine your incomes and benefits when you do this comparison.

Even if your spouse is not yet collecting benefits, you must add in your spouse's income when trying to determine whether or not your Social Security benefits will be taxed.

If the only income you receive is from Social Security, your benefits most likely will not be taxable. You may not even have to file a tax return. If you do have income in addition to Social Security, you will have to file an income tax return even if you don't owe any money.

Calculating your income

The IRS has worksheets for everything and, yes, there is even one to help you figure out whether your Social Security income will be taxed. (Your Social Security benefits will be reported on form SSA-1099, by the way.) In this section, I not only walk you through the calculation, but I also give you some examples as well as tips on avoiding a tax bill come April.

Figuring out if your benefits are taxable

Use the following steps for the calculation to determine if your Social Security benefits are taxable:

1. **Write in the amount from box 5 on all of your SSA-1099s.** Include the full amount of any lump-sum payments received in 2006. If you are a railroad retiree, you will get a similar form called RRB-1099.

2. **Enter one half of the amount on line A.**

3. **Add your taxable pensions, wages, interest, dividends, and other taxable income and write in the total.**

4. **Write in any tax-exempt interest (such as interest from municipal bonds), plus any exclusions from income.**

5. **Add lines B, C, and D and write in the total.**

When calculating income, you must include wages and any other compensation you receive for services. You also must include interest, dividends, rents from any rental property, royalties, income from partnerships, estate and trust income, gains from sales or exchanges of assets, and business income of all kinds.

Compare the total you get using the steps above to the base amounts allowed according to your tax filing status. If your total (Step 5) equals or is less than the base amount for your filing status, then none of your Social Security benefits are taxable for that year. If your total in Step 5 is more than your base amount, then some of your Social Security benefits may be taxable.

If your income exceeds the base amount, then 50 percent of your Social Security benefits will be taxable. Now that does not mean you will pay 50 percent of your benefits in taxes. What it does mean is that 50 percent of your Social Security benefits must be added as income when filing your 1040 form with the IRS. This amount will then be taxed at your current income tax rate. This will be true until your income exceeds $34,000 if you are single or $44,000 if you are married and filing jointly.

Once your joint income tops $44,000 or your single income tops $34,000, more than 50 percent of your Social Security benefits will be taxable at your current tax rate, and the amount taxable can go as high as 85 percent depending on how much you are earning. But, remember, that's taxable benefits, not the amount you are taxed. The amount you are taxed will depend on your current income tax rate.

For example, suppose married couple Tom and Judy added up all their income, which included $12,000 in Social Security for Tom and $10,000 in Social Security for Judy for a total of $22,000 from Social Security benefits. Tom also earned an additional $20,000 from a part-time job.

To calculate the amount to compare to the base amount, they would need to use one-half of their total Social Security benefits, which would be $11,000 ($22,000/2) plus $20,000 in part-time income. So their total income would be $31,000. The base amount allowed for a married couple filing jointly is $32,000, so their Social Security income would not be taxed.

Checking your status

Income tax rates vary depending on your filing status and income earned. They range from 10 percent to 35 percent. Just to give you an idea of how to find your tax rate, Table 7-4 is an example income tax table for a couple filing jointly. Use the IRS Web site www.irs.gov/formspubs/article/0,,id=150856,00.html to find the most current tax rates.

Table 7-4		Example Income Tax Rates for a Married Couple Filing Jointly
If Taxable Income Is Over	*But Not Over*	*Your Tax Rate Is*
$0	$15,100	10% of the amount over $0
$15,100	$61,300	$1,510 plus 15% of the amount over $15,100
$61,300	$123,700	$8,440 plus 25% of the amount over $61,300
$123,700	$188,450	$24,040 plus 28% of the amount over $123,700
$188,450	$336,550	$42,170 plus 33% of the amount over $188,450
$336,550	no limit	$91,043 plus 35% of the amount over $336,550

So, you can see from this chart, as long as your total income is below $15,100, you only need to pay a 10 percent tax on your income. Income over $15,100 is taxed at a 15 percent rate until your income exceeds $61,300. If you work during retirement and have a total income of more than $61,300, you would then be kicked up into the 25 percent tax bracket.

Avoiding a tax bill

Okay, so you can't avoid the tax bill altogether, but if you prefer not to be stuck with a tax bill at tax time, you can request that the federal government take more income taxes out of your Social Security benefits. You do that by filing form W-4V with the IRS, which is similar to the W-4 forms you filed when you were working. You can download this form at http://www.irs.gov/pub/irs-pdf/fw4v.pdf.

Another route, which I recommend, is that you file quarterly estimated taxes rather than asking the government to take additional money out of your Social Security check. You can do that by downloading the instructions and forms from the IRS Web site at http://www.irs.gov/pub/irs-pdf/f1040es.pdf.

The reason you are better off using the estimated tax method is that you control the amount of additional taxes you want to pay each quarter. Your income situation could change during the year and it is a lot easier to adjust your quarterly payment than it is to get the government to change the amount it is taking out of your Social Security check.

Taxes on pensions and retirement savings when collecting

I discussed taxes on pensions and retirement savings in Chapter 6. The way that you calculate how much you'll pay in taxes on the money you get from your pensions or retirement savings does not change whether or not you are collecting Social Security. What does change is that if you do get a pension, plus take more of out of your retirement savings, you could end up kicking yourself over the line and being forced to pay taxes on your Social Security benefits or having to pay a larger percentage of taxes on those benefits.

As you plan the amount you want to withdraw from your retirement savings, consider what impact that amount might have on your Social Security benefits. Follow the steps in the section "Figuring out if your benefits are taxable" above to compare the income you plan to take out with the base amount you are allowed based on your filing status. If you can avoid paying taxes on your Social Security benefits, you will save money and it might be enough so that you don't need to draw as much from your savings.

For example, suppose you and your wife have a total of $20,000 a year in Social Security benefits. You plan to take out $23,000 per year from your retirement savings. You will then have to pay income tax on one-half of the $20,000 Social Security benefit. In the following sections, I compare how your taxes may be impacted below if you take only $22,000 and avoid paying taxes on your Social Security benefits versus taking out $23,000 and paying taxes.

Scenario one — Taking out $22,000 and avoiding taxes on benefits

In calculating your comparison income amount, you would use $22,000 in retirement savings income plus $10,000 in Social Security benefits (remember you only use ½ of your Social Security benefits for this calculation) for a total of $32,000. Your base income allowed as a married couple filing jointly is $32,000. So your Social Security benefits would not be taxable.

Income tax would be based on the $22,000 retirement savings income only. You can then claim a standard exemption of $3,200 for each of you plus a standard deduction of $10,000 as a couple, which means you could subtract $16,400 from $22,000. That means your income would be only $5,600 and your taxes would be only $560 ($5,600 x 10%).

Scenario two — Taking out $23,000 and paying taxes on benefits

In this scenario, your total income for comparison would be $33,000 ($13,000 from retirement savings and $20,000), which means you exceed your allowable base amount by $1,000.

In this scenario, you do have to include ½ of your Social Security benefits when calculating income for income tax purposes. Income tax would be based on $23,000 retirement savings plus $10,000 (half of your Social Security benefit) for a total income of $33,000 that is taxable.

You can subtract $3,200 in exemptions for each of you plus $10,000 for a standard deduction for a total of $16,400, so your taxable income would be $16,600. You would have to pay $1,510 plus 15 percent of the amount over $15,100 or $1,500, which is an additional $225. So your total tax bill would be $1,735 ($1,510 + $225).

So you can see if you're sitting on the edge of whether or not your Social Security benefits will be taxable, test to see if it's worth taking out the additional money. As you can see from this example, taking out that extra $1,000 resulted in an extra $1,175 in taxes ($1,735–$560).

What isn't taxed?

Believe it or not there are some types of income you can get in retirement that will not be taxed. These include the following:

- Compensation for sickness or injury (such as workers compensation) is not taxable.

- Benefits you collect from an accident or health-insurance policy are not taxable as long as you paid the premiums or the premiums paid by your employer were included in your gross income.

- Payments from long-term care insurance companies generally are not taxable.

- Life insurance proceeds paid after the death of an insured person are not taxable unless the policy was turned over for a price.

- Veterans' benefits from the Department of Veterans Affairs are not included in gross income.

- Payments you receive from a state fund as a victim of a crime should not be included in your income, but you cannot deduct as medical expenses any expenses reimbursed by the fund.

- Some government benefit programs designed to help the elderly cope on a fixed income are not included as gross income. For example, benefits from the Nutrition Program for the Elderly would not be included when calculating your income.

Chapter 8

Delaying Social Security and Working

In This Chapter

▶ Collecting pensions and working

▶ Saving after retirement

▶ Increasing Social Security by delaying

▶ Knowing when to stop delaying

You decided to retire from your job, or maybe you were offered an early retirement package, but want to keep working elsewhere. You've got lots of decisions to make regarding how to handle your retirement nest egg while still working. If you are eligible for Social Security, you're probably wondering whether you should start collecting or delay collecting until you stop working.

In this chapter, I explore the issues of what to do with your employer-based pension and savings plans, if you continue to work after you've left where your funds are still being held. I also discuss how you should figure out when you can and should start collecting your Social Security benefits. And because new pension legislation has begun to change the rules by which traditional pensions were governed, I take you through the old and new rules for pensions so you can better understand how you may be affected by the change.

Taking a Look at Pension Legislation

If you're thinking of going back to work for your company part-time or as a consultant or independent contractor after you retire, be sure you can do that at the same time as you're collecting your retirement pension. Most companies don't allow their retirees who are collecting pensions to work for them in any capacity.

Companies don't discriminate against you by not letting you come back to work for them. Numerous federal tax and pension rules made it difficult, if not impossible for companies to hire people to whom they are paying traditional pension benefits if those people are younger than the pension plan's normal retirement age. However, Congress changed these pension rules through the Pension Protection Act of 2006 passed in August, but because no one can determine how quickly each company will begin to change its rules based on the new legislation, you need to understand your pension's past as well as its future.

Checking out the past on pensions

The rules that made it difficult for a company to hire people who are younger than the pension plan's normal retirement age but to whom it is paying traditional pension benefits can be found in the two key laws that govern aspects of traditional pension plans, as well as in the tax codes.

The two key laws are

- **ERISA (Employee Retirement Income Security Act of 1974):** This law governs the operation of most employee benefit plans including traditional pensions as well as employee retirement savings plans, such as 401(k)s.

- **ADEA (Age Discrimination in Employment Act):** This prohibits discrimination in employment. The law governs early retirement benefits and voluntary early retirement incentive plans.

Rules developed based on these laws made it nearly impossible for companies to rehire workers who retired early and then wanted to come back to work. The rules mandated by ERISA and ADEA were eased somewhat with passage of the Pension Protection Act of 2006. Under this law, companies will be able to pay employees age 62 or older a partial pension if they decide to stay on the job part time. Employees who are younger than 62 and receive a pension from the company still can't work for that company.

The barriers in place prior to the 2006 pension law that prevented you from working for a company from which you receive a pension included the following:

- Tax rules required that a person separate from his employer to be legitimately considered retired. If pension benefits are paid before the employee is separated, severe penalties could be imposed and the tax-qualified status of the pension plan could be at risk. The problem was that the IRS had never put out a rule specifying how long an employee must be separated from a company to be considered legitimately retired.

✔ ERISA rules created problems for companies that rehired employees. These companies ran the risk of losing the tax-qualified status of their retirement plans, which would hurt all employees as well as the company.

✔ Rehiring workers could cross paths with ADEA rules involving voluntary early retirement. The ADEA rules were meant to protect workers from age discrimination and being forced out against their will with early retirement packages.

✔ Some companies put their employees on an independent contractor status after they've retired, but the way the work is designed after retirement doesn't actually fit the definition of an independent contractor. If the IRS questions the designation, severe tax penalties are possible. Companies don't pay benefits or Social Security taxes for independent contractors. The IRS could require the company to pay back taxes and back benefits if an employee is paid as an independent contractor incorrectly.

Looking to the future

After you reach age 62 or older, these rules will no longer be a barrier to your being rehired by your old company once the 2006 pension law is fully in place (see the section earlier in this chapter, "Checking out the past on pensions," for more info on the pre-2006 legislation rules). If you decide you do want to continue working for that company part-time or as a consultant or independent contractor, the new rules based on the 2006 law should make this possible. (I discuss more about going back to work for your old company in Chapters 15 and 16.)

If you are retiring in the next couple of years, 2007 to 2009, you may find the barriers are still in place at your company. The Pension Protection Act was signed into law in August of 2006 and the rules based on that law still had to be written while I was working on this book.

I don't know exactly what the rules will say or when the new rules will be available for companies that want to design programs for their workers to return after retirement. Once the companies get those rules, they will then have to work within their own corporate structure to change the rules internally that govern their retirement plans, as well as rules that govern employees that want to come back to work.

All this rule changing could take some time to work through the system. I can't predict how fast companies will change their rules, which of course will vary company to company.

Some companies are actively rehiring workers through temporary agencies or consulting firms. That was how they skirted the rules mentioned above. The temporary agency or consulting firm officially hired and paid the person, who was then contracted back to the company after retirement.

Companies with systems already in place to rehire workers after retirement likely will move more quickly to revise their rules to match what will now be allowed under the 2006 pension law. They could decide to continue doing business with the outside companies or they could decide to bring all hiring back inside the company.

If they rehire workers directly, then they have to pay benefits, which they don't have to pay if they hire the workers through an outside firm. So, if you do work for a company that has established a rehire program through an outside temporary agency or consulting firm, you may not see any changes.

Going the way of dinosaurs

Traditional pensions are rapidly becoming extinct, and the new pension law likely will hasten their demise. The new law does give companies incentives to freeze or close their pension plans as well as automatically enroll employees into 401(k) plans. The following sections cover the ins and outs of these possibilities.

Freezing pension plans

When a company freezes a plan, it can be a hard freeze (no additional enrollments allowed [no new employees qualify] and no more accrual of benefits) or a soft freeze (all new employees are locked out of the plan).

Major companies announced freezes of their pension plans as final passage of the new bill was being considered or shortly after it was signed into law. Some big names in this group include IBM, Verizon, Motorola, and Hewlett Packard. Delta Air Lines and Northwest followed suit soon after as they worked their way out of bankruptcy. DuPont announced within days after the bill was signed that it would cut all contributions to its pension plan and instead increase contributions to its employee retirement savings plans.

Why are companies rushing to drop their pension obligations to long-term employees who were counting on these pensions in retirement? People are living longer, so the costs of providing this benefit continues to increase. Any shortfalls a company has in meeting its pension obligations must be subtracted from a company's net worth under the new law. That could negatively impact a company's market value (stock price), as well as make it more expensive for the company to borrow money.

Also, according to provisions in the new law, most companies must fund their pension plans 100 percent by 2017. Some companies in bankruptcy, such as the major airlines, have an additional seven years to fully fund their plans. Estimates are that private pension plans are underfunded by $300 billion to $450 billion. Rather than try to make up this shortfall, many companies will instead just freeze their pensions.

Getting automatically enrolled in a 401(k)

Through the new pension legislation, companies also got the green light to automatically enroll employees into a 401(k). So if you take a new job with a company that has a 401(k), some portion of your salary will likely be taken out for your company's retirement savings plan. If you are earning too little and can't afford the deduction, you will have to opt out of the 401(k) in most companies after this law is fully in place.

Why is automatic enrollment a good thing? Many people never get around to enrolling in their 401(k). They end up having very little saved for retirement. The powers that be hope that by making enrollment in an employer-sponsored retirement plan automatic, people will be less likely to make the effort to opt out and more people will save for retirement.

The new law also opens the doors for companies to provide investment advisors to their employees. These advisors will primarily represent the firms that are handling the savings programs, usually mutual fund companies, insurance companies, or other types of financial institutions. Some are concerned that the advisors will not be independent enough and may steer people to mutual funds or other investments that will make more money for the financial company giving the advice. The choices may not be what's best for the employee.

If your company does offer you access to a financial advisor for your employer-sponsored retirement, check out the advisor's background. You may be better off finding your own independent advisor rather than working with someone who stands to make a profit from his advice.

Understanding the fate of your funds

How does the new legislation impact you if you've already left the company? That depends on the financial state of your pension fund. If the company's pension funds are in serious trouble and are less than 60 percent funded, you will not be able to get a lump sum of your pension obligation. To avoid being locked out of your funds, you may want to take a lump sum rather than risk the possibility that your company's funds may fall below this threshold.

Major changes for retired public service workers

Policemen, firemen, teachers, and other public service workers will have more options for going back to work under the 2006 pension law.

Public safety workers, who frequently retire at age 50 years or earlier, will no longer be penalized for collecting their early retirement benefits between the ages of 50 and 55. Under the old law, these public safety workers had to pay a 10 percent penalty if they started to collect their pensions before age 55. Many public safety workers stay on the job 20 years and retire, which can often be when they are in their mid-40s. Now they only have to wait until age 50 to start collecting their pension without a penalty.

The new law made it easier for all public service employees to buy back lost years in order to collect a full pension. For example, if a teacher taught in a public school system for 15 years and then moved to a private school system for five years, she could buy back the five years lost in the public system to qualify for a 20-year pension. For many public retirement systems, pensions are significantly lower for people who worked less than 20 years. Money saved in a 403(b) plan can be used to buy back these years.

How will you know whether your company's pension plan is in danger? The 2006 law requires companies to report the financial health of their pension plans to all its pension plan beneficiaries within 120 days after the end of the fiscal year. If you do have funds sitting in a pension plan at a company you no longer work for, ask to get a copy of this report.

If your former company's pension fund is short of being 100 percent funded, read carefully what it intends to do to meet the requirements. You may find it difficult to interpret the report. If you're not sure what it says, contact your accountant or financial advisor and get a good explanation of the company's pension plan prospects.

Rolling out your funds into a retirement portfolio you manage or one that is managed by your financial advisor may be a better option for you. You may find that there is less risk in having total control over the funds than letting them stay in a company fund that is in trouble. Not all pensions are set up with provisions that allow you to take the money as a lump sum, but most are.

You will need to check with your company's benefits coordinator in charge of retirement issues to find out the policies that govern your company's retirement plan. If there is a provision within your pension fund agreement that allows you to take a lump sum, and you question the solvency of your company's pension fund, you're safest bet is to roll the funds into a IRA. You certainly don't want to wait around until your company falls below 60 percent and you can no longer get your money out.

Retiring Early — Not Eligible to Collect Social Security

If you've spent 25 to 30 years with one company or as a public servant with a state or federal government agency, you may end up retiring well before you reach the age of 62, (which for most people is the earliest age you can start collecting your Social Security benefits).

Although you probably have some form of retirement benefits from your former employer, you may or may not be able to collect them. Some companies require you to reach full retirement age (whatever age that company sets) before allowing you to collect any retirement money. Others allow you to get benefits at a significantly reduced level if you want to start collecting early. Still others, who want to reduce their payroll expenses, encourage higher-paid workers to retire with attractive early retirement packages.

You have a lot of decisions to make about how to be paid your retirement pension (if you are eligible for one) and how to manage your retirement savings over which you likely will have full control (such as funds from your 401(k) or other employer-sponsored retirement savings plan).

You will also need to manage your retirement savings portfolio to be sure you don't run out of funds. I talk more about managing retirement portfolios in Chapter 5.

Taking pensions while still working for your company

If you are one of the lucky few who are eligible to collect money from your company's pension plan (only about 30 percent of people retiring from private companies in 2007 have traditional pensions), you do have to decide whether or not you want to take them early (before full retirement age). You also must decide how you want to be paid those funds from your company. I talk more about the options for pension payments and managing withdrawals in Chapter 6.

Trying out retirement part-time

The new pension law did give the green light for companies to allow employees who are at least 62 years old take a partial pension payout and stay on the job part-time. If you are younger than 62, you probably will not be able to go back to work directly for the company from which you just retired. (I discuss the new pension law in-depth in the section, "Taking a Look at Pension Legislation," earlier in this chapter.)

You will need to find out if the company is hiring ex-employees through a third party. I talk more about how to find that out in Chapters 15 and 16.

What the new law does do is open the door for what many people call a phased retirement program, where you can collect a partial pension and continue working part-time. I talk more about phased retirement programs and how they work in Chapter 15.

Withdrawing a lump sum

When you leave your job, but are not ready to stop working, you may decide you want to take the lump sum value of your traditional pension plan. Not all companies allow you to do this, but some do.

If your company does allow you take a lump sum, you will need to be fully vested (have worked long enough to earn the right to take out 100 percent of the funds) to get the full cash value of your pension. Should you decide to take out your pension funds in one lump sum, you should then roll out the funds into an Individual Retirement Account to avoid taxes and penalties.

Don't just spend it! If you spend it, you risk running out of money during retirement (when you finally do decide to stop working). You will also have to pay hefty tax penalties if you spend it rather than roll it into a qualified IRA. You'll have to pay a 10 percent penalty for any funds you withdraw and spend before you reach the age of 59½. In addition, you will have to pay tax on the money you withdraw at your current income tax rate no matter what age you are.

Given that your pension fund will likely total hundreds of thousands of dollars, you will be hit with taxes at the highest tax bracket — 35 percent. Adding the 10 percent penalty plus 35 percent in income taxes, your total tax hit would be 45 percent. That means almost half of the money in your retirement pension would be lost to the government in the form of income taxes and penalties.

You will not have to pay the penalties if you spend the lump sum immediately, but are already older than 59½. But either way, you will have to pay the income taxes.

Seeking help if you do take the money

The total amount in your pension fund will be a large sum of money. Complicated financial calculations of present cash value can dramatically impact how much you get, so seek financial advice from an independent accountant or financial advisor who you know is looking out for your best interest. Your company will be looking to save money and minimize how much it pays to you.

An independent financial advisor can review the calculation as well as your company's pension payout rules and help you determine whether it is better for you to leave the money in the pension fund or take a lump sum. If you don't know an advisor, get recommendations from friends.

You can also find a certified financial planner at the Financial Planning Association (http://www.fpanet.org/public/). There you will find basic information about the planning process, as well as a search tool to find a planner near your home.

Withdrawing employer retirement savings

When you leave your job, you're usually offered the options to keep your 401(k) or other employer retirement savings in the account managed by your employer, or you can roll those funds into your own individual retirement account (IRA) and manage them yourself. Whether or not you do that depends on the investments permitted in your employer retirement savings plans.

You may find that the options are limited and you're stuck with a large portion of your 401(k) in your company's stock. The options offered may not give the opportunity to properly diversify your retirement portfolio. Luckily in the new pension law, companies are required to let you sell company stock much sooner and convert it to a different type of investment that will give you more diversity.

I talk more about proper asset allocation in Chapter 5. If you don't like your investment options in your employer retirement savings plan, then you should definitely roll the funds out into an IRA and pick your own investments or have a financial advisor help you do so if you don't know much about managing a portfolio.

If you do decide to take out your retirement savings, don't spend them. You will have to pay a 10 percent penalty if you withdraw funds before the age of 59½.

Continuing to save

If you retire early and take another job, you may be earning enough so you can continue to save. If so, the following sections give you some ideas on the best vehicles to put your savings in.

Catching up on IRA contributions

After the age of 50, the government allows you to do what are called catch-up contributions. That means you can save even more money in a traditional or Roth IRA than someone under the age of 50.

The new pension legislation not only affected the rules for pension funds, it also made permanent many of the rules that let older workers save more. These catch-up contributions can be critical, especially if your retirement savings fall short of what you'll need to live comfortably in retirement.

The savings rules allow you to put $4,000 into an IRA in 2007. It will increase to $5,000 in 2008 and then be adjusted by inflation after that. People who are 50 years old can benefit by additional contributions that are allowed just for them. If you are 50 or older, you can add an additional $1,000. If the new law hadn't passed in time, your contributions to IRAs would have dropped back to just $2,000 per year in 2010.

If you are working for a company that has a 401(k) or other qualified employee retirement savings plans, there are catch-up contributions available for those plans too that were made permanent under the new law. In 401(k) plans, all workers can contribute up to $15,000 annually. Workers who are 50 and older can also contribute an additional catch-up contribution of $5,000.

If the change in law had not been made, you would have lost the ability to make catch-up contributions. Also, the maximum you could put into an employer-sponsored retirement savings plan would have gone back to $13,000 in 2011.

Taking credit if you don't earn much

Many people who decide to go back to work after retiring earn considerably less than they did when they were working full-time. If you do take a job at which you are not earning much, you may become eligible for the Saver's Credit. This is another benefit for retirement savers that was made permanent in the new pension law.

Lower and middle-income taxpayers can qualify for this credit based on the amount they put into a qualified retirement savings account. This includes both an IRA and an employer's qualified retirement savings plan. The tax credit can be subtracted from your income tax bill.

A tax credit can be a more powerful tool than a tax deduction. That's because a tax deduction is subtracted from your taxable income. Then you calculate your taxes based on the lower income. A tax credit is subtracted from the tax due amount and lowers your tax bill directly.

You are eligible for the Saver's Credit if your adjusted gross income is $25,000 or less for singles ($50,000 or less for married couples). These adjusted gross income figures will be adjusted for inflation beginning in 2007. So expect the maximum allowable salary to increase.

If you do qualify, you may be eligible for a deduction as much as 50 percent of the first $2,000 you deposit in a retirement savings account. The IRS provides a worksheet with your Form 1040 filing instructions to help you figure your tax credit.

This gives your contribution to a tax deductible IRA double power to reduce your tax bill. You can use the amount you contributed into your IRA as a deduction to lower your gross income tax. Plus you can use it to figure the Saver's Credit you'll be allowed.

Delaying Benefits — Deciding Not to Collect

You can start collecting Social Security when you reach age 62, but your benefits will be reduced significantly and this reduction is something you must live with for the rest of your life.

You can find out more information about the reduction and how to calculate that in Chapter 7. I also talk about collecting Social Security and working in that chapter.

In this section, I focus on the benefits of continuing to work and not collecting Social Security. This can improve your ultimate Social Security benefit and give you more money every month throughout your retirement years.

Improving future Social Security benefits

You can improve your monthly Social Security benefits in three ways if you delay collecting your benefits beyond age 62 (the age when you first become eligible for benefits):

✓ **Your benefits won't be reduced as much the closer you get to your full retirement age.** I discuss the rules related to collecting Social Security early in Chapter 7.

✔ **Continue to work and delay retirement.** Your benefits may actually increase, especially if you had some years in your 35-year work record when you made no money or very little money. By continuing to work, you can replace these very low or zero-dollar earning years with higher earnings.

Social Security uses your 35 highest-earning years to calculate your Social Security benefit. If some of your work history includes years where you did not earn any money or years where your income was very low, the money you earn after retiring, but before you start collecting Social Security, can help to improve the amount you will end up collecting.

✔ **Work past your full retirement age.** Your benefits could increase even more if you decide to continue working past your full retirement age. The amount you can collect from Social Security goes up each year that you wait.

Whenever you work, you must pay into Social Security. Your employer matches your contribution. Each quarter (a quarter is three months of the year), your employer reports your earnings to Social Security. So if you continue to work, your work record just gets longer. It can never hurt you, but it might help you.

For example, suppose you stayed home to raise a family for 15 years and didn't earn any money. In this scenario, about 40 percent of your work history could be $0 earnings years. If you continue working after retirement, those zero dollar earnings years will be replaced gradually, increasing the amount you will be able to collect when you do decide to take Social Security.

Once you do start collecting Social Security, if you continue working, your benefit amount is automatically adjusted each year and improves your earnings history. You don't need to do anything. Social Security will adjust it based on earnings reported by your employer.

Understanding the benefit of delaying benefits

The biggest benefit of waiting past your full retirement age to collect Social Security is that each year that you wait, your benefit will go up between 6 and 8 percent, depending on when you were born. Table 8-1 shows you what your yearly increase will be by year of birth.

Table 8-1	Social Security Benefit Increases for Delayed Retirement	
Year of Birth	*Yearly Rate of Increase*	*Monthly Rate of Increase*
1935-1936	6.0%	½ of 1%
1937-1938	6.5%	¹³⁄₂₄ of 1%
1939-1940	7.0%	⁷⁄₁₂ of 1%
1941-1942	7.5%	⅝ of 1%
1943 or later	8%	⅔ of 1%

The percentage of benefit increase differs by year of birth because full retirement age is gradually increasing to age 67 from age 65. People who can retire at age 65 will have 5 years to accrue additional benefits, while people who can retire at 67 will have only three years to benefit from waiting.

So what does this mean for someone born in 1943 whose full retirement age is 66 (Chapter 7 has a chart that shows the change in retirement ages by year of birth.), but decides to wait until 70? Each of the four years the person waits after the age of 66 will result in a benefit increase of 8 percent.

To show you how much waiting can help you, I used the Social Security Web site's benefits calculator to find the benefits for a fictitious retiree named Sally. She earned an average of $30,000 per year during her 35-year work history.

Sally was born in 1944, so she could start collecting benefits as early as 2006 at age 62. She could also decide to wait until 2010, when she will reach full retirement age. Or she could put it off until 2014 when she will be 70. Here are her three options in today's dollars according to the Social Security benefits calculator (www.ssa.gov/planners/calculators.htm):

    Sally at age 62 = $684

    Sally at age 66 = $955

    Sally at age 70 = $1,320

You can see that by waiting until she is 70 rather than collecting early at age 62, her monthly benefit will be $636 more, almost double what she could have gotten at age 62. If you haven't saved enough for retirement, this can certainly go a long way to helping you make ends meet.

Social Security benefits do increase each year based on the cost of living, called the COLA (cost of living adjustment). Social Security announces the amount of the COLA increase for the next year in October of the previous year. For example, in October 2007, the COLA increase will be announced for January 2008.

Unfortunately, at the same time the COLA is announced, Social Security also usually announces the premium increase for Medicare Part B. Often this increase is about the same amount as the COLA, so your Social Security check won't change by much when you start collecting. I talk more about Medicare and its costs in Chapter 10.

Social Security is one of the few retirement benefits that increase each year based on a COLA. Most private pensions do not increase at all. The amount that you are promised at the time you retire is the amount that you must live with for the rest of your life.

Calculating your best time to start collecting Social Security

I'm sure you're wondering how to figure out when the best time is for you to start collecting Social Security. That depends on your expected lifetime. But who really knows how long they will live?

No one can be sure how long they will live, but you can use the MSN Life Expectancy Calculator to guesstimate it. You can find the calculator at `http://moneycentral.msn.com/investor/calcs/n_expect/main.asp`.

To show you how to figure out your best option, I assume three different ages for Sally to die — 70, 80, and 90. I calculate the total benefits she will receive before each age of death depending on when she started to collect.

Started collecting at age 62

If Sally dies at age 70, she will collect Social Security benefits for a total of 96 months. She'll collect these benefits for 216 months if she dies at age 80. She'll collect these benefits for 336 months if she dies at age 90. The total amount of benefits she will collect if she started collecting Social Security at age 62, based on a monthly amount of $684, is

By age 70 = $65,664

By age 80 = $147,744

By age 90 = $229,824

Started collecting at age 66

If Sally dies at age 70, she will collect Social Security benefits for a total of 48 months. She'll collect benefits for 168 months if she dies at age 80. She'll collect benefits for 288 months if she dies at age 90. The total amount of benefits she will collect if she started collecting Social Security at age 66, based on a monthly amount of $955, is

By age 70 = $45,840

By age 80 = $160,440

By age 90 = $275,040

Started collecting at age 70

If Sally dies at age 70, she will collect Social Security benefits for a total of 0 months. She'll collect benefits for 120 months if she dies at age 80. She'll collect benefits for 240 months if she dies at age 90. The total amount of Social Security benefits she will collect if she started collecting at age 70, based on a monthly amount of $1,320, is

By age 70 = $0

By age 80 = $158,400

By age 90 = $316,800

You can see from these calculations that if your family has traditionally long life spans past the age of 80, you may be better off waiting until 70 to start collecting Social Security. Of course, you must also consider your own health status. But, provided your health is good enough, you likely will live as long as your other family members.

On the other hand, if it's common in your family for people to die before the age of 70, you're best off starting to collect Social Security as soon as possible at age 62. That way you will have more money to use during your early retirement years.

Deciding not to wait any longer

Your benefits of waiting to collect do have an end point. Once you reach the age of 70, there is absolutely no benefit to waiting any longer. If you forego your Social Security benefits after the age of 70 because you still haven't retired, you're just giving your money away.

If you are still working, you can always bank your Social Security check. You won't have any penalties if you continue working. You won't face any reduction in your Social Security benefits.

If you do still work at the age of 70 and you improve your earnings history by replacing some $0 earnings years, your benefits will be adjusted upward automatically. But, that will happen whether or not you are collecting.

Chapter 9

Trying to Stay Healthy —
Before Age 65

In This Chapter

▶ Finding individual health insurance

▶ Knowing what to do when benefits are cut

▶ Joining a group

▶ Footing the bill

Retirees, especially those who retired before age 65, often find they can't afford to stay retired because they can't get health insurance — or can't afford to pay for it. Some early retirees must choose to go back to work not for the money, but instead just to get access to group health benefits.

This chapter will look at the difficult job of finding health insurance after retirement, but before you qualify for Medicare.

Exploring Health Insurance Types

When looking for health insurance, if you can figure out how to stay in a group plan after retirement rather than be forced to apply for individual plans, do so. While the monthly premium may seem high to you, I can guarantee that comparable coverage, if you were able to find it, would be more expensive through an individual plan. I talk more about health insurance costs in the section, " Finding and Paying for Health Insurance . . . After You Retire but Before Medicare," below, but first I want to explore the various types of health insurance on the market today.

Group health plans

Most of you probably had group health insurance at least at some point in your working life. Many companies give people a choice of coverage among a number of different options — Health Maintenance Organization (HMO), Preferred Provider Organization (PPO), Point-of-Service Plan (POS), Indemnity Plan, and High Deductible Health Plan (HDHP) with Health Savings Account (HSA).

Health Maintenance Organization (HMO)

HMOs are the oldest type of a managed-care plan. They offer not only care for illness, but also preventive care. They can be formed in two different ways:

- Some are set up where doctors, nurses, and other medical personnel are hired as employees of the plan. When you seek care, you must go to specified HMO facilities and get help from one of the medical personnel on the staff of the HMO.

- Another type of HMO structure involves contracting with physician groups or individual doctors who will see you in their private offices. The HMO will pay these doctor groups a set amount per patient per month, no matter how often the doctor sees you in a given month. If you join this type of group, beware, you may be seeking a new doctor on a regular basis. Arguments about treatment and payment arrangements frequently result in the doctor leaving the group, whether by choice or not. This is managed care, and sometimes the private doctor doesn't agree with the HMO's managers.

Here are some characteristics common to HMOs:

- **Co-payment:** No matter what type of underlying structure, HMO facilities or private offices, you as a patient will only have to pay a co-payment when you see a doctor. Co-payments can be as low as $5 per visit or as high as $25 for the primary care provider and $50 for specialists. You will get a list of fees when you apply for the plan.

- **Primary care provider (PCP):** Each person in the HMO is assigned a PCP. This is the doctor you must see for everything. In some managed-care systems, you are assigned a doctor, or in others, you can pick a doctor from a list of providers given to you.

- **Referrals:** You can only see a specialist about a medical problem you're having, if your PCP decides you need to see a specialist. Then you will be given a referral slip. Don't go to see a specialist without a referral from your PCP, or the HMO won't pay for it.

- **Rules for reimbursement:** Even when you travel, you may have difficulty getting reimbursement, except for emergency care in this type of closed system. If you do select an HMO, be certain you understand the rules for seeking medical care while you are traveling before you go on your trip. If an emergency does arise, the last thing you want to do is try to find out the rules while you're sitting in an emergency room or the office of an urgent-care doctor.

Point-of-Service Plan (POS)

Many HMOs offer a bit of a twist to their HMOs called a Point-of-Service (POS) plan. In this type of plan, your primary care physician (PCP) will usually make referrals to specialists who are part of the HMO network. But, if you want to see someone outside the network of providers approved by the HMO, you can get some reimbursement. HMOs do pay less of the bill if you use a provider outside the plan. For example, the HMO may pay 100 percent of costs after your co-pay of $50 if you see a doctor in the HMO network, but only 50 percent or 70 percent outside the network.

Sometimes the PCP may decide to refer you to a specialist outside the network. If that happens, then the plan will pay most if not all of the bill.

If you do get a referral outside the HMO network, be sure you know how much you are going to have to pay out-of-pocket before seeing the specialist. You don't want to find out after seeing the specialist that you're going to be socked with 30 or 50 percent of the bill. PCPs have been known to make a mistake because specialists, as well as primary care doctors, drop in and out of the network. When you make an appointment with the specialist, make sure he or she will accept your HMO as the paying insurer.

Sorting out the maze of an HMO can be a full-time job if you're sick. Take the time to learn the ropes before you need the care.

Preferred Provider Organizations (PPO)

A PPO is a type of managed care, but it operates much more like a traditional health insurance plan that you had when you were growing up, which today are called Indemnity Plans. PPOs contract with doctors, hospitals, and other medical care providers who agree to accept lower fees to be part of the insurer's network.

You may wonder why doctors would agree to accept lower fees. Well, if they want patients today, they probably don't have a choice. Few people can get Indemnity Plans (see the section "Indemnity or Fee-for-Service Plan," below) through their workplace today. Even if they are offered, the cost of these plans is too high for most employees.

As long as you see a physician inside the PPO network of providers, you will pay a co-payment specified in the plan, usually between $10 and $25 for your primary care provider (PCP) and $25 to $50 for a specialist. You can seek care outside the PPOs network of providers, but you will likely have to pay co-insurance. For example, a PPO likely will pay all charges above the co-pay if you see a doctor inside the network and only 50 or 70 percent of the charges outside the network.

Indemnity or Fee-for-Service Plan

An Indemnity Plan is most likely the type of plan you had when you were growing up. You could see any doctor without having to worry about whether or not they were in the network of providers for your health insurer. Your parents likely paid 20 or 30 percent of the doctor's bill and the insurance company paid the rest.

You can find Indemnity Plans on the market today, but you will probably decide the monthly costs are too high. Since you can see the doctor of your choice, the insurance company most likely has not negotiated rates with the doctor and will be forced to pay the full fee, rather than a discounted fee that would have been negotiated with a doctor who is part of the insurer's network.

Few companies offer this choice any more for their employees, and for those that do, the cost is so much higher that many people choose not to pay for them. I've seen employers charge $200 or more per month to employees who decide they want the Indemnity Plan for their family. Most employees that choose to pay the extra premium do so because there are doctors they want to see regularly that are not in the PPO or HMO network the employer offers.

High Deductible Health Plan (HDHP)

A new type of plan, called the High Deductible Health Plan (HDHP), that first became available to the group health insurance market in 2004 is growing very slowly in popularity. With this type of plan, you have a high deductible, which you must pay out-of-pocket before the insurance company pays anything.

Deductibles can be as low as $1,000 for an individual and $2,200 for self and family, but they can also be as high as $5,000 for an individual and $10,000 for self and family. So if you choose this type of plan, be sure you understand how much you could be paying out-of-pocket if you get sick.

Promoters of this type of plan believe that they put you in the driver's seat to control the rising costs of medical insurance. But, if you do sign up for this plan, it won't take you long to realize that it's a false promise. You will find it very difficult to get information to be able to compare fees. Even if you try to call for a quote by phone, you likely will be told it depends on what the medical provider has to do, and the list of fees are so long that they can't provide you with a quote. You may be able to get a quote for one particular day after the doctor sees you, but by then you've already seen the doctor and will have to pay the fees anyway.

On top of the doctor's bill, you'll also get bills from the lab for any blood tests or other tests run. If the doctor sends you for an x-ray, you'll get billed for both the x-ray and for the radiologist who reads the x-ray. You'll be amazed at how quickly a doctor's visit for a wellness exam can turn into a $500 or $1,000 bill or even more.

If you choose to see a doctor in the HDHPs network of providers, you will receive a discount on your bill. As long as you stay in the HDHP's network, you likely will see discounts of 20 to 60 percent on the bill. It all depends on the fees the network provider negotiated with the HDHP. I have found that if you choose a doctor in a group connected with a hospital, you tend to get a better discount if billed through the hospital system.

Health Savings Account (HSA)

HSAs are tax-free savings plans that you can open and deposit up to $2,700 per year, provided your deductible is at least that high. If you do sign up for an HDHP, make sure that the plan is HSA compatible. Some are, but some are not.

Any money put into these savings accounts can grow tax-free and be taken out tax-free as long as you use the money for allowable medical care. Any unused funds in a given year can be rolled over to the next year. The savings account is yours to keep throughout your life, but you can only add to it when you are enrolled in an HDHP that is compatible. Once you start on Medicare, you can no longer add to the savings account, but you can still draw funds from this account to pay Medicare co-pays and deductibles. I talk more about your out-of-pocket costs while on Medicare in Chapter 10.

Money put into the HSA is tax-deductible in the year you deposit the money. If you are over the age of 50, you can put an extra $700 per year into the plan to help you catch up in saving for medical care when you are older. Catch-up contributions are permitted with many retirement savings plans, such as Individual Retirement Accounts (IRAs) and 401(k)s. So if you are still adding to yours, you may be able to save more and reduce your tax bill at the same time.

Medical expenses for which you can withdraw money tax-free from the HSA include the costs of diagnosis, cure, mitigation, treatment, or prevention of disease, and the costs for treatments affecting any part or function of the body. They include the costs of equipment, supplies, and diagnostic devices needed for these purposes. They also include dental expenses. You cannot pay expenses that are just beneficial to general health, such as vitamins or a vacation. These funds can also be used to pay premiums for qualified long-term care services and limited amounts paid for any qualified long-term care insurance contract.

Losing a Group Plan

After you retire, you could find out at some point that your company no longer offers health insurance to its employees as part of their retirement package. Even if you are initially offered the coverage, the company doesn't have to guarantee that it will offer it for the rest of your life or until you qualify for Medicare.

Needing coverage . . . quickly!

If you find out that you are no longer eligible for a group plan, act quickly to check out your alternatives. Once you are without group coverage for 60 days, it becomes much more difficult, if not impossible, to find coverage for any pre-existing conditions.

By the time you reach 50, you're likely to have at least one pre-existing condition. For example, if you take medicine for high blood pressure, a company could determine that is a pre-existing condition and not offer coverage or offer coverage at a much higher rate per month than if you did not have the health problem. They also could exclude coverage for anything related to your high blood pressure. When an insurance company adds this type of exclusion, it's called a *rider*. A rider can exclude coverage for the medical condition for which you need coverage the most.

Health insurance companies are famous for cherrypicking who they will insure and who they won't. That means they only pick the best cherries (healthiest people) on the tree, all others are left to fend for themselves. Often if you have even one thing wrong with you, such as high blood pressure or diabetes, you will not be able to get individual health insurance from most companies — even if you can prove you've kept it under control for years. Those that do offer coverage will charge outrageous sums. If you have a more serious illness, forget about it. I know couples paying over $20,000 per year just for their health insurance.

Checking out your options

So before you give up on the idea of being part of a group, check carefully into your options, which include

- ✔ **COBRA:** You may be able to continue coverage under COBRA. You should be able to keep your group coverage for 18 months more as long as you pay 100 percent of the premiums. Federal law makes it mandatory for a company to offer you continuing coverage under COBRA if you've lost your job or you've experienced a change in your family life, such as a divorce. A divorcee who was covered on the ex-spouse's plan can get COBRA coverage for up to 36 months.

- ✔ **Conversion:** You might be able to convert your group plan into an individual plan. Sometimes this can be done without taking COBRA for 18 months, and sometimes you can't apply for a conversion until after you've exhausted your COBRA benefits. If you can convert to an individual plan, you won't have to worry about being denied coverage for pre-existing conditions.

- ✔ **Professional or Social Associations:** If you belong to professional or social associations, you may be able to get a group policy through one of those associations. Contact any association to which you belong to find out if they have access to group health insurance for their members.

Group insurance does offer you the best rates and more comprehensive coverage, so if you can find a way to stay within a group, do so. I explore your other options below, including COBRA, association health plans, individual health plans, and state guaranteed issue insurance pools.

You may also find health plans that offer a discount for services rather than insurance. These are not health insurance plans, but they may save you money if you can't find a way to get health insurance. But be careful, many of these plans are not accepted by doctors even if the doctors' group may be listed on the promotional materials. I had one for a short time and called 15 doctors' groups on the list only to find out that most of them had never heard of the plan. If you are considering a discount plan, call the doctors on the list for the plan and find out if the doctor has heard of the plan and will honor it.

Understanding state influence

Another thing that makes it so difficult to find health insurance wherever you're living is that health insurance is managed by the states, so insurance companies lobby for the easiest rules they can get in each state. You will find very different health insurance rules state by state. For example, if you had a good plan when you were living in New Jersey, which has some of the strongest consumer-oriented health insurance laws, you won't find the same type of coverage in Florida, which tends to bend more easily to insurance company wishes.

Some states have rules that make it easier for you to get health insurance if you are a small business. For example, in Florida, the state makes it possible for self-employed individuals to join the small business group. So if you live in Florida and run a small business out of your home, you can get group health insurance. You can find out which states offer this option at Health Insurance.org (www.healthinsurance.org). You will find links there to insurance Web sites for the states that do have special provisions for small business owners.

COBRA

COBRA is short for a 1985 law (Consolidated Omnibus Budget Reconciliation Act of 1985) that guaranteed continuing group health coverage for employees working at companies with 20 or more people. You are entitled for COBRA benefits if:

- ✔ You work for a company that has more than 20 workers.

- ✔ You were covered on a group health insurance plan prior to the change in your work or family life. You can check with your human resources person to see if you are in a plan covered by COBRA.

- ✔ You lost your coverage because of a change in your work or family life that qualifies, such as you change jobs, you get divorced, or your spouse loses coverage at his or her workplace.

You must send your company a notice within 60 days of any life change event that qualifies. The company must let you know if you are eligible for COBRA within 14 days of receiving your notice.

If you do qualify for coverage, then you will need to pay for 100 percent of the health insurance costs. This likely will be a huge jump in monthly premiums you must pay out of pocket. Most companies subsidize health insurance; very few pay for it completely. Most employers today expect employees to pay between 20 percent and 40 percent of their health insurance premiums, so your health insurance premium bill likely will jump by 60 to 80 percent depending on how much of it was paid by the employer previously.

Don't get angry and drop the insurance without first researching your options and finding alternative health insurance coverage. If you are without group health coverage for 60 days, you will find it difficult to get coverage for any pre-existing conditions.

When you do your search, you probably will find out that an individual health plan will cost you a lot more money, if you can even qualify for that plan. If you or a member of your family has pre-existing conditions, most individual health insurance won't consider covering you or will put a hefty surcharge on your monthly premium. This is called rating you up and it can be as much as 100 percent more than you would have to pay if you didn't have the condition. That means a $350 monthly premium could all of sudden turn into a $700 monthly premium for an individual. Family health insurance is even higher.

Association health plans

If you can't get COBRA or convert your group plan into an individual plan, you may have one other choice before entering the maze of seeking individual health coverage — association health plans. Many professional and social associations provide their members with a way to get group health insurance. Check with any professional or social associations in which you are a member to find out if they offer access to a group health insurance plan.

AARP

The AARP started offering a Personal Health Insurance Plan to its members aged 50 to 64 who do not yet qualify for Medicare. The Plan offers insurance through the United HealthCare Insurance Company.

You won't be able to access the AARP's plan in all states, but as of September 2005, it was available in these 15 states: Alabama, Arizona, Arkansas, Colorado, Connecticut, Florida, Illinois, Maryland, Missouri, Nebraska, Ohio, Oklahoma, Pennsylvania, Texas, and Virginia.

If you are having difficulty finding a health insurance plan, you may want to check out the AARP plan online at `http://www.aarp.org/aarp_benefits/offer_health/aarp_personal_health_insurance_plan.html`. I'm not aware of any other group plan available for this age group.

The AARP has numerous options available for you as part of this plan. For comprehensive coverage, you can choose from deductible levels of $1,000, $2,000, and $5,000. There is also a plan that offers limited coverage with a $2,000 deductible. Premiums do vary state by state.

Individual health plans

Options for individual health plans are similar to those available under group plans. You can find HMOs, PPOs, POSs, HDHPs, and Indemnity Plans, but you likely won't find that their coverage is as comprehensive as that available on a group plan. You'll have to carefully scour the list of what they cover and what they don't.

When picking an individual health plan, be sure you understand how much the plan will pay for services. Some plans provide coverage based on a schedule of fees. If your doctor charges more for any type of procedure listed on the schedule, you have to pay the difference out of pocket. For example, if the plan lists the fee for a specific operation as $15,000 and your doctor charges you $25,000, you'll have to pay the difference out-of-pocket.

Be sure to read the fine print of any individual health plan that you choose. If you find something written in your contract that you don't understand, ask questions until you do. Definitely do not wait until you need the care to find out what kind of coverage you have. That will be too late to fix the problem with your coverage.

State guaranteed issue health insurance pools

State guaranteed issue insurance pools should always be your last resort. They provide the least amount of coverage for the most amount of money. When my COBRA ran out and before I found the current small business group I could join, the best quote I could find through guaranteed issue was $780 per month for a high deductible health plan, and other options were considerably higher.

Contact your state health insurance commissioner to find out if guaranteed issue health insurance pools are offered in your state. If your state does offer these types of pools, they will include a list of health insurance companies that can be contacted for coverage.

Finding and Paying for Health Insurance ... After You Retire but Before Medicare

Your health insurance premiums will skyrocket once you lose the coverage you've come to depend on through your workplace. In fact, many people after they start to research health insurance costs, decide they can't afford to retire early and must wait until they are closer to qualifying for Medicare.

If you do work for a company that offers COBRA coverage, that does allow you to retire at least 18 months early and still carry your group insurance coverage.

As you start to make your plans for early retirement before you qualify for Medicare, make sure you check out your health insurance options carefully and what they will cost before you take the leap. You won't be able to rectify this mistake easily if you find out you're going to lose your health insurance.

Researching coverage exclusions

As you age, you have to face the fact that health problems will appear. For example, most people over 50 have some signs of arthritis — that can result in being rated up for higher premiums and possibly total denial of health insurance in some states because of what insurance companies would consider a *pre-existing condition*. In others, even if you can find coverage, the health insurance company will write the policy only if you accept an exclusion for anything related to your pre-existing condition of arthritis.

When you consider how many joints can be affected by arthritis, if you're told by the health insurance company that it's excluding coverage for anything related to arthritis, you likely won't have coverage for anything involving your joints. You can be sure they'll deny payment on the basis of arthritis if you need joint surgery.

It's very difficult to find out what a company may or may not exclude in coverage. All of this is part of the secretive world of underwriting. No insurance company puts out an extensive list of things it will or will not cover. You can only find out if you have a coverage problem with a specific insurance company after you've filled out their extensive questionnaire and provided them with a comprehensive health history. I can guarantee if you haven't been through this process, you will find it one of the most intrusive things you ever have to do.

Recruiting retirees

Many people end up going back to work after retiring solely to get health insurance coverage. I live near Orlando, Florida, and know many people who took full-time jobs a Disney not because they needed the money, but because they wanted access to a group health insurance plan. I know couples who were paying over $1,500 per month to get health insurance, prior to joining Disney. Other neighbors and friends are luckier, and have continuing health coverage through their former place of employment as part of their retirement health package.

Disney has had so much success recruiting workers in my retirement community, that their recruiters come to the community once a month to find new workers. Health insurance is not the only driving force. Many are looking for free tickets and other discount benefits they can use when their grandchildren are visiting.

In addition to the questions they will ask you, they can use a secretive database available to health insurers that lists all the payments that were made on your behalf by all the insurance companies. So they know what types of medications you've taken in the past, as well as whatever diagnoses you've received from the doctor.

You can be denied coverage based on information in your file, but you can't get a copy of your file to find out if it is correct. When you do get denied or coverage gets excluded, only then can you ask for details about why the company has denied coverage. If you think the information in your file is wrong, you have the onus of paying for a doctor's appointment and getting whatever information you may need to prove the information in the file is not correct. If that involves additional tests, you pay for the tests out-of-pocket unless you have existing health insurance coverage that has not yet expired.

The underwriting process can take 30 days or more. That's why you should start seeking replacement coverage at least 60 days before your current coverage expires.

Finding insurance coverage

When looking for health insurance, the insurer definitely has the upper hand and holds all the cards. You may be able to look for health insurance options and try to find the best price on the Internet. But, the quotes you'll receive from all these Web sites are based on someone in excellent health with no problems.

You won't actually know what your health insurance will cost you until after you fill out an online questionnaire and answer a verbal list of questions from the underwriter. In addition, the underwriter will ask you to send medical records related to the questions you answer. The entire underwriting process can take more than a month, and when it's over, you may not like the price you get. You then have to start the entire process over again with another insurance company.

You do have a couple of options for making the most of your time during your search:

✓ **Start the underwriting process at the same time with a number of companies.** You will find that after the underwriting process, some companies will reject your application, some will increase your monthly rate considerably because of certain medical conditions, and others will not cover a chronic disease. The process can take 60 to 90 days, so it's a good idea to apply with several companies. That way when the final offers come in after underwriting, you can choose the company that offers you the best option at the best price.

✓ **Find an insurance agent that specializes in health insurance.** That's not an easy person to find in most states. Agents don't make much money selling individual health insurance policies because so many of their successful sales fall through. Many times the individuals who apply for insurance don't qualify. Individual health insurance agents find out very quickly that they'll run around to see potential customers, but few will turn into successful sales. It's not hard to get someone to fill out the application, but it is hard to get someone through the underwriting process. The agent only makes money if someone qualifies. So, you may find it difficult to find an individual health insurance agent who has been around for awhile and can help you. Ask your friends and neighbors if they know someone that can help.

Uncovering hidden costs

Premiums are not the only thing you must consider when picking a health insurance plan. In addition to premiums, you likely will have to pay:

✓ **Deductibles:** The amount you must spend before the health insurance company will pay any part of your medical bills is called a *deductible*. Deductibles can be as low as $100 and as high as $5,000, depending on the type of health insurance plan you choose.

✓ **Co-payments:** A *co-payment* is a set dollar amount you will pay each time you see a medical provider. For example, you may have to pay $20 each time you see your primary care provider.

✔ **Co-insurance:** *Co-insurance* is usually a percentage you will pay of the allowable charges a doctor or other medical provider bills for your care. For example, if the insurance company pays 80 percent of your hospital bill, then your co-insurance will be 20 percent of that bill.

Also, you need to check whether or not the insurance company has pre-certification requirements. These are common when you need surgery or other major medical procedure. If you fail to get pre-certification before the surgery or procedure, the insurance company can refuse to pay the bill.

You may also find that some companies charge you to even apply for their coverage, called an application process charge or administrative fee. These fees will likely be in the $50 to $100 range. They do have to pay their underwriters, and you foot part of the bill for that intrusive process.

Figuring Out When Your Health Coverage Will End

Whatever coverage you choose after retirement, but before Medicare, will end when you become eligible for Medicare at age 65. At that point, you'll have to decide among numerous options to figure out what type of health coverage you want. I talk about health coverage options under Medicare in Chapter 8.

Before that time, there are a number of ways your coverage can end:

✔ **You send a note to the insurance company to drop the coverage.** You must do this in writing. Hopefully before you do this, you do have another health insurance plan lined up. You don't want to have a break in coverage, because you will find difficulty getting another plan if you have pre-existing conditions, and you may not have coverage for these conditions if you have a break in coverage of more than 60 days. So don't act in anger if you find your plan is not providing the coverage you expected. Act slowly and carefully to protect your rights to continuing health insurance coverage.

✔ **You fail to pay the premium.** If you don't pay the premiums on time, the company can drop your insurance and you will have to start the application process all over again. You can be denied coverage even if you pay the bill late. If a new medical condition has developed since your initial application, you probably will be denied coverage. Don't forget to pay those health insurance premiums on time. Many health insurance companies will set up an automatic payment process that takes the money out of your bank account. You may want to consider that option to avoid this mistake.

✔ **You reach a certain age.** Some companies will specify that they will only cover you up to a certain age. If the age is less than 65, don't consider the policy. Find one that will cover you until you are eligible for Medicare. You don't want to have to search for insurance again and risk denial because of a pre-existing condition. The number of medical conditions you face do increase as you age.

✔ **Making fraudulent misstatements.** If you tried to hide a health problem during your application process and the health insurance company finds out that you provided false information, the company does have the right to cancel your coverage as though you never had it. Even an omission can be interpreted as a fraudulent misstatement.

Finding health insurance as an individual may be one of the most difficult processes you face when you retire. You'll find it frustrating and you may end up deciding you have to go back to work just to get the medical coverage you need. Your only comfort will be that you are not alone. Many people return to work because they can't find or can't afford individual health insurance.

Chapter 10

Exploring Medicare's Maze of Benefits

In This Chapter

▶ Medicare's jumble of benefits

▶ Coverage options

▶ Paying for what Medicare doesn't

▶ Covering long-term care

*I*f you think you had a hard time figuring out health insurance benefits when you were covered in a group plan through your company, you've not seen anything yet. Medicare's maze of benefits with its Parts A, B, C, and D can be difficult to explore even if you have a PhD in healthcare. In this chapter, I sort out myriad benefits and rules to help make your journey through this maze a bit easier.

Getting Started with Medicare

You probably have heard about the As, Bs, Cs, and Ds of Medicare but aren't sure what these letters mean. Keeping it brief — the devil's in the details below — I list the basics in their simplest form:

- **Part A** covers hospitalization.

- **Part B** covers doctors and most of your other medical needs.

- **Part C** includes all managed-care options to Parts A and B.

- **Part D** covers drugs.

You likely did pay for Medicare through payroll taxes your entire working life. You contributed 1.45 percent of your paycheck, and your employer contributed a matching amount.

Because medical expenses continue to rise each year, and the taxes for it have not, Medicare is facing a financial crisis. Medicare's coverage options could change dramatically while you're in retirement. You need to carefully read news stories about changes to Medicare coverage each year. A great Web site that keeps you up to date on Medicare is the Medicare Rights Center (www.medicarerights.org).

Starting coverage

You might be wondering how you start your Medicare coverage. If you're 65 and already collecting Social Security, Part A coverage should start automatically. You should get your Medicare card in the mail without having to do anything. This automatic enrollment works for people who started to collect Social Security before the age of 65 or people who apply for Social Security at age 65.

The only coverage that doesn't involve paying a monthly premium is Part A. You will have to pay for Parts B and D. Part C you only have to pay for if you choose a managed-care plan. I talk more about Part C in the section, "Medicare Advantage Plans — Part C," below.

Missing Medicare deadlines

If you're not already collecting Social Security, and that will be true for more and more people as the full retirement age to collect Social Security gradually increases to 67, you will need to sign up for Medicare about three months before your 65th birthday.

Unlike Social Security, you have a limited time to apply for Medicare. You must apply some time during a seven-month window, which starts three months before your 65th birthday and ends four months after. If you miss this window, you will have to wait for the next general enrollment period, which happens between January 1 and March 31 each year. Missing the deadline means paying more for Medicare Parts B and D as well as paying penalties. (See the next section, "Facing penalties," for more on the financial details of missing Medicare application windows.)

Facing penalties

If you delay your application and miss the deadline, you'll end up paying more for Medicare Parts B and D for the rest of your life because you'll incur penalties for both of them if you don't take all parts immediately upon becoming eligible. The following penalties get added to the monthly premium you pay for these Medicare options when you do sign up:

- ✔ **If you miss the deadline for Medicare Part B,** you'll get a 10 percent penalty added to your monthly premium for the rest of your life for every 12 months you miss.

- ✔ **If you miss the deadline for Medicare Part D,** you'll get a 1 percent penalty added to your monthly premium for every month you miss.

These premiums have increased at a rate of 10 to 12 percent each year as medical costs increase, so expect increases in these premiums in the future as well. Medicare Part D premiums vary widely, since this option is provide by private insurers, but premiums average about $20 to $30 per month for the basic plan. More comprehensive coverage is higher. If you miss the deadline and have to wait a year for Parts B and D, then a $9.84 penalty would be added to your future Part B monthly premium. The penalty for your Medicare Part D payment will vary depending which private plan you choose.

Delaying coverage because you're covered at work

You can avoid these penalties, if the reason you delayed signing up for Medicare was because you had coverage through your place of work. You can continue your coverage at work if you're still working at age 65 for a company that has at least 20 employees. If you are working and have benefits, compare the health insurance benefits offered by your workplace to those offered by Medicare. Pick whichever one will be better for you.

What are the rules if you delay signing up for Medicare because you do have coverage at work? You must apply for Medicare within eight months of leaving your job. If you don't, you will be liable for the penalties discussed above for Parts A and B.

Traditional Medicare — Parts A and B

Traditional Medicare is structured like an Indemnity Health Insurance Plan. You can go to any doctor that will accept Medicare reimbursement. You pay 20 percent of the medical provider's allowable charges and Medicare picks up 80 percent. Your 20 percent is called the co-insurance.

In addition, there is a deductible that you must pay before Medicare starts to pay for things. That deductible depends on the type of medical care you need and under which part it is covered — A or B. You can also buy additional coverage that will pay any medical costs that Medicare doesn't cover. I talk more about that later in this chapter in the section, "Paying for Things Medicare Doesn't Cover."

Part A

You receive automatic coverage under Part A when you turn 65, but what exactly gets covered? And what exactly do you have to pay? I break it all down for you in the sections that follow.

Knowing what's covered under Part A

Part A covers the inpatient portion of your medical care, including care in the hospital, at skilled-nursing facilities (as long as you go directly to the nursing home from at least a three-day hospital stay), in your home after a hospital stay, and hospice care. When you are in a hospital or skilled-nursing facility, Medicare will pay for a semi-private room, meals, general nursing, and other hospital services and supplies.

The only time that Medicare Part A will pay for your stay in a skilled-nursing facility is if you went directly from at least a three-day stay in a hospital to a skilled-nursing facility. Sometimes a physician will decide to order in-hospital testing for three days rather than outpatient testing just to make it possible for a patient that needs skilled-nursing care to qualify for that care under Part A. If you go home between a hospital stay for a few days and then go into a nursing facility, Medicare will not pick up the bill.

After a hospital stay you can get coverage for home healthcare needs, as long as your doctor recommends it. Many different types of care can be ordered by the doctor including part-time skilled-nursing care, physical therapy, occupational therapy, speech-language therapy, home health aid services, medical social services, durable medical equipment (such as wheelchairs or a hospital bed), oxygen, medical supplies, and any other medically necessary services deemed important by the doctor.

People diagnosed with a terminal illness can also get coverage under Medicare for hospice care. Hospices specialize in assisting people and their family after a doctor has determined the person has six months or less to live. Hospices help with the legal, financial, and emotional needs and decision making of both the patient and his or her family. Care can be provided in the home, at a hospice facility, or in the hospital.

Detailing what Part A doesn't cover

You won't get coverage for private duty nursing or a telephone or television in your hospital or skilled-nursing facility room. You have to pay for those items out-of-pocket if the skilled-nursing facility or hospital charges extra for them. You also have to pay the extra costs of a private room unless your doctor can make the case that it was medically necessary.

Unfortunately, Part A doesn't cover 100 percent of your inpatient care. You will have to pay both a deductible and co-insurance for each hospital stay. The deductible and co-insurance amount is adjusted each year by the Centers for Medicare and Medicaid Services, an agency of the U.S. Department of Health and Human Services.

In 2007, the inpatient deductible is $992. Coinsurance is $238 a day for the 61st to 90th day of inpatient care. Co-insurance then jumps to $476 a day for the 91st to 150th days of inpatient care, as long as you haven't used up your lifetime reserve days. You are responsible for all costs after the 150th day of care in a hospital.

Calculating the costs of inpatient care

So how do you figure out the costs of inpatient care? Say you needed to be in the hospital for 100 days. Here is what you would need to pay out-of-pocket if you don't have some additional coverage that pays for what Medicare does not:

Day 1 to Day 60:	$992 deductible
Day 61 to Day 90:	$7,140 co-insurance
Day 91 to Day 100:	$4,760 co-insurance (as long as you still have lifetime reserve days available)
Total cost out of pocket:	$12,892

This deductible and co-insurance is based on something unique to Medicare called *benefit periods*. A benefit period starts when you enter a hospital or skilled-nursing facility and ends when you've been out of the hospital or skilled-nursing facility at least 60 days. If you need additional hospitalization or skilled-nursing care within that window, you don't need to pay an additional deductible. But, if your need for care falls outside that window, then you will have to pay a new set of deductibles and co-insurance.

Using lifetime reserve days and understanding benefit periods

Lifetime reserve days add another unique twist to Medicare coverage. Officially you can only get 90 days of inpatient coverage during a benefit period. A benefit period under Medicare starts when you enter a hospital. It ends when you've been out of the hospital or a skilled-nursing facility for at least 60 days. In addition to the 90-day limit, Medicare recipients also get 60 lifetime reserve days that can be used any time you need more than 90 days of inpatient care. But, you only get a total of 60 days for your entire life, so it's important to use them sparingly. Once you've used them up, you'll have to pay 100 percent of all inpatient costs.

You must pay the deductible each time you enter the hospital during a new benefit period. The good news is that when you start a new benefit period, it restarts the clock for co-insurance as well. That means you can be in the hospital another 90 days if needed. Sometimes family members are forced to take a sick family member home when their family member has maxed out his or her in-patient days. They must find a way to keep their loved one alive until the benefit period runs out — 60 days after the family member leaves the hospital or skilled-nursing facility.

Coinsurance for a skilled-nursing care facility is less. You won't have to pay a deductible because you must be transferring into the facility from at least a three-day hospital stay and have already paid your deductible for that benefit period. Medicare will cover the first 20 days in a skilled-nursing facility 100 percent. After that your cost per day is $119 a day for the 21st to 100th day. Sometimes you can find a nursing facility that will charge you less than the $119 a day.

Working around the rules for Part A

You are responsible for all costs after the 100th day. You can avoid these costs if you are able to go home for at least 60 days. Then your doctor can restart the clock with a new benefit period by putting you in the hospital for tests for at least 3 days. You will have to pay a new deductible, but then you will be able to get Medicare coverage for another 100 days in a skilled-nursing facility.

Yes it is a maze, and as you get deeper into that maze it becomes much trickier. Luckily, most hospitals and skilled-nursing facilities have social workers who spend their entire day helping people work within and around the Medicare rules. It's good to understand them, but you won't be alone trying to navigate them.

If you are ever told that your time has run out for care in a hospital or skilled-nursing facility, be sure you talk with the social worker assigned to your case to see what alternatives there might be for you. But sometimes, the only alternative will be coverage through long-term healthcare insurance, which I discuss below in the section, "Paying for Things Medicare Doesn't Cover." Otherwise you have to pay cash or apply for Medicaid, a healthcare program for the poor. There are strict income and asset levels that determine whether you're allowed to qualify for Medicaid.

Part B

Because you're automatically covered under Medicare Part A, you're probably wondering why you'd want to pay for coverage with Part B. Well, check all that Part B covers (and don't forget to review what it doesn't cover!), and when you see how much you'll pay for coverage, you'll understand that Part B is the cheapest health insurance plan on the market.

Checking out what Part B covers

Part B covers your outpatient medical care. In addition to covering your doctors appointments, Part B covers outpatient medical and surgical procedures, diagnostic tests, ambulatory surgery center fees for approved procedures, and durable medical equipment including wheelchairs, hospital beds, oxygen, and walkers. Part A pays for durable medical equipment if it was ordered as part of a home healthcare plan after a hospital stay. You can also get coverage for second surgical opinions and outpatient physical, occupational, and speech therapy.

Part B also pays for many preventive care screenings and services including

- **Bone mass measurements:** Your and your doctor will determine how frequently you need this test. Medicare patients with a diagnosis of osteoporosis will need this test more frequently than those who do not have the disorder.

- **Cardiovascular screenings:** You can get Medicare to pay for screening tests for cholesterol, lipid, and triglyceride levels every five years.

- **Colorectal cancer screening:** You and your doctor determine your level of risk for colorectal cancer and how frequently you need preventive screening tests. These tests can include Fecal Occult Blood Test, Flexible Sigmoidoscopy, Colonoscopy, and Barium Enema.

- ✔ **Diabetes screenings plus services and supplies:** You can get Medicare to pay for screenings to check for diabetes every year if you have any of the following risk factors: high blood pressure, abnormal cholesterol or triglyceride levels, obesity, or a history of high blood sugar. Medicare also will pay for screenings if you have two or more of these characteristics: age 65 or older, overweight, family history of diabetes, or a history of diabetes during pregnancy. In addition to screenings, Medicare pays for glucose monitors, test strips, and lancets as well as diabetes self-management training.

- ✔ **Glaucoma screening:** Your Glaucoma screening will be paid by Medicare once every 12 months. It must be done or supervised by an eye doctor who is legally allowed to do this service in your state.

- ✔ **Mammogram screening:** Women on Medicare can get coverage for a mammogram once every 12 months. Medicare also covers new digital technologies for mammogram screening.

- ✔ **Pap test and pelvic examination:** Medicare will pay for a woman's Pap test once every 24 months, if you have no evidence of cancer risk. You can be tested once every 12 months if you are at high risk for cervical or vaginal cancer. Medicare does not cover a clinical breast exam.

- ✔ **Prostate cancer screening:** Men are covered by Medicare for a digital rectal examination and a prostate-specific antigen (PSA) test once every 12 months.

- ✔ **Shots (vaccinations):** You can get Medicare to pay for a flu shot once a year in the fall or winter. You can also get a Pneumococcal pneumonia shot (one shot may be all you ever need; ask your doctor). Hepatitis B shots are covered by Medicare for people at high or medium risk for Hepatitis B.

- ✔ **"Welcome to Medicare" Physical Exam:** When you first sign up for Medicare, you get a one-time review of your health, as well as education and counseling about preventive services, within the first six months of coverage under Part B. This exam is required if you choose to accept Part B. It will include screenings, shots, and referrals for other care if needed.

Understanding what Part B doesn't cover

Medicare Part B does exclude a number of medical services from its coverage. The most important is that you can't get a routine or yearly physical. The only physical included as part of your coverage is the first "Welcome to Medicare" physical mentioned above.

You also won't get coverage for any prescription drugs under Part B, but if you pay an additional monthly premium, you can get that coverage under Part D. Other exclusions from coverage include custodial care, acupuncture, dental care, cosmetic surgery, hearing aids and exams, orthopedic shoes, routine foot care, routine eye care, and most shots except for those listed above.

Calculating the coverage costs for Part B

You pay a monthly premium for Part B coverage, but that premium is cheaper than any other health insurance plan on the market. The monthly premium for 2007 is $93.50 per month and more if you earn over $80,000 per year (see Table 10-1). In addition to the monthly premium, your deductible for Part B is $131. After that you pay 20 percent of all your covered medical costs and Medicare pays the rest. The only exception to this co-payment is if you need mental health care. Medicare Part B only pays 50 percent of that type of care.

In 2007, Medicare Part B premiums will be set through means testing, which means you pay more if your income is above $80,000 (filing single) or $160,000 (filing jointly). If your income is under $80,000 (as an individual) or under $160,000 (filing jointly), you will pay $93.50 per month. Table 10-1 shows you Medicare Part B premiums beginning in 2007.

Table 10-1	New Medicare Part B Premiums for 2007
Income	*Part B Premium*
Under $80,000 for single ($160,000 if filing jointly)	$93.50 per person
Between $80,001 and $100,000 for single ($160,001 and $200,000 if filing jointly)	$105.80 per person
Between $100,001 and $150,000 for single ($200,001 and $300,000 if filing jointly)	$124.40 per person
Between $150,001 and $200,000 for single ($300,001 and $400,000 if filing jointly)	$142.90 per person
Above $200,000 for singles ($400,000 if filing jointly)	$162.40 per person

When you are on Medicare, you must check to be sure you doctor will accept *assignment*. This is another of those Medicare-specific terms you'll get to know quickly. If the doctor doesn't accept assignment, it means he or she will not take the responsibility of billing Medicare and waiting to be paid. You will have to pay the entire bill at the time you receive services. If your doctor does not accept assignment, you may want to consider finding another doctor. Be sure to check this out before your appointment or you could be shocked at the end when you have to come up with $100 or considerably more.

Medicare Advantage Plans — Part C

Medicare Advantage Plans are a managed-care alternative to traditional Medicare that you can purchase through private insurers. You must pay for Parts A and B in order to apply for Part C, but you may find a managed-care plan in which you won't have as many out-of-pocket costs as you do by just paying for Part B.

Examining the plans

Medicare offers several managed-care plans as alternatives to traditional Medicare. All Part C options are available through private insurers rather than the government, and the following sections describe how each of the various plans work.

Medicare Health Maintenance Organizations (HMOs)

If you choose to enroll in an HMO, you can only use the doctors, hospitals, or other providers in the HMO network. You must select a primary care doctor, who then serves as a gatekeeper to decide when you can see a specialist and which specialist you can see. Neither Medicare nor the HMO will pay for unauthorized visits to specialists. They also will not pay for visits to medical providers outside your HMOs network. For an additional premium, you may find an HMO that offers partial coverage for point-of-service (POS) benefits outside the plan, which means you can choose your own doctors but you'll pay more. HMOs usually provide more benefits than traditional Medicare, which includes coverage for some of the out-of-pocket deductibles and co-payments mentioned above, as well as more preventive care, such as annual physicals. How much more you'll pay in monthly premiums will depend on the level of coverage provided by the HMO. Each private insurer sets its own premium rates, but Medicare does monitor these rates. Some HMOs also include drug coverage as part of their plan, so you don't need to pay for Medicare Part D separately, but you will pay a higher premium to get drug coverage through the HMO.

Medicare Preferred Provider Organizations (PPOs)

If you want more flexibility regarding which doctors you can see, you might prefer a PPO to an HMO. More of your costs for medical care will be covered if you see in-network doctors, but you can get reimbursed for care from doctors or hospitals outside the network. You don't have to see a primary care physician before being permitted to contact a specialist. You will pay higher premiums for a PPO than an HMO to get this increased flexibility.

Finding Medicare Part C alternatives

Medicare Part C options vary state by state. Health insurance programs are managed on a state-by-state basis and not at the Federal government level. You can search online to find out which Medicare Advantage Plan options are available in your state. In fact, you may find that options vary city by city or among regions in your state because it depends on where the health insurance providers set up a doctor's network. You'll find more options if you live near a major city than you will if you live in a rural area. Use Medicare's Personal Medical Plan Finder at www.Medicare.gov/MPPF/home.asp to check out your options. If you're not comfortable searching online, you also can get the information about specific plans by calling 1-800-MEDICARE (1-800-633-4227).

Provider-Sponsored Organizations (PSOs)

Medicare is experimenting with a new type of organization called Provider-Sponsored Organizations (PSOs), which are medical-provider owned and sponsored ventures that operate much like an HMO. The big difference is that rather than being owned and managed by an insurer, they are owned and managed by a medical-provider group (which can include doctors, laboratories, and hospitals). You may find it hard to find this option in your state. The rules for this option vary state by state, so do a lot of research in your state before choosing one of these. The best place to start your research in your state's health insurance regulator.

Private Fee-for-Service Plans (PFFS)

If you want a traditional Indemnity plan, but prefer to work with a private insurer rather than the government, you may want to consider a PFFS if you can find one. There aren't many out there. You pay an initial premium for the plan plus deductibles and co-payments.

Medical Savings Accounts (MSAs)

Congress hoped to engage in an experiment allowing 390,000 Medicare recipients to open MSAs. Under this experiment, you can choose to save for your own medical costs in tax-advantaged medical savings accounts. With this option, you can buy a high-deductible insurance plan (usually with a deductible of $1,000 to $3,000) and pay all medical costs up to that deductible. As of August 2006, there were no MSAs available for Medicare recipients, but you can learn more about how they will work if they do become available at http://hiicap.state.ny.us/medicare/msa.htm.

Figuring out which plan is best for you

How do you decide what is best for you? It depends on what is more important to you. Read the following statements and find which one you identify with most to determine which plan will work best for you:

- ✔ **You want to keep your doctors.** If you use a specific group of doctors, specialists, or hospitals and don't want to risk having to change them periodically, you will be safest staying on traditional Medicare. While you may find your doctors in the network of the HMO or PPO, that doesn't guarantee you they will always be in that network.

- ✔ **You want more benefits or you want to reduce your medical costs.** You may be able to reduce your out-of-pocket costs and likely find more benefits in one of the Medicare Advantage plans. After paying the premium for these plans, your co-pay will be a set amount, usually between $5 and $25 depending on the plan you choose rather than the 20 percent co-pay required for traditional Medicare. But, be sure you understand what is being covered before you sign up. Many of these Medicare Advantage insurers prefer to cover only the healthiest seniors and do not provide good coverage if you have a chronic health condition. Before you switch to a Medicare Advantage plan, be sure you ask a lot of questions about the coverage provided for your specific health conditions and how much that coverage will cost.

- ✔ **You have good supplemental coverage from your former employer.** Some retirees have coverage that pays for anything not covered by Medicare, such as the deductibles and 20 percent co-pay for traditional Medicare. If you do have retiree health coverage, check with your former employer before signing up for a Medicare Advantage plan. You could lose your retiree health benefits if you sign up for a Medicare Advantage plan.

- ✔ **You receive Medicaid benefits.** If you currently receive Medicaid benefits, be sure to coordinate any decision about your Medicare coverage before considering a change. Contact your state Medicaid office and be sure you pick a plan that will be acceptable under the Medicaid rules in your state. Your state may even pay the premiums for you to switch to an acceptable Medicare Advantage Plan, but if you choose the wrong one, you could lose Medicaid benefits.

Prescription Coverage — Part D

If I had to pick one word to describe Medicare Part D, that word would be confusing. I don't believe the government could have designed a more confusing plan to cover your prescriptions if the powers that be set out to do just that.

Yes, all the complaints you hear about this plan are true:

- ✔ **You will find it difficult to sort out the more than 40 options available in most states.**

- ✔ **You will find it difficult to figure out your annual costs for each plan option.** The U.S. General Accountability Office (GAO) even found that customer service representatives got it wrong 86 percent of the time during calls made by GAO researchers to test the accuracy of the information Medicare recipients received from these private insurers.

- ✔ **You will find it difficult to figure out whether or not the drugs you are taking are covered by the plans you are considering.** Insurers may even list your drug as being covered, but when you need to actually pick up a prescription, you find out that the coverage is for a dosage level lower than the one you take.

- ✔ **You will find it difficult to get approval for coverage for a drug not currently covered.** If you find out your drug is not covered, you and your doctor have to go through an extensive process to get approval for you to take the drug, and it's not guaranteed you ever will get the coverage. Without that approval, you must either change drugs or pay for your prescription out-of-pocket.

Are you ready? In this section, I take Plan D step by step, but I warn you: The plan can be confusing. Take it slowly and read carefully so you can best understand how this coverage can benefit you.

The worst mistake the government made in setting up Part D was to make it illegal for the government to leverage the power of the 43 million Medicare recipients to reduce prescription drug costs. The government cannot negotiate lower drug prices for seniors, but it can negotiate lower drug prices for veterans.

Demystifying the basic drug benefit

You can choose from several options when choosing your drug coverage. Congress made this a plan available through private insurers rather than through Medicare, but, of course, the government foots the bill anyway. Insurers have great flexibility in how they can design their plans, as long as they meet the minimum requirements outlined in the following list:

- ✔ Anyone who is covered by Medicare Parts A or B is eligible for Part D.

- ✔ Your enrollment in Part D is voluntary, but if you do decide to enroll in the Medicare prescription drug plan, you will pay a monthly premium for the plan and that premium will depend on the private insurer and the specific plan you choose. Remember, you have more than 40 to choose from in most states.

✔ You have to pay a deductible of $250, which means you'll have to spend $250 on drugs before your drug costs will be covered under the plan.

✔ After you've met your deductible, you have to pay 25 percent of prescription costs and the insurer will pay 75 percent of the costs. The 25 percent is your co-pay. This division of payments continues until you spend $500 out-of-pocket on drugs and you receive drugs worth $2,000.

✔ You then lose all coverage until you spend another $2,850 on drugs. This is what you've probably heard called the *donut hole*. That's a nickname given to this gap in coverage, because you have to pay 100 percent of your drug costs at this point. By the time you get coverage again, you'll have to spend a total of $3,600 out-of-pocket since the beginning of the year (the $250 deductible, plus the $500 co-pay, plus the $2,850 donut hole).

✔ Once you've spent $3,600 out-of-pocket (that includes the $250 deductible, plus the $500 co-pay, plus the $2,850 in the donut hole) and the total value of drugs received is $5,100 ($250 deductible, plus $2,000 paid by insurer, plus $2,850 paid by senior once the donut hole is reached), then you will only pay 5 percent of all future drug costs and the insurer will pay 95 percent. The amount of co-pays to be paid out-of-pocket will be adjusted yearly.

Insurers have many alternatives that give you more coverage as long as you are willing to pay more money in monthly premiums. Most of the alternatives cover the $250 deductible, and many offer coverage during the donut hole.

Obtaining Plan D prescription coverage

There are two ways to get Medicare's Plan D prescription coverage: through the stand-alone Prescription Drug Plan (PDP) or through the Medicare Advantage Prescription Drug Plan (MA-PD). The average PDP costs $32 per month nationwide, but there are options in some states for less than $2 per month or more than $100 per month. I tell you how to sort out the options for PDP and MA-PD plans below in "Finding the right plan for you — it can happen!"

You also must be careful about how you sign up for Medicare Part D if you qualify for SSI and get help with your Medicare Part B premiums. You must pick a plan that meets the requirements set by the Centers for Medicare and Medicaid Services. If you choose one that has premiums that are too high, you will have to pay out-of-pocket for the additional premium and possibly co-pays. Be sure to check with Medicare to make sure you pick a plan that gives you fully paid coverage.

Knowing what to do if you have drug coverage from another source

You may be eligible for Part D coverage, but you might not want to sign up for it. Many people who are eligible already get their prescription drugs from other sources, such as state plans, retirement benefits from a company or union, or an alphabet soup of other plans including COBRA, TRICARE, VA, FEHB, PACE, ESRD, ADAP, and SPAP. If you do get prescription drug coverage from somewhere else, check with your current provider before signing up for the new Medicare plan.

If you do get prescription coverage from another source, you need to find out whether or not your current provider offers a *creditable* plan. If your plan is creditable, that means that its coverage is at least as good as Medicare and probably is even better. If you are currently in a creditable plan, don't sign up for Part D. If you sign up for Part D, you likely will lose your existing drug coverage and you may even lose your coverage for other medical needs, so proceed with caution. Check with your current medical insurance provider before signing up for Part D or a Medicare Advantage Plan.

The sections that follow describe what you should do if you do have prescription coverage from another one of these sources.

Employer or Union Plan

You may still have prescription coverage through your former employer or union. Most did continue offering prescription coverage in 2006. In fact, 93 percent of employers who provided prescription drug coverage to their retirees prior to 2006 continued doing so after Part D was available. The future doesn't look as rosy though for this coverage, which is usually better than what is offered under Medicare Part D. By 2010, 50 percent of employers indicate they might not continue to offer prescription drug coverage. Employers do get an enticement from the government to continue offering prescription drug coverage, which ranges from about $640 to $825 per individual covered depending on the type of coverage offered.

State Pharmacy Assistance Program (SPAP)

You may live in a state that still offers a SPAP program. Some states decided to continue offering these plans after Part D came on the market, others cancelled it when Part D started in 2006. To find out more about how your state is handling prescription drug coverage, as well as other health coverage for seniors, go to www.statehealthfacts.org and click on the tab for individual state profiles.

COBRA

If you have drug coverage through COBRA (which permits you by federal law to continue your employer-provided health insurance plan for 18 to 36 months after you leave the job), check with your insurer to see if your coverage is creditable. If your coverage is creditable, you may want to keep the COBRA coverage in place. You must make this decision before enrolling in Medicare Part D. Many COBRA plans will not let you drop your prescription drug coverage in that plan if you do want to keep the coverage for your other medical needs. If you decide to keep your COBRA plan and it is not creditable, and then eventually sign up for Medicare Part D, you will have to pay a penalty of 1 percent for each month you did not enroll in Medicare Part D after being eligible, plus you will have to wait to enroll in Medicare Part D until the Annual Coordinated Election Period (November 15 to December 31 each year). I talk more about annual enrollment below.

VA or TRICARE

If you receive your prescription drug coverage from the Department of Veterans Affairs (VA) or the Military Health Care System (TRICARE), your drug coverage is creditable and you don't need to sign up for Medicare Part D. If you lose your VA or TRICARE benefits in the future, you will have 63 days after losing those benefits to sign up for Medicare Part D, as well as other parts of Medicare, without a penalty.

FEHB

If you receive your prescription drug coverage through the Federal Employees Health Benefits, your coverage is creditable and better than Medicare Part D. You probably do not want to enroll in a private Medicare Part D plan.

PACE

If you receive your prescription drug coverage through PACE (Program of All Inclusive Care for the Elderly), do not sign up for Medicare Part D. If you do so, you will lose your PACE coverage.

ADAP

Each state designs its own AIDS Drug Assistance Programs, so you will need to contact your state to find out whether or not you should sign up for Medicare Part D. In some states, the plans are creditable and even better than Part D; in other states, the plans are not as good as Part D.

ESRD

If you receive your prescription drug coverage from Medicare because you are in end-stage renal disease, contact your benefit specialist to determine whether or not you should sign up for Medicare Part D.

Ensuring the drugs you take are covered

Another major mess created with this plan is trying to find a plan that covers all your medications. Each private insurer has their own drug formulary, which lists all the drugs that plan will cover. Medicare did develop basic guidelines for formularies and each insurer must include drugs that are commonly used to treat common conditions, but insurers don't have to cover all drugs available on the market, and different brand-name drugs are covered on different plans. The key is to find the private plan that best matches your drug needs.

Formularies also are developed using a tier structure. Tier 1 are generic drugs covered by the plan. Tier 2 are the preferred brand-name drugs. Some plans also have a Tier 3. These are the more expensive, non-preferred, brand-name drugs for which you may be able to get coverage.

In addition to the formularies and tiers, you'll also find that most of the private plans limit use of certain types of drugs. Plans can limit use in one of three ways:

- ✔ **Prior Authorization:** They can require that you get prior authorization from the insurance company before your physician can prescribe the drug if you want the plan to pay for it. Your physician will have to prove that your condition requires this drug rather than other drugs on the formulary that are likely cheaper but don't work.

- ✔ **Limit the Quantity:** Plans will only coverage a certain dosage of many common drugs. For example, if you normally take 30 mg of a drug, but the more common dosage is 10 mg, the insurer may not cover the higher dosage unless your physician proves to the insurer why you need the higher dosage.

- ✔ **Step Approach:** Your insurer may require that you try a series of cheaper drugs and prove that they don't work for you before they will pay for the more expensive drug. This is called "step therapy."

If you have been on a particular drug therapy for a while and the drug plan you choose does not cover that drug, then the insurer must work with you and your doctor to transition you to another drug therapy. Plans are supposed to provide you with a 30-day supply to give you and your physician time to change your prescription or apply for an exception to the formulary. Each drug plan has a different process for filing for exceptions. You should be able to find information about the exception process on the plan's Web site or call the customer service number for the plan.

Finding the right plan for you — it can happen!

If you explore the Part D mess I describe throughout this chapter, you're probably wondering how you can possibly find a plan that is right for you. Luckily Medicare did develop a decent tool for sorting all this out at its Web site www.medicare.gov. There will be a link on the Web site called "Compare Medicare Prescription Drug Plans." This link will walk you through the process of picking a plan. You can also call 800-633-2273 to work with someone by telephone.

You will need to know the names of all the drugs you take as well as your dosage in order to use the tool. You'll need to put in both the name of the drug and the amount of the drug you take each day or every 30 days.

Once you select a plan, you can only change that plan during the Annual Coordinated Election Period (ACEP). This period will occur each year from November 15 to December 31. Even if you are happy with the plan you have, you probably should check out any new plans that might be better for you during ACEP. Plans can and will make changes each year as this new program gets sorted out. Plans can change the list of drugs covered, change the premiums, and change the co-pays each year.

You can only change plans outside the ACEP if one of these three things happen:

✔ You move out of the area served by your current plan.

✔ You enter or leave a nursing home.

✔ Your plan changes and no longer covers your service area.

Adding up the costs

Your total drug cost will depend on four elements:

✔ **Monthly premium:** This is the amount you must pay each month to buy the Part D benefit.

✔ **Deductible:** This is the amount you will need to pay out of pocket before the insurer will pay anything. For the standard plan, it's $250, but some plans do offer a $0 deductible.

✔ **Co-pay:** This is the amount you will pay each time you pick up your drug from the pharmacy. Co-pays vary greatly among drug plans, so be sure you look closely at the data.

✔ **Donut hole:** Some plans offer no coverage during the donut hole, others provide full coverage.

The most important number to look for is your total annual costs. Since there is so much variation regarding types of drugs covered, the amount of your co-pay, the dosage that may be covered, and whether or not you will have a deductible or coverage during the donut hole, it's important to look at the annual cost number.

Donut hole coverage may be critical for you. Remember that's the point in the plan where you get no coverage after you've spent $500 and gotten $2,000 in drugs. Some plans do cover you in the donut hole. Their monthly premium may be more expensive, but when you look at the total costs of your drugs for the year, you may find that the coverage during the donut hole will actually save you money by the end of the year even if the monthly premium is higher.

Paying for Part D coverage

You can pay for Part D in three different ways:

✔ You can have the premium deducted from your bank account.

✔ You can have the premium taken out of your Social Security check. The Part B premium also is taken out of your benefit check.

✔ You can mail the company a check or money order each month. I don't recommend this method. If you forget to send the check, you could lose your coverage.

If you can't afford to pay for Part D, you may be eligible for the Extra Help program. There are three levels of assistance:

✔ **Group 1** includes individuals with incomes below $9,570 (or couples with incomes below $12,830). Assets cannot exceed $7,500 for individuals or $12,000 for a couple. People in this group do not have to pay a premium for Part D and can get their generic drugs for $1 and their brand-name drugs for $3.

✔ **Group 2** includes individuals with incomes below $12,919 (or couples with incomes below $17,320). Assets cannot exceed $7,500 for individuals or $12,000 for a couple. People in this group can get their generic drugs for $2 and their brand-name drugs for $5.

✔ **Group 3** includes individuals with incomes below $14,355 (or couples with incomes below $19,245). Assets cannot exceed $11,500 for individuals or $23,000 for a couple.

Your house and vehicles are not counted as part of your assets for this test. Less than half of your earned income will be counted, so if you think you are close to passing the test, you should apply and find out.

Paying for Things Medicare Doesn't Cover

You can encounter a lot of out-of-pocket expenses for Parts A and B, but you can get supplemental coverage for those costs. If you don't have coverage through a supplemental plan offered by your former company or union, you may want to consider a Medigap or Medicare Advantage Plan (Part C; you can find more info on these plans earlier in this chapter under "Medicare Advantage Plans — Part C").

Medicare Advantage Plans

The Medicare Advantage Plans (Part C) do offer coverage for the deductibles as well as lower co-pays than you'll find with Parts A and B. You do need to pay for Part B before you qualify for Part C, but you may be able to save money by signing up for a Part C plan.

I talk about the pros and cons of the Medicare Advantage Plans in the section "Medicare Advantage Plans — Part C," earlier in this chapter. The key thing you lose is complete flexibility in what doctor you can choose, but the cost savings might make sense for you.

Medigap

Another alternative that can give you more flexibility in choosing your doctors is a Medigap supplemental insurance policy. These policies pay your costs that Medicare doesn't cover.

Discovering what Medigap can and can't cover

How much of your costs will be paid depends on the type of Medigap policy you choose. Your choice will also determine how much your premium will be. Options available in a Medigap policy include

- ✔ Coverage of the Medicare hospital deductible.

- ✔ Skilled-nursing facility daily co-insurance.

- ✔ Coverage of the Part B $131 deductible.

- ✔ Coverage while traveling outside the U.S. (This is only available for the first two months of your trip.)

- ✔ Coverage of doctor's fees that exceed the Medicare approved charges.

- ✔ Medically necessary home care costs not paid by Medicare.

- ✔ Preventive care coverage.

You can't get coverage for custodial care (such as feeding, bathing, or grooming) at home or in a nursing home or other long-term care facility under the Medigap plan. You also can't get coverage for prescription drugs, vision care, dental care, or a private nurse.

Searching for the right-priced policy

Shop carefully for a Medigap policy. They do differ state by state because they're based on state health insurance laws. You'll find up to 12 different types of Medigap policies in your state and the insurance companies have three different ways to price them:

- ✔ **Community rated premiums:** These are based on the cost of providing coverage in your area. They are not based on age. Premium increases are based on inflation.

- ✔ **Issue-age rated premiums:** These are based on the age at which you first buy the plan. Premiums do not increase as you get older. Inflation is the only reason your premium can go up. The younger you are when you first buy this insurance, the cheaper your premium will be.

- ✔ **Attained-age rated premiums:** These premiums change each year based on your age. You will find lower premiums when you first sign up at age 65 for this type of policy, but as you get older you may not be able to afford the increases to these premiums.

Look for discounts when you shop around for Medigap insurance. Some companies offer better discounts for women. Some offer discounts for nonsmokers. Some also offer discounts for married couples that sign up for a Medigap plan at the same time.

Monthly premiums do vary greatly state by state. You can find them as low as $53 for Medigap A, which is the most basic level of coverage, and as high as $900 for some of the more comprehensive types of Medigap. Most range between $100 and $400 monthly.

Long-term healthcare

Medicare coverage for long-term healthcare maxes out at 150 days. If you need inpatient care for longer than that, you need to have private health insurance to cover the costs of that care. This includes care in a hospital, skilled-nursing facility, assisted-living facility, or even home healthcare services.

Understanding the need for long-term care insurance

Over $140 billion dollars is spent each year on long-term care services. More than $60 billion of that is paid by Medicaid and about $24 billion by Medicare. In order to qualify for Medicaid, you must first use up most of your assets.

Long-term care includes anyone who has difficulty performing two or more activities of daily living including bathing, dressing, toileting, eating, and transferring from one location to another. Nearly 80 percent of seniors who need assistance with daily living live at home or in community-based settings, such as assisted-living facilities. About 20 percent live in nursing homes or other institutional settings.

If you want to have some control of the level and type of care you'll be able to receive, you should buy a long-term healthcare policy. Without it you're limited to facilities that will accept Medicaid if you run out of money and need long-term care as you get older.

An extended nursing home stay can quickly use up any assets you might have saved for retirement. Nursing homes cost an average of $3,000 per month and can be as high as $100,000. For seniors, the average nursing home stay is 19 months.

Finding and purchasing a policy

Long-term care insurance can pay for most of that and allow you to avoid digging into your retirement assets, which you'll need for other costs of living, such as food and housing. If you purchase long-term care insurance over the age of 65, premiums can be high. They range from $2,000 to $10,000 annually.

But, you can lock in a much lower premium level if you buy the insurance at a younger age. Usually the best time to buy it is between age 55 and 60 to get the best rates. But, be sure you buy a policy that locks in your premium level for life. It doesn't help to start coverage early if your premium can go up. The primary reason most people end up dropping long-term life insurance as they age, when they may have the greatest need for it, is because the premiums jumped too high and they could no longer afford to pay them.

Selecting a long-term care insurance policy can be difficult. They are filled with hard-to-understand legal fine print. You might not even realize that the policy you choose will actual fall short of what you need until it's too late.

Your task of picking the right one can be even harder because many policies are sold through a slick sales presentation in which the salesperson may overstate what is actually being covered. When you need the coverage years later, the salesperson will be long gone. Many of these sales presentations are designed to scare people into buying them.

Don't rush to make the decision and never sign a contract for a long-term care policy without taking the time to read it and compare it with other possible offers. Carefully research options available in your state and seek at least three proposals before making a decision. You may want to ask an attorney who is familiar with long-term care contracts to review the contracts you are considering. The money you spend for that review can save you a lot of headaches later if you find out that coverage you were expecting is not included in the contract.

You also want to check out the insurance company that is offering the policy. If the insurance company does not have a good financial rating, then there is no guarantee that company will still be around when it comes time to pay for your benefits. There are two key financial ratings services you can check online — A.M. Best (www3.ambest.com/ratings) and Standard & Poor's (www2.standardandpoors.com). If you don't have Internet access, you can find these ratings in a public library.

Getting Medicare Coverage, If You Don't Qualify

Some people were not required to pay Social Security and Medicare taxes while they were working. If you worked most of your life for the state or federal government, this could be true for you. The government entity you worked for may have started taking out for Medicare late in your working career.

To be eligible for Medicare, you must have worked 40 quarters in which you paid into the Medicare system. That equates to 10 years of work because you earn 1 quarter for every three months. You may also be eligible for Medicare if you were married to someone who worked for 10 years and paid Medicare taxes.

If you have less than 30 quarters of work, you may still be able to buy into Medicare coverage at age 65. If you have fewer than 30 quarters, your premium for Part A will be $393 per month. The Part B premium will be $98.40 for a total of $491.40. If you have between 30 and 39 quarters of Medicare-covered employment, you can get Medicare Part A for $216 per month and Medicare Part B for $98.40 per month for a total of $314.40.

To determine whether or not you qualify, contact the Social Security Administration at 800-772-1213 to find out if you have enough quarters to qualify for Medicare.

Part III
Finding Your Next Job

The 5th Wave   By Rich Tennant

"I'm updating my resume to make me appear more youthful. I'm including a street name. What do you like — 'PR-Diddy,' 'JJ Kool-Data,' or 'Ice-Cubicle?'"

In this part . . .

You've likely been out of the job-search arena for a long time, and things have changed. In this part, I help you rebuild your job search skills and get ready for some tough interview questions you'll likely face as a retiree trying to find a job. You may also need help battling some myths many hiring managers believe about older workers, so I give you ammunition for that as well. Finally, I explore the various alternatives to working full time.

Chapter 11

Rebuilding Your Job Search Skills

∙ ∙

In This Chapter

▶ Writing your resumé

▶ Using your network

▶ Exploring Internet job sites

▶ Using traditional advertising

▶ Seeking support

∙ ∙

*I*f you're looking for a job during retirement, you probably haven't looked for a job in a long time. Searching for a job is so different today than it was when you first got out of school.

To help you in the hunt, this chapter reviews the skills you need to conduct a successful job search in today's high-tech environment. In addition, I discuss what to include and not to include on your resumé. You can also use this chapter to figure out how to find jobs that are available.

Building Your Resumé

If you haven't needed to build a resumé and look for a job for 20 years or more, be ready to totally change your idea of how to write a resumé. In today's fast-paced world, where jobs are posted on the Internet and people can easily respond with the click of their mouse, companies are inundated with hundreds of resumés for every job posting.

Often screening of resumés is done by computer using a program that looks for a set of key words that have been developed specifically for each job available in the company. If your resumé doesn't include the requisite key words, it likely won't even be looked at by a human being.

Even if a human being does sort through the resumés, initial screening of each resumé will be done in a matter of seconds per resumé. You must be certain that you've hit the key points in the opening paragraph or two, which should be a highlight of your accomplishments. In the sections that follow, I give you all the information you need to build your best resumé.

Keeping up with change

Rules for resumés have changed dramatically over the years. Know today's rules before drafting your resumé.

Going over one page

Keeping your resumé to one page is no longer the rule. You should give yourself enough space to highlight your critical skills and experience, but you don't need to write a book. Keep your resumé to two pages, unless you're looking for a job in academia. Academic resumés frequently can be four to five pages long if your experience warrants it.

Nixing the line "references available upon request"

You don't have to include that phrase at the bottom of resumés anymore. Everyone assumes that to be the case.

Keeping just the key words

You don't have to list every single job you ever had. Not only will that date you, but it will also give you little room to highlight your accomplishments that match specifically the position you're hoping to get.

Remember, whether it's a computer program scanning the resumés or a human being spending just seconds looking at them, you don't want a lot of extraneous information on the resumé. You want the resumé to be packed with the key words that say, "Yes I'm the perfect person for the position you have."

Your resumé should be a marketing piece that highlights the most critical aspects of your career. It doesn't need to have every detail of your working life. Its only purpose is to get you into the interview where you can really sell yourself.

Selecting your job history carefully

You don't have to limit your job history to the last ten years. Pick and choose the jobs that are the best match for the position you are seeking. Focus on listing the jobs that are most relevant to the position you are seeking, no matter how long ago you did that job.

Tailoring your resumé

You don't need to design one resumé that you use for every job application. In fact, you probably should design several resumés if you are seeking several different types of positions. Each resumé can highlight your past work experience that best matches the type of work you're seeking.

Your resumé doesn't have to be limited to paid work either. You may have worked as a volunteer for many years, while you earned money doing something else. Now in retirement you want to get paid for the type of work for which you volunteered in the past. Build a resumé for that type of work based on your successes as a volunteer.

Avoiding snail mail

You probably went to a copy store and printed out 50 or more copies of your resumé on top-quality linen stationary in the past. Don't bother spending the money. In most cases, you'll be sending your resumé by e-mail or responding to a job posting on the Internet. Few people use snail mail to send their resumé today. If you do, that will date you!

Also, if you get into the habit of just printing out your resumé as you need it, you can then tailor each resumé specifically to the job for which you are applying. You can be sure that the skills and key words mentioned in a company's ad are clearly spelled out in your resumé. If not, tweak it so it's a better match.

Preparing your resumé

You should prepare your resumé in a standard Word format that you can use to print out the resumé or that you can use as an e-mail attachment. You can buy a package of quality stationary for the resumés you'll need to take with you on a job interview or for the rare occasion when someone asks you to send in a resumé.

Even if you've sent your resumé by e-mail or posted it using an Internet job site, you should always bring a copy with you to an interview. Many times your resumé prints out differently than intended when you send it electronically, so bring a good-looking, clean copy with you.

You should also prepare a resumé in text format that you can cut and paste into online forms. If you cut and paste from a Word document, you'll also copy some formatting codes that will drive the online form crazy. Then you'll have to correct all those strange format errors.

Here are the steps to save a Word document in text format:

1. Click on file and click "Save As."

2. In the "Save as type" field, click on the down arrow and select "Plain Text." You should also give the document a different name. For example, if you named your resumé "Writing Jobs," you might want to call this one "Writing Jobs_Plain Text," so you can quickly differentiate the document when you scan down your list of documents.

3. You will get a warning that you'll lose all your formatting, pictures, and objects in the file. That's okay. You want to lose those things in a plain text document. You'll be given the option to save it using Windows (which will be the default), MS DOS, or other encoding. Use the Windows default.

4. Open the document in the new plain text version and fix any problems created when you lost the formatting. Yes, it will be a lot of work, but it's much easier to do it once on your home computer than do it each time you cut and paste your resumé into an online form.

Using the employer's needs

Hiring managers often tell their human resources staff that they just want to see the top 10 or 20 resumés. You can only be one of those top 10 or 20 resumés by being as close to a perfect match as possible, which means you probably need to show that your knowledge and experience meets all the key skills wanted.

The computer programs likely will be looking to find key words that match the experience and skills necessary for the job. Even if human beings are screening resumés, they will not do the hiring. Initially all screening is done by a lower-level employee who is working off a list developed by the hiring manager. They want to please the hiring manager by finding resumés that fit the list.

Researching the employer's needs

Before even starting to write your resumé, research the types of jobs you want by reading the advertisements on the key job-search Web sites (such as Career Builder). As you look at the detailed job descriptions, you'll see the key words that are commonly used by employers when they write a job description for a particular type of job. I talk more about Internet search sites in the section "Tapping the Internet."

For each type of job you are seeking, you will probably find 10 to 20 key words or types of skills that all employers want for that type of job. Keep these in mind as you develop your resumé.

For example, suppose you decided that you'd like to work as a bank teller. Reviewing several advertisements on Career Builders, I found these key skills listed:

- ✔ Proven customer service skills
- ✔ Cash handling skills
- ✔ Effective verbal/written communication skills
- ✔ Ability to complete a teller training program
- ✔ Basic computer skills

If you were looking to apply for a bank teller position, you would then use this list to develop your resumé.

Your research on the key job sites should give you all that you need to develop a list of key words that should be found easily in your resumé. Don't be afraid to repeat key words in several descriptions of your past jobs if appropriate.

Highlighting skills that meet those needs

As you begin to write your resumé, highlight skills that meet the needs of employers seeking to hire people for the types of positions you seek. Pick the jobs you've worked in over the years that best match the ones you are seeking even if it means highlighting a job you did more than ten years ago.

For example, when building your resumé for a bank teller position, you should have a paragraph at the top of the resumé that highlights your experiences directly related to the key skills listed above, even if they were learned doing work for a different type of business.

Review your former positions and write descriptions for each position that include some of the key words and skill sets. For example, if you ever worked in retail sales or for a fast-food restaurant and had to handle cash, be sure to highlight that job and its cash-handling aspects, as well as the customer service skills you demonstrated in that position. Or if you ran events for a volunteer organization and were responsible for the cash collected, you can highlight that position.

Don't be afraid to use the same key words in several job descriptions. Many computer scanning programs score the resumé, and you get the highest score by having more years doing the required skills. If it's a human being quickly scanning through the resumé, the easier it is for him to find the key words the better chance you'll get put in the interview pile.

Emphasizing accomplishments

Company recruiters look for a sign that you've been successful in the past. They want evidence that you did produce in former jobs and will produce for their company. So, follow these tips to ensure your accomplishments stand out:

- ✔ As you write your job descriptions, think about what you accomplished in each job. Use active words such as "developed," "organized," "implemented," or "established" to show your successes.

- ✔ Also put a number to your successes when appropriate. For example, if you were responsible for selling $3 million in a year, state that. Don't leave out the numbers. Quantify your successes when possible.

Avoiding dating yourself

Your resumé needs to show that you are current, and the following two things will date you quickly if you can't prove that you've kept up with times:

- ✔ **Terminology:** Each industry has its own type of "industry speak," so be sure the terms you use on your resumé match what is currently being used in your industry.

If you've got old job descriptions that you plan to reuse, be sure to first read through publications from professional associations within your industry. As you look through articles on their Web sites, you will likely pick up some catch phrases and other terms that are used commonly today. You may find these common terms are different from terms you've been using over the past 20 years. Be sure to update your job descriptions using the more recent terms and phrases.

- ✔ **Technology:** Also, if you've been on a job for 20 or 30 years, you may not be working with the most current technology for the industry. It all depends on your former company and whether or not they kept up with the changing times. Or you may have continued supporting the older hardware and software as your company gradually switched over to the new technology.

Review job listings in your industry and see what types of technologies are needed for the jobs that are available. If you do want to stay in your industry, you may need to go back to school to update your skills before looking for another job. You probably can find adult-education classes at local community colleges or possibly even online. I talk more about educational opportunities in Chapter 19.

Taking advantage of writing tips

Writing a resumé can be the hardest thing for most people to do. As you write your resumé, keep these points in mind:

- **Mind your length.** You don't have to limit your resumé to just one page, but more than two pages could hurt you. Few will read the entire resumé and some may even be turned off by its windiness. Remember, you only want to highlight the positions you've had in which you can focus on the key skill sets the person doing the hiring will want to see.

- **Avoid personal info.** Don't include information about your family or your hobbies, unless the information is relevant to the type of job you are seeking. Also, don't include your height, age, weight, sex, or religion, unless it's somehow related to the position. For example, if you are applying to work at your church or synagogue, you certainly want to indicate your religious affiliation.

- **Keep it relevant.** Be sure all the information you include on your resumé is relevant to the position you are seeking. Don't include nonwork experience, unless it helps to demonstrate skills that you believe are relevant to the type of job you want. For example, if your hobby is woodworking and you're looking for a position where those skills would be helpful, include information about your hobby.

- **Address work gaps.** If you took time off to raise your family or care for a sick parent, you should briefly address that time and turn it into a positive. You certainly learned skills that could be useful. For example, if you are thinking of applying for a position as a home health aide, the skills learned caring for an elderly family member would be relevant to your job search.

- **Check your spelling and grammar carefully.** You could be the perfect person for the job, but if the hiring manager sees typos on your resumé, you may not even make it into the door for an interview. Errors on the resumé indicate to an employer that you're not detail oriented.

Formatting Your Resumé

Traditionally resumés have been formatted in chronological order. That may not be the best thing for you if you are thinking about going back into the workforce after retirement, especially if you don't want to work at the same type of job from which you just retired.

If you're changing fields, it's possible that your hobbies or volunteer work may be more relevant than your most recent jobs. Many people who go back to work after retirement seek jobs that they would enjoy doing. But, they couldn't take the risk of changing careers when a steady income was so critical.

For those of you looking to change careers, your best choice may be a resumé that shows your chronological work history, but highlights your functional skills. Here are the parts of this type of combination resumé:

- **Contact info:** You should include your name, address, telephone number, and e-mail address. Many human resources departments prefer to contact candidates initially by e-mail rather than play phone tag.

- **Highlights or summary:** Summarize the highlights of your career. Be sure to use the key words that match the list you compiled researching the necessary job skills for the type of position you are seeking.

- **Experience:** Don't list your job history in this section. Instead prepare a series of paragraphs that talk about your skills and prove that you have the skills needed for the job. For example, looking at the skill list for the bank teller above, you would write a paragraph about Cash Handling, Customer Service, Verbal/Written Communications, and Computer Skills. Write these paragraphs using brief sentences that highlight your accomplishments. In the Cash Handling paragraph, you may talk about your volunteer work where you handled cash, such as managing the collection of over $100,000 at each event you ran for Junior Achievement.

- **Work history:** Use this section to provide a list of your previous jobs in chronological order. Each job can be just one line that includes your job title, your company, and your dates of employment.

- **Education:** List your degrees and the schools you've attended with any related information about your course emphasis.

- **Certifications or technical skills:** If you have related certifications or technical skills that are relevant to the type of job you seek, include them in this section.

I give you an example of how this resumé looks in Figure 11-1.

Name
Address
City, State Zip
(Area Code) Telephone Number
Email Address

Summary
Write two or three sentences that summarize the parts of your former career that highlight your accomplishments directly related to the position you are seeking. Remember to use the key words in this summary.

Experience

Skill One (i.e. Cash Handling Skills)
Write a summary that highlights your skills in this area. Be sure to start each sentence with an action word that emphases your accomplishment, such as "managed," "organized," "implemented," or "developed."

Skill Two (i.e. Written/Verbal Communication Skills)
Again write a summary as described in Skill One.

Skill Three (i.e. Computer Skills)
Again write a summary as described in Skill One.

Work History

Job title	Employer	Years Worked
Job title	Employer	Years Worked
Job title	Employer	Years Worked

(List your jobs in chronological order, you don't have to go back more than ten years but if you want to show experience that is older than that you can if relevant.)

Education
Degree, School Attended, Year Completed
Course Emphasis (if appropriate)

Degree, School Attended, Year Completed
Course Emphasis (if appropriate)

Certifications
If you have related certifications or technical skills that are relevant to the type of job you seek, include them in this section.

Figure 11-1:
A sample resumé using a combination of functional highlights and chronological work history.

Using Your Network

While many people spend most of their time searching the Internet job sites or answering ads in the newspapers, the reality of the situation is that 80 percent of jobs are filled through networking and only 20 percent are filled from job ads in the newspaper or on the Internet.

Your networking will do more to help you find a job than hours spent quietly in your home writing the best resumé and top-notch cover letters. In Chapter 4, I talk about the six steps to building and maintaining your network. If you don't know how to build a network, review those steps.

Once you've got an active network in place, you won't have any trouble tapping into it for job leads and job introductions. Remember, hundreds of people answer each job posting, whether it's on the Internet or in a newspaper advertisement.

 If you want your resumé to get to the desk of the person making the job hiring decision, it helps to have an inside contact. With so many unknown people coming through human resources, a known entity recommended by an associate or friend often is more likely to make it to the top of a job interview list.

Tapping the Internet

You'll find a wealth of information on the Internet. In addition to job listings, you can research how to improve your job-searching skills, as well as do research about the companies that you plan to approach. The more you know about a company, the better you can target your cover letter and your resumé to match the company's needs. You'll also present yourself as a much stronger candidate when you get to the interview. So don't only think of the Internet as a communication and job-search tool, also plan to use it for research so you can make a better overall approach for the job you want.

Scouring job-listing sites

Most people looking for a job will visit the well-known job Web sites such as Career Builder (www.careerbuilder.com) and Yahoo! careers (careers. yahoo.com). But, there are many others out there that you might find better. The big Web sites may have lots of job listings, but they also get lots of visitors, so that means you'll be competing with hundreds if not thousands of applicants for each job.

You may want to visit the lesser-known Web sites that are more targeted to the types of jobs searches you're interested in pursuing. In Chapter 4, I mention a few good ones that focus on seniors including YourEncore (www.yourencore.com), Seniors4Hire (www.seniors4hire.org), Employment Network for Retired Government Experts (www.enrge.us), and Senior Job Bank (www.seniorjobbank.org). You can find out more about what each one of these job sites offers in Chapter 4.

Posting your resumé online

When you post a resumé online, it's like putting up an ad about you that anyone can read, even folks you may not want to hear from, such as spammers or scammers. Be aware that if you do decide to post your resumé, you will get a lot of garbage e-mails.

So, if you plan to post your resumé, your first step is to get an e-mail address that you'll use solely for online posting. You can get them easily for free at Yahoo! or Google, if your provider doesn't let you set up a unique address or if you want to limit the mail coming directly into your computer. When you use the online e-mail services, you pick up your mail online and then decide if you want to forward it on to your primary e-mail account on your computer. This gives you an extra veil of protection against viruses and other sorts of bugs, as well as limits the amount of mail you get on your home computer.

Also, if your resumé is more than one page, consider adding key words to your second page to be sure all computer scanners recognize those skills and alert recruiters who may be looking for your particular set of skills. You can do that by hiding your key words on the second page of your resumé at the bottom of the page. You certainly don't want people to see those words, so change the text color for those key words to white before posting the resumé. That way your key words won't print out when the recruiter gets your resumé, but a scanning program will pick them up.

Another good place to find alternative, less busy job sites is to use the Google directory (www.google.com/Top/Business/Employment/Job_Search), which lists over 50 job search sites. You'll also find job sites grouped by industry, executive search, seasonal, staffing services, and worldwide.

If part of your retirement dream is to spend a lot of time traveling, check out the worldwide firms listed at Google. You may find some interesting opportunities that can help your dream come true. In addition to job listing sites, you'll find sites for resumé building and interviewing advice.

Checking in on company Web sites

Company Web sites provide you with a wealth of information. In addition to scouring a company's job openings, you can find a great deal of information about the company, its mission and goals, and its future plans.

Take the time to read the most recent annual report to find out more about what the company did during the past year and what it plans to do in the future. You may have looked at annual reports before, but didn't read the fine print. Many people just enjoy looking at the pretty pictures and reading the large, glossy text. That's not where you'll find the most useful information. Unfortunately, to get the most useful information, you will have to read the fine print. Get out those magnifying glasses!

Your best place to look for key information about what the company did over the past year and what it plans to do in the future is a section of the annual report called, "Management's Discussion and Analysis." You can use the information to find out about key future plans. Once you have a good idea of where the company wants to go, you can use that information to develop your cover letter.

If you read about a project planned for the future that you think would be perfect for you, use the company's language as you develop your letter spelling out your prior experience directly related to that new project. You could just hit the right cord and be picked out of the pack of hundreds of applicants just because you showed that you do your homework, making you a good potential asset for the company.

You may want to start by looking up the best companies for people over 50 to find a few companies that you want to target in your area. In Chapter 14, I talk extensively about the AARP's program for recognizing top employers that actively recruit people over 50. In most cases, these employers provide benefits packages directly targeted to meet the needs of retirees that want to go back to work.

Once you've picked a few companies that interest you from AARP's list, visit their Web sites, find out more about each company and its programs for people over 50, and then search for available jobs on the company's Web site.

You can find the list of best employers at AARP's Web site: `www.aarp.org/money/careers/employerresourcecenter/bestemployers`.

Looking through the Classifieds

You can also search for jobs using a more traditional approach by reading advertisements in newspapers or looking for jobs on job-posting boards at places that you frequent.

Newspapers

Your daily and weekly newspapers probably have an employment section. Most often the best day to use the newspaper's employment section is Sunday, when the greatest number of job ads can be found.

But, you may not realize that many newspapers also offer their advertisers the ability to post the job listings on the newspaper's Web site. That way you can check for jobs regularly as the newspaper gets new ads throughout the week. You can even use the newspaper's Web site search capabilities to quickly find job listings that match your key words. That can be a lot faster than looking through pages and pages of job ads that don't interest you.

Grocery stores

You may not think a grocery store is a likely place to find job listings, but many of the larger food store chains do have boards where people can post all kinds of things, such as jobs available, items for sale, or pets that need a home. Often a small business that doesn't want to be inundated with hundreds of resumés and that wants to find a person that already lives nearby will post an announcement on these types of job boards.

Senior centers

Many communities have senior centers that offer daily activities for older members. You can find them at YMCAs, Jewish Community Centers, as well as at centers run by community groups.

Often one service offered by these centers is to help members find jobs and to help employers find seniors to fill positions. If you are a member of a community center, find out if they do have a program for seniors that includes job-searching services.

Churches or synagogues

Don't forget to contact the church or synagogue to which you belong. Many religious institutions today do provide job assistance to their members.

Your church or synagogue likely has a job board where members can post information about positions open in their company to help other members of the church or synagogue who are looking for work.

If your church or synagogue doesn't do this, it might be a good way for you to serve the institution if you help them start such a service. While you're doing it, you may find just the right job for yourself!

In addition to being the first person who will learn about all available positions, you will also be able to expand your network of people who can help give you an introduction to the hiring manager. The best way to get an interview is to know someone who can recommend you directly to the hiring manager.

Counting on Your Support Groups

Job searching can be very depressing, especially if you're getting a lot of rejections or not getting any responses at all. Don't be discouraged, but do look for support.

Your friends and family likely will offer some support, but they may also be wondering why you want to go back to work in the first place. They may not be your strongest support network. You should look to support groups that are in place and who can provide you with the emotional boost you'll likely need as you look for jobs.

In Chapter 4, I talk about how support groups work. If you want to find out more details about support groups, you can read more about them there.

Senior centers

As I mentioned above, senior centers can be a good source for job listings, but they can also be a place where you'll find support groups. Contact the senior centers you have worked with before or that are located in community centers with which you are familiar.

If you don't know of any, call your local YMCA or Jewish Community Center and they may be able to help you find senior centers or support groups for job seekers. Your city or town may also have a senior services department who can help you locate support groups.

Health centers

If you find you are getting depressed, you shouldn't wait too long to seek help. You're facing a lot of changes in your life related to the loss of your daily work routine and the loss of your network of co-workers. At the same time, you're also trying to search for a job.

Many people do face depression during times like these because they are times of major job stress. Contact your doctor to get references for help if you are feeling depressed. You can also contact the local mental health center to find out about support groups in your area.

Churches or synagogues

Another good place to find out about support groups is your church or synagogue. Often these groups are run privately without a major announcement. Check with your religious leader to find out what support groups are operating through your religious institution and how you can plug into them.

Chapter 12

Surviving the Interview — Especially Those Tough Questions

In This Chapter

▶ Psyching yourself up

▶ Dealing with interview basics

▶ Answering the tough questions

▶ Checking out your checklist

Getting past the interview can be the hardest part of getting a new job, especially for someone who is a retiree looking to get back into the work force. Actually, interviews are rough for everyone, not only for older workers.

This chapter will review the types of interview questions retirees may find hard to answer, and give you alternatives for how to answer them. I also discuss good basic interview preparation tasks that can help you improve how you present yourself during an interview.

Getting Ready for the Interview Mentally

For most people, the hardest thing to do before an interview is calm down enough to think and answer questions strategically. Even though you've done all your homework, researched the company, and made sure you can clearly tell your interviewer how your skills match the job, your nerves may make you forgot all your research and interview preparation.

Understanding the need to stay calm

You need to find a way to calm down. The more relaxed you can be during the interview, the better you'll do. You'll then be able to focus on what needs to be said and present your real self.

When you present yourself calmly in an interview, you'll be in a better state of mind to say what you want to say. Also, you'll be more aware of any negative impressions the interviewer may have and try to correct them. I talk about how to do that in more detail below, when I review dealing with the hard questions.

Reducing stress before an interview

You can use a number of stress-reduction techniques. Some take a lot of practice, such as meditation, yoga, and tai chi. But, others you probably can learn quickly and use successfully. Pick one or two of these and practice using them before you start interviewing for jobs. Use the one that works best for you.

Visualization

Pick something that makes you feel calm, such as a walk along the beach or watching a sunset. Close your eyes and picture yourself there. Focus on this image for two or three minutes. If you are able to focus on the picture and kick out any other thoughts, you'll be amazed at how quickly this can calm you down.

If you need some help, get a CD of nature sounds that match your image and listen to it at the same time. On the day of your interview, bring a photo that depicts your favorite place. That will help you visualize in a particularly stressful situation.

You may even want to paste the image to the inside of your notebook or calendar that you plan to bring to the interview. Take a quick look at it while you are waiting in the office before your interview. The picture could help you maintain a sense of calm, as you get more and more nervous waiting. I know that sometimes waiting can be worse than the actual interview.

This relaxation technique is particularly good if you tend to worry a lot before an interview. Looking at a relaxing image can take the place of worrying.

Deep breathing

Take a long deep breath through your nose for four or five seconds, then hold your breath for another four to five seconds, and finally breathe out through your mouth for the same four to five seconds. If it's working for you, you should notice that you feel a sense of relaxation that takes over in your chest, your shoulders, and other tense muscles.

Repeat this method of deep breathing for at least two to three minutes. The first few times you try this you may need to make some noise as you breathe in deeply to help get you started. After you've practiced doing this for awhile, you'll find you don't need to make the noise and will still benefit from deep breathing quietly.

You certainly don't want to do this noisily waiting to be interviewed. You'll attract too much attention and may make a negative impression. Most will think you're really nervous if they hear you deep breathing. Some may even think it's the sign of a medical emergency. You certainly don't want to bring unnecessary attention to you while you wait.

This relaxation technique can calm the nerves throughout your body and let you sit in a more relaxed position. You'll present yourself as calm and confident in the interview if your body is relaxed.

Thought blocking

You may find that during a stressful situation, your mind constantly second guesses itself. You're constantly worrying that you may say something wrong or have already done so. Or you may frequently criticize yourself as you think through the answers to questions and don't really listen to what the interview is asking. You should instead be focusing on what you want to say next.

Thought blocking helps you control unwanted thoughts. If you are constantly thinking, "oh no," I shouldn't have said that or some other critical phrase, practice stopping yourself in everyday conversation.

Each time you start being self-critical, just say the word "stop" quietly to yourself. Don't say it out loud or people will start looking at you weird and wondering what you want them to stop doing. You may want to add the practice of deep breathing when you say stop to help you release tensions and clear the negative thoughts from your mind.

This relaxation technique should help you gain more control over what you are thinking and give you the opportunity to concentrate on what you need to say in the interview.

Reviewing the Basics for Answering Interview Questions

As a retiree who wants to go back to work, you have more of a challenge during the interview process than younger workers. Your life has been so full of work experiences that you tend to have too much to talk about and don't focus on the key things specific to the job for which you are applying. So follow these guidelines to give the best interview:

- **Gather relatable experiences.** As you prepare for the interview, think about your experiences that you want to talk about. The experiences that you pick should be directly related to the job you are seeking.

  If you've done your homework about the company and its culture, you should think about experiences in your background that will demonstrate how you can fit in. Once you get to the interview, if you see that it's a very young workforce, talk about experiences you've had in the past working side-by-side with younger workers.

- **Let the interviewer know that you will be comfortable being in that type of the work environment.** Do it subtlety though, don't create a barrier that may not be there.

- **Read the interviewer's body language.** You should be able to judge by the interviewer's body language whether or not the interviewer is comfortable talking with you. If you find the interviewer is very nervous and seems to be looking for a way to get you quickly out the door, you can either make him more comfortable or just accept that it's not the right company for you and move on.

- **Avoid talking negatively about your former employers or co-workers.** You'll look like a complainer and will likely turn off the interviewer. Instead, if asked about something you didn't like about your former job, turn a negative into a positive by giving an example of how you corrected a problem and improved the working environment for everyone.

- **Never criticize the company.** Don't tell the interviewer that the company is doing something wrong and you know how to do it better. You don't want to appear combative or overly critical, but you can make suggestions more gently about how you could improve what they are doing.

- **Be ready to ask questions.** Make a list of questions based on your research, and ask several during the interview to show your interest. You'll also show how well prepared you are and that you do your homework.

- ✔ **Always show enthusiasm for the job.** Even if it's something that you're planning to do just to make a few extra bucks, show your enthusiasm. No one wants to hire someone who isn't even enthusiastic during the interview. If you're not exited about the job during the interview, your interviewer will certainly assume you're not going to be enthusiastic when you start work.

- ✔ **Prepare yourself and practice.** Prepare a response for questions you think you will be asked. Do some research, develop your answers, and then practice your responses until you are comfortable talking about the issue. You may want to develop a list of the tough questions and then ask a family member or friend to use them to do a mock interview. If you'd like and you have the video equipment, tape your interview. Then you can watch yourself and improve your responses. (You can get a list of questions just by checking out the section, "Dealing with the Tough Questions," later in this chapter, where I discuss specific interview questions.)

Answering Basic Questions

Everyone gets asked certain basic questions on interviews, so anticipate them and think about how you can best answer them to emphasize the key points you want to make. The three most common interview questions are

- ✔ Can you tell me about yourself?
- ✔ Why do you want to work here?
- ✔ What are your goals?

These questions are actually ice breakers. How you answer them will set the tone for the interview, so think about your responses and how you can influence the rest of the interview so that the interviewer focuses on the key things you want to present.

But, remember these questions are ice breakers. The interviewer is not expecting a long-winded response. Keep your initial response brief and bring out the key points you want to make. If the interviewer is interested, he will then ask a follow-up question about a specific point.

You can control where the interview goes, by saying just enough to peak the interviewer's interest and encouraging his desire to learn more. That way he asks more questions about what you want to talk about.

Getting to know you

When you're asked, "Can you tell me about yourself?" the interviewer is not looking for your life history, so don't go into a long-winded story about your childhood and how you got to where you are. No one ever wants to hear your entire life story in an interview situation where they are meeting you for the first time.

Before you even get into the first interview, think about how you do want to answer this question. Plan to mention a few personal things that are relevant to the job you are seeking, point out a few job-related things, and talk about any educational background that you have that is relevant.

Testing your knowledge of the company

With the question, "Why do you want to work here?" the interviewer is testing your knowledge of the company and its products or its services. If you did your homework, you should be well prepared to answer this question based on the research you did on the company's Web site.

Pick out a few things you want to talk about related to the company's goals and missions that you can tie directly to the type of position you are seeking. Don't be afraid to even use the company's wording as you develop your answer to this question.

If the company actively recruits older workers, mention some of the programs it promotes to attract older workers that you are particularly interested in, but only if that program fits the type of job you are seeking. For example, you may want to discuss benefits that the company promotes to seniors, such as long-term care insurance. That way you let the recruiter know the company's recruitment advertising is working.

Don't bring up a benefit if it's not appropriate for the position you are seeking. For example, if the company talks about telecommuting as an option for its workers and you're applying for an onsite sales job, it's obviously not something you want to discuss as a benefit. Pick the benefits for people over 50 that won't conflict with the job you want.

Sizing up your longevity

When asking, "What are your goals?" the interviewer is testing how long you'll stay around on the job. He probably wants to know if you just want the job for a year or two or if you think it's something you'll take for a lot longer.

Don't talk about goals you have outside the company unless they somehow relate to how you'll be staying around the area. For example, suppose you just bought a new retirement home near the company, talk about how you want to find a way to supplement your retirement income with a position close to your home.

If you are thinking of starting a small business or doing something else once you get settled in your new retirement home, and you know that this job is just a short-term bridge to get some extra bucks, definitely don't talk about that. Think instead about how you can answer this question to give the interviewer the impression that you will be at the job for awhile.

Dealing with the Tough Questions

Retirees do get some tough questions that probably aren't asked of younger candidates. While age discrimination is against the law, there are lots of ways you can pick up clues that you may actually be sitting in front of someone that just doesn't want to hire you because you are an older worker.

The types of questions asked by an interviewer can certainly give you a clue to their age bias. In fact, if you are asked many of the questions in this section, it could be a sign that your age may be a barrier to your getting the job.

Tough questions for older workers usually fall in one of two areas — questions related to your qualifications and questions related to your longevity with the company. Be prepared to answer these questions before you go in. Practice your answers, so you can answer the questions calmly and in a way that will be beneficial to your getting the job. You also may need to deal with a lot of myths people doing the hiring believe. You can get some ideas on how to answer those in Chapter 13.

Sometimes if the hiring person just won't hire workers over 50, there is little you can do. Yes, you can file a compliant with the Equal Employment Opportunity Commission, but you'll be waiting months and possibly years for it to settle. At the same time, word could also get out on the rumor mill that you are a troublemaker, which can make it harder for you to find a job, especially if you are looking for one in a small, tightly knit industry. You can find out more about age discrimination laws in this excellent article at AARP's Web site: www.aarp.org/money/careers/jobloss/a2004-04-28-agediscrimination.html.

Dealing with age discrimination

Don't be surprised if you recognize signs of age discrimination as you look for work after you've retired. You do have protections under the Age Discrimination in Employment Act (ADEA), but they can be difficult to enforce.

The ADEA states that there must be a lawful reason that is not connected to age when making employment decisions. You fall under the aegis of the ADEA if you are age 40 or over and you are applying for, or working in, a company with at least 20 employees. Sometimes age can be a factor in hiring. For example, if a director needs a teen to play a particular role in a play, he can decide not to hire a person over 40.

Even if you are applying for a job in a company with fewer than 20 employees, you may have some age discrimination protections in your state. Many states do have laws that protect against age discrimination that cover smaller companies.

The ADEA makes it unlawful for job ads or other materials to mention age requirements or state that a certain age is preferred, unless of course it falls under an exception, such as the need for a teen to play a particular part in a play. Also, a company cannot set age limits for training it offers. Age can't be a factor in hiring decisions, when making decisions about promotions, or when deciding who to lay off.

ADEA also protects you from being forced to retire at a certain age, but there are exceptions for certain types of position. For example, many times people who work in public safety positions are encouraged to retire at a younger age.

If you do file a complaint with the Equal Employment Opportunity Commission, the company can't take action against you if you are still working for them, but you may find that information about your claim gets passed quietly among other business managers in your area.

How to deal with qualification questions, like . . .

While all applicants are asked questions about their qualifications, the types of questions older workers are asked often differ. In this section, I point out some of the most difficult questions you could be asked and give you some ideas of how to answer them effectively. Handled properly, you may even be able turn a negative into a positive.

You're overqualified . . . won't you get bored?

Talk about how impressed you are with the company and its products or services. Tell the interviewer how much you would enjoy working for such an excellent company. Remind him that your experience is exactly what the company needs.

Also point out that with your experience, he won't need to waste as much time and money training you. When you're hired, you can hit the ground running and begin earning your paycheck much faster than someone with less experience.

Can you keep up with this fast-track company?

Imagine an employer asking someone in their 20s this question? Sure it's one of the clearest signs that age discrimination is lurking somewhere nearby, but don't get angry. Discuss your technical knowledge that matches what the company needs and the strategies you use to stay current on all the issues related to your field, as well as keep up with technology changes.

If you're an athlete or have some other story to share to talk about your ability to stay at the top of your game, you may want to share it when you hear this question. You can also show your interviewer that you are on the fast track by talking about your energy and attitudes. You can also discuss how you dealt with rapid change in your former company and how much you got done in a day on your last job.

You've never worked in this industry; can you transfer your skills?

This question probably is not as related to age as it is to experience, and could be thrown at anyone seeking to change industries. If you've done a good job of research, you should be prepared with a list of examples of skills you have that can easily be transferred to the skills needed.

As you prepare for the interview, jot down some ideas that you can discuss about what you did during your career that matches what you think this company made need based on its products and services. Talk about how you think these experiences and skills will make it easy for you to quickly become a valuable employee.

Can you relate your past experiences to our current business needs?

You're likely to be hit with this type of question if you're changing industries or type of work. As you prepare for the interview, make a list of past experiences that you think are relevant to the industry in you which you plan to seek employment or the type of position you are seeking.

Compare this list of past experiences with the industry or job you want to move into. Identify any skills that you think are relevant, and be prepared to discuss how they would meet the needs of the hiring manager.

Don't hesitate to talk about your ability and eagerness to learn new things. Discuss how quickly you learn things and how much effort you put into anything you do. If you've taken some coursework to prepare for the job change, be sure to discuss the coursework and how that will help meet the new company's needs.

How to deal with longevity questions, like . . .

Most hiring managers hate the process of hiring people, and hope to find candidates who will stay around awhile, so they don't have to go about hiring someone again too soon. Older workers frequently will be asked about how long they plan to stay.

Expect to be asked and decide how you want to respond to longevity questions before you start interviewing. That way when the discussion starts, your response will sound sincere and well thought out.

I see you've been out of work for over six months, why?

If you've been out of work for a while because you lived the life of a retiree for about six months or more, don't be afraid to say that. Talk about how you tried retirement and it didn't work for you. Let the interviewer know that you enjoy being more active and believe you have many years of productivity left.

You can also talk about how you wanted to take time off to think about what to do next and, after carefully researching your options, you've chosen to do the type of work you're applying for at the new company. Talk about your research and make the hiring manager comfortable that you have thought things through and know what you want to do.

Don't ever give the interviewer the indication that you were looking around and this job sounded like something you wanted to try out. Be more positive than that and make your reasons for choosing the particular line of work clear and decisive.

If you took time to learn a new skill, that's a great reason to be out of work for a while. Retraining will show the hiring manager how interested you are in the job change. Talk about the skills you've learned and how you believe they will contribute to the company.

You've moved around a lot, can you explain?

Many older workers have been forced to go from job to job, especially if they were victims of downsizing in the 1980s and 1990s. Your resume may look very spotty because of all the job changes you had to take after losing the career position you had.

Be ready to talk about and explain your reasons for your job changes. If you changed fields or industries, you may want to discuss how you had to work your way back up the ladder, which required job changes to broaden your knowledge or skills. If you changed jobs for promotions, be sure to point that out and how quickly you learned and moved up in your new career.

If it's relevant to your reason for job change, you can discuss the economy and how you've had to make changes to meet the challenges of an ever-changing economic world. Talk about your willingness to learn new industries and new skills to stay competitive through this period of dramatic change.

You can easily change the negative of moving around into a positive about managing and responding to change effectively, but you do have to prepare and practice your response before the interview so it sounds sincere and convincing.

You've been working as a consultant, is that just a way to say you were out of work and looking for a job?

Many people try to make their resumes look better by filling in a long gap without work with their own consulting business. Hiring managers see it all the time, so be prepared to talk about your consulting work if that is on your resume.

If you continued working for your former company as a consultant so you could complete several ongoing projects, talk about those projects and why the company wanted only you to finish them. You should be able to make yourself sound indispensable and build your credibility.

Now that you've finished the projects, you're ready to start work on something new and exciting. Talk about how the position fills your desire for a new challenge.

If you have just used "consultant" as a filler, you may want to joke about it, but you're probably better off not trying to hide the fact that you were out of work. Instead, talk about what you did do to keep yourself competitive in the marketplace.

Be ready to discuss how you filled your day, which could include reading professional journals to keep up on the most current information in your field or maybe to catch up because you just didn't have the time to read all that stuff when you were working full-time.

You may just have been looking for work, so be prepared to handle the question without sounding guilty. Know what you want to say, because if you have a significant gap on your resume. You will be asked about it.

You've been at one company so long, can you adapt to our company?

You may be someone who worked all your adult life at one company, or least for the past 20 or 30 years before retiring. While that makes you look like a very stable person, it also may make you look like you'll have a hard time getting used to a change.

You can handle this type of question in several different ways. One way is just to say that you're looking forward to a change. You waited around to get your retirement benefits, but now that you qualify, you're eager to do something different. After much research, you've decided this is exactly the right type of position for you. Talk about the research you did and how you came to the decision to seek work in the field for which you are interviewing.

You can also talk about all the changes your former company went through over the years and how you thrived during those periods. If you led the change during one or more of those periods for your former department or company, be ready to discuss your change-management skills and what you learned about change. This will help to convince the hiring manager that you handle change well and are worth considering for the position you are seeking.

Preparing an Interview Checklist

I'm a big believer in preparing lists, especially when I expect to be nervous about doing something. Everyone tends to forget things when they are nervous. So the day before an interview, use the checklist in Figure 12-1 to be sure you've reviewed all the key points for the interview and you're ready to make a great impression.

I recommend you review the checklist the day before the interview, so you have time to fix any last-minute problems. You should also take one more quick look at the checklist before you walk out the door for the interview, just to be sure you're not forgetting anything — like your Social Security `card, driver's license, or other documentation you planned to bring.

Job Interview Checklist

	Ready	Needs Work
1. You can discuss five things that make you the right candidate for the job.	_____	_____
2. You are ready to discuss every item on your resume.	_____	_____
3. You can list the skills and experiences that qualify you for the job.	_____	_____
4. You are prepared to discuss the education and/or training that qualifies you for the job.	_____	_____
5. You know which hobbies or activities you want to discuss that are relevant to the job.	_____	_____
6. You can write down your employment history on an application accurately or you have the detail with you that you need. This should include addresses and telephone numbers.	_____	_____
7. You have the names, address, and contact information for your references.	_____	_____
8. You have any documentation that you might need such as Social Security number, driver's license and certifications.	_____	_____
9. You have directions and have made arrangements, if necessary, to get to the interview on time. If you have the time and you're traveling to a location for the first time, do a test run before the day of the interview to be sure you know where the interview will take place and how long it will take you to get there.	_____	_____
10. You have prepared some questions you plan to ask your interviewer.	_____	_____

Figure 12-1:
Use this Job Interview Checklist the day before an interview to be sure you are ready.

Chapter 13

Overcoming Myths About Older Workers During Your Job Search

In This Chapter

▶ Debunking training myths

▶ Pounding productivity myths

▶ Dealing with cost myths

Myths about older workers can do more to damage your chance of being hired than anything you write in your resume or say in an interview. Unfortunately, myths about older workers abound, and many times you don't even know if the person doing the hiring believes them. You need to understand these myths and counteract them when they rear their ugly head. This chapter will review the myths and arm you with the facts you can use to disprove them.

Going Toe to Toe with Training Myths

Many employers still believe these two well-debunked training myths:

> **Myth 1:** You can't teach an old dog new tricks.

> **Myth 2:** Training older workers is a lost investment because they will not stay on the job for long.

Both have been disproved in study after study. I give you the ammunition you need to quickly disprove these myths in a conversation with employers who seem to be hinting that they don't think its worth the time and expense to train you for the job.

Emphasizing your ability to learn

Many employers think you can't teach an old dog new tricks. However, although you may experience a negligible loss of cognitive function as you age, the experience, knowledge, maturity, and loyalty you bring to a company quickly overcome any of the negatives. Older workers do tend to take longer to absorb completely new material, but their better attitudes toward studying new things, as well as their accumulated experience, more than makes up for the time. In fact, the experience and knowledge older workers bring to the table actually lowers the costs of training them. In fact, people 50+ are one of the fastest-growing populations on the Internet. Those in the 50+ age group have the financial resources, and, if needed, can get help from their children and grandchildren.

When interviewing, be sure to discuss your experience in learning new technologies both on the job and at home. Tell potential employers how much you enjoy learning new technologies. If they buy into the myth that you can't learn anything new, you can dazzle them with your love of learning.

Leveraging your longevity

Many employers believe that older workers aren't worth training because they won't stay long enough with the job, but this myth couldn't be farther from the truth. In reality, people over 50 are more likely to stay with a job than their younger colleagues. Younger workers frequently are still trying to find their niche, changing jobs to experiment with career alternatives and company choices.

Mid-career employees have been there and done that. They've navigated their job changes and chosen their career directions or redirections, as the case may be. And the trend in desire to change jobs levels out in the 50s.

Older workers tend to be more engaged in their work and more committed to their organization. In fact, human resources managers list loyalty and dedication as the number one quality for older employees. The number two quality is commitment to doing quality work. Certainly two excellent reasons to train the older worker.

When it comes to technology, how long of a commitment does the employer need from a worker after he or she is trained? Since new technology arrives at workers' doorsteps every two to three years, and even more frequently in some fast-paced industries, there is little chance that over-50 trainees won't outlast the technology they are being taught today.

Home Depot believes "Passion Never Retires"

Home Depot, one of the leaders in debunking the over-50 myths, actually designed an entire recruitment campaign to attract older workers called "Passion Never Retires." Home Depot has an immense need for skilled, knowledgeable, and passionate employees. They've found that over-50 workers bring extensive experience and provide good leadership, which benefits their stores nationwide. Home Depot even has a program called the "snowbird special" to attract retirees who want to return to work after retirement. Snowbirds usually live half the year in the north (during the warmer months) and half the year in the south to avoid the cold. Home Depot lets them work in both places.

Talk about your experiences and how they have helped you to find just the right job for you based on your knowledge and experience. Discuss how the job that's on the table fits your profile for the ideal job and that you are less likely to look for something new once you find that ideal job. The best way to debunk the myth that you won't stay long is to prove that the job available is a perfect match for you given your knowledge and experience.

Poking Holes in Productivity Myths

When it comes to productivity, three myths can be particularly difficult to overcome when you talk to employers who believe the following myths:

> **Myth 1:** Older workers are not as productive as younger workers.
>
> **Myth 2:** Older workers are less flexible and adaptable.
>
> **Myth 3:** Older workers are not as creative or innovative.

All three myths have been debunked by study after study. I discuss each of these myths in the sections below and give you the ammunition you need to disprove them if you suspect your potential employer believes any of them.

Pointing out your increased productivity

The official definition for productivity by the U.S. Bureau of Labor Statistics is "the ratio of output of goods and services to the hours of work required to produce that output." No one actually collects information by age and job, so there are no specific numbers to debunk the myth that older workers are less productive. Instead, you must look at studies that have been done that focus on the relationship between productivity and aging to give you the facts you need to debunk this myth.

Some studies that seem to support this myth (and probably these are what fuel the misconception held by many employers today) conclude that worker productivity begins to decline between the ages of 30 and 40. These studies focused on manual dexterity and work-and-motion observations. Others found there was no significant relationship between productivity and age.

Studies that will help you debunk this myth focus on acquired knowledge and how that can compensate for age-related effects of declines in mental efficiency. One key study was done by Neil Charness, who studied experienced chess players versus less experienced ones. He found experienced chess players can remember more detail about familiar, structured chess positions than players with less experience and skill. Charness's finding has been confirmed by researchers studying the productivity implications of aging. Study after study has proven that experience in a domain can offset cognitive declines that may occur with age.

Companies tend to avoid hiring older workers for fast-paced jobs that require speed of execution, but study after study shows that communication skills and decision-making skills continue to sharpen with age, which can more than compensate for any declines in manual dexterity. For example, one study that looked at hotel clerks found that while older clerks handled calls more slowly, they achieved a higher success rate by making more bookings than the younger clerks.

Don't let employers use the excuse that you're too old to handle a fast-paced job. Give them examples of how your communication and decision-making skills can more than make up for any decline in your manual dexterity.

Advertising your adaptability

Employers may be fooled into thinking that older workers are less flexible than younger workers. However, although older workers may not be able to turn cartwheels the way they used to, they're just as adaptable to change as younger workers.

Older workers are more likely to ask why, but that's not because they're trying to be difficult. Older workers have seen many changes in processes and procedures during their work life in the past. Too often these changes have been abandoned in midstream because they didn't bring about the expected rewards quickly enough. So, older workers will question the reasons for the change and help to make that happen more quickly once they buy into the process.

In fact, one researcher, Dr. Tracey Rizzuto, at Louisiana State University, studied the ability of younger versus older workers to accept change when she looked at the upgrade to computer systems in the state of Pennsylvania. She found that older workers were more willing to learn the new technology than their younger counterparts. Although she found some isolated examples of older workers who resisted change, generally the older workers saw the value of the change and felt an obligation and loyalty to their co-workers to learn and implement the new technology.

You can easily debunk this myth by talking about change processes you've experienced in the past and how you have helped to make the change happen.

Capitalizing on your creativity

No myth could be further from the truth than the one that has employers believing that older workers aren't creative or innovative.

Creativity can be found in two forms: completely new ideas never tried before and new ideas that expand upon or change current practices. Although younger people primarily come up with new ideas that have never been tried before, the older, more experienced worker can better come up with new ideas that expand on or change current practices, based on experience. So older workers are creative from a different perspective.

Organizations need both types of creative talent. There's no question that today's workplace needs the employee commitment and knowledge that comes with experience. In today's competitive environment, experience can be a far more important driver in the workplace. Companies do need the younger minds who can create things from pure novelty, but they also need the older minds who can look at what's being done and use their experience and knowledge to find new and better ways of doing things.

When applying for a job, talk about the innovations you put into place over the years at your former workplaces. Show that you can be creative and how your experience can help the company find new and better ways to improve their processes.

Factoring in creativity in the over-50 set

If anyone tries to tell you that once you hit 50 you're over the hill and not creative, you just need to remind them of some of our greatest thinkers and most creative people in history:

✔ Giuseppe Verdi composed *Ave Maria* at age 85.

✔ Martha Graham performed until she was 75 and was a choreographer into her 90s.

✔ Benjamin Franklin invented bifocals at 78. He needed to find a way to correct his own vision problems.

✔ Frank Lloyd Wright worked on his design for the Guggenheim Museum into his 90s. He died at the age of 91.

Coping with Cost Myths

All companies look for ways to cut their costs. Labor costs definitely take the largest chunk out of most companies' budgets. That's what makes the myths related to costs some of the hardest to overcome when you're a retiree looking to reenter the workforce. The three common cost myths are

Myth 1: Older works cost more than hiring younger workers.

Myth 2: Benefit costs are higher for older workers.

Myth 3: Accident costs are higher for older workers.

Unfortunately, if the employer has already bought into these myths, you probably won't even get called in for an interview. You may be able to overcome these myths if you hear about them when networking with others already inside the company. I debunk the myths with facts in the sections that follow.

If you suspect cost issues are a factor when trying to get an interview with a company, try using some of these facts in a creative way when writing your cover letter — especially if you can talk about your cost-cutting expertise you developed during your past work experiences.

Keeping reality in check when it comes to your paycheck

Yes it's true that the 55-year-old worker who's been with a company for 25 years or more likely will earn more than a 30-year-old worker who's been in the same job for only 5 years. But, the older worker likely assumes greater responsibility and performs at a higher productivity level because of his or her experience.

When you are a retiree returning to the workforce at a new company, you won't command the same income level as the person who has worked for the company for 30 years. Today's employers pay according to the market rate for a position regardless of age. Service, position, and performance are the primary drivers of cash compensation, so age shouldn't be a factor in determining cash compensation. No significant difference in pay should be expected for a 45-year-old or 55-year-old doing the same job at the same level of performance.

Don't expect to command the same salary you did at your former company. While job hunting, if you seek a lot more than the market rate for a new employee in the type of position for which you are applying, you likely won't get the job.

Telling the truth about benefit costs

The three key benefits that cost the most for any company include healthcare costs, retirement costs, and paid time off. In the following sections, I sort out the actual cost factors and how you can reveal the truth about these cost factors to potential employers.

Healthcare costs

Rising healthcare costs worry all companies that provide health benefits to their employees. How to deal with these costs continues to be one of the biggest concerns for all companies. Use the following list to overcome some misconceptions you may hear during your job hunt when the issue of healthcare costs is discussed:

✔ Although as people age they are more likely to use more medical services, companies must also consider that older workers likely have fewer dependents, which helps to offset some of the rising claims costs.

✔ Although age factors into how much workers utilize healthcare, some of the key risk factors, including high blood pressure, obesity, high cholesterol, smoking, and alcohol use, drive up healthcare costs more than age alone and can be an issue for much younger people.

✔ Healthcare costs incurred by older workers may not be as high as expected because older workers have proven that they're better partners than younger workers in finding ways to become better consumers in healthcare purchasing, such as looking for generic drugs when available. They also are more willing to accept the fact that they must pay a larger share of their health services than younger workers.

Retirement benefit costs

You shouldn't need to discuss retirement benefits when looking to return to work because retirement benefit costs for workers returning to the workforce after they already retired are no different than those costs of newly hired, younger workers. In today's world, most companies offer a 401(k)-style retirement plan, where both the company and the employer contribute to the plan. In some cases, the employer doesn't even contribute to the plan.

Age is not a factor in determining what the employer contribution will be. The primary factor is the amount of time the employee has worked for the company and his salary.

If you are returning to work for the same company from which you have retired, be sure to talk with your benefits specialist to find out how that might impact any retirement benefits you are now receiving. Each company has a different set of rules regarding their retirement benefits.

Paid time off

You shouldn't have to worry about paid time off being a negative factor for cost considerations of hiring older workers. Vacation, holidays, and personal days depend on a person's length of service with a company. Age should not be a determining factor for paid time off.

Older workers going back to work after retirement may want to discuss the possibility of more unpaid time off. If you do want to go back to work, but want more flexibility to take time off unpaid to be able to travel or do other "retirement" type activities, be sure to discuss that up front during the interview. While it may not cost the company anything when they don't have to pay you, if they don't have a plan for how to get the work done while you're gone, you may not have a job when you come back. Find a company and a job that allows you that unpaid time off flexibility.

Accident costs are higher for older workers

If an employer expresses concerns that as an older worker you may be more at risk of being involved in an accident, remind him that studies show older, more experienced workers are less likely to drive accident costs up for a company. In fact, older workers take fewer risks in accident prone situations. They've learned from experience what they can do safely and what they should avoid. Statistically, older workers have fewer accidents than younger workers.

Chapter 14

Working 9 to 5 or Not! Exploring Your Hourly Options

In This Chapter

▶ Going part time

▶ Locating employment agencies

▶ Working from home

▶ Reviewing the top part-time jobs

You don't have to look for a full-time job. You may decide you want to work part-time or just work certain days of the week. Know how much you want to work before you start looking, and then look for opportunities that meet your time requirements.

This chapter discusses the variety of opportunities seniors can find in the workplace, from working part-time at a job location to working at home through telecommuting. Also, I discuss employment agencies that seek to place workers over 50.

Seeking Part-Time Work

If you're like most people, as you get near your full retirement age, you're looking forward to slowing down. You may not be ready to spend 100 percent of your day figuring out what to do in retirement though. Instead, you want to find less stressful work that requires fewer hours so you can do some of the things you've been putting off for years while working in a highly stressful full-time position.

Other people find once they start retirement that they just don't have enough money to make ends meet. They would like to make some extra cash, but don't won't to get back into the daily grind of a full-time job.

Considering your needs and wants

When looking for a job, you're not in the same position you were in when you first got out of school. You know what your ideal working conditions would be and you know what you absolutely don't want to accept in working conditions.

Looking for your own ideals

Whatever your reasons for wanting to go back to work part-time, you will find many different options depending on your interests and skills.

The three key things most older workers seek when looking for a new job include

- ✔ **Ability to set your own hours:** Older workers want more flexible schedules. Many employers do offer flexible scheduling where workers can choose when they want to begin and end their work day. You will find that the employer usually sets a core time of the day when you must be in the office.

- ✔ **Ability to take time off when needed:** Older workers often have family members who they must care for or they find they must deal with other life priorities. Many retirees who go back to work part-time want the type of job where the company can be flexible about time off.

- ✔ **Benefits that answer your needs:** Older workers have specific needs, such as healthcare insurance, long-term care insurance, and assistance with eldercare or grandchild care issues.

Finding a job that factors in what's important to you

If you're looking for specific things that are important to you (see the list in the section earlier in this chapter), be sure to discuss them even before you get hired. You and the employer should have a clear agreement on these issues or neither of you will be happy when these issues crop up.

How do you find these types of ideal working conditions? One good way is to watch for clues that the company's hiring processes, training, benefits, and alternative work arrangements welcome older workers. Here are some clues you should watch for:

- ✔ **Recruiting:** Companies whose ads mention that they are looking for maturity, decision-making skills, and work experience likely will hire older workers. A really good sign is an employment ad that is designed to appeal to older workers.

✔ **Training:** Companies that indicate they offer training to workers of all ages clearly welcome older applicants. If during the hiring process the employer makes it clear that you should take advantage of all training opportunities, you know that the company is serious about the training being offered and that it will be available to older workers.

✔ **Health benefits:** Companies seeking to hire older workers will include some benefit options that are critical to people as they age, such as long-term care insurance. Read the benefit package that is being offered. If you see that it appeals to workers of all ages, you've found an age neutral employer.

✔ **Flexible work arrangements:** If you find an employer that offers flexible work schedules, such as flextime or telecommuting, you've found a good place to work. The best possibility is a firm that has already established a phased retirement program (I talk more about them in Chapter 15). If this type of program does exist in a company, then it won't be hard for you to discuss your needs for a flexible work arrangement. The company already recognizes the needs of its older workers if they have a phased retirement program.

Finding the best of the best for part-time work and flexible schedules

Your quickest way to find the best employers for older workers is stopping by AARP's "Best Employers for Workers Over 50 Program" at www.aarp.org/money/careers/employerresourcecenter/bestemployers/. At this site, you can find a list of all the companies that have been named a best employer during the seven years since AARP started the program (www.aarp.org/money/careers/employerresourcecenter/bestemployers/winners/2006.html). You can click on the link for any employer listed and get details about the employer's innovative programs for workers over 50, as well as a link to the employer's Web site so you can find out what types of jobs are available.

Just to give you an idea about the innovative programs AARP has found through its "Best Employers for Workers Over 50 Program," I want to focus on the number one winner of this award in 2005 and 2006 — Mercy Health System in Wisconsin (see the sidebar, "Mercy! What a great job!" for more info). If more companies realized the benefits of these innovative programs, your job search would be easy.

Mercy Health System is innovative in so many aspects of its hiring and benefits that I review some of its key programs in the sections that follow so you know what to look for and ask about as you conduct your own job search near your home.

Mercy! What a great job!

Mercy's Health System recognized the shortage of healthcare employees and realized there was a large untapped resource of potential workers over the age of 50. It developed its human resources program with that focus in mind. In 2006, 28 percent of Mercy's workforce was over the age of 50 and 16 percent of the new hires in the past year fit in the age group.

Rather than losing the older health worker, as many hospitals are facing today, Mercy's employees stay around thanks to its innovative programs. The average tenure of its workers over the age of 50 is 10.25 years.

Mercy won the AARP award for the second year in a row because of these flexible work options:

✔ **Weekender program:** Employees can choose to work on weekends only.

✔ **Traveler Option:** Employees can take work assignments based on 6- to 13-week assignments and travel in between.

✔ **Registry pool option:** Employees can work between 48 and 96 hours per month and still get full benefits.

✔ **Work-to-retire program:** Employees can work reduced hours or seasonally as they get closer to retiring. Employees who are 55 or older with 20 years of service can work just 1,000 hours per year at their discretion and get benefits for the entire year.

Recruiting

Mercy conducts recruiting using e-cards (e-mails in the form of a card sent to potential employees) and direct mailings to targeted lists of mature workers and retirees. It also recruits new employees by sponsoring booths at job and product fairs that target senior populations. Personal recommendations from other happy employees are another tool Mercy uses to find workers over 50.

Cultural and learning opportunities

Many different types of cultural and learning opportunities are offered to both its full- and part-time staff including tuition reimbursement, in-house classroom training, on-line training, and certification programs. Employees must work at least 20 hours a week to be eligible for the tuition reimbursement program and certification classes.

Health benefits

Both full- and part-time employees who work at least 20 hours a week get individual and family medical and dental coverage including prescription drug coverage. In addition, they get long-term care insurance and short-term disability insurance. Employees must work at least 36 hours a week to get long-term disability benefits. Health benefits for employees 65 and older include spousal medical and drug coverage, dental insurance, and long-term care insurance. Even new hires are eligible for these health benefits when they retire.

Working with winners

Healthcare employers are not the only ones recognized as best employers by AARP. Here is a brief overview of some other innovative programs that won in different industries:

✔ **Education:** Brevard Public Schools in Veira, Florida, won for its "Life Hub" program. The school system offers a confidential, no cost service to employees and their families so they can address issues related to child care, grandchild care, and elder care. The school system also holds an annual Wellness Conference that features health screenings, biometric assessments, as well as presentations that increase awareness about good health and disease prevention. Forty percent of the school system's employees are age 50 or older. Retired school principals serve as recruiters to help hire new teachers at school fairs. The school system also taps retired educator organizations to recruit new teachers.

✔ **Financial:** The Principal Financial Group, based in Iowa, offers a "Wellness Time Off" program that allows employees extra time away from work to take care of health and wellness needs. In addition, it has a "Happy Returns" program that helps retirees return to work with the assistance of Manpower staffing service.

✔ **Theme parks:** Anheuser-Busch Adventure Parks, which include SeaWorld and Busch Gardens in Florida, offers an on-line and telephone service called "Life Assistance Services" to assist employees with selecting day care services and elder care services. Employees can also get advice on finding the right nursing home. Busch's long-term care policy is available not only to employees, but also to the employees' parents and grandparents. Another innovative program is its "Legends Ambassadors," which is a team of people aged 55 and older who are committed to helping SeaWorld and Busch Gardens provide quality employment and job satisfaction to the 55-plus population. The Ambassadors are selected annually to help new hires learn the ropes and offer suggestions, concerns, and ideas to Human Resources. Ambassadors also participate in job fairs, recruiting efforts, and training. Busch also uses senior placement agencies to target mature workers and retirees for employment.

You'll find more than 75 companies all around the country that have developed innovative programs on AARP's Web site. I've just given you a brief overview of the variety you can find there.

Financial benefits

Mercy offers both a 401(k) and a cash-balance retirement to its full- and part-time employees. Employees age 50 and older can make catch-up contributions to their 401(k) account, which can be as high as $5,000 per year. Catch-up contributions became permanent under the new 2006 pension law. You can find out more details about that law in Chapter 8. The hospital also offers referral services for elder care and child care for employees' children and grandchildren.

Alternative work arrangements

Mercy offers a number of different types of work arrangements including flex time where employees can set their own hours within certain guidelines; telecommuting, which allows employees to work at home provided that is possible for the type of work they do; a phased retirement program (I talk more about how phased retirement programs work in Chapter 15); and job sharing, where two employees share one job. Full-time employees can also move to part-time work on a permanent or temporary basis.

Maintaining relations with retirees

Mercy currently has 100 retirees and it hired an individual whose direct responsibilities include retiree relations. The hospital stays in touch with its employees on a regular basis and invites them to organization events and celebrations. It also provides retirees with ongoing access to retirement-planning workshops.

Retirees can choose to come back to work on a temporary basis. They can work as consultants or do contract work. Telecommuting from home, working full-time, or working part-time are all options for retirees that decide they'd like to work again.

While many hospitals around the country are struggling with hard to fill vacancies, Mercy has shown them how to maintain their needed workforce for years to come. This is crucially important given the fact that the workforce is aging and soon there won't be enough workers to fill their shoes unless companies find innovative ways to attract and retain their older workforce.

Finding Temporary Agencies that Specialize in 50+ workers

One of the best ways to find jobs once you're 50 or older is through temporary agencies that specialize in placing workers 50 and older. One thing you will find consistently in the descriptions for most of the companies that won AARP's "Best Employers" award is that they recruit through senior placement agencies or agencies that focus on mature workers (www.aarp.org/money/careers/employerresourcecenter/bestemployers/).

There are a number of top agencies out there. You can probably find one near you by looking in the yellow pages of your local telephone book. Kelly Services won one of the "Best Employers" awards from AARP in 2005. Manpower Services was named by a number of "Best Employers" as their source for mature workers.

If you don't find any specific mention of seeking "mature workers" or other clues I mention above, call the temporary agency and ask whether they provide placement services for older workers. If they answer you enthusiastically that they do, you probably do have a match. I find that when an employment agency gives a pat answer about nondiscrimination, they probably won't make any special efforts to help the older worker find a job.

Working with the nation's largest senior placement and training service

The nation's largest senior placement and training service is Experience Works (www.experienceworks.org), which started out as Green Thumb 40 years ago. It was originally chartered in 1965 as a small, rural demonstration program.

Today, Experience Works helps seniors get the training they need to find good jobs in their own communities. It is one of the leading providers of training, employment, and community service for low-income older people.

Checking out its services

Experience Works provides its services through older-worker training projects across the country. Projects include training in occupational skills, classroom training, or on-the-job training:

- **Occupational skills:** This type of training helps older workers develop skills for high-growth occupations such as home health aide, nurse assistant, and computer operator. Experience Works identifies the high-growth occupations within each specific project locality before setting up the training.

- **Classroom training:** Classroom training is customized depending on the needs of the participants. This type of training is focused on developing the basic skills some participants need in order to become ready to work at a job.

- **On-the-job training:** Sometimes employers will ask Experience Works to develop and coordinate training for participants with specific jobs that require special skills. The employer that requests this training can get partial reimbursement for the extraordinary costs that may be associated with training a particular individual.

Checking out its largest program — SCSEP

Experience Works's largest program is the Senior Community Service Employment Program (SCSEP), which is funded under Title V of the Older Americans Act as well as state and local grants. Thousands of low-income people age 55 and older have been helped under this program throughout the United States.

Seniors can get training, counseling, and community service assignments at faith-based and community organizations in their communities, which will help them transition into a paid position in the workforce. Initially, participants are placed at host agencies where they will be paid the minimum wage for an average of 20 hours per week. Host agencies can include either a private nonprofit organization or a public agency operated by a unit of government.

SCSEP has had great success training older workers and finding them jobs. After completing the program, 38 percent of Experience Works's SCSEP participants found permanent jobs, primarily as teachers' aides, emergency dispatchers, care providers, and clerical assistants.

Participating in SCSEP

You can qualify for this program as long as you are 55 years of age or older and a resident of a state where the SCSEP program operates. Your annual family income must not be more than 125 percent of the established federal poverty income guidelines. You also must be eligible to work in the United States and be currently unemployed.

To find out if there is a program in your state, go to the Web site. Near the top-left side of the Web site, you will see a box that says "For Seniors." Choose your state from a drop-down list and enter your county to find out if there is an Experience Works program near you.

For example, to test the system, I put in a Florida county and found that 2,000 seniors are helped annually in Florida. There are nine regional offices in that state.

To make contact with Experience Works, you can either send an e-mail or call the numbers given for your state. There is no cost for the training programs and you can earn while you learn.

Using online resources

Resources can be as close as your computer, or your grandson's or granddaughter's computer. You'll find lots of good information on the Web for locating companies that hire older workers. Here are some good places to start.

National Council on Aging resources

The National Council on Aging (www.maturityworks.org) maintains a job database for the senior network. To find available job postings, click on "Job" near the top left of the Web site.

You can search job listings there. People searching for a job can post their resume for free on the Web site. Employers can post a job listing for free if they are a member of the council, but must pay $50 per listing if they are not.

Senior Employment Resources (SER)

Senior Employment Resources (www.seniorjobs.org) focuses on helping people age 50 or older who want to work in the Washington D.C. area, primarily in Northern Virginia. SER is a registered 501(c)(3) nonprofit organization that receives a small portion of its funding from Fairfax County. SER is an equal opportunity service.

Seniors4Hire

When the Forward Group started Seniors4Hire (www.seniors4hire.org), they were actually planning to start a job site for teens called Teens4Hire. They were inundated with requests by companies that wanted to hire seniors, so Seniors4Hire was born.

Companies that encouraged the Forward Group to start the site include Bank of America, RadioShack Corp., and Regal Entertainment Group, and they are still actively involved in the site. You can join the site for free as long as you are at least 50 years old.

In 2006, the site had over 200,000 job seekers age 50 or older and more than 550 employers that posted jobs. Industry groups that post on the site include financial services, retail, telecommunications, and healthcare.

Senior Job Bank

One of the oldest senior job-placement sites on the Internet is Senior Job Bank (www.seniorjobbank.org). You'll find hundreds of jobs available there each day. Listings are organized by state. Access to the site is free for seniors, but employers must pay $89 per job posting. A wide variety of jobs are available, from entry level to senior executive.

Finding work if you're a scientist or engineer

Eli Lilly Company and Proctor & Gamble started YourEncore.com (www.yourencore.com) to reconnect with their retirees. In 2006, the site is flourishing as a place that job seekers who were scientists, engineers, or product developers can find work.

Most of the jobs posted on this Web site are short-term projects that are designed to solve a specific problem. In addition to the two founders, you'll also find projects from Boeing, National Starch, 3M Co., and Ethicon Endo-Surgery. Yourencore.com was started to bypass the pension rules that made it difficult to rehire workers that were drawing a pension from the company.

The 2006 pension law lifts some of the barriers to hiring retirees who are collecting a pension and are at least 62 years old, but the barriers do still exist if you are younger than that, so this Web site will probably continue to operate after the 2006 law is fully in force.

Searching for jobs if you're a retired government expert

Yup, there is even a Web site dedicated to helping former U.S. government workers find work after retirement in the private sector. It's called the Employment Network for Retired Government Experts (www.enrge.us). This Web site focuses on building a job network for former U.S. government workers who want to try working in the private sector.

You must be a retired federal, state, or local government employee, or a government employee within 12 months of a scheduled retirement, to use this free service. Government contractors, entrepreneurs, venture capitalists, human resource managers, investors, inventors, industrialists, small, large, and emerging business owners, and other employers use this site's database of candidates. Jobs offered through this site tend to be contract-based, but some are full- or part-time. Employers pay $1,000 to access the database for an 18-month period.

Telecommuting — Not Telemarketing!

Telecommuting is becoming more and more popular. More than 24 million workers telecommute at least one day a week. About 25 percent of these workers work at home every day.

Understanding telecommuting

A telecommuting job is in no way a telemarketing job (where you call people on the phone in the middle of their supper or favorite television show to sell them something they don't want and don't need). *Telecommuting* simply means you work somewhere other than the regular workplace for the company. Most often that place is your home, but it can be a satellite office or telework center.

A *telework center* is a place where computers, Internet access, and other office equipment are available. Some companies that allow telecommuting set up these workspaces for workers who live far from the regular office. These employees can work at the telework center rather than travel all the way into the office for at least part of their work week.

If you do want to telecommute from home, you will need to have an office set up in your home and be able to stay in close contact with your employer throughout the day. Sometimes employers will even provide the equipment workers need to telecommute from home.

The biggest advantage of telecommuting is that you can set your own hours. If you have something to do at home or must errands outside the home, you can take care of those things and then make up the time later in the day.

Finding a telecommuting job

How do you find telecommuting jobs? Some of the Web sites mentioned earlier in this chapter do list contract work, which often can be done by telecommuting. You will also find telecommuting jobs on Internet job sites. If you know that you can do the job from home, even if telecommuting is not listed, it never hurts to ask during a job interview whether telecommuting is a possibility.

One of the largest Web sites for contract work, freelance projects, and part-time jobs that does include telecommuting is Sologig (www.sologig.com), which boasts that it lists 10,000 jobs daily. A wide variety of jobs are listed on the site including Web and graphic design, marketing, writing, editing, translation, programming and database development, networking, engineering, architecture, business and administrative support, and sales.

Sologig is affiliated with Career Builder.com. In fact, if you indicate that you want to work freelance or on a contract basis when applying for a job on Career Builder, you will be sent to Sologig. Job seekers do not have to pay a fee for the service, but if you want priority placement when an employer searches for a freelancer, there is a premium membership that costs $39.99 per month.

To get started with Sologig, you develop a personal profile that focuses on the types of projects or jobs you're interested in finding. Then you can search the database for projects, which Sologig says numbers 100,000. If you find a project that interests you, you can apply for the project online. Employers will then view your profile and contact you if they are interested.

Each employer sets its own rules regarding hiring processes, project parameters, and compensation. Sologig.com does not charge any fees per project that you accept.

Most Popular Part-Time Jobs for Older Workers

You may be wondering what types of jobs are the most popular among older workers who do want to work part-time. Well, you'll find there are lots of different job types available to people 50 and older.

The following sections list the most popular part-time jobs older workers are choosing:

Bank teller

Banks prefer to higher older workers because they are reliable, responsible, and have excellent customer-service skills that they have developed over many years of working. Teller positions give you a lot of opportunity to interact with people throughout the day.

Many banks also offer tellers part-time hours and flexible schedules to attract and keep good workers. Often part-time positions are available at busy times of the day, such as lunch time. Check with the banks in your area to find out if they have any jobs available. Even if there isn't a job in the branch nearest you, your branch will likely know how to apply for a position with another branch nearby that does have openings.

Customer greeters

You probably saw customer greeters for the first time at your local Wal-Mart. They are the people that stand near the entrance to the store and greet customers as they come in.

Wal-Mart started a trend that has become very popular in many other retail businesses. Car dealerships and banks are two of the retailers that often employ customer greeters today.

Take notice as you walk into various retail stores in your area. If you do see a customer greeter near the entrance, that's a good place to check to see if there are any openings. Even if there are no openings in the specific store you are visiting, the employment office can give you information about other locations that might have openings.

One of the nice benefits of working at a retail store is that you get employee discounts that will make it much cheaper to buy gifts for your grandkids.

English instructor

If you like to travel, working as an English instructor might be the perfect opportunity for you. To learn more about teaching English abroad, visit the Web site Transitions Abroad (`http://www.transitionsabroad.com/listings/work/esl/index.shtml`). There you will find information about certification training and employers that hire people to teach English abroad.

You will need some training to learn how to teach English as a second language. Once you're certified, you will be able to find work and get a work permit abroad in countries throughout Asia and Eastern Europe. Many other English teaching jobs exist around the globe.

Countries that have jobs for English teachers and that are listed on Transitions Abroad include Canada, Chile, China, Costa Rica, Czech Republic, France, Italy, Japan, Korea, Mexico, Russia, Spain, Taiwan, Thailand, and United Kingdom. There are also opportunities in the United States if you don't want to travel abroad.

College or university faculty member

If you enjoy teaching and have at least a Master's degree, you may be able to find a faculty or instructor position at a local community college or through one of the nationwide private universities, such as the University of Phoenix. Contact your local community college to find out what types of teaching opportunities are available.

The University of Phoenix hires instructors at satellite facilities all over the country who teach inside the classroom, through a program called FlexNet (that is partially online and partially in the classroom) and through classes entirely online. The university seeks faculty members with extensive work experience to teach, so it makes a perfect fit for retired workers.

I do have some direct experience teaching there. I am a faculty member for the Graduate Business and Management program at the university's Tampa campus. Each faculty member is contracted on a course-by-course basis for four- to six-week courses. So it's easy to set your own schedule, teach, and then travel in-between contracts.

Floral assistant

If you enjoy being around plants and want flexible schedules, a floral assistant might be your best choice for a part-time job. You'll even get some health benefits from this choice because flowers have been shown to decrease depression and enhance memory for older people.

You will need to work many holidays if you choose this type of position. Floral shops, of course, are their busiest during the holiday seasons.

Home care aides

If you've already cared for an elderly parent or spouse in your home, you know what a home care assistant needs to do. As the U.S. population ages, the need for home care assistants grows rapidly.

You can find out more details about the scope of duties for Home Care Aides at the Department of Labor Web site (http://www.bls.gov/oco/ocos173.htm). In some states, all you will need is on-the-job training, which you can get through your future employer.

Other states do require formal training, which you can get through local community colleges, vocation schools, elder care programs, or home healthcare agencies.

You can get a national certification as a home care aide through The National Association for Home Care and Hospice (NAHC) (www.nahc.org), but certification is voluntary. If you do decide to get certified, it requires completion of a 75-hour course and written exam developed by NAHC. After the test, home care aides seeking certification are evaluated on 17 different skills by a registered nurse.

Mystery shopping

Do you like to shop? If you do, you can get paid for it by working as a mystery shopper.

Remember all those times you've gotten bad service and wanted to tell someone about it, but there was no one around to tell or you didn't want to take the time to do it? Well, mystery shopping lets you get out some of that frustration.

Many retailers, including fast-food restaurants, grocery stores, banks, car dealers, and new home builders, use mystery shoppers. Almost any area that you enjoy shopping in probably hires mystery shoppers.

WARNING! Be careful though, many Web sites on the Internet or job listings on job boards offer you mystery shopping opportunities provided you pay a fee to join. Don't do it! You don't have to pay to be a mystery shopper, and the good companies don't charge.

The best place to find out more about mystery shopping is the Mystery Shopping Providers Association (www.mysteryshop.org/shoppers). They do offer two levels of certification — Silver and Gold. It does help to have at least a Silver certification to get picked up by the better mystery shopping firms. You can get that certification online for $15 at www.mysteryshop. org/shoppers/certification. You will read through a quick course on the basics of how to mystery shop and take a short exam online. After you're certified, you can use the association's resources to search for shopping opportunities.

Three good mystery shopping firms to work with include Service Intelligence (www.serviceintelligence.com), Maritz (www.maritz.com), and Jancyn (www.jancyn.com). Most of your better mystery shopping firms do value your getting the Silver certificate. You have a better chance of getting picked up if you can give your certificate number when applying to be a mystery shopper.

Teacher's assistant

Do you like working with children? Many school systems around the country are looking for teacher's assistants as classroom sizes continue to grow.

Some school systems even provide on-the-job training for teacher's assistants. If you think this might be a good match for you, you can find out more about the job requirements at the U.S. Department of Labor's Web site (www.bls.gov/oco/ocos153.htm). You can also find out about training programs that are offered in your state at your state department of education Web site or by contacting your county's school system.

About 40 percent of teacher's assistants work part-time, and you can likely find a part-time job that fits your schedule, especially since many school systems have a great shortage of workers.

Each state sets its own rules about educational requirements, which can vary greatly. In some states, you may find that all you need is a high school diploma, while others require some college training.

If you do have experience working with special education students or can speak a foreign language, you will find that you are in even greater demand.

Tour guide

If you enjoy giving tours, you may find lots of opportunities near your home at museums, parks, resorts, casinos, and other hospitality-based businesses. Many of these types of facilities use older workers to explain the attractions and inform customers about the various services and amenities offered.

Large new home developments also hire tour guides who give a basic tour of the community and free up salespeople to work with serious buyers.

If this type of job interests you, stop by museums, parks, resorts, or new home developments near you to find out if they do hire tour guides and how you can apply for the spots.

Part IV

Revisiting Your Former Career or Starting Your Own Business

The 5th Wave   By Rich Tennant

"For 30 years I've put a hat and coat on to make sales calls and I'm not changing now just because I'm doing it on the Web in my living room."

In this part . . .

You may decide you don't really want to change jobs or that you'd like to work as a consultant for your former company or within your former industry. Or maybe you'd like to follow your dreams and run your own business. In this part, I talk about creative ways to stay on your current job part time or convince your boss to let you work as a consultant. I also explore how you can start your own consulting business providing services to other companies in the industry you know best. Finally, I help you explore various alternatives you may want to consider if you'd like to run your own business.

Chapter 15

Staying on the Job Part-Time

• •

In This Chapter

▶ Going part-time

▶ Sharing your job

▶ Working from home

▶ Contracting independently

▶ Temping awhile

▶ Retiring in phases

• •

*Y*ou may be ready to slow down, but not ready to stop work completely as you near full retirement age. Many companies do offer alternative working arrangements for their older workers, including part-time work schedules, job sharing, telecommuting, and independent contracting. More and more companies are realizing the value of retaining their older workers as they find it harder and harder to hire well-qualified candidates to replace all the baby boomers ready to retire.

In this chapter, I look at the alternatives to a full-time position, explain how they work, and give you some suggestions on how to make them happen.

Unfortunately, some of you will be working for a company that has not seen the value of retaining their older workers and the powers that be won't be willing to consider these alternatives. If that's the case, you'll find some great ideas for how to continue working part-time for a different company in Chapter 14.

Switching to Part-Time

The traditional way to slow down on a job is to reduce your time at work by switching to a part-time position, which would be any work assignment below what your company considers full-time — usually 35 to 40 hours a week. Part-time positions can be structured as five half days, three days a week, four days a week, or any other combination of days depending on what you and your boss can work out. But to switch to part-time, you need to restructure your day and get approval for the switch. I discuss both of these ideas in the sections below.

Developing a restructuring plan

You need to do your homework before talking to your boss about working part-time. Follow these steps:

1. **Develop a detailed list of everything you do.** This should be a much more extensive list of your daily functions than your job description. You should include even the most mundane tasks in this list, such as filing — yeah, unfortunately everyone has to do some of that — copying, or other support functions that may not be in your official job description but are part of your daily routine.

2. **Figure out what you *must* do.** Obviously, if you do get permission to go part-time, you can't do everything that you were doing full-time, unless you have a job that really doesn't require a full-time employee. So you need to look at your list of daily functions and determine what you must do, what could be passed on to a co-worker or another department, and what could be eliminated.

3. **Create a new job description.** Be sure that you can handle this description given the work week you prefer. Keep the tasks that are critical to your current skills and talents. Also be sure to list tasks that have been assigned to you because they are a priority of your boss or your company and you've been designated as the best person to do them — even if you hate doing those tasks. You want to show your boss that you will continue being a team player even as a part-timer.

4. **Evaluate the leftover tasks.** Determine if the tasks left can be eliminated because they really are "busy work" or no longer needed. Be ready to make the case for their elimination and be sure you don't put a task on that list that you know is important to your boss even if you don't think it's important. Trying to make the case against something your boss wants when you are trying to get something for yourself will just give your boss ammunition to reject your entire request to go part-time.

   You're sure to have some tasks left on your list that still need to be done, but you believe others in your department or possibly another department can take over those tasks. You may or may not want to recommend who should take over those tasks.

5. **Make the call about how far your recommendations should go based on your relationship with your boss.** You may think it's better to just list tasks you don't think are critical for you to do or you may find it better to develop a plan for who should do them.

If you're a manager or a supervisor, you'll be in a stronger position to recommend restructuring. If you're not in a supervisory role, it's probably best to leave the restructuring to your boss, but be ready to make some suggestions if he asks for them.

Proposing the change

Obviously, your best shot at getting what you want is to ask for the change when your boss is praising you for your work. So develop your proposal and sit on it until the timing is right. If you're scheduled for a review and you're expecting it to be a good one, that may be the best time to bring up the discussion. Another good time is shortly after you've completed a project for which you were praised. (I talk more about how to write the proposal and prepare for the approach to your boss in the section below, "Convincing Your Boss.")

You do take some risks proposing a part-time arrangement. If your boss says no, he may then question whether you are still willing to put in a full-time effort or may be thinking about leaving the job. Your relationship with your boss, as well as your outstanding job reviews, could be hurt. So tread carefully and be sure you are ready for a possible negative impact on your standing within the company if your proposal is rejected.

Sharing Your Job

Job sharing became popular when women reentered the job force after having a child. Many women did want to go back to work, but not full-time. They wanted more time to spend raising their family. So they talked with other co-workers in the same boat, found a partner who also wanted to job share, and then proposed it to their boss. If you want to job share, you need to follow the same route — I take you through it in the sections that follow.

Finding the right fit

In order to job share, you'll need to find someone else in the company that has similar or complementary job skills and also wants to work part-time. The two of you can then propose to share one job instead of two. That way the company only has to hire one person and keeps two people already trained in the job, who can then help train the new person.

Today, job sharing is a popular alternative for workers nearing retirement. For example, suppose you are in a department that has a total of six workers and four of them are near retirement age. If the four workers near retirement age would like to cut back on their hours and reduce their stress as they near retirement, job sharing might be the best alternative.

The company could make two of the four positions job-sharing positions and only need to hire two new employees. The four job-sharers could then serve as mentors to the new hires and make the transition much smoother for both the company and the employees.

The key to getting a job-share arrangement to work is finding someone who is not only willing to share a job with you, but is willing to share that job during the hours you don't want to work. For example, suppose you want to work in the mornings from 9 to 1. You would need to find a job-share partner who is willing to work from 1 to 5.

Companies that do permit job sharing usually structure the job-share partnerships in the following three different ways:

- ✔ **Skill sets:** When a job-sharing arrangement is based on skill sets, each member of the job share brings skills and experiences that complement the other member of the arrangement. Working together, they meet the full expectations of the job. For example, one person may be a very good number cruncher while the other person on the job-share team is good with managing people or projects. Pairing them can create an even more effective working environment for the company.

- ✔ **Mentor/subordinate:** When a job-sharing arrangement involves a team with a supervisor or manager and subordinate, each one handles the tasks that best meet their skills and experience. The supervisor won't be bogged down with tasks that can be handled by someone at a lower level with less experience, which frees him up to focus his time on managing people and organizing the department or function. This type of job share can be the most cost effective type of job share and it also serves as the ideal mentoring relationship in which the subordinate can be trained to take over when the supervisor is promoted or moves on.

> ✔ **Geographic shares:** Many companies need regional coverage, but don't need full-time people at each location. A job-sharing arrangement can involve two people in two different parts of the country. This kind of arrangement can help the company meet its geographic coverage needs. Many times this type of job-share team doesn't work in the same office.

Creating a winning job-sharing team

The key to any successful job-share team is communication. It's critical that both members of a job-share team openly communicate about the tasks they are working on, so when one of them is out of the office, the other person can cover questions about ongoing projects or duties. Responsibilities must be clearly defined upfront. Everyone involved, including the job sharers, the boss, and other co-workers, must understand who is responsible for which tasks.

One big advantage of job-sharing arrangements is that job sharers can cover for each other when one goes on vacation or is sick. To help sell the plan to your boss, be sure to let him know that each of you will work extra hours if needed when one partner in the job share must be out of the office during his normal work hours.

Once you've found your job-share partner, both of you need to write detailed descriptions of your daily tasks. Then you should work together to develop a plan for how you can share your job and also what tasks you may need to pass on to others. Since you will be sharing one job, there will be a second position open that the company can either decide to fill or not, depending on what is needed.

You will find that some of your tasks will need to be a shared responsibility. This includes things that could be needed throughout the day no matter who is in the office. Other tasks may fall to one partner or the other depending on skills or experience.

Once both partners agree on a plan, then it's time to write up the proposal and approach your boss. I talk more about how to write the proposal and prepare for the approach to your boss in the section below, "Convincing Your Boss." Carefully pick a time when you know he is most receptive to hearing new ideas. If you've just worked on a successful project together, that can be the best timing to suggest a job-share arrangement.

Telecommuting from Home

Telecommuting means that you will work from your home rather than go into the office every day. You should plan to go to the office at least one day per week to maintain good relationships with your co-workers and attend crucial meetings. You may need to go into the office on days you're scheduled to be home if a crisis arises at your company and you're needed for meetings or other activities.

If you do want to think about this option, you must have a place in your home that you can dedicate as office space and be prepared to spend the money you need to buy all the office equipment. You can't plan to do this on your kitchen table. You will need a room where you can close the door and concentrate without being disturbed. Some companies that permit telecommuting do provide office equipment, but if you're making the case for telecommuting the first time in your company, don't expect any help financing the move.

To telecommute, you must be the type of person who is self-motivated, highly focused, and dedicated. If you meet these criteria, you'll probably find that you can get more done in your home than in the office where there can be constant interruptions. But, you also must be someone who does not need the camaraderie that comes by being in the workplace. Working at home, alone, can be difficult if you are a people person.

If you think telecommuting is the way you want to go, then sit down and write a detailed description of all your work duties. Determine which duties can be done just as efficiently, or possibly even more efficiently, from your home. Figure out the duties that must be done in the office.

Group the duties that must be done in the office together and determine whether or not they can be done on the one or two days you plan to go to the office. If not, determine whether they are duties you can pass on to someone else.

Develop a proposal for your boss that lays out what duties you believe you can do from home, what duties you will do the one or two days you go to the office, and what duties you propose giving up as you shorten your work week and become a part-timer. I talk more about how to write the proposal and prepare for the approach to your boss in the section below, "Convincing Your Boss."

Convincing Your Boss

If any part-time alternatives are already permitted in your company, getting approval for the arrangement should be relatively simple because the rules for doing so already exist. But, if your company has never allowed any of these types of arrangements, then you'll have to sell your boss and your company on the idea of alternative work arrangements before you can even propose one for yourself. The following sections not only tell you how to develop your proposal, but also where you can find some great help.

Taking steps in the right direction

Here are the steps you should take to make the case for an alternative work arrangement:

1. **Research your company's policies and current work arrangements.** Start this task by reading your employee manual to see whether there are any current human resource provisions for working part-time, job sharing, telecommuting, or other alternative work arrangements, such as flex time. Also research the company's position on benefits for employees who work part-time. This will give you the ammunition for your proposal. If there is no mention of alternative work arrangements, you do have your work cut out for you to make the case for them. Your proposal will need to be more extensive, talking about how the arrangements have proven good for both employees and employers. There's lots of research out there. I'll point you to some good resources later in this section.

2. **Make an appointment to discuss your plans with a co-worker who utilizes alternative work arrangements.** If you know of anyone in your company who has an alternative work arrangement, make an appointment to talk with them, find out details about their arrangement, and find out how they got the company to agree to their arrangement.

3. **Find out who will have to approve your request for an alternative work arrangement and figure out when the best time is to approach that person with your request.** For example, would they be more receptive to hearing new ideas in the morning or afternoon? Is early in the week better for them or are they more relaxed toward the middle or end of the week? Do they prefer to discuss new ideas face-to-face or to read about them in a written proposal sent by e-mail or letter. Figure out the best way to initiate this discussion.

4. **Once you've got all your ducks in a row, write your proposal and plan your strategy for presenting it.**

Finding help online

Developing your proposal on your own may all sound very scary to you. If you're not comfortable trying to do this all on your own from scratch, there is an excellent Web site you can use for proposal development called Work Options (www.workoptions.com). Pat Katepoo, who developed this site, has been convincing companies of the benefits of alternative work arrangements since 1993.

She's even pulled together resources specifically for people aged 50 and older who want to consider an alternative to their current working arrangement at http://www.workoptions.com/fiftyplus.htm. To make things even easier for you, Pat Katepoo has developed excellent templates that you can download and personalize for your company and job situation at http://www.workoptions.com/wherestart.htm. She not only gives you a template in which you fill in the blanks for your situation, she also takes you carefully through the steps — researching, writing an effective proposal, and developing you strategy for presenting the proposal. She does charge $29.92 for each template.

A good place to find research publications about changes in the workplace is the Families and Work Institute (famliesandwork.org). You'll find a number of studies on older workers and changes in the workforce that you can use to build your case. Boston University's Center for Work and Family Balance (www.workandfamily.org) is another good source for research on changes in the workforce that you can use for developing your proposal.

In Chapter 14, I discuss AARP's "Best Employers for Workers Over 50 Program." Read through the descriptions to get some ideas of what other companies are doing in regards to alternative work arrangements. You can get more information about all the employers that have won recognition from AARP at www.aarp.org/money/careers/employerresourcecenter/bestemployers/.

A good Web site developed from the employer's perspective that has some excellent articles you can use to build your case is Employee Retention (www.hermangroup.com/retentionconnection) developed by the Herman Group, a management-consulting firm.

Proposing an Independent Contractor Arrangement

You may also want to consider leaving your company completely and working as an independent contractor. Do be careful though if you decide to take this route. Often these positions are not designed as true contractor arrangements and are instead just a way for the company to avoid paying benefits.

As an independent contractor, you should truly be able to set your own schedule, and decide where you want to work and how you want to work, as long as you are able to meet the specifications in the contract you write between you and the employer.

You should be hired on a project-by-project basis. Your duties and responsibilities should be carefully spelled out, as well as who will be responsible for materials, supplies, and other items that may be needed to complete the project. If you plan to hire assistants to help you with the project or subcontract out some of the work, be sure your costs for these items are specified in the contract as well.

When you're an employee, both you and your employer pay half of your taxes for Social Security and Medicare, which means each of you pay 6.2 percent of your income for Social Security taxes (up to an income level of $94,200 in 2006) and 1.45 percent for Medicare taxes. As a contractor, you'll have to pay both employer and employee taxes, which means you'll have to pay 15.3 percent of your income toward Social Security and Medicare taxes to cover both the employer and employee taxes.

The IRS uses the following 20-question test to determine whether a person is truly working as an independent contractor:

- ✔ **Is the individual's work vital to the company's core business?** If you are still an employee, the answer to this question is yes. You can only be considered a contractor if the services you plan to provide are nonessential business activities.

- ✔ **Did you train the individual to perform tasks in a specific way?** If your company provides training, then you are considered an employee. Contractors should be skilled professionals who require no training to perform their services.

- ✔ **Do you (or can you) instruct the individual as to when, where, and how the work is performed?** Employers can control where, when, and how work should be performed for the company, but they can't do that for an independent contractor. If you become a contractor, you must be able to determine where you perform the work based on industry specifications.

- ✔ **Do you (or can you) control the sequence or order of the work performed?** For employees, the answer to this question is yes as well. On the other hand, as a contractor you will be held accountable only for outcomes, not the way in which you complete the work.

- ✔ **Do you (or can you) set the hours of work for the individual?** Employers can set schedules for employees. As a contractor, you must be able to set your own work hours as long as you meet agreed-upon deadlines.

✔ **Do you (or can you) require the individual to perform the work personally?** Employees are required to do the work personally. As a contractor, you can delegate work to your own staff or subcontract the work to others.

✔ **Do you (or can you) prohibit the individual from hiring, supervising, and paying assistants?** The company decides whether assistants can be hired for employees and pays those assistants. As a contractor, you get to make the choice to hire assistants for yourself. The contractor also pays the costs of assistants who perform all or part of the project.

✔ **Does the individual perform regular and continuous services for you?** Employees work regularly even if they do not have full-time jobs. Contractors work on a project-by-project basis with new contracts drawn up for each new project.

✔ **Does the individual provide services on a substantially full-time basis to your company?** Employers can control whether full-time employees work for others. As a contractor, you have the right to work for more than one company provided you perform the requirements of your contract on time.

✔ **Is your company the sole or major source of income for the individual?** For employees, the answer to this question is yes. Contractors usually work for multiple clients at the same time.

✔ **Is the work performed on your premises?** Employees usually work on-site unless telecommuting has been approved. As a contractor, you have the choice to work on-site (if space is available) or at an office of your choosing.

✔ **Do you (or can you) require the individual to submit regular reports, either written or oral?** You can ask employees to provide status or activity reports on a regular basis. Contractors are responsible to deliver their product on time. You cannot be required to provide interim reports unless those reports are part of the initial contract agreement.

✔ **Do you pay the individual by the hour, week, or month?** Employees are paid at fixed intervals. Compensation for contractors is determined by project or is based on a fixed fee.

✔ **Do you pay the individual's travel and business expenses?** Employees who incur work-related expenses are usually reimbursed for those expenses. Contractors normally include out-of-pocket expenses as part of their project fee rather than being reimbursed for them as they occur.

✔ **Do you furnish tools or equipment for the individual?** Employees generally use company-provided supplies. Contractors usually provide their own equipment and supplies, unless otherwise specified in the contract.

✔ **Does the individual have a significant investment in facilities, tools, or equipment?** Employees typically use the company's facilities, tools, and equipment. Contractors usually pay their own expenses related to workspace, equipment, and other needs.

✔ **Can the individual realize a profit or loss from his or her services to your company?** For employees, the answer to this question is no, because employees can usually expect steady paychecks. Contractors, on the other hand, run the risk of nonpayment if a project is not completed according to contract specifications.

✔ **Does the individual make his or her services available to the general public?** Employees do not sell their services to the public. Contractors publicize their services to a wide range of potential clients using direct mail, advertising, and other means.

✔ **Can the individual terminate the relationship without liability?** Employees can quit at any time. Contractors are legally obligated to complete projects according to contract provisions, or they may face penalties for noncompletion as set forth in the contract.

✔ **Do you have the right to discharge the individual at any time?** Employees can usually be let go "at will" by their employer. Contractors can be discharged only if they fail to perform contracted services.

Use this 20-question test to develop the provisions of any independent contract you agree to sign. If a company regularly uses independent contract agreements for former employees who have retired, you may find that the company will supply you with a contract. Don't sign the contract without testing its provisions against these 20 questions. In fact, it's always a good idea to pay an attorney familiar with labor law to review any independent contract before you sign it.

Be sure you clearly define the scope of any project for which you will work as an independent contractor. Make sure you clearly spell out in writing what you will be responsible to do, when you will be responsible to complete the work, and who will pay for all the materials and supplies needed to get the work done.

Going Back to Work as a Temporary Worker

You may decide that you want to work again after you've already left your position. You don't want to take on the responsibilities of a full- or part-time employee year round. Instead you'd just like to take periodic temporary assignments to make some extra money.

You will be able to do that without any problem provided your company does have a system for hiring temporary workers. You may find that your company actually uses a temporary agency for all its temporary workers and you will have to sign up with that agency to get any work.

You could have a problem though if you are collecting a pension from the company. Federal tax and labor laws does prohibit a company from rehiring its retirees who are receiving a pension. The provisions of these laws were eased for retirees with passage of the Pension Protection Act of 2006. The actual rules related to this new law were not yet written at the time I was writing this book. I talk about the provisions of the new law in greater detail in Chapter 8.

Your company may or may not ease its restrictions on rehiring employees who are collecting a pension. If you do collect a pension, be sure to check with your human resources department regarding the rules about working and collecting a pension before talking with your ex-boss about a temporary position.

Using a Phased Retirement Arrangement

You might like to cut your hours gradually and work toward retirement rather than go cold turkey from work to retirement. It can be very stressful to be at work one day and be at home with no structure for your day the next day.

You may want to consider one of the alternative work arrangements I discuss in this chapter, but can't afford to take the cut in pay unless you can get a least part of your pension benefits. Thanks to the 2006 pension law, the doorway was opened to companies who want to start formal phased retirement arrangements.

Prior to the new law, companies risked tax penalties, as well as the qualified status of their pension plans, if they continued people on their payroll who were receiving pension benefits. Under the new law, once an employee reaches age 62, the company can pay partial pension benefits to that employee while he's still working.

The official rules for phased retirement programs were still being developed by the Internal Revenue Service, regarding rule changes needed for issues related to tax codes, and by the Department of Labor, regarding rule changes related to provisions of ERISA and ADEA. ERISA stands for the Employee Retirement Income Security Act of 1974, which governs the operation of most employee benefit plans including traditional pensions as well as employee retirement savings plans, such as 401(k)s. ADEA stands for Age Discrimination in Employment Act, which prohibits discrimination in employment. The law governs early retirement benefits and voluntary early retirement incentive plans.

Changes will be needed in both ERISA and ADEA rules to make it possible for companies to rehire employees who are collecting pensions from their employers. If you aren't collecting a pension, you won't face the same problem.

People who do want to continue working under an alternative work arrangement such as part-time, job sharing, or telecommuting, but need to supplement their income to make up for the reduction in income, do have the option of officially retiring, rolling out their employer-retirement savings program into an individual retirement account (IRA), and then taking needed withdrawals to cover any shortfall in income.

This can be a good way to fund a phased retirement if you don't have a pension plan at work. But, be careful. You don't want to retire too early and take out so much money in early retirement that you run out of money during retirement.

A key provision that you will want to look for in any phased retirement program is a continuation of benefits, especially health benefits, at least until you qualify for Medicare. Once you get past the age of 50, you'll likely have some ongoing health problems that could make it impossible for you to get health insurance on your own before you qualify for Medicare.

Many companies that do want to retain their older workers are making it possible for their part-time workers to get access to group health insurance benefits through the company. You probably will have to pay more of the premium if you decide to work part-time or under one of the other alternative work arrangements discussed in this chapter. Another benefit many older workers seek is long-term care insurance.

Remember, you likely will be living 15, 20, or more years in retirement, so you do have to be careful not to withdraw the funds too quickly. I talk more about managing distributions from your retirement savings in Chapter 6.

Chapter 16

Consulting for Your Former Company

· ·

In This Chapter

▶ Qualifying to consult

▶ Exploring consulting projects

▶ Opening the door

▶ Setting fees

▶ Contracting

· ·

Sometimes your knowledge and experience are so important to a company that they just aren't ready for you to leave. Consulting after retiring from a full-time position can be very lucrative for the former employee.

This chapter will discuss how you set up consulting arrangements, as well as how to figure out what you should charge.

Understanding Consulting

Anyone with a specialized set of skills or knowledge can be a consultant. The key for you is whether or not you can sell the company on paying for your knowledge and skills.

When you start talking about retirement, if your boss starts talking about how he can't possibly imagine operating the department or company without you, you probably have a good chance of arranging for a consulting agreement provided that's what you want to do. But there could be a big barrier in the way of your consulting for your company. If you'll be eligible for traditional monthly pension benefits in retirement, your company may not be able to hire you.

Thanks to the Pension Protection Act of 2006, that barrier has been partially knocked down, and as long as you are at least 62 years old your company may already have changed the rules for their retirees. In Chapter 8, I explain the reasons for the barrier, if you want more details.

If you are younger than 62 and collecting a pension, you probably won't be able to work directly for your company. Some companies do hire consultants who are former employees through third-party consulting firms. If you know that the company does have a number of consultants on contract, talk with them to find out how they made their arrangements.

Checking out the advantages

Consultants pretty much can do anything a company needs but does not want to hire an employee to do or believes that a specialist can do more effectively and/or efficiently. As a retiree, your biggest benefit is that you set your work hours and you pick the projects you want to work on.

As a consultant, if the project doesn't interest you, you can always say no and move on to something else. If you want to travel at the time the project must be done, you can either negotiate a different schedule or pass on the project. Try doing that when you're a full-time employee. You won't get that type of flexibility.

For example, suppose you've been working on product development in the marketing department for 20 to 30 years. You know all the product lines extremely well, as well as the company's competitors. You could probably develop an analysis for the potential of a new product, as well as its marketing plan, fairly rapidly because you won't need to do as much research as a newer employee without the knowledge of the company and its competitors. Your company may decide to hire you as a marketing consultant to periodically work on new product development or other marketing dilemmas.

Reviewing the required skills

Consultants come in all stripes and sizes. If you search the Internet using the word *consulting*, you will probably find consultants in the fields of advertising, computers, construction, entertainment, financial services, law, politics, resume building, theater, telecommunications, and dozens of other areas.

The only limit to the types of consulting you can do is your experience and knowledge. Before someone will pay the big bucks for a consultant, you have to prove to them its worth paying you for your knowledge and skills.

What skills do you need? Skills you must have fall into three categories — technical skills, project-management skills, and personal skills.

- ✔ **Technical skills:** These include any skills in which you have a specialty because of your functional expertise (accounting, writing, or whatever area you've been working in for the past 20 to 30 years).

- ✔ **Project-management skills:** These could include creating the product, negotiating, interviewing, presenting recommendations, problem-identification, problem-solving, time management, client service skills, proposal development, and team-building and management skills.

- ✔ **Personal skills:** These include communications, listening, management, collaboration, interpersonal, marketing, promotion, and leadership.

If you think you may be weak in any of these skill sets, you should probably find a partner for your consulting work. All these skills are needed by a consultant at one time or another.

Seeing how consultants work

Basically, consultants are hired to solve a problem. You do so by working through these five major steps:

1. **Investigate the problem.** You figure out what's gone wrong or what needs to be done. As part of the investigation step, you'll talk with people in the organization, research information, and collect data so you'll be able to analyze the problem. As an insider, you know where the "bodies are buried," so to speak. From your experience, you probably have a good idea where the weaknesses are and who you need to talk with about the problem. You probably know who's protecting what fiefdom and how someone might be creating resistance to the solution. You will need to talk with the key people putting up the barriers to the solution to get their side of the story. Don't assume your solution is right until you've done a full investigation. Remember, you want to look at this from a fresh perspective and not just the perspective you might have had while working full-time in one department of the company.

2. **Analyze your data.** Next you need to analyze the problem to figure out the causes and symptoms. For example, as you start your research regarding the launch of the new product, you may find the sales manager has some serious concerns about how it will fit in the product line. He also might believe that the new product could cut into sales of other products. When you talk with the manufacturing manager, you might find that the new product cannot easily be built along side other products in the line and that you'll need to consider outsourcing manufacturing. You

need to collect all the pros and cons about the new product and how it will fit in the organization.

3. **Make recommendations.** After your finish your analysis, you'll need to come up with a set a recommendations that directly respond to the questions that were posed to you when you first took on the project. For example, if your task is developing a marketing and sales plan for the new product, your recommendations would include designing that plan. But, as an outside consultant, you also would want to discuss recommendations for how to handle any objections you might have heard from various department heads during the investigation.

4. **Develop a plan for change.** If part of your recommendation includes a major shift for the organization in how it handles the type of problem you analyzed, you should talk about how to manage the change. For example, if during your analysis of the new product plan, you find you need to recommend significant changes, you could be put in the role of advocating your set of recommendations. It's likely, if the company wants you to be involved in change management, that would be an additional project and you would need to negotiate an extension of the contract to do the work necessary to implement the change process.

5. **Implement your recommendations.** In some cases, your contract may include a provision that you help implement your recommendations even if change is not involved. For example, you could be asked to spearhead the introduction of the new product. Once the product is launched, you would pass the day-to-day operations to a product manager who is a full-time employee who has been working with you throughout the project. Because it is very hard to determine what your charges should be for implementation of your recommendations prior to developing the recommendations, you should protect yourself with a clause for negotiating hours and fees, once the recommendations have been accepted, that will be based on what all agree is needed.

Learning how to listen

No matter what type of consulting work you do, the most important skill you must develop is listening. As a consultant, you don't want to do too much of the talking, especially as you're collecting your information and developing your recommendations. The best way to get information is to say as little as possible to encourage people to talk, and sit back and listen.

Initially, you need to listen to what your client wants to accomplish by hiring you as a consultant. You have to ask the right questions and listen carefully to the answers. You certainly don't want to put in hours on a contract just to find out that the finished product of the contract does not satisfy the original needs of the company. You're wasting your time and the time of the people who hired you if you don't listen carefully.

Starting to Talk with Your Employer About Consulting

If you think consulting is the right thing for you after retirement, start talking with the managers and executives in your company who will ultimately make the contracting decision.

Don't start out a conversation saying you want to be a consultant. You should instead slowly build the case for the type of project you think you want to do. Once you've got them convinced that the project is necessary, then you can start making the pitch for your handling the project after retirement.

Often as you prepare to turn your work over to others in your department pending your retirement, you can slice out a piece of the pie (a part of your position) that you enjoy doing the most and would like to continue doing even after you leave the company full-time. As you sort out your key tasks, make a list of those things you think you would be able to do very well as a consultant.

Be sure that you pick the things for which you are well respected and seen as the top specialist in the company. If you cut out that piece of the pie just right, your case for becoming a consultant should just about make itself.

Researching Compensation Issues

One of the hardest things for any consultant to do is to figure out the fees they want to charge. You definitely don't want to sell your time cheap, but you also don't want to price yourself out of the market. Whatever fees you decide to charge, be sure you're ready to defend and justify them.

Researching fee structures

As you develop your fees, your first step should be researching what other consultants doing similar work in the field are charging. You've probably been privy to several contract negotiations in your department with outside consultants, and you can use their fee structure as a starting point.

If you know of others who are consulting for the company, you may be able to discuss fees with them, but that can be a very delicate decision. You don't want to create problems by stepping on company rules that forbid people from discussing compensation, so tread very carefully in this area.

You can also research fees for your area on the Internet. One good Web site is HotGigs (`www.hotgigs.com`). You can register for free, pick your top-five skills, and get an estimate for hourly fees in the areas you want to work. If you do decide to use the network to find consulting projects, you will need to subscribe. It's $50 to try it out for three months, and $125 for 12 months. HotGigs boosts that it has arranged over $700 million active gigs through its network.

If you belong to a professional association for your specialty area, you can contact the national or regional office for your association. They may collect data on consultant fees for your specialty in the areas of the country you want to work.

Setting your fees

Once you've collected all the data about fees, you can then figure what fee you want to charge. Remember, as a consultant, you will have to pay all your benefits (health insurance, disability insurance, retirement savings, and other benefits you may currently enjoy from working for your company).

Often, benefits add another 35 percent to your actual income. For example, if you earn $30 per hour, your benefits probably cost the company about an additional $10 per hour. You will also need to pay all the costs to set up, equip, and maintain your home office. Administrative costs for a company usually run about 40 percent per employee, so that adds another $12 per hour in costs for the company. In actuality, a person earning $30 per hour is probably costing the company $52.

Many consultants simply set their fees as double or triple their hourly wage. In addition, if you are planning to charge by the hour, be sure to set up a minimum number of hours for you to come to the office. For example, you may want to put in the contract that you bill a minimum of four hours per day. You certainly don't want to be regularly called in for a 30-minute meeting. Because you're working outside the office, that meeting will end up costing you about four hours by the time you get ready, drive to the office, attend the meeting, and return home.

There are other ways to set fees, too:

- ✔ **You can set a daily rate for consulting.** You simply calculate the rate by multiplying eight hours times your hourly rate. If your hourly rate is $50, then your daily rate would be $400.

- ✔ **You can set a rate per project.** You would need to carefully estimate the number of hours you expect to spend on the project and then multiply that number by your hourly rate. But, if you do set a rate per project, be sure you specify in detail what that rate includes. One big benefit of project fees is that you don't have to report your hours. If you can get it done more quickly, you will still be paid the same fee and pocket that difference as additional profit. Remember, the company is paying you for your specialized skills, not the number of hours you work.

- ✔ **You can set fees based on performance.** If you expect a share in future revenue, profits, or commission, then you want to establish a fee based at least partially on the results of your work. You should still have a base fee for the initial work you do plus a percentage based on the performance aspects of the project. For example, if you are going to design a new product launch and then get a share of the profits after implementing the launch, you would set a fee for designing the launch, a fee for your day-to-day involvement in the actual launch, and the percentage of the company's profits.

- ✔ **You can set up a retainer fee.** Some companies want a consultant to guarantee to be available at least a minimum number of hours per month. This can be a common arrangement for former managers and executives. If you can arrange for a retainer fee, you would get paid a set amount per month, no matter how many hours you work, but you would have to be available when called. In the fee agreement, you should specify a number of hours you are guaranteeing each month. If the company requires your services for more than that number of hours in any given month, you should set an hourly fee that you will be paid during for months when more of your time is needed.

However you decide to set your fees, the key is to be sure you are going to make enough money to recover your expenses and earn a profit. You should be sure to spell out very carefully in any written agreement who will pay for what when it comes to expenses such as travel, entertainment (if appropriate for the type of project you'll be working on), copying, long-distance calls, and any other expenses that you incur as part of your work for the company.

Negotiating Contracts

Negotiating contract terms that are a win-win for both you and the company are critical to a successful consulting agreement. Contracts spell out the expectations for both sides. They should include all the necessary detail about the scope of the project, who will be responsible for what aspects of the project, and what the deadlines are for the project.

As a consultant, you likely won't be responsible for every piece of information you will be analyzing. Often there are several people inside the organization that serve on the project team and help you get whatever internal documentation you may need.

If your company regularly hires consultants, it probably has a standard contract form with blanks that must be completed regarding the specifics of the project you'll be hired to do. You also may just write a one- or two-page formal letter of agreement that spells out the details of who will be responsible for what tasks and by what time each of the tasks will be completed. Of course this letter should also include your compensation for the project.

Since you've been working with the same people for many years, contract negotiations should be relatively simple, but you should be sure that everything is in writing before you start any project as a consultant. Too often consultants agree to do a project for a manager or executive they know and then find out as they near completion that they started out the project with two different things in mind. The consultant is then stuck with doing what is needed to satisfy the person who hired him or accept a reduced fee. You can avoid this potential pitfall by carefully spelling out everything up front.

If you or your company wants to develop a more detailed or specific contract, you may want to read the more extensive discussion about contracting in Chapter 17, where I talk about consulting for your former industry rather than your former employee. These types of contracts are usually much more detailed with a lot more clauses.

Confidentiality

You likely already have a confidentiality agreement in place with your company that spells out your limitations with whom you can discuss certain company confidential details. If you plan to continue as a consultant, you should be sure this confidentiality agreement is updated to reflect your new working arrangement with the company.

You may decide that you like consulting and want to actually build a consulting business in retirement. Your agreement with your company will probably have a non-compete and nondisclosure clause that limits your ability to work for a competing firm for at least 90 days and sometimes can be at least a year, if you are working with highly confidential company information.

Whether or not you are planning to do consulting, you are likely to be asked to sign a non-compete and nondisclosure agreement while you are on the job, as well as when you leave the job. You will not be able to compete or work with a competitor of your employer for the time specified in the agreement as an employee, independent contractor, owner, part owner, or investor, depending on what is specified in the agreement.

When companies ask you to sign a non-compete or nondisclosure agreement as part of your severance or retirement package, they usually offer you some benefits in exchange for signing, such as additional pay. If you refuse to sign, the company can actually take you to court to prevent you from working for a competitor or starting your own business.

Whether or not your company's non-compete and nondisclosure agreements are legal and binding depends on the laws in your state or locality. If you do decide to do consulting for a competitor, be sure you understand your company's agreements as well as the state laws governing those agreements.

In some states, these agreements are generally not legal. For example, if your company is based in California, it cannot enforce a non-compete agreement unless the agreement is part of the sale of a business. In California, courts will enforce a non-complete clause only if it involves a business owner who sold his business and agreed not to compete with the new owner as part of the deal. Otherwise, California employees cannot be required to sign anything that would restrict their ability to earn a livelihood.

In many other states, non-compete and nondisclosure agreements are legal. While these states don't want to restrict employees from earning a living, their laws tend to protect companies as long as the agreements are reasonable in scope and necessary to protect the company's business interests. Common restrictions allowed include that you can't work for a competitor for six months or within a 25 or 50 miles radius of the company.

If your job ended because your employer laid you off or encouraged you to voluntarily retire, the non-compete clause may not hold up in court. Courts do tend to side with the employee if the employer terminated the employment and it was not the employee's fault.

Another issue that could come up if you are being challenged on a non-compete clause could be the compensation you received for signing the agreement.

When non-compete clauses lose in court

May Department Stores Company, which runs stores such as Lord & Taylor and Marshall Fields, tried to enforce it's non-compete clause when Victoria's Secret (the lingerie store) hired a top May's executive as its Chief Operating Officer. In this case the judge ruled that these stores were not in "material competition" and the non-compete clause was unenforceable.

At first glance you might think that Victoria's Secret stores do compete directly with some of May's department store brands — both sell millions of dollars of lingerie. But the judge didn't agree that there was "material competition" for the purposes of this agreement and decided that any confidential information about May's department store that the executive knew would not give Victoria's Secret a competitive advantage over May.

May's definition of competing business included "any . . . specialty store or other retail business that sells goods or merchandise of the types sold in May's (or its subsidiaries' or divisions') stores at retail to consumers." The court decided that this definition was too broad and would not enforce the agreement.

For example, if you signed a non-compete agreement that restricted your working for a competitor for six months, and part of that agreement was that you were paid six-months' income as severance, the court will likely consider that reasonable compensation and uphold your company's non-compete clause.

In some cases, employers will ask you to sign a non-compete clause even if it's not enforceable in your state. This can be an intimidation tactic, so be sure to check with an attorney if you signed a non-compete clause and decide later you want to break it. Companies that use this tactic count on the fact that employees don't know the law and, in fear, will abide by the provisions of a non-compete agreement when they leave a job even if they don't have to do so.

You also can contact your state's Department of Labor (http://www.dol.gov/esa/contacts/state_of.htm) if you have any questions about the terms of a non-compete or nondisclosure agreement that you signed. If non-compete agreements are legal in your state, your former employer may have legitimate cause to sue both you and your new employer, especially if your former company warns your new employer and the new company doesn't fire you.

Even if the non-compete agreement is legal and binding, you may still be able to work around it. Using your power of persuasion, you may be able to get your former employer to allow you to break the non-compete agreement. If he says he will, be sure you get that in writing with an effective date and signatures from someone who has the legal right to allow you to break the agreement.

Expenses

Be sure to make a detailed list of all anticipated expenses for your consulting project. Determine what types of expenses you will pay out of pocket (mostly expenses relating to your home office and car) and what expenses you plan to bill to the company.

While you don't what to present an absolute total of what your expenses will be, because things always change once you get started, you should give your company an idea of what you expect those expenses to be. If the company balks at your estimate of expenses, you may need to narrow the scope of the work or negotiate a different arrangement.

It's better to get an agreement about the expected total expenses, as well as how and when they will be paid, before starting the project. For example, if you are planning to have your house painted, the contractor normally will ask you to pay certain expenses at the time you sign the contract so he can buy the paint and other materials needed to do the job. You want to do the same thing for any out-of-pocket costs you may need at the start of the project.

Deadlines

Deadlines must be clearly spelled out in any agreement. Often if you are working on a project that will last longer than a month or two, you likely will have several preliminary deadlines for update reports or meetings, as well as a final deadline for the project.

Don't overcommit and agree to deadlines that you know you can't meet. That's the best way to lose a contract or kill any chance that you will get another project in the future.

Your best bet is to actually promise less than you know you can do and provide even better service than you promised. That's how you keep a client for many years to come.

Things do happen that make it impossible to meet a promised deadline. There can be a family emergency, another project that you took on required more time than you expected, or numerous other reasons. As soon as you know you may miss a deadline, be sure to contact your clients. You usually can salvage a relationship as long as you promptly warn about any delays and set a new schedule that fits the needs of both you and the company.

Getting Paid

Finally, you want to be sure you get paid for your work. You will need to keep records of the hours you worked and be ready to invoice the company either monthly or at previously agreed upon intervals. Your payment intervals should be clearly spelled out in any written agreement or contract.

Activity log

Each time you work on a project, you should keep a daily activity log that specifies the time spent on the project and a brief description of what you did. That way when it comes time to bill the client, you'll have all the detail you need.

If you are billing hourly, it's much harder to try to reconstruct the number of hours you worked at the end of the month than it is if you write it down daily. One good way of keeping track is the calendar section of Microsoft Outlook. You likely already are keeping track of meetings on the calendar, so just start tracking work at home as well.

Invoices

As a consultant, you will need to invoice your time to get paid. Invoices can be rather simple, but you will need to include your name, address, Social Security number (or other federal ID if you have one), telephone number, and project name or number. Your company may specify other information that's needed on the invoice as well.

If you are billing hourly, it's a good idea to include some detail of the type of work you did for each hour or group of hours you are billing. If you're billing by the project, you should develop your invoice based on the agreed upon payment intervals. For example, these could be monthly or they could be based on a percentage of work done, such as 25 percent, 50 percent, and 100 percent.

Chapter 17

Consulting in Your Former Industry

In This Chapter

▶ Testing your skills

▶ Networking

▶ Reviewing legal barriers

▶ Specializing

▶ Pricing

▶ Contracting

▶ Writing proposals

▶ Checking out tips for success

After many years of work in an industry, you've surely made lots of contacts. When you're getting ready to retire, you may decide you'd like to keep your fingers in the pot.

If you do want to start a consulting business after you retire, the good time to start is while you are still working and maintaining regular contacts with your network. This chapter will discuss the key issues in setting up a consulting business.

Being Your Own Boss After Retiring — Try Consulting

If you'd like to earn extra money after retiring, but don't want to be required to show up at a particular location every day, you may want to consider setting up a consulting business. As a consultant, you get to set the hours and pick the projects you'd like to work on. You set up your workspace just the way you like it. You also get to pick the people you want to work with and for.

Anyone who has 20 to 30 years of experience in a particular field can qualify to be a consultant. It's up to you to package and sell yourself as an expert, so other people will want to buy your services. In Chapter 16, I talk about the steps involved in consulting, so I won't repeat them here.

You will find that you take on many different roles as a consultant, such as:

- **Problem-solver:** Helping a company sort out a problem and coming up with a solution.

- **Detective:** Figuring out what the problem is and how it can be corrected.

- **Wise Man:** Reviewing decisions that have already been made and validating them.

- **Counselor:** Helping the company figure out what is getting in the way of success. You almost become a therapist for the business owner.

- **Facilitator:** Helping a company achieve its goal. For example, you could be called to implement a major change if your specialty is change management.

Assessing Your Skills to Be a Consultant in Your Industry

First, you need to determine if you have the technical, project-management, and personal skills to be successful as a consultant. Here is what you need to think about:

- **Technical skills:** You must identify your specialty in a particular technology or function, such as computer programming, Web site design, accounting, management, or tax. Any technical expertise that you possess and you think companies would hire you to provide can fit these criteria.

- **Project-management skills:** You must be good at running projects. Some of the tasks you may need to perform as a consultant include creating the product, negotiating, interviewing, presenting recommendations, problem-identification, problem-solving, time management, client service skills, proposal development, and team-building and management skills.

- **Personal skills:** You must be a very good communicator and be an excellent listener. Your management, collaboration, interpersonal, marketing, promotion, and leadership skills will also be needed to be successful as a consultant.

If you think you may be weak in any of these skills, you'll need to find a partner for your consulting work. All these skills are needed by a consultant at one time or another.

Picking Your Niche

You probably have lots of different experiences that you could develop into a consulting business. It's important to define your consulting business around one or two specialty areas in which you can truly sell yourself as a specialist.

As you review your background, pick out things that you accomplished that you believe are unique or groundbreaking in your industry. You must be careful not to trade confidential company information. Not only could you get sued, but you also will lose a lot of respect and trust among other companies.

Building and Using Your Network

For consulting, your business success depends totally on your ability to network. In Chapter 4, I talked about the basics of building your network. In this chapter, I focus on how to build and use your network to increase your possibility of success as a consultant. If you're not sure of the basics, read Chapter 4 for more details.

Finding contacts for your network

Your initial network will be co-workers and vendors who you worked with regularly during you career. You may be able to get a few projects to get your business going from this group of people, but you'll have to build your network beyond this group to truly develop a successful consulting business.

A good place to find networking contacts in your local area are events run by your local Chamber of Commerce. Make an appointment with a membership representative at your local chamber to talk about the various business groups that operate through the chamber. You likely will find at least one group, if not more, that will serve as a good contact for building your network.

 Another good source for networking is Business Network International (BNI). BNI's entire purpose is to offer its business and professional members the opportunity to share ideas, contacts, and most importantly, referrals. You probably can find a local chapter near you. Visit BNI's Web site (www.bni.com) to locate the nearest chapter and find out more about the organization.

When networking to build a business, it's not enough to just get a bunch of introductions and contact information. You need to really get to know the person and work yourself up to a level where the person will want to recommend you.

Getting to know your contacts

Your first step in getting to know someone is to actually call people whose business cards you collected at a party or other business function. After getting their card, jot down a few notes regarding your conversation on the back of the card as well as ideas for follow-up based on your conversation.

Do this as soon as possible after the conversation so you don't end up with a bunch of cards and have no idea who each person is or what you talked about. I know this can be difficult during a business function, but you likely will forget some key details if you don't try to find a quiet, inconspicuous place periodically during the event to jot down some key points on each card.

Set up a time to meet them for coffee or lunch as soon as you can after the event. When you call for an appointment, remind them of your discussion and entice them to join you with some ideas related to a topic in which they expressed an interest.

When you do meet, if appropriate, volunteer to discuss some tips for how they can handle a problem they mentioned that relates to your business. Don't start pushing for business right away unless the conversation naturally flows in that direction.

Remember, this first meeting is a "get-to-know-you" session, not a sales session. If you come on too strong, you may never get to the next steps, which permit you to build a long-lasting relationship.

Becoming a known entity

As you get to know each other, you may mutually decide you want to get to know each other even better. That's when you can start building a business relationship. People do business with other people with whom they feel comfortable working with. You want to get into your potential client's comfort zone.

As part of this process, do a lot of listening and asking questions. Show you are truly interested in the other person and his business. You'll find out a lot more about the other person and how you might help them by listening rather than talking. As you talk, offer some simple tips or solutions to build up your credibility with your potential client.

When you become a known entity, the person may mention you to someone else, but they won't feel comfortable enough to recommend you. They'll be able to tell others about your expertise and background, but won't put their reputation on the line by encouraging someone else to work with you.

Becoming someone to recommend

When your contact feels comfortable to highly recommend you to others, you've successfully built a strong addition to your network. This is when your contact starts selling you.

You probably won't get to this point until you've actually done one or two projects for your contact, but you may be able to reach this point more quickly by helping them out of a few quick binds and offering tips or advice during a lunch or telephone conversation.

You might be able to get to this point rather quickly with someone who you've worked with over the years either at your former company or at a company with which you did business. Don't forget to keep in contact with those who have known you for years. Be sure to let them know what you're planning to do. They can't help you if they don't know your plans!

Understanding Your Non-Compete Clauses

When you retire, you are likely to be required to sign a non-compete clause that could limit your ability to consult for companies that compete with your former company for 6 and possibly as long as 12 months. If you are asked to sign a non-compete clause, be certain you are getting compensated for signing that clause, especially if you are considering starting your own consulting business.

If you signed the clause already and decided to start a consulting business several weeks or months after you retired, you will have to live with it, but take it to an attorney for review. Each state has its own set of rules about how non-compete clauses can be written. Sometimes companies write clauses that are really not enforceable. I talk more about this problem in Chapter 16.

Pricing Your Services

Pricing yourself is the most difficult task you'll face. You must carefully balance your need to earn a certain amount of money to cover your expenses and make a profit with your ability to stay competitive and not price yourself out of the market.

If you've done a good job of developing your reputation as a specialist, your ability to set your price high is greatly improved. Companies that know you can get the job done based on projects you've already done for them or based on strong recommendations they've gotten from others will be more willing to pay you top dollar.

Networking with others to gather pricing details

Your best way to find out what people charge for similar consulting work is to bring the issue up for discussion at various networking events, such as those mentioned above through your local Chamber of Commerce.

Another good place to network in order to find pricing information is your professional association. You'll likely find others who attend association meetings that also consult for a living for either the same industry in which you plan to work or another industry. They will likely be willing to discuss fee structures, especially if you won't be competing with them for the exact same projects.

Setting your price

You likely will set your price differently with each type of consulting opportunity. In some cases, you may find it best to price a rate per hour, in others you may quote a daily rate. You also may want to set a price for an entire project, regardless of the number of hours you spent working on it. I talk more about setting prices in Chapter 16.

Whatever price you set, you want to be sure you cover all your expenses and time, as well as leave room for some profit. You should also specify carefully what is included in the price and what expenses you will bill for separately. For example, if part of the project involves a significant amount of travel, you should set up your contract to bill those travel expenses separately.

You can also set a monthly retainer fee, once you have developed a strong working relationship with the company. Your retainer fee would guarantee your availability to the company for a certain number of hours per month. If you work more than that set number of hours, you would then include an hourly or daily rate for the time spent working for that company beyond the retainer fee guarantee.

Writing Your Contracts

Once you've picked your niche and established your fee structure, it's time to sit down with an attorney and draft a basic contract. You won't use the exact same contract for all clients, but you will find that there are many basic clauses that can be used with minor adjustments for each consulting job you take.

Remember, the primary purpose of a contract is to protect yourself and the earnings you expect to receive from your clients. While verbal agreements can sometimes hold up in court if someone doesn't pay you, it's very hard to prove what was agreed to verbally. It's best to put everything in writing before you get started.

Finding an attorney

Use the opportunity to build a relationship with an attorney you can call on for emergencies that crop up. You can set up appointments with the attorney periodically to review any problems you've had during the year and possible changes you may need to your standard contract or the way you do business.

Attorneys can help:

- ✔ You decide upon and set up your business structure, which will likely be a sole proprietorship (one owner) or partnership. But if you think you have a great risk of being sued, you may want to consider establishing yourself as a limited liability company or a corporation. As you discuss your business plans with your attorney, he can advise what might be best for you.

- ✔ Advise you on regulations that could affect your business and assist you with filing paperwork for necessary licenses, permits, or registrations. If you plan to work out of your home, you need to be sure that you understand any limitations to doing so depending on homeowner association covenants or local ordinances.

✔ Advise you on what types of business insurance you may need and possibly even refer you to a good agent.

✔ Assist you if you have problems collecting from a client. Sometimes a letter from your lawyer can be enough incentive to pay, avoiding a more costly collection battle.

✔ Advise you on how to avoid possible lawsuits as a consultant and defend you in court if it becomes necessary. Hopefully by working with an attorney long before you face any problems, you'll have the skills and knowledge to minimize any hostilities and avoid a costly lawsuit.

Depending on your type of consulting business, you may find it useful to hire an attorney on retainer, so you have someone to call on in emergencies who knows your business. The best way to find an attorney is through referrals from friends and associates who run their own business. Another good source for recommendations is the local Chamber of Commerce.

Understanding contract parts

How detailed your contract will need to be depends on the type of consulting business you plan to run and the type of clients you'll be working with. You may find that a two- or three-page letter of agreement will suffice, or your attorney may recommend that you work with something more extensive to protect your interests.

While you may not use all these elements, I review the key parts of a contract so you don't forget to include any important ones when you draft your agreements. All contracts will have the names and addresses of the parties involved in the contract. It's also important that the contract be signed and dated. This date can be critical if a dispute crops up later on. Here are the other key parts of a contract.

Writing a short summary of the project

You should start any contact with a brief section that provides some background for the agreement. In this section, you should include a brief description of the parties, their interest in an agreement, and the project that is the subject of the contract.

For example, suppose Mr. ABC is a human resources consultant who assists companies with upgrades to their personnel software. In this scenario, you can say that ABC Consulting, a consulting company owned by Mr. ABC, agrees to provide recommendations regarding the type of human resources software that would be best for XYZ Company, a manufacturing firm in the auto industry. Mr. ABC will review the current system, interview XYZ Company executives and managers, and then make recommendations for the company. If the recommendations are accepted, XYZ will consider a second contract for implementation with details to be worked out at that time.

Defining the promises made

In this section, you would list what each party promises to do as part of the contract. Depending on the project, it could be the amount to be paid and the services to be rendered in exchange for the amount paid.

For example, if part of the project entails selling something, you should lay out specifics of what will be sold, for how much, and by whom. You also should detail who pays what expenses, such as manufacturing, shipping, and so forth.

If the project includes specialist consulting services, you likely will need to include an attachment that details those services. You should also be sure to spell out the expectations of both parties in detail. Not only will this help to define the project and be sure everyone is on board, it will also protect you later if the client is not happy with your work.

While, in the name of good customer service, you should always try to satisfy the client. Sometimes you may decide to do additional work just to make a customer happy, other times you may need to walk away from a situation where your client continues to raise the bar of expectations beyond what you promised. As long as you carefully spelled out expectations up front, you will have the ammunition you need to put your foot down, say no, and expect to get paid.

Specifying a deadline

You should specify the date by which the work must be done, as well as who will get what work done when. Many times both you and your client will need to meet deadlines in order for the project to be completed on time. You want to be sure you have a detailed list of these deadlines and what each party to the contract is required to do to meet these deadlines.

For example, if there are a number of pieces that must be completed before the final analysis can be done, you should set up a work schedule for both parties. This schedule should list all the information needed, who will be responsible for gathering each piece of information, and a date by which the information gathering must be completed.

Any part of the schedule that is critical should include the words, "time is of the essence." If you end up in a dispute later and these words are missing, the judge could decide to give more leeway to the timing and not enforce the deadlines.

You will also want to specify for how long the contract will be in effect. While you can extend any time frame, you do want the ability to renegotiate elements of the contract, such as price, if the time frame exceeds an agreed-upon end date. Everyone's costs of operating increases over time. You need to protect yourself by not setting your fees permanently, but providing for a renegotiation of fees after a set number of months or years.

Establishing your price and how you'll be paid

You definitely must include the price for your services, or if you don't have a set price for the project, you should include the method that will be used to determine your fee. For example, you may specify an hourly or daily rate for the life of the agreement. If your compensation includes pay for specific performance, you need to specify what that pay will be and how performance will be determined.

You also should specify terms for payment, whether you will be paid monthly or according to some set schedule. For example, suppose you agreed to divide the project with a series of due dates for different parts of the project. When you meet the deadline for each part of the project, your contract will specify that you be paid an installment toward the full fee. You should specify when those installments must be paid and what portion of the total contract fee will be paid at each installment.

Terminating the contract

You should always include a clause that spells out how the contract can be terminated and what must be paid if the contract is terminated early. For example, if you've completed half the work and the client decides to kill the project, you want to protect yourself with a termination clause that requires the client to pay some portion of your services. Your client will likely want protection as well from your walking away in the middle of a contract without proper notice.

You may have damages when a client decides to terminate a contract, such as expenses that you incurred as part of the project or time you spent on the project. Your contract should specify damages for terminating a contract and how those damages will be determined. Damages are paid by the person who breaches the contract.

Assigning the work

If you think you would like to hire someone else to do part of the project, you will need a clause that specifies that you have the right to assign the work to a person of your choosing. Your client might not like such a blanket statement and may want the right to interview and refuse to work with a person you are thinking of hiring.

You need to spell out how work can be assigned and if there are any provisions for the company to review your selection. You, of course, want as much freedom to hire others, but the company could object.

As long as your contract specifies that you can assign work, the company can't forbid you from doing so. But, if a dispute about a particular person you hired or a company to whom you subcontracted comes up, you must be willing to work out a compromise to keep the project or risk the possibility that the company will terminate the contract.

Handling disputes

You should lay out how the parties to the contract will handle a dispute situation if one should arise. For example, you may specify that disputes should be handled by arbitration or mediation. Both parties may then be able to avoid a lengthy court battle.

You also want to specify who pays attorney's costs if a dispute arises. For example, you could state that the party who breaches the contract will be responsible for both parties' attorneys' fees and legal costs.

You should also specify where notices of disputes or defaults should be sent and the amount of time each party has to respond to the notices.

Picking state law

If you and your client operate in different states, you should specify in the contract which state's laws will apply if there is a dispute. Laws vary from state to state, so you need to establish the state's laws that will take precedence.

Designing your contracts

You may find that many of the sections in your contracts will be the same with each contract, or only minimal changes will be needed. You could ask your attorney to develop a contract with blanks that can be used to fill in any details that change with each contract.

You may want to do a bit of research to collect contracts that other consultants in your field are using. Trade associations can be a good source for sample contracts. People in your network may also be able to help with this research.

If your company hired consultants frequently, you might want to review some of the contracts and take notes to help you with designing your own contract.

Writing Proposals

You will find yourself writing proposals frequently, but before you even start writing, be sure you understand the scope of the project and what it is your client really wants to achieve. Consultants usually are called in when there is a major problem and no one inside the company knows how to fix it.

Even if you are writing your proposal based on a formal request for proposal, set up an appointment with the person in charge of the proposal process or someone that person designates. Carefully review the request for proposal and prepare some incisive questions about the project before the appointment. At the appointment, gather as much information as you can about the company's expectations. The more you know, the stronger your proposal will be. This meeting also will give you an opportunity to establish rapport with one of the decisions makers.

You should always start your written response to a request for proposal with a brief summary of what the client wants. Then include one or two sentences that state something that will get the client's attention and make him eager to read the rest of your proposal.

Follow carefully the guidelines laid out in the request for proposals. If you don't, you could just be knocked out of the game for not following directions. Companies design these instructions based on how they want to select possible candidates. If they have to do too much work to figure out your response to their request for proposals, you could get you knocked out of the running as well.

You'll usually find that companies give you a list of specific tasks that they want done as part of the project and what must be accomplished with each task. When you design your response, be sure to use these tasks as heads for each section of your response. Make it as easy for them to find the information as possible.

Companies will also ask you for your relevant experience and expertise, which you should be able to provide in a brief paragraph or two in most instances for a short proposal. If you become one of the final candidates, you will likely then be asked for a more detailed discussion of your expertise and experience.

You'll also be asked to specify your fees. You probably don't want to specify your fees too early in the process, but you could come up with some line that gives a range of fees depending on what is needed. This gives you a lot of negotiating room at the time of final contract.

Setting Up a Successful Consulting Business

Your consulting business will only be successful if you start out by defining what you want to do and how you want to do it. If you're serious about wanting to have a consulting business, don't start looking for clients while developing the business on the fly. You should develop a business plan, and figure out who you want in your network and how you'll use your network to get business.

Developing a business plan

You probably have written or been involved in the development of business plans for your former employer. You should make the same effort to develop a business strategy for your own company.

You must figure out your business mission and goals to know where you'd like it to go and how you want to sell yourself. You must determine your business's niche and what knowledge and expertise makes you the expert in that field.

Once you've defined your business and how you want to sell yourself, then you need to decide what your ideal client might look like and how you would recognize one when you see him.

Finally, you have to figure out what you might use to attract your ideal client to do business with you. Now you're ready to begin building your network for your consulting business.

Networking effectively

Start building your network by identifying the types of business or social groups where you are most likely to find your ideal client. Former co-workers and vendors who fit the profile should be the first ones you contact to let them know your plans. They can become the core of your new business network and possibly lead you to some other good prospects.

As you start making the rounds to network at the various business and social groups on your list, practice becoming a good listener. You've probably been to a lot of these types of functions before and couldn't stand the people who were always looking for business that talked incessantly about themselves. You know how bored you were and couldn't wait to get away from them. Don't become them!

Instead, learn to listen and ask astute questions. Develop a few good one-liners to pique people's interest about you and your business, but always try to find a way to switch the conversation back to the other person by asking a question to show interest in your potential client.

By asking thought-provoking questions, you can get your potential client looking at his business in a different way. As you talk, you can share a tip that helped you solve a similar problem he is now facing or tell him about a resource where he might be able to save money or time.

People don't pick people to do business with because they understand what it is you do. Instead, they pick people who they believe understand what they do. When they decide to hire you as a consultant, it's because they've become convinced that you understand their problem and you can find a solution.

Be careful not to try to sell yourself or your business too early in any conversation. People who are perceived as pushy, seeking business or referrals too early in the conversation, can be seen as rude. People will just find an excuse to get away from you as quickly as possible.

Instead, use these initial contacts to make new friends. Connect with people who you think share similar interests and get their contact information. Then call them to meet for lunch or a drink where you can begin the process of developing a long-term business relationship.

Following-up regularly

When you get back to your office, review the business cards you collected at the networking event. Prioritize the cards into an order in which you will make follow-up contacts with each potential client.

People with whom you believe you had a strong connection, and you think may have an immediate need for your expertise, should be among the first that you contact for follow-up. Call and set up a lunch date as soon as possible and start the process of getting to know them better.

You should follow-up as soon as you can after a networking event with all the people you met that you'd like in your network, even if you don't believe they will have any business for you anytime soon. You want to at least have one "get to know you" conversation while the initial meeting is still fresh in your mind, as well as in the mind of the person you'd like to add to your network.

Don't always be on the hunt for new business. When doing follow-up, be on the hunt to learn more about your network participants. As you develop your credibility, your services will be sought. Always be on the alert for information that may help you identify a business opportunity, but be certain the timing is right to make the pitch for your services.

Offer your network members suggestions that will help them solve minor problems. As they find your ideas beneficial, they will seek you out for solutions to major problems. That's when you can start to sell your consulting services.

Chapter 18

Buying or Starting Your Own Business or Franchise

- -

In This Chapter

▶ Building your own business

▶ Buying an existing business

▶ Franchising

- -

Some people are using their retirement as a time to start the business they dreamed about all their working life. Others decide they don't want all the work of starting a business from scratch, so they look for an existing business that matches their dream.

Another option you can consider if you want your own business is franchising. You may find this an attractive way to start a business, especially if you would like the support of a national brand.

In this chapter, I review the pros and cons of these three options, as well explain the basics you need to get started in each.

Starting Your Own Business

Many people dream about being their own boss and running their own business. Some people retire from their company so they can roll out their employer-based retirement savings and use some of that money to fund the start-up of their dream. Others find they just don't have enough money in retirement and start a small business to supplement their income rather than go back to work for someone else.

You can start the business with two different goals — to build a going concern (a company that has the resources to continue to operate — in other words, a company that's not bankrupt!) and fully fund your retirement or just to supplement a decent retirement income.

Supplementing your retirement

If you're just looking to supplement a decent retirement income, you should consider a start-up business that doesn't require a huge upfront investment. That way you won't put any of your retirement savings at risk.

In the active-adult community in which I live, many of the retirees started their businesses based on a hobby from which they found a way to make a profit. For example, some folks who enjoy painting started a paint contracting business. Woodworkers do small carpentry jobs for their neighbors. Many quickly find they have more work than they really want.

Carolyn-E's Dry Cleaning Valet Service

Dick and Carolyn Bernstein found that rising healthcare costs were eroding their retirement plans. Dick retired from Honeywell with a decent retirement, and Carolyn retired from real estate. They toyed with a number of business ideas before starting their dry cleaning valet service.

The idea grew out of total frustration with the one dry cleaner in the neighborhood who overcharged for poor-quality service. They searched the Orlando area for a good dry cleaner and finally found one with decent pricing about 27 miles away. This gave them the idea for what is now their new business: Carolyn-E's Dry Cleaning Valet Service. They worked out a deal with the dry cleaner in Orlando who gave them enough profit to pick up and deliver dry cleaning from their neighbors.

Their first advertising did get them a few customers, but ticked off a bunch of neighbors. They put hangers on people's doors with the company name. It was windy and the hangers blew everywhere. While the first marketing idea did cause some problems, it also got them their first few customers and their business has blossomed from there, doubling in size month after month.

They've expanded this business by finding some commercial accounts, where they stop by area businesses and pick up dry cleaning from individuals at those businesses. Business people especially like the idea of someone who can pick up and deliver dry cleaning so they don't have to run out themselves. They've found great success approaching car dealerships and real estate companies.

Dick was not new to starting and running a business. He was involved in his family business when he was younger and started several other businesses before beginning what turned out to be a 23-year stint with Honeywell.

Dick drew up a brief five-year business plan for himself for his current business. He's on target with his initial projections. He didn't need to write an extensive plan to take to banks for funding because the start-up costs were so cheap.

The biggest drain on the business's profits were rising gas prices, which put his profits at risk during much of the first year in 2006 when gas prices hit more than $3 a gallon. He almost had to increase prices, but knew that could result in lost customers, which can really hurt a business that just started. The only major purchase they made was a new vehicle that would be better for this type of business than the one they had.

Dick's day starts with a round of golf, while Carolyn handles calls for pickups. She gives him a list of stops when he gets back from golf. He makes his pickups, delivers the clothes to the dry cleaner in Orlando, and picks up whatever is completed from the day before. He then delivers the clean clothes and often picks up the next batch for cleaning at the same time. It's a simple business to run and one that can easily be done from home and still give Dick and Carolyn time to enjoy their retirement. In addition to handling the business calls, Carolyn helps with the pickups and deliveries in the community.

In addition to starting his dry cleaning business, Dick also serves as a consultant for other small businesses in the area to earn some additional money.

Others who retired from a family business, and passed their old business on to their kids, start something smaller that they promote just within their neighborhood. For example, one person who owned a construction business started a new home inspection business. Another person who owned a large hair salon, opened a small business doing neighbors' hair in her home. Still others found a service missing in the community and started their own small business to fill the need.

A common thread in all the businesses is that they all retired and wanted to make some extra cash, but didn't want to put in the hours they had when they worked or ran their business full-time. They don't have to depend on their business to live because they do have retirement income, but they want to supplement that income. Starting from that perspective, one doesn't have to plan a massive marketing effort. In fact, word-of-mouth is what has worked the best for all of them.

You can get some good ideas about how to start and run a business through the Small Business Administration (SBA; www.sba.org). I talk more about what's available in the next section. In the "Getting started — developing a business plan" section, I talk about how to develop a business plan and get your business off the ground.

Funding your retirement

If you need your business to fund your retirement, you essentially should expect to work more than full-time and earn very little for the first few years. That's when a sizeable rollover of your employer-based retirement savings can help to fund your personal needs through the early years of the business. If you do choose this route, you will be taking a great risk that you could run out of money during retirement if the business does not succeed, so tread carefully and seek help to determine if your plans are solid.

Luckily, there's a lot of free help available for you, so don't try to go it alone. Here are some of the best resources you can count on if you do want to start a small business.

Free courses

The Small Business Administration offers an extensive array of free courses for small-business owners. You'll find courses about how to get started, business management, financing, marketing and advertising, business planning tools, government contracting, risk management and cyber security, e-commerce, and taxation.

You can find them at http://www.sba.gov/training/. You'll also find links to national training events, an extensive online business library, and online university and college business courses.

Service Corps of Retired Executives (SCORE)

SCORE (www.score.org) enables retired executives to offer their volunteer services to business owners. You can get help developing your business plan and finding funding for it. In Chapter 20, I give you more details about SCORE and how it works.

Small Business Development Centers (SBDCs)

The SBA administers the Small Business Development Center program as a cooperative effort among the private sector, the educational community, and federal, state, and local governments. By working with an SBDC, you can get needed management and technical assistance.

There are 63 lead SBDCs in the country with at least one in every state, the District of Columbia, Guam, Puerto Rico, Samoa, and the U.S. Virgin islands. These lead SBDCs support a network of more than 1,100 service locations that can be located at colleges, universities, community colleges, vocational schools, chambers of commerce, and economic development corporations.

You can get SBDC assistance that is tailored to your needs as a small-business person. Each center develops services in cooperation with the local SBA district offices to ensure statewide coordination with other available resources. You can find the SBDC service location closest to you at www.sba.gov/sbdc/.

Each center has a director, staff members, volunteers, and part-time personnel. Qualified individuals recruited from professional and trade associations, the legal and banking community, academia, chambers of commerce, and SCORE (the Service Corps of Retired Executives) are among those who donate their services. SBDCs also use paid consultants, consulting engineers, and testing laboratories from the private sector to help clients who need specialized expertise.

Women's Business Centers (WBCs)

If you're a woman and want to start your own business, the SBC also provides a network of 80 educational centers designed to assist women start and grow small businesses. WBCs operate to level the playing field for women entrepreneurs who still face unique obstacles in the world of business. To find out more about their services, go to http://www.onlinewbc.gov/wbc.pdf.

Getting started — developing a business plan

Before you even think about asking for help, you must be able to answer these two questions: "What do I want to sell?" and "Why should people want to buy it from me?" If you have a business dream in mind, you'll probably find it easy to answer the first question, "What do I want to sell?", but you may find it much harder to answer the second question, "Why should people want to buy it from me?"

As you try to answer that second question, make a list of your unique skills and services you might offer in conjunction with the product you want to sell to make your product or service stand out in people's minds. For example, Dick and Carolyn Bernstein, featured in the sidebar about their dry-cleaning valet service, added the pickup and delivery features to make their business unique. Not only did it minimize their start-up costs because the business could be run completely out of the home without having the costs of setting up a retail store, but they also offered something rather unique in dry cleaning in the area — pickup and delivery.

It's that type of innovate planning that can help your business take off. You may hate the idea of writing a business plan, but if you do take the time, it will help you think through what you want to do and improve the success of your business.

You should think about these key points as you develop your business plan:

✔ **Detail your proposed business idea and why you think this business makes sense given the current market conditions.** Don't only think about your great idea as you sort this out. Be sure to look at the competition you'll face, as well as the state of the economy.

✔ **Sort out your start-up finances.** Be sure you estimate how much money you'll need to get your business started and operate it during the first year. You certainly don't want to get started with a great idea just to find out six months down the road you can't afford to keep it going.

✔ **Figure out when you think you can recover your initial investment and when you think the business will show a reasonable profit.** You need to estimate initial sales and project sales growth, then subtract any expenses you expect for running the business, including buying your products, marketing and advertising, and administrative expenses.

✔ **Develop a list of challenges you expect to face as you start your business.** Then figure out a plan for how you will overcome the challenges and make your business a success.

If you've never developed a business plan before, I highly recommend that you take the online business-planning course at `www.sba.gov/ starting_business/startup/guide.html`. Click on "Online Business Planning Course" in the "Supporting Resources" section.

Marketing your business

As part of the initial planning phase, you should determine how you will market your business. Start by doing a market and industry analysis. This should include the following:

✔ **Describe the market for your product or service.** You should detail all the research you did regarding the size of your market, the number of potential customers for your product or service, and your projected growth rates for your business, as well as the industry in which in plan to operate.

✔ **Take an overview of your competition.** You must determine what companies currently offer products or services similar to what you offer. Remember, the customer seeks a product to solve a problem. Think about the problem you'll be solving and then think about the products or services that may solve that same problem in a different way.

For example, people want to communicate with their friends and family. They can do that using lots of different means: telephones, e-mails, Internet phone service, or cellphones. So even if you plan to sell Internet phone service and you think this is a new and innovative field, you must remember that the customer won't only be looking at your Internet phone service versus other Internet phones services, he also will be looking at other ways to do what he wants — talk to his family and friends.

So don't limit your review of competition too narrowly. Think of it from what you are providing that the customer wants and all the ways the customer may be able to satisfy that desire.

✔ **Learn from your competition.** As you collect information about your competition, take the time to look at what they are doing right and what they are doing wrong in marketing their product. You can pick up the good ideas and improve on the bad ones as you develop your own marketing plans.

But, be sure you don't overstep your bounds and infringe on trademarks or copyrights. You could be stuck with large legal bills defending yourself if you use something you shouldn't. For example, you can copy add-on services a similar company offers, but you can't use their marketing logo (or trademark) and you can't copy their advertising designs.

Funding your business

After you've collected all the information you need to detail your product or service and what it will cost to offer it, assess your competition, project your potential sales, and design your marketing plans (see the earlier sections, "Getting started — developing a business plan" and "Marketing your business," for more information on these topics), you'll be ready to put together some numbers to figure out how much money you need to get started. Use this information to develop a budget for the first year and project a five-year budget.

Your budget should be as truthful as you can make it, but it doesn't have to be carved in stone. Even well-established companies draw up budgets each year and might need to make adjustments during the year if market conditions change.

The primary purpose of this initial budgeting process is to give you an opportunity to figure out all the details of how your business will operate and how much money you'll need during the first year. You need to take a stab at analyzing your cash flow and where it will come from in order to have any chance of success. Many businesses fail in the first two years because they failed to accurately project their cash flow needs and ran out of money. In fact, it's the second most common reason for failure. The number one reason is poor management.

Avoiding trademark trouble

A classic example of a major corporation getting in trouble and spending millions of dollars is the ongoing battles between the Beatles's recording company, Apple Corps Ltd., and Apple Computer. When Apple Computer decided on its name and icon, they settled a dispute with Beatles by signing an agreement in 1977 detailing how Apple Computer could use the name.

In 1990, Apple Corps filed suit because it said Apple Computer had breached its agreement when it started offering the iPod and called it AppleMusic. The Beatles won that suit and Apple Computer had to pay Apple Corps $26 million to settle the claim. The battle started again when Apple Computer introduced iTunes.

Without the money you need to market and sell your product, as well as pay any staff or consultants you might need to hire, your business will need to cut back, likely causing its demise. You can't sell a product or service without marketing it. Yet many businesses in trouble start cutbacks by skimping on marketing. In the section on funding a franchise below, you'll see that the franchisor recommends that marketing and advertising get the lion's share of funds available for a home-based business in the first year.

If you do plan to start from home, your start-up costs will be much less than if you have to pay the lease for retail or other commercial space. If you can start the business with your spouse as your partner and put off hiring staff until your business starts earning enough money, you can reduce your funding needs.

If you do need to raise funds from others to get your business started, you can find other possible sources to tap — just check out the sections that follow.

Personal savings

While you might have a sizeable retirement nest egg that you can use, be certain you're not putting your entire retirement savings at risk on one business idea. Remember the adage you heard from a very young age — "Don't put all your eggs in one basket."

Starting a new business is a high-risk venture. Retirement is not the time to invest all your savings in something with such high risks. Rather than take out your retirement funds, you may want to consider a small personal loan through your bank. Some people start businesses using credit cards, but beware they have the highest interest rates, making it even more difficult to fund your business long-term as interest eats up any profits.

Friends and families

You may be able to tap family members or friends for cash as early investors. If you do know someone interested, you may be able to get money interest free or at a very low interest rate.

Banks and credit unions

You will need a well-thought-out business plan to have a chance at getting a loan through a bank or credit union. Your best bet is to work on getting a Small Business Administration loan through a participating bank, but be prepared for a complex and long application process. You can find out more about SBA financing at `www.sba.gov/starting_business/financing/applyloan.html`.

Venture capital firms

This source of funds is primarily for businesses that have already proved successful and are looking for an investor to expand and get to the next level of operations.

Deciding your business location

A key decision in all of this is whether you plan to start your business at home or in commercial office or retail space. That decision will drive your budget and your method of operations. While working from home is by far the cheapest way to go, it might not make sense if you're thinking of starting a retail business.

Many communities have limitations on what type of business you can run from your home. Most limit traffic into and out of the home for business purposes. So, if your business requires frequent visits from your customers, you should definitely check on the rules for running a business out of your home before you get started.

Buying an Existing Business

Starting a small business from home to supplement your income might be a great idea for retirees, but if you truly need an immediate cash flow from your business to pay your mortgage and other major bills, you're probably better off buying a business that is already successful. Building a business that will provide significant cash flows can take 10 to 15 years or more, so you can't really count on a business for cash flow to meet significant personal needs in the early years of operation.

Buying a going concern (a company that has the resources to continue to operate) that already proved it can make money and provide you with a good cash flow is a much better bet for many retirees who need almost the equivalent of their previous full-time income. By buying a business, you can also reduce the start-up costs of time, money, and energy.

Your cash flow from the business can start immediately because you'll have inventory and receivables (money due from customers). You also can count on an existing customer base and an easier time raising capital, because you'll have a proven cash flow from the business.

But remember, buying an existing business will require an initial investment that is much greater than starting a business from scratch. While it's great to have all the business basics in place — cash flow, customers, and inventory — you do have to pay for it all.

Deciding what type of business to buy

Your first step is to decide what type of business you want to buy. Don't look at something you don't enjoy doing. For example, you could find out about a great deal on a bakery, but if you don't know anything about baking or running a bakery, it's not the right choice for you.

Tropics

Howie and Sandy Brecher looked at starting a business from scratch and buying an existing small business after Howie was downsized as a top executive in a chemical manufacturing firm in his early 50s. They quickly ruled out starting a business from scratch because they knew it would take too long to generate a decent cash flow.

At first Howie thought he would buy a chemical manufacturing firm, a field he'd worked in for his entire career, but as he evaluated the businesses on the market, he found major problems facing all of them. So he started considering other options.

While he did work with a business broker, he ended up hearing about the business they now own from a friend — retail stores on the Jersey shore called Tropics and Coconuts. When they bought the business, the operation included three stores, and this year they decided to open a fourth that offers plus sizes called Tropics Too.

The stores sell primarily high-end beach fashions with near-exclusive rights to a top brand, Fresh Produce Sportswear. Their stores carry the comprehensive inventory of this popular line, so they attract customers from all around New

Jersey and the Philadelphia area. They do carry other products from a total of about 60 vendors.

Howie didn't know much about fashion or running a retail operation, but Sandy did. Sandy takes responsibility for making the fashion buying decisions and hiring the staff, while Howie manages the finances. They formed a good partnership with each contributing unique skills, and continue to build a successful business.

Howie said the most important thing to do when buying a business is careful due diligence. You need to do a lot more than just look at the numbers on a piece of paper. He said it's important to go into the operation and observe what goes on. As long as you know enough about the type of business, you should be able to observe sales and determine if the numbers make sense.

You also must understand the demographics for the business and whether you believe those demographics will continue to work in favor of maintaining an ongoing business. For example, Sandy grew up in Jersey and knew the economics of the Jersey shore. She was able to quickly determine that the market was a good one and would likely be so for a long time to come.

You best bet is to buy a business related to the field you've in worked before. Or you could consider buying a business related to your favorite hobby or some other passion. In fact, if you've been working for a small business and you know it's doing well, you might find out if that business is for sale. Owners will rarely let employees know that a business is on the market, so it can't hurt to ask.

Finding businesses for sale

Occasionally you'll see a sign posted on a small business indicating it's for sale, but more often than not you'll never know that a business you walk into every day is for sale. The following sections detail the number of ways to find businesses that are for sale.

Newspaper ads

You can check your local business newspapers for a listing of businesses for sale, but don't count on this as your primary source for finding opportunities. Very few businesses will advertise publicly that they are for sale.

Business professionals

You should check with bankers, lawyers, accountants, insurance agents, and real estate brokers that you know for possible opportunities. They are usually the first to hear that a business may be on the market. If you don't know anyone in this network of professionals, call friends who you think may be connected.

Business suppliers

Another good network you can tap is suppliers for the type of business you'd like to buy. They often know who might be thinking of selling their business. For example, if you'd like to own a small hardware store, check with suppliers that sell tools and other items sold in hardware stores.

Trade associations

Most businesses have a trade association related to their type of business. For example, if you want to buy a bookstore, find out if there is a local booksellers' association. Often employees of the association will be aware if one of their members wants to sell.

Actual owner

You can always approach an owner of a business you frequent and ask if they are thinking of selling. You never know if a person is thinking of retiring or moving and just hasn't taken any action yet. Yes, it's probably a long shot, but it could be your best bet.

Business brokers

Business brokers should be your last resort. These are people who earn commissions from the business owners who want to sell their businesses. They represent the interests of the person selling a business because that's who pays them. They only make money when they successfully sell that business, so you can't depend on them for quality advice.

If you do find a business through a business broker, don't depend on them to help you through the process of due diligence, which is when you scour the business and its financial statements to determine if it's a good buy. Instead, hire your own accountant and attorney to look over the deal.

You also may want to hire a business appraiser who can value the business for you. You can find out more about business value appraisers and what they offer you at the Web site of the American Society of Appraisers (www. bvappraisers.org/).

Assessing the value of a business

Trying to set the value of a going concern (a company that has the resources to continue to operate) can be very difficult. While setting a cash value to things you can touch — inventory, store fixtures, equipment, and other tangible assets — can be relatively simple, it's much harder to put a value on intangible things (things you can't touch), such as customer base and location.

As the new owner, you do have a customer base from which to build your business, but remember, most small businesses are a success because of the owner — his relationship to customers, his vision, his management skills, and his other unique talents. This can be very difficult to duplicate.

Many times when a business changes hands, old customers disappear. Your best bet is to put into the contract for buying the business that the selling owner must be involved with the business during your first year of operation. You should clearly spell out their specifics of that involvement. That's not unusual, and many small-business owners see their business as their child and want it to continue to succeed even after they are gone.

Whatever you agree to with the owner, be certain that your business purchase contract clearly states that the prior owner and management agree not to start or buy a competing business for five years or more. This non-compete clause of the contract can be by geographical area or business type depending on the type of business, but the last thing you need is to buy a business and find out that you're losing customers to the old owner or his managers. You may want to set up a consulting agreement with the prior owner and/or some of his key managers to best protect your interests and your business's future.

Sandy and Howie Brecher found just such an owner, who actually worked side-by-side with them during their first year of operation. The owner ran a similar business on the Florida coast under the same name, so he wanted to be sure they did succeed and do well. In fact, they've remained friends with the former owner and still discuss business issues even though they bought the business four years ago.

When you're trying to evaluate the health of the business you're thinking of buying, as well as its future potential, you should ask to see certain records, which I discuss in the following sections.

Profit and loss statements and balance sheets for the past five years

Few small businesses actually do these consistently, and the business owner may need to generate them for you based on historical financial records. It can sometimes take a long time to get these numbers.

When you do get them, don't just read them and accept them. You need to do your due diligence, observe the business operations and determine if you think the numbers are realistic based on what you are seeing. For example, if the owner indicates that he has a $100,000 sales volume per month, but you can't figure out how based on the number of sales you see in a day, ask a lot of questions.

Tax returns for the past five years

Find out what the owner has actually reported to the IRS and how that compares to the financial statements he's showing you. While it's not surprising if the owner shows you profit figures that are much higher than what he reports to the IRS, be sure you understand how he got to those lower profit figures he reported to the IRS. You may find that what he reports to the IRS is actually more truthful than what he gave you in financial statements as you dig into the figures.

Loan documents if you expect to assume any loans

Be sure you understand the terms and what your repayment obligations will be. If you think you can lower the interest rates by getting a larger loan from the Small Business Administration, you may want to add that to your loan application.

Leases and/or building ownership

Be certain to review any lease agreements or ownership documents to find out what your obligations and rights will be under those leases or deeds. For example, you may find the lease runs out in two years on the store location. If that location is important to you and the success of maintaining the business, that could be risky.

You may want to find out if you can extend that lease prior to signing the deal. When you open discussions with the property owner, you may find out he intends to increase the monthly rent obligation beyond what you consider feasible to keep the business financially viable. That could mean you'd have to move the business soon after buying it, which can be the kiss of death to any business.

If you don't like the location of some of the retail stores, but do like the business operation, it's extremely important to find out the terms of the lease and how long you must hold any lousy locations. A bigger problem can sometimes be a lease that gives the landlord approval over you as the purchaser. They may have someone else in mind (maybe a son-in-law) and will disapprove of the purchase. Or the property owner may be looking for some type of payment or renegotiation of the lease as the quid pro quo for agreeing to transfer it to a new business owner. The best leases are those where the landlord cannot do much to impede the sale, as long as he has been given notice and your financials and business plan are not much different from what currently exists.

If any of these problems exist, the location, which may have looked great to you, actually may have little value.

Patents, trademarks, copyrights, and licenses

These intangible assets can be very important to the exclusivity of the business you are thinking of buying. Find out if the owner intends to sign these rights over to you. Also find out if any of them are running out soon.

For example, you may find that you are buying a business that owns a patent for its key product, which protects it from competition. This patent can be very valuable and make the business more expensive to buy. It likely also is critical to the business's continued success.

But, as you do your due diligence, you may find out that the patent runs out in a year or two and you could lose your exclusive rights to the product. That makes the patent almost worthless. You'll likely see aggressive competition for your business fairly quickly.

You also want to be sure that you have the rights to the continuing use of any trademarks or product names that are unique to the business. You should have your attorney do a search for any conflicting trademarks or names and find out what has been registered. You certainly don't want to buy a store because of its name just to find out you have to change it in the future. You also want to protect yourself from the owner using the name you just bought to open a competing business.

Licenses owned by the business can be critical to its future success as well. For example, if you're buying a restaurant with a liquor license, you want to be sure that license is transferable. It can take months to get a liquor license. If your customers are used to ordering liquor with their meals and all of a sudden can't, you could lose a lot of customers quickly. You need to plan for that and figure the loss in any price you offer for the business.

Legal problems

Ask to see information about any pending legal actions against the business. This can include lawsuits that have been filed, administrative proceedings pending with governmental agencies, or claims that have been filed against the business.

Have your attorney review the information and figure out your potential liability. Be sure your purchase contract clearly spells out who will be responsible for what regarding any pending legal actions.

Accounting reports

Ask to see all reports from the business's accountant. There are three types of reports that a Certified Public Accountant can provide — compilation, reviews, and audits. Here is what each involves:

- ✔ **Compiled:** Compilation reports are merely an organized look at the business's finances with a professional presentation of the balance sheet, income statement, and other financial reports. The accountant has not reviewed or audited the owner's figures.

- ✔ **Reviewed:** The accountant takes a compilation one step further by questioning the employees and the owner about the numbers. While he hasn't done a full audit, he can certify that he or she is not aware of any material modifications that are necessary for the information to conform to generally accepted accounting principles.

- ✔ **Audited:** For these types of financial statements, the accountant actually examines the numbers by going to the business and verifying the accuracy of the numbers himself. While an auditor will not actually open every record or individually count the inventory, he will do a series of tests on parts of the financial records to be sure they are accurate. For example, he may review 10 to 20 percent of the customer records to see if they accurately reflect the numbers presented in accounts receivable. If he doesn't find any problems with his tests, he will sign a statement saying that the financial statements are accurate and do conform to generally accepted accounting principles.

While there is no doubt that audited financial statements are your best bet, few small businesses actually pay for them to do done.

In addition to the financial statements, you should also ask to see a list of all assets and a schedule of depreciation for those assets. Depreciation schedules can give you a good idea of the age of the assets and how long they may still be useful to the business. For example, if you find that most of the assets are almost fully depreciated, it's likely that you will be spending a lot of money on replacing those assets or repairing them. If assets are primarily new with a lot of value left after depreciation, your repair and replacement costs will be significantly lower.

Title and title insurance

If the business owns any property, be sure to review the title and title insurance policy. Have your attorney recheck the title for any encumbrances, such as a lien against the title for past unpaid vendor bills. You also want to check any ownership documents for vehicles or other major equipment owned by the company that is being transferred to the new owner. Liens can also be taken against major assets, so you want to be sure your attorney checks for liens against vehicles or major equipment.

Workers' compensation and unemployment claims

You should check with the workers' compensation insurance carrier to find out the claims history for the company and its current insurance rates. If many claims have been filed, this could indicate a major problem with the business, and it also means your future insurance rates could go up dramatically.

The same is true about unemployment claims. If the business owner frequently laid people off and has a significant claims history with the state unemployment office, you will find your payroll taxes will be higher than other similar businesses, which can be a drain on future profits.

Employee benefits

You should review the benefits currently being offered to employees because you likely will have a morale problem if you decide to cut those benefits as a means of improving your profit margin. If part of your plan to improve the profitability of the business is to cut salaries or benefits, you can expect to have some very unhappy employees who will likely leave.

Trade secrets

You may not find that the business you are buying has many trade secrets, but these secrets can be valuable assets, so be sure you protect them in your contract to buy the business. For example, the most valuable trade secret for any business is its customer lists. Be sure you know who has copies of these lists and that they are protected by confidentiality agreements.

Zoning

Your lawyer should check on any special zoning arrangements that might be in place. For example, you could find out that the store is operating under a temporary zoning variance or conditional use permit. This could mean that you will be severely limited on what you can do on the property. You may have some great ideas on how to expand the business or attract new customers, but your conditional use permit may not allow you to do what is planned.

You also could find that the special zoning rights given the current owner will not transfer to the new owner. For example, the current owner may have been granted a temporary zoning variance to continue operating a business that no longer fits the current zoning codes. Those temporary rights could be lost when the business changes hands.

Toxic waste

If the business you are buying involves the disposal of toxic wastes, review the records detailing how toxic waste has been handled in the past. You certainly don't want to be stuck with the costs of cleaning up someone else's negligence. For example, if you buy a car repair shop, you want to know how its owner handled the disposal of fluids taken out of cars.

Talking with the neighbors and customers

While all the legal and financial information you have gathered is very important, don't forget to talk with the company's neighbors, vendors, employees, and customers. You can get a good feel for how respected the business is and how well it treats its customers.

A business that has a good reputation with its customers and neighboring businesses will have a much better chance of success than one that does not have a good reputation. While posting signs indicating the business has changed hands may help, you are starting in a deficit position if the reputation is bad.

Listen carefully for subtle clues. Many times when you talk with suppliers, former employees, and others who have good inside information, you will find that they are reluctant to talk for fear of reprisal. You probably won't get a straight answer if there are problems, but you might be able to tell by the tone of a person's voice or by a clear sign of evasiveness that there is a problem.

Intending to buy, but . . .

If you get to the point that you've decided yes this is the business for me, but you do want to take time to investigate certain areas more deeply, such as financial issues or legal issues, then you can sign a "Letter of Intent to Purchase." This will buy you some time to investigate further while securing your rights to buy. That will give you some additional time to involve other professionals you trust, such as your lawyer, accountant, or business advisor.

You will need to give the seller an earnest money deposit to show the seriousness of your intent, but since final purchase details have not been worked out, you should have the right to a full refund.

When you do get to the point of actually offering a sales agreement to buy the business, this will be the key document that protects your rights. You will likely go through several drafts of the agreement with each draft being reviewed by your attorney and the seller's attorney.

Don't get impatient with what might seem like a long time to get it right. While you may be excited that you finally found just the right business, you don't want to rush this most crucial step and end up with problems later.

Funding the purchase of a business

As mentioned above, buying an existing business will be a lot more expensive than starting one from scratch, but the existing cash flow of a going concern can be worth the difference. In the section on funding a business in "Starting Your Own Business" above, I review the options for funding a business.

While the same options exist for buying a business, you'll likely find the best option is a loan guaranteed by the Small Business Administration. You can get an idea of the types of loans possible at the SBA Web site (www.sba.gov/financing/sbaloan/snapshot.html). Be prepared for a lot of paperwork.

Howie Brecher said his final application for an SBA loan was 100 pages long including his business plan. He needed to submit 12 copies of the application, which also included pictures, maps, and three five-year scenarios for the business, one that outlined his expectations, one that outlined a five-year plan if everything went wrong with the economy and how the business would survive, and one that indicated what would happen if everything went great. He also needed to develop an exit strategy.

Finding a Franchise

When you buy a franchise, it's like buying a business in a box. You get all the basics of how to set up your business and how to sell the product. The information you get is based on lessons learned while the franchisor developed and ran his own business.

Franchises can be a great alternative to starting your own business, especially if you don't have a lot of business or management experience, but don't expect to make much money in the first few years while you build your business, and do expect to work long hours. Well-known franchises will help you attract customers, but buying a franchise is more like starting a new business than buying an existing business.

What is franchising?

When you buy a franchise, you're actually buying a business relationship between yourself and the company that distributes a product or service nationwide. You actually buy a limited license from the company for the right to sell or distribute the product or service within a given area.

You will find that there are two types of franchises:

- **Product distribution franchises** involve an agreement between you and the manufacturer. You are granted rights to sell the manufacturer's product, but cannot operate under the manufacturer's name. Car dealerships are an example of this type of franchise.

- **Business format franchises,** which are more common today, involve an agreement where you not only get the right to sell the product or service, but you also get an entire system for running your franchise. You do get the right to operate your business under the national brand name. McDonald's or Wendy's are examples of this type of franchise.

The person or company who sells the rights to you is called the franchisor and you become the franchisee when you sign on the dotted line and buy the franchise.

Business format franchise

Because business format franchises have become so popular today, the government's gotten involved. You do get some protections granted by the government if you decide to buy a business format franchise. The Federal Trade Commission requires that three key elements must exist in order for there to be a franchise business relationship:

- ✔ You must be granted limited rights to use the company's trade name, service mark, logo, or other advertising symbol.

- ✔ You must get the rights to use systems or methods associated with operating the core business.

- ✔ You must pay the franchisor something in return for being granted these two rights.

You can find out more about the FTC rules and recommendations you should read before buying a franchise at http://www.ftc.gov/bcp/edu/pubs/consumer/invest/inv07.htm.

One big advantage you can expect when deciding to buy a business format franchise is that you will get training, marketing materials, and operating systems. You should also get a manual that spells out how to operate your business. A good franchise package will include extensive management systems to help make your business a success.

Don't be naïve. You're not getting all this solely to help you succeed. The franchisor wants all his franchisees to run the type of business the exact same way with the same quality of products and services. If you don't run the business according to his systems, your business will not match the other franchises.

That's a big problem for the national brand and company image. Customers of a particular franchise brand expect products or services worldwide to be the same no matter where they walk into the franchise.

Wouldn't you be disappointed if you walked into a McDonald's and ordered a Big Mac just to find out that it didn't taste like the hamburger you were expecting? Now maybe you don't even like BigMacs and would be pleasantly surprised by a franchisee that was making a better hamburger, but if you were a BigMac fan, you'd probably complain to the company.

Whatever brand you're looking for, whether it's a UPS Store, a Wendy's, a Cracker Barrel, or whatever franchise restaurant or store you visit regularly, you know what you want when you walk into that business and you expect to get it. The franchisor wants to be sure you do. That's why a good franchisor gives such extensive training and support to all his franchisees.

You should get lots of advantages if you decide to buy into a franchise system:

- ✔ You can expect national advertising that helps drive customers to your business. If you're considering a franchise for which you never see advertising, you need to ask a lot of questions about how the franchisor plans to help you promote your business. Be sure you get those promises in writing.

- ✔ You get access to the purchasing power of a large, national operation which should enable you to buy needed supplies at a lower price.

- ✔ You can take advantage of marketing techniques that have worked for others in the franchise before, so you don't have to reinvent the wheel to get your business going.

- ✔ You get operational systems that include tools, controls, and procedures to help make your business successful.

- ✔ You can take advantage of the national brand awareness that already exists for the product or service you want to sell.

Product distribution franchise

If you're buying a product distribution franchise, then the rules are different. You'll find these types of arrangements most commonly when setting up a franchise in the automobile or oil industry.

For example, I'm sure you've noticed that most car dealerships open under the name of the person who owns the franchise or some other name he chooses, such as World Toyota or Frank's Chevy's. In these situations, the franchise owner has bought the right to sell the specific brand of car, but does not get an entire package to run the business. He cannot name his car dealership General Motors or Ford Dealership. These corporations don't want to give the customer the impression it's a corporate owned business.

I won't discuss this type of franchise further because in most cases you must have millions to buy a distributorship and get involved in product distribution franchising. You'll find that most of these types of franchises are sold to people who are already running one for the manufacturer. For example, a Buick dealer might decide to buy the rights to open a Saab dealership from General Motors.

Other common product distribution dealerships include gas stations for the major oil companies or bottling distributorships for the major soda manufacturers. If you are interested in this type of franchise, then you'll definitely need to do a lot of additional research before pursuing this option.

Finding franchise opportunities

You've probably heard of the major fast-food franchises, such as McDonald's, Wendy's, and Burger King, but you may not be aware that there are over 200 industry categories in which you can find a franchise today.

The primary professional association within the franchise industry is called the International Franchise Association, which groups franchises in 18 main categories. These categories include automotive, baked goods, building and construction, business services, child-related businesses, education-related businesses, fast food, healthcare, lodging, maintenance services, personnel services, printing, real estate, restaurants, retail, service business, sports and recreation, and travel. You can find more detail about the industries at the IFA Web site — www.franchise.org.

Just so that you have an idea of what each of these major industry categories include, let's take a closer look at one of them — retail. Under retail, you will find beauty, clothing and accessories, computer products and services, party-related goods and services, pet-related goods and services, photographic products and services, general retail stores, and video stores. Taking that one step further, under beauty-related you would find diet and fitness franchises, entertainment and fashion franchises, hair care and cosmetic franchises, tanning and skin care franchises, and vitamin franchises, just to name a few.

You get the idea. After seeing these lists, it's not hard to imagine how many different types of franchises there are and how easy it will be to find one that closely matches your skills and the type of business you might want to run.

While fast-food franchises far exceed all other types of franchise systems, they're not necessarily the best one for you. If you haven't run a restaurant before and know nothing about the restaurant business, that's a good combination for sure failure. Take the time to find what matches you best.

The IFA is a good place to start your research about franchising in general, as well as a good source for franchise opportunities. It's the world's largest clearinghouse on franchises. If you find that the franchise you're considering is not a member of the IFA, tread very carefully.

Researching and finding the right franchise for you does take a lot of time. You can shorten that a bit by working with a business broker. But, do be aware that business brokers are primarily interested in earning their commission and may not always put your interests first. The good news is that the broker is paid by the franchisor, so it won't be an out-of-pocket cost for you.

Here are three franchise business brokers you may want to contact if you do want help finding the right opportunity:

- ✓ **FranChoice (www.franchoice.com):** This is the broker recommended by the IFA.

- ✓ **FranNet (www.frannet.com):** FranNet is the world's largest network of franchise consultants. They help you learn about your choices and find the right one for you. FranNet has 50 offices that are individually owned and operated.

- ✓ **Entrepreneur Source (www.theesource.com):** Entrepreneur Source focuses on consulting and training to help you succeed in your own business. They start with interviews and assessments to help you understand your goals, needs, and expectations, to be able to find options best suited for you.

If you know exactly which company you want to work with, go directly to their Web site for details. You don't have to use a broker to find a franchise, but no matter what you do, you should be sure to have an attorney who understands franchise law and can advise you throughout the process.

Key things to consider before signing a contract

In order to buy a franchise system, you must sign a franchise agreement that spells out what you are buying. You could be buying just one franchise store, or you may want the right to build several store locations.

If you do decide franchising is for you, be sure to have an attorney who is familiar with franchise law review your contract. All offers to buy a franchise must comply with the Federal Trade Commission standards for a Uniform Franchise Offering Circular (UFOC), but even under the rules of the UFOC, there are different types of franchise agreements you can be offered.

To find out more about franchising and its contracts, read *Franchising For Dummies* by Michael Seid and Dave Thomas, who started Wendy's (published by Wiley).

Another thing to consider is location. You may want to buy the rights to own and run all the stores within a particular geographic area, but unless you plan to work more than a full-time job in retirement, you certainly don't want to get too big.

Contracts are set up in four different structures — single-unit franchises, multiple single-unit franchises, area-development franchises, and master franchises. Each of these structures involves a different type of agreement. The following sections give you the basics of each type of structure.

Single-unit franchise

If you just want to own and operate one store or franchise unit, then you would sign an agreement for a single-unit franchise. This is the simplest form of franchise ownership.

You don't even have to be thinking of operating out of a storefront. You can do it from your home. For example, service franchises, such as carpet-cleaning franchises or house-cleaning franchises, frequently are from the franchisee's home. Your customers will find you through advertising in the telephone book, in local newspapers or community newsletters, on bulletin boards, or even by radio, depending on how you decide to advertise your business.

Multiple single-unit franchises

If you're successful and the franchise bug bites you, you may want to buy more than one franchise unit from the same franchisor. It's not unusual for a franchisee whose first unit proves profitable to sign a second agreement with the same franchisor for another location. This would be called a multiple single-unit franchise agreement.

Since you're already familiar with the operation and the people involved, you can get that second or maybe third unit up and running much more quickly. Both you and the franchisor benefit from quicker start-up with less initial costs and time for training. You may even help a fellow retiree get started by buying a second or third franchise location as partners.

Area development franchises

If you're really successful and want to build more than one unit at a time, you might think about an area development franchise. This gives you the right to all franchises in a particular geographic area. You can protect yourself from some invading your territory.

With this type of agreement, you would need to sign both an area development franchise agreement, as well as single-unit development agreements for each franchise you open. The area development agreement specifies development rights, but the unit development agreement governs the terms for how each unit will be run and the franchise fees for the unit.

Master franchises

If you're ready to really build something big, you can go for the highest level franchisee by signing a master franchise agreement. This not only gives you the right to develop a certain number of units within a geographic area, you also get the right to offer and sell the franchise to other franchisees. You essentially become franchisor for some of the units you sell.

The master franchise agreement is similar to the area development agreement, where you get the rights to develop a set number of franchises in a particular geographic area within a set time period. With this type of agreement, you don't have to develop all those units yourself. You can find others to develop most of the individual units.

Your agreement will likely require you to open and operate at least the first single unit yourself and will likely require that you open and operate at least two units. Once you have those two up and running, you can begin selling the rights to additional locations in your area to other franchisees, who will be called your sub-franchisees.

A master franchise could be a good idea if you and a bunch of other retirees would like to operate similar businesses in the same area, but you probably will need to find retirees who want to live outside the U.S. You probably won't find many master franchise agreements available in the United States. Most franchisors in the U.S. today prefer to have a direct relationship with each of their franchisees.

But, U.S. franchisors who want to expand outside the states do prefer to offer master franchise agreements in other countries to just one individual or company. Franchisors realize that cultural, political, and economic differences make it critical to have one point person who can lead their franchise unit development who has significant experience developing businesses in that country.

So if you've lived and worked for a long time in another country for your former corporation and think there is potential for a franchise system there that doesn't currently exist, a franchise could be your best opportunity for developing an international business operation.

Funding requirements

You can find franchise opportunities that will let you get started with just $20,000 to $30,000, but they won't be well-known names. If you want to buy into a well-established franchise, expect to need at least $100,000 in cash.

Just to give you an idea of what a business run out of the home might cost in initial investment, I pulled the information from a successful cleaning service franchise, Maid Brigade. Table 18-1 shows what Maid Brigade estimates in start-up costs.

Table 18-1	Maid Brigade Estimated Start-up Costs
Expense Item	*Cost Range*
Initial Franchise Fee	$29,500 to $58,500
Opening Inventory	$5,000 to $7,500
Advertising/Marketing Budget	$50,000 to $80,000
Working Capital	$20,000 to $31,000
Total Initial Investment	$104,500 to $177,000

If you wanted to set up the same kind of business without the Maid Brigade name, you could save the $29,500 to $58,500, but you would not get the benefit of the national name brand. You also would not have access to their training and operations manual. That's the biggest advantage that purchasing a franchise offers you — a business in a box.

Part V

Knowledge to Philanthropy: Opportunities to Broaden the Mind and More

The 5th Wave   By Rich Tennant

City School of Interpretive Dance

"Believe me Mrs. Wilcox, this isn't the type of school you can just waltz into, pick up a degree and waltz out of again."

In this part . . .

You may not want to go back to work, but you also don't enjoy the retirement lifestyle. In this part, I explore opportunities you may want to consider other than getting back to the working grind. I explore both traditional educational opportunities, such as going back to college, as well as less traditional ones that give you an opportunity to learn new things. I also talk about various volunteer opportunities you may want to consider to give back to your community, or possibly another community around the globe.

Chapter 19

Going Back to College: Expanding Your Knowledge and Skills

● ●

In This Chapter

▶ Discovering educational opportunities

▶ Finding senior learning hangouts

▶ Traveling and learning abroad

▶ Organizing your own learning opportunity

● ●

Many seniors decide that the best west to stay young in retirement is to learn something new. Colleges and universities throughout the world are designing educational opportunities for retirees. Some are designed to earn a degree, but many are just short-term learning opportunities.

You may want to just expand your horizons and learn something new, but you also may want to retrain for another career. In this chapter, I introduce you to myriad learning opportunities around the world for retirees. And if those don't fit the bill, I give you some pointers on how to start your own learning experience or even become a teacher yourself.

Your opportunities for learning are limited only by your imagination. With all the resources available on the Internet today, you can find just about anything that interests you. If you're not sure how to make use of the Internet, I recommend that you start by taking a course through a SeniorNet Learning Center (see the section, "SeniorNet," later in this chapter). Or if one is not near you, contact your local community college (see the section, "Local community colleges") and see if it offers basic computing courses.

Popular Senior Learning Opportunities

As a retiree, now that you have much more control over your schedule, you can easily decide to take off for several weeks or several months to pursue something you've wanted to learn more about for a long time. Many colleges around the world have recognized that adult learners, especially those who have retired, can be an excellent source of new students.

In this section, I discuss some of the top programs that are being offered specifically for people over 50. I also give you some tips on how to find programs close to your home.

Elderhostel

People 55 and over have been enjoying programs run by Elderhostel (www.elderhostel.org), a nonprofit organization, for more than 30 years. Today, Elderhostel runs educational programs for adults 55 and older in all 50 U.S. states as well as in 90 countries around the world.

More than 150,000 people sign up for the 8,000 educational trips run by Elderhostel each year. Many of the trips are run in conjunction with an area college or university, so they include both a lecture series and touring.

Programs run by Elderhostel are all-inclusive. That means they include meals, lectures, field trips, cultural excursions, tips, and medical and travel insurance coverage. Air fare is priced into many of the trips overseas as well.

Trips vary greatly in length. They can be a one-day discovery trip in a particular city or a short five-day adventure, such as a visit to three barrier islands off the coast of Georgia (St. Simons, Sapelo, and Jekyll) to learn more about the culture in the area and explore the islands, run in conjunction with Georgia Southwestern State University. These trips cost under $500 per person and include hotel, 15 meals, and tours of the three islands, in addition to lectures. Two- to three-week trips are available too.

If you want to travel outside the U.S., Elderhostel also runs programs that include travel to Africa, Asia, Australia, Canada, Europe, and the Americas. You'll find programs offered by Elderhostel in these seven areas:

- ✔ **Active outdoor:** Participants explore the wonders of the natural world. These programs can include hiking in the Grand Canyon or exploring central France by barge. You will exercise both the body and mind, but you do need to be able to participate in extensive physical activity.

Active outdoor trips are fast paced and include strenuous physical challenges.

✔ **Discover:** Participants explore the landscape and cultures of both the U.S. and Canada. You could tour the national parks or explore a cosmopolitan city with an expert leading the group.

✔ **Individual skills:** These programs focus on giving you the opportunity to learn a new skill, such as Southwestern cooking, watercolor, yoga, or pottery making. These courses are led by experienced craftspeople and expert guides.

✔ **Intergenerational:** Travel with a grandchild or other younger relative or friend to explore something that interests you. These trips include interactive lectures and field trips run to offer experiences that can bridge generational differences.

✔ **Liberal arts:** Participants explore topics of interest in university settings around the U.S. You can take a course in Shakespeare, analyze Freud, or study classic opera. Programs include lectures by distinguished university faculty, backstage ventures with theater professionals, as well as discussions with historians, authors, diplomats, and philosophers.

✔ **Service learning:** These programs give participants an opportunity to make a difference in a community, an ecosystem, or the life of an individual. You could tutor children or help restore a forest habitat for wildlife. Or you might sign up to assist with artifact restoration or assist with museum curatorial work.

✔ **Adventures afloat programs:** Participants explore and learn history from the deck of various types of floating classrooms, such as yachts, barges, and cruise ships.

Elderhostel programs tend to attract people primarily between the ages of 65 and 75. A similar program for younger folks, between the ages of 50 and 60, called Road Scholar (www.roadscholar.org) is being developed by the Elderhostel organization. This program is a bit more upscale and less structured than the Elderhostel programs.

TraveLearn

A leading educational tour operator whose clientele are primarily people 50 and over is TraveLearn (www.travelearn.com), which has been putting together educational tours for more than 25 years. You'll find land tours, land/cruise tours, and cruise-only tours to places such as, Alaska, Antarctica, China, Costa Rica, Ecuador, Ireland, and Morocco.

TraveLearn trips use more luxury accommodations than you'll find on Elderhostel tours. Groups can be as small as eight travelers and never more than 20. All trip leaders are experts in the area in which they are leading a trip. You can sign up for a free travel newsletter on TraveLearn's Web site to keep up-to-date on the trips available.

Osher Lifelong Learning Institute (OLLI)

If you are lucky enough to live in the San Francisco area or can visit there for an extended period of time, you may want to consider attending a session of the Osher Lifelong Learning Institute (http://www.cel.sfsu.edu/olli/) run by San Francisco State University.

These programs are run primarily for people who want to learn about a topic, but don't want the pressures normally associated with a college course. You won't be assigned extensive homework, even though occasionally there is some. You also won't get grades or receive credit for the classes.

Here's a sampling of the types of coursework you'll find in the program:

- **Artmaking and storytelling:** Students explore and experiment with their imagination through photography, creative writing, and storytelling, particularly memoir writing.

- **Urban curriculum:** Students examine the economic, social, cultural, and political forces that shape the San Francisco area.

- **Redefining aging:** Students explore issues involving personal and professional choices as they age. Discussions include entrepreneurship, investing, spirituality, and interior design.

- **International affairs and current events:** Students analyze global events and their impact on the San Francisco area. Topics include global climate change, schools, Mexico, Islam and the West, and globalization.

- **Technology and the future:** Students are introduced to new software and other technologies as part of a project-based course. Topics include digital photography and Photoshop, as well as an introduction to the Internet and e-mail basics.

The Institute also runs an Artist-in-Residence program where students can work with top artists in various fields. One continuing project that was started under this program is the Geezer Theater, where aspiring writers and actors work with the Artists-in-Residence and write and perform original theater performances.

You may be able to find similar adult learning programs near you. Check with your state university system. Many offer senior adult learning programs that might be just what you are looking to find.

SeniorNet

If you want to learn more about how to use your computer, visit the Web site SeniorNet (www.seniornet.org). This nonprofit organization, which was founded in 1986, provides adults aged 50 and older with computer instruction so they can use the computer to enhance their lives and share their wisdom and knowledge.

More than 240 learning centers are supported by SeniorNet throughout the U.S., as well as in Sweden, Malaysia, and Japan. You can locate the one nearest you on its Web site at http://www.seniornet.org/php/lclist.php.

Even if you don't live near one of the learning centers, you can benefit from newsletters published by the organization, as well as from discounts on computer-related products and services.

SeniorNet also sponsors an active online community with hundreds of discussion topics called the SeniorNet RoundTables (http://discussions.seniornet.org). Computers are not the only thing discussed. You'll also find discussion topics including

- Arts and entertainment
- Books and literature
- Civic and social issues
- Crafts and collectibles
- Culinary arts
- Culture
- Financial topics and legal issues
- Gardening
- Genealogy
- Health
- Religion and spirituality
- Retirement living

- Volunteerism, activism, and philanthropy
- Working seniors and careers
- Writing, language, and word play

When it comes to leaning more about your computer, you can get help from SeniorNet members to learn how to touch up your digital photography, send and receive e-mail, desktop publishing, manage personal and financial records, and communicate with people around the world. You'll even find help on how to write your own autobiography.

SeniorNet grew out of a research project originally funded by the Markle Foundation in 1986. Today it's an international, nonprofit organization based in Santa Clara, California. Funding for SeniorNet comes from membership dues ($40 a year), Learning Center fees, and individual donations. SeniorNet also receives donations from companies and foundations.

Membership in SeniorNet makes you eligible for computer training at its learning centers where the adult technology curriculum is run by other senior members. You can also get free computer and Internet access at the learning center computer labs and access to advanced equipment including scanners, printers, and digital cameras. Members also get a free subscription to the monthly e-newsletter and discounts on computer software and hardware.

Local community colleges

If you want to learn close to home, one of the best places to check out is your local community college. Many community colleges offer adult learning classes that include computer basics, financial management, and other lifestyle classes.

Or you may be interested in getting training for a career change to a new field, if you think you might want to go back to work. You can earn an associates degree or get the coursework you need for a professional certification.

Learning online

Many universities also offer online courses that you can take from your home computer. You can research what's available and find out more about each school's program at the Guide to Online Schools (www.guidetoonline schools.com).

The Guide to Online schools provides a directory of over 2,500 online degree programs that include accredited online colleges, online universities, and distance learning programs. You can earn an associate's degree, bachelor's degree, master's degree, or a PhD.

You'll find coursework in business, counseling, criminal justice, design, education, engineering, healthcare, human services, nursing, paralegal, psychology, religion, and technology. Some schools offer classes that a partially done online and partially in a live classroom.

Learning Abroad

You may decide that you'd like to learn abroad. Senior studies programs are available at overseas colleges and universities as well. I review some of the best programs you might be interested in exploring.

University of Strathclyde's Senior Studies Institute

The University of Strathclyde in Glasgow, Scotland, hosts the Senior Studies Institute through its Centre for Lifelong Learning (www.cll.strath.ac.uk/ ssi.html). The university established the institute in 1991 to offer older people a place they could go for lifelong learning. Today, more than 3,000 students participate in coursework each year. The university offers three primary types of learning opportunities:

✔ Lifelong learning encourages continuing personal growth and intellectual stimulation through daytime classes, seminars, and other learning opportunities.

✔ Useful learning courses provide older people with an opportunity to learn life skills, which they can then use to help in their community as volunteers or entrepreneurs.

✔ Widening access gives students access to other university courses and offers opportunities to work within the community.

If you don't want to learn in Scotland, but would like to improve your writing skills, you might be interested in Strathclyde's Online Creative Writing Classes called BLAZE (www.cll.strath.ac.uk/ssi/classlists/ writing.htm).

Adult Residential Colleges Association (ARCA)

You can join more than 150,000 adults each year who take short-term residential coursework at one of the small residential colleges in England or Wales through a collaborative program called the Adult Residential Colleges Association (http://www.arca.uk.net).

Courses focus on helping you learn throughout life for personal satisfaction. You can attend courses that are run over a weekend, during the week, or as summer schools. Most of these courses are offered for the enjoyment of learning and you don't need to meet academic requirements to enroll.

Often these colleges are in historic houses set in the countryside. Accommodations vary greatly. You may stay in a small comfortable room or a grand suite depending on what is available near the school you choose.

Archaeology Abroad

If you think you might like to travel and do a bit of digging at the same time, the University of London publishes Archaeology Abroad, which is a guide to fieldwork opportunities outside the United Kingdom. The guide provides information on hundreds of archeological fieldwork opportunities around the world.

You can get an annual subscription to the guide for $65 by subscribing online at http://www.britarch.ac.uk/archabroad/subscribe.html.

Using information found in the guide, you can sign up for a few weeks or a few months depending on the project. You can also get information about Fieldwork Awards that help Archaeology Abroad subscribers with their excavation expenses, including travel costs and participation, regardless of your age, nationality, or level of fieldwork experience.

You'll find projects that accept participants with little or no previous archaeological training or experience. The university does recommend that you do learn some basic archaeological techniques before venturing abroad.

Before joining a project, keep the following in mind:

✔ You will find that conditions do vary considerably from site to site, so be sure to check out your living conditions before accepting a fieldwork assignment or traveling. Accommodations can be quite rustic and may just be tents or involve shared rooms and facilities.

✔ You may be expected to share shopping and cooking as well. Sometimes there will be a location where all field workers meet before traveling to the site. Other times you may need to find your own way to the excavation site.

✔ Costs will vary greatly depending on the sponsor of the dig and how it's funded. The sponsor may have been able to raise money from a sponsoring institution or government entity to help defray costs.

✔ If you've never done archaeological fieldwork and would like to take a training course through a field school, you will find that there are significant fees, but many times those fees include food, accommodations, tuition, and field trips. The guide includes information about field schools as well.

✔ You do need to be physically fit in order to participate in archeological field work. This type of work usually involves strenuous physical labor. You should ask your doctor for at least an anti-tetanus vaccination before leaving, if you haven't had one in the last ten years.

✔ In addition, you may need other vaccinations depending on where you are traveling. You can find out if there are any travel alerts for a particular location at the U.S. State Department Web site (`http://travel.state.gov/travel/cis_pa_tw/cis_pa_tw_1168.html`). You should also be sure to have your own health and travel insurance in case of personal injury or transportation cancellation.

Adult cultural program — France

You can learn more about French culture in two- to four-week programs where you live and study in the medieval city of Montpellier, which has one of one of the oldest universities in Europe. The program is part of the Institut Méditerranéen de Langues (`http://www.iml.fr`).

While you enjoy the French Mediterranean, you'll take coursework with other retirees on topics such as French civilization and culture, French cooking, and wine and cheese tasting. You'll also travel to area towns as part of the program.

Specialists in history, sociology, French southern civilization, and politics will teach as part of the program. You also have the option to do volunteer work, which can be an excellent way to interact with the local people and learn more about French culture.

Taking art in Italy

Would you like to live and work in the Italian mountains as you seek to improve your fine-arts skills in drawing, painting, collage, mask making, digital photography, fresco, or clay sculpture? The Abruzzi Mountain Art Workshop offers fine-arts classes in a rustic mountain village that is about an hour from Rome.

You can learn more about the classes at www.artworkshopitaly.com. You can also choose to work at 12th-century sites or abandoned abbeys. Independent studio space is also available.

A weeklong workshop includes seven nights of hotel accommodations, five hours of instruction each day, daily excursions to islands and coastal sites, daily lunch or dinner, and all materials and supplies. Also, your work will be critiqued daily as part of the workshop.

Learning a language

If you'd like to learn a new language and travel at the same time, check out the directory provided by AmeriSpan (http://www.amerispan.com/language_schools/). You'll find course availability for learning 20 different languages.

AmeriSpan can help you find courses in Argentina, Austria, Bolivia, Brazil, Canada, Chile, China, Costa Rica, Dominican Republic, Ecuador, Egypt, Greece, Guatemala, Honduras, Israel, Italy, Japan, Mexico, Morocco, Panama, Peru, Poland, Portugal, Puerto Rico, Russia, Spain, Switzerland, Thailand, Uruguay, and Venezuela. Some courses even combine learning a language with cooking, wine-tasting, sailing, golfing, and dancing.

You may want to avoid taking courses in June, July, and August, which is when they are filled with college-age students. The times you'll find the most retirees in classes are from February through April or September through December.

Becoming a Teacher Yourself

You may like to become a teacher yourself, but you never took any teacher certification courses. The National Association for Alternative Certification works with a number of states to help them develop alternative certification programs. You can find a list of current programs at `http://www. alt-teachercert.org/program_sites.htm`.

Each state has its own set of rules and requirements. You will find a link to the state's alternative certification Web site at the link above.

In order to qualify for one of these programs, you must have a bachelor's degree or be a paraprofessional with at least 60 hours or more of college credit. If you want to teach math, science, or special needs children, you'll be in demand in most states because that is the type of teachers sought most often. High school teachers also are in high demand in many states.

If you do qualify, the state programs often pay tuition assistance, provide training, give financial incentives, and provide mentor support. Many states get federal funding for programs that help people transition to teaching.

To give you an idea of what is entailed to get an alternative certification, I looked at Florida's program, which includes the following components:

- **Survival training:** Candidates are first given an initial period of preparation before assuming responsibility in the classroom.

- **Support team:** A support team is in place to coordinate and support the professional development of each new teacher.

- **Peer mentor:** Each new teacher is assigned a peer mentor, who provides face-to-face feedback and assists the new teacher throughout the learning experience.

- **Online tutor:** Teachers have access guidance, feedback, and assessment of work products that are developed as part of the program's learning activities.

- **Online professional preparation learning activities:** Learning activities are provided in-depth online to give each new teacher training in the Florida Educator Accomplished Practices. Topics covered include assessment, communication, critical thinking, diversity, ethics, human development and learning, knowledge of subject matter, learning environments, planning, role of the teacher, and technology.

- **Database tracking system:** This system is used to document the progress of each teacher as various tasks are completed that demonstrate the new teacher has learned the Florida Educator Accomplished Practices.

- **Professional education test:** This test is administered at the end of the program to demonstrate attained knowledge.

After successfully completing this alternative certification process, you can be certified to teach in Florida. Each state does design its own program, but the basic design is similar.

Starting Your Own Learning Group

You may decide that none of these opportunities are right for you. You can always start your own learning opportunity that you design based on your own learning priorities.

You may enjoy starting your own book club with people who enjoy reading the same genre of books that you do. Or you may want to set up group tours designed to meet your specific needs. Another idea might be to start an investment club where you can share ideas for how to manage your retirement portfolio.

Forming a book club

One common learning opportunity you'll find in many senior centers or active adult retirement communities is a book club. If you don't know of one in your community, check with your local library.

Many libraries do offer meeting places for book clubs. Your local librarian can probably point you in the right direction for a book club near you or possibly help you start one if there are none in your area.

If you do decide to start a new one from scratch, you can find some excellent resources at Book-Club-Resources.com (www.book-clubs-resource.com). Here are the basic tasks you need to think about to start your own club:

- ✔ **Plan your size and where you'll meet:** Before you can even start recruiting members, you need to determine the size of your book club and where you'll meet. Size will be very dependent on where you decide to meet because if you decide to host meetings in your home, you must figure out how many people you can invite to comfortably meet in your home. If you don't have enough space, talk with your library or community center to see if it is possible to use a room there.

- ✔ **Recruit Members:** You could start by recruiting friends, but if you don't find enough members that way, you can post flyers at your local library.

Book clubs are a great way to make new friends who share similar interests.

✔ **Set guidelines:** At your first meeting, you should start to draft guidelines. Items can include how often you want to meet, how many books you plan to discuss during each meeting, and how you will decide which books you want to read. It's a good idea to pick one consistent time and place to meet. People tend to forget about a meeting if it doesn't become part of a routine schedule. For example, you could decide to meet at 11 a.m. on the first Tuesday of the month.

✔ **Find a discussion leader:** You can decide to hire a professional leader to moderate your book club meetings or you can lead them yourself. If you do want to hire a professional leader, contact your library or a local community college for suggestions. If you decide to lead the discussion yourself, you can take advantage of the reading group guides you can find online (`www.book-clubs-resource.com/guides`) to make your task easier.

Putting together a travel group

Traveling with friends is always fun. You can put together your own travel group. Your group can either decide to go together on one of the organized trips I talked about above or you can work with a travel agent to put together a trip that better meets your needs.

If you do decide to organize trips yourself, find a good travel agent whom you can count on to help with the logistics. Setting up a trip takes a lot of effort and knowledge, and unless you've done this before, don't try to do this all by yourself.

Starting an investment club

Investment clubs can be an excellent way to share information about managing your retirement portfolio and researching investment opportunities. BetterInvesting of The National Association of Investors Corporation (NAIC) provides you with excellent materials about how to start your own club at `http://www.betterinvesting.org/clubsandchapters/`.

You may want to start by finding an existing club near you before trying to start your own. If you do prefer to join an existing club, you can use

BetterInvesting's search tool to find a club near you at `http://www.better investing.org/clubs/findaclub.html`.

BetterInvesting is an independent, nonprofit organization that is dedicated to teaching individuals how to become successful, strategic, long-term investors. You won't find stock recommendations on the Web site and there are no commissions or fees from your investing activities.

Chapter 20

Volunteering in the Business and Community World

In This Chapter

▶ Reviewing your volunteer skills

▶ Finding opportunities in businesses

▶ Searching for opportunities in communities

▶ Volunteering internationally

▶ Becoming a virtual volunteer

*I*f you don't need to make money, but you want to continue using the skills you've learned throughout your life, you can take advantage of the numerous opportunities to volunteer.

You can decide to stay in the business world and help small-business people in trouble. Or you can decide to give back to your community instead and take on leadership or other volunteer roles in community organizations.

In this chapter, I review the volunteer opportunities in both the business and community world.

Understanding That You Have Something to Offer

You — and all retirees — have experience and knowledge you've built over the years that you can offer to someone else, if you want to offer the time. After spending a few months doing all the things around the house you wanted to get done, you probably have a lot of untapped energy.

You also may find that you want to do something more creative than playing golf or cards all day or hanging out at the pool. You have a lot of creativity left in you, but you're not sure what to do with it. You don't want to go back into the workforce, but you do want to give back to your community.

You can do that in many different ways. If you've been a business person your entire life and just love the challenge of helping another business get on its feet, your may want to work as a small-business volunteer.

If you're tired of business or never worked for a business at all, there are many volunteer opportunities from which to choose. First, I review possible business volunteer opportunities, then I explore community volunteer spots, and finally I look at ways you can both volunteer and travel worldwide.

Being a Volunteer in the Business World

Many small businesses need help to get off the ground or to fix an internal problem. You can go through two key organizations if that's the way you want to volunteer your time — SCORE and Volunteers in Medical Clinics. If you prefer working with small-business start-ups, you may want to volunteer at a small-business incubator. I explore all of these options in the sections that follow.

SCORE

SCORE (www.score.org), which uses the tagline "Counselors to America's Small Business," is by far America's premier source of free and confidential small-business advice for entrepreneurs. Since being formed in 1964, SCORE has helped over 7.5 million small-business owners by providing counseling, training, and advice on a volunteer basis.

Today, SCORE has over 375 chapter offices nationwide. You can also find helpful "how-to" articles and business templates on its Web site. If you join SCORE, you can become part of a network of over 10,500 volunteers. SCORE volunteers share their business acumen and lessons they've learned over the years in business. SCORE volunteers are working and retired business owners, executives, and corporate leaders.

As a SCORE volunteer, you serve as a resource partner with the U.S. Small Business Administration to assist small-business owners seeking help. Depending on your expertise, you could help a small-business owner develop a business plan, improve his marketing, increase his cash flow, or any number of other critical aspects needed to keep a business alive.

You can decide to offer business advice online. Over 1,400 SCORE counselors respond to e-mail requests for help. Or, you can decide you prefer to do face-to-face counseling. That is done through one of SCORE's local chapter offices. For more information about being a volunteer, go to http://www.score.org/volunteer.html.

Volunteers in Medicine clinics

Retired physicians, nurses, dentists, social workers, pharmacists, and others who worked in the medical field may find volunteering in a Volunteers in Medicine (VIM; http://www.vimi.org/volunteer.shtml) clinic very satisfying. VIM clinics serve in areas where healthcare is most needed.

The first VIM clinic was formed in 1993 at a time when Hilton Head had no access to healthcare. A free health clinic was started that uses retired health-care professionals in the area. Almost immediately, the clinic had 55 physicians, 64 nurses, and 15 dentists who volunteered to give some time.

In 2005, more than 160,000 retired physicians, 350,000 nurses, and 40,000 dentists volunteer time to one of the VIM clinics nationwide. Many of the retired healthcare workers that become involved in VIM not only want to practice, they find they need to practice. They find serving this community in this way is therapeutic.

Patients served by the VIM clinics are people surviving on limited resources. Today, thanks to the VIM clinic, every person who lives or works on Hilton Head Island has easy access to healthcare. You can find out more about the VIM clinic on Hilton Head at www.vimclinic.org. Clinics similar to that one now operate in Alabama, Florida, Georgia, Indiana, Kansas, Louisiana, Massachusetts, Missouri, New Jersey, North Carolina, Ohio, Oregon, Pennsylvania, South Carolina, Tennessee, Texas, Washington, and Wyoming.

The amount of time you decide to give to a clinic is up to you. VIM does recommend that retired physicians volunteer at least a half-day per week. Some volunteers actually choose to work every day. Continuing education is provided to all professionals who decide to volunteer for VIM.

Small-business incubators

If you enjoy working with entrepreneurs and don't want to work with SCORE, you may also find your talents needed at a small-business incubator.

Many business owners don't have the space or desire to start their business out of their homes, but they can't afford renting space or the essential support function. Instead, they turn to small-business incubators, which are usually affiliated with a university or college in the area.

At *small-business incubators,* business owners get help from business students as well as from retired business people who volunteer their time. Business incubators are designed specifically to help start-up firms, and provide

- ✔ Flexible space and leases often at very low rates

- ✔ Fee-based business support services, such as telephone answering, bookkeeping, secretarial, fax and copy machine access, libraries, and meeting rooms

- ✔ Group rates for health, life, and other insurance plans

- ✔ Business and technical assistance either on-site or through a community referral system

- ✔ Assistance in obtaining funding for the business

- ✔ Networking with other entrepreneurs

If working with business start-ups is a better fit for you, then you may want to check with your local college or university to see if they know of one in the area. You can find a listing of small-business incubators throughout the U.S. and the world at Small Business Notes (http://www.smallbusinessnotes. com/incubation.html).

Helping Out in Your Community

Options for volunteering in your community are extensive. In this section, I focus on the organizations that seek retirees, but in reality you can find many other opportunities through local religious groups, the United Way, and other local service organizations. Essentially any task that you think you would like to consider volunteering to do, you will likely find a way to do it.

Executive Service Corps Affiliate Network

The Executive Service Corps Affiliate Network (ESCAN; www.escus.org), which is a nationwide network of 34 nonprofit consulting groups, provides a variety of high-quality, affordable services to nonprofit organizations, schools, and government agencies.

Volunteer consultants, who have had senior-level positions in business, government, and nonprofits, provide most of the services. Their goal is to help strengthen the management of nonprofit agencies so that they can more effectively perform their missions.

The areas in which volunteer consultants provide services include strategic planning, coaching and mentoring, financial management, marketing and public relations, merger support, business plan development, board governance, leadership development, facility management, fundraising, human resources, information systems, cost reduction, income generation, endowment planning, and organizational assessments.

To find out more about how you can become affiliated with Executive Service Corps, go to `http://www.escus.org/where.html` and contact the affiliate office nearest you.

AARP

AARP offers many different ways you can volunteer your time. You can find articles and information about how to volunteer at `http://www.aarp.org/about_aarp/community_service`. AARP's founder, Dr. Ethel Percy Andrus, believed it was important "to serve, not to be served." Her vision helped shape AARP's volunteer programs at the national, state, and local levels.

Today, you'll find a wide variety of community events that inform, protect, and empower adults age 50-plus on a range of important issues. AARP volunteers and staff work together to enhance the quality of life for everyone as they age by achieving positive social change through information, advocacy, and service.

Consider volunteering in one of the AARP programs I discuss in the following sections.

AARP Day of Service

Each year AARP designates a Day of Service (check for this year's date by checking out `www.aarp.org/about_aarp/community_service`). AARP encourages its members to consider devoting the day to volunteer service with an organization of their choosing. If you don't want to work for an organization, AARP recommends that you spend the day helping your elderly or handicapped neighbors with errands, household chores, and other basic tasks.

AARP Benefits Outreach Program: Low-income help

AARP volunteers help older people with low or moderate incomes find public and private benefit programs for which they may be eligible to help pay for prescription drugs, groceries, doctor bills, heating bills, property taxes, and more.

About 5,000 low-income older persons get the benefits they need to strengthen their financial security with the help of AARP volunteers. To find out if this program is available in your community, e-mail bopvolunteer@aarp.org.

AARP chapters

AARP chapters, which total more than 2,400 in the U.S., Puerto Rico, and the Virgin Islands, are the core of AARP's volunteer efforts nationwide by fostering community volunteerism and fellowship, and offering a range of service programming that includes mentoring activities, food and clothing drives, friendly visits, and much more.

Chapters also lend direct support to AARP State Office advocacy and legislative efforts, and often combine forces with groups like Habitat for Humanity and Meals on Wheels, to make life better in communities where AARP families live and work.

You can find out more information about AARP chapter activities in your state or area by contacting AARP Community Networks at 601 E St. NW, Washington, DC 20049. You can also contact this group by e-mail at chapters@aarp.org, or call its toll-free number: 1-888-OUR-AARP (1-888-687-2277).

AARP Driver Safety Program

If you'd like to teach driver safety, you can join a network of 10,000 volunteers who help older drivers learn ways to avoid a collision and cause injuries to themselves and others. This eight-hour classroom refresher course is designed especially for drivers age 50 and older, but there's no age requirement.

Topics include the normal changes in vision, hearing, and reaction time and discussions center around practical techniques to compensate for these changes. In 2005, there were about 630,000 course graduates.

In a majority of states, people who take these courses benefit from discounted auto insurance. This program is available nationwide and is taught in many convenient locations. An online version of the AARP Driver Safety Program refresher course is available online at http://www.aarp.org/drive. You can call 888-227-7669 for more information.

AARP Money Management Program

If you enjoy helping others with daily money management assistance, you may want to volunteer for AARP's Money Management Program. Volunteers help older or disabled people who have difficulty budgeting, paying bills, and keeping track of their finances, but have no family or friends able to help them out.

The program works with state and local community service agencies to help people maintain their financial independence, to remain in their homes, and to provide an added level of protection against financial exploitation. You can find out more information about this program at www.aarpmmp.org or call toll free (1-888-687-2277).

NRTA: AARP's Educator Community

If you'd prefer working with children, you may enjoy volunteering with your local retired educators' associations through the NRTA's *With Our Youth!* Program.

Volunteers work with children and the broader community through tutoring, providing school supplies and books, and helping to run food and clothing drives. Also, retired educators can help new teachers and administrators by assisting them using their years of experience and knowledge. You can find out more about the program by writing to NRTA, 601 E Street NW, Washington, DC 20049.

AARP Tax-Aide

Are you one of those rare people that enjoy helping others prepare their tax returns? AARP Tax-Aide volunteers provide free tax preparation services to millions of low- and moderate-income taxpayers, with special attention to those age 60 and older. Electronic filing and online counseling are also offered by the program.

AARP has offered this service for 36 years and now has over 32,000 volunteers. In 2006, it served about 1.9 million taxpayers at 8,500 sites. Program volunteers also answer tax-related questions year-round online. If you'd like to volunteer for this program, you can find out more information about it at www.aarp.org/taxaide or you can e-mail taxaide@aarp.org. You can also reach the program by calling 1-888-227-7669.

National and state volunteers

If you'd enjoy taking on a leadership role, there are many possibilities at the national and state levels. Working for AARP, you would help set national policy and serve in key advisory roles. AARP policy and legislative decisions are made at the national level by the volunteer Board of Directors. And, the volunteer National Legislative Council provides valuable input.

AARP volunteers also serve as state volunteer leaders to help develop and advance state priorities. You can also assist with communications to individuals, groups, and the media about the organization's programs and priorities, or you can train other volunteers on key issues. You'll be involved in advocating for issues affecting Americans aged 50 years and older.

If you want to work from home, you can sign up for free e-mail updates and action alerts from AARP. You can become an AARP Citizen Advocate and respond to action alerts that involve national and state issues. To learn more about how you can become an advocate, go to www.aarp.org/issues/become_advocate. For more information on how you can become a state volunteer, go to www.aarp.org/states.

Environmental Alliance for Senior Involvement

If you'd like to volunteer to improve the environment and work with other retirees at the same time, you may want join the Environmental Alliance for Senior Involvement (EASI; www.easi.org) as a volunteer. This organization was established in 1991 as a national nonprofit coalition of environmental, aging, and volunteer organizations. It was formed as the result of an agreement between the U.S. Environmental Protection Agency and the AARP.

EASI seeks to increase opportunities for older adults to play an active, visible role in protecting and improving the environment in their communities. Through its national network of 12,000 local organizations, EASI selects local hosts to recruit, train, and recognize senior volunteers who carry out a wide range of environmental activities.

Three programs that might interest you include

- **Local Senior Environment Corps Initiatives:** These projects focus on energy conservation, environmental education, environmental health, environmental monitoring, environmental restoration, and pollution prevention. One project run by EASI volunteers is helping to develop environmental legislation in a special effort for its state legislature.

- **Senior Leadership Corps:** This program provides leadership for local Bureau of Land Management volunteer projects and helps to manage various projects involving hundreds of volunteers.

- **Volunteer Senior Ranger Corps:** This project, supported by a grant from the United Parcel Service Foundation, is a cooperative effort run by EASI, the National Parks Service, and the National Park Foundation. Volunteers help to meet priority needs at eight of America's national parks through partnerships between the Park and its surrounding communities.

You can find out more about these and other volunteer opportunities offered by EASI by going to `http://www.easi.org/` and clinking on the tab for programs.

Experience Corps

Experience Corps (`www.experiencecorps.org`) provides you with a way to help disadvantaged youth in 14 cities. Today there are more than 1,800 Corps members who serve as tutors and mentors to children in urban public schools and after-school programs, where they help teach children to read and develop the confidence and skills they need to succeed in school and in life.

Research shows that Experience Corps boosts student academic performance, helps schools and youth-serving organizations become more successful, strengthens ties between these institutions and surrounding neighborhoods, and enhances the well-being of the volunteers in the process.

Currently, Experience Corps operates in Baltimore, Boston, Chicago, Cleveland, Indianapolis, Minneapolis, New York, Oakland, Philadelphia, Port Arthur (Texas), Portland (Oregon), San Francisco, Tucson (Arizona), and California. To find out more about the existing programs, go to `http://www.experiencecorps.org/join_us/index.html`.

If you don't have an Experience Corps program in a city near you, but would like to be involved in starting one, go to `http://www.experiencecorps.org/join_us/guideposts.html` to find the ten guideposts for starting a program near you.

Generations United

Generations United (GU; `www.gu.org`) seeks to improve the lives of children, youth, and older people through intergenerational strategies, programs, and public policies. GU represents more than 100 national, state, and local organizations and individuals, which in turn represent more than 70 million Americans.

GU, which opened its doors in 1986, acts as a catalyst for stimulating collaboration between senior, children, and youth organizations. Go to `www.gu.org` to find out more about volunteer activities that might interest you.

North Carolina Center for Creative Retirement

The North Carolina Center for Creative Retirement (NCCCR; http://www.unca.edu/ncccr/), which was established in 1988 as an integral part of the University of North Carolina at Asheville, promotes lifelong learning, leadership, and community service opportunities for retirees. Besides serving the greater Asheville area, NCCCR collaborates with organizations in North Carolina and across the country.

NCCCR works to encourage the development of an age-integrated society. As the U.S. population ages, NCCCR serves as a laboratory for exploring creative and productive roles for a new generation of retirement-aged people, many of whom want to blend education with post-retirement careers.

Two programs that might interest you are

✔ **Leadership Asheville Seniors:** If you're retired and living near UNC Asheville, you can participate in eight day-long sessions around the Ashville community. Participants meet with community leaders, activists, and politicians to learn more about the area's history, people, institutions, challenges, and opportunities. Many people who participate in this program use it to reevaluate their choice of volunteer roles and find new ones. After completing the program, you can stay in touch with other alumni by joining the Leadership Asheville Forum.

✔ **Creative Retirement Exploration Weekend:** Offers a unique learning vacation for those considering relocating in retirement — whether to western North Carolina or elsewhere. Topics covered include how to determine what a community offers you and how to assess if you'll enjoy living in a place as much as you do visiting there. You'll also explore how to answer questions such as: What should I be doing right now to make my retirement what I want it to be when I get there? What lifestyle changes should I consider as I approach retirement? And what new opportunities can I find in a new community? The Retirement Exploration Weekend usually includes about 150 people from more than 26 states.

Volunteer leaders guide NCCCR programs and services through a Center Steering Council who collaborate with the center's professional staff.

Year-round programs serve people in the greater Asheville area. The center also offers periodic workshops, seminars, and retreats for people from all over the U.S. You can find out more about NCCCR's programs at http://www.unca.edu/ncccr/ or by calling 828-251-6140.

OASIS

You can work with children and help improve their learning opportunities as an OASIS volunteer (www.oasisnet.org/volunteer/index.htm), who have offered many tools and talents to strengthen and serve their communities since 1982 and helped children learn to read through OASIS Intergenerational Tutoring. Other volunteer opportunities include teaching classes, providing support to peers, promoting improved health, planning lifelong learning programs, mentoring young people, as well as many other roles through OASIS centers.

More than 14,000 volunteers work through OASIS programs around the country. You can find OASIS centers in Arizona, California, Colorado, Illinois, Indiana, Maryland, Missouri, New Mexico, New York, Ohio, Oklahoma, Oregon, Pennsylvania, Texas, and Washington, D.C.

To help you figure out if OASIS is the right opportunity for you or if other volunteer opportunities may be better, go to http://www.oasisnet.org/volunteer/fit.htm.

Peace Corps

You probably never thought you could volunteer for the Peace Corps (www.peacecorps.gov) in your 50s or 60s. Well think again!

Although in 1964, only 2 percent of Peace Corps volunteers were people over the age of 50, today, about 7 percent are over 50 years old and hundreds serve overseas as Peace Corps volunteers. Many senior Peace Corps volunteers serve as married couples. While you can offer the Peace Corps many different types of skills, most people over 50 work in education or business.

You can work in emerging and essential areas, such as information technology and business development. Healthcare is another key area where volunteers are needed, especially for the President's Emergency Plan for AIDS Relief. Peace Corps volunteers seek to help individuals who want to build a better life for themselves, their children, and their communities.

If you do decide to serve as a Peace Corps volunteer, you must plan on setting aside 27 months for what could be grueling work. Peace Corps looks for people with determination, flexibility, patience, and a sense of humor. Applying to the Peace Corps involves five steps with paperwork required at each point along the way. This includes a lengthy application you must complete, an interview process, medical and legal clearance, assessment of skills and suitability, and then, if successful, a placement offer.

To find out more about the process, go to www.peacecorps.gov and click on "How Do I Become a Volunteer." You may also be interested in other key links, such as "What Do Volunteers Do?"; "Where Do Volunteers Go?"; and "What's It Like to Volunteer?"

Senior Corps

Senior Corps (www.seniorcorps.org) connects people who are age 55 and over with people and organizations that need them most. You can become a mentor, coach, or companion to people in need, or you can contribute your job skills and expertise to community projects and organizations.

Senior Corps was created during John F. Kennedy's presidency. Today, it links more than 500,000 Americans to service opportunities. Your skills, knowledge, and experience can make a real difference to individuals, nonprofits, and other community organizations throughout the United States. Today, Senior Corps is part of the Corporation for National Service, which was authorized by Congress in 1993. Its predecessors were ACTION and VISTA.

You can serve in several different ways after guidance and training. These include

- **Foster Grandparent Program:** This program connects volunteers age 60 and over with children and young people with exceptional needs. Volunteers mentor, support, and help some of the most vulnerable children in the United States.

- **Senior Companion Program:** This program brings together volunteers age 60 and over with adults in their community who have difficulty with the simple tasks of day-to-day living. You will be able to help others on a personal level by assisting with shopping and light chores, interacting with doctors, or just making a friendly visit.

- **RSVP Program:** This program connects volunteers age 55 and over with service opportunities in their communities that match their skills and availability. RSVP volunteers choose how and where they want to serve — from a few hours a month to over 40 hours a week. RSVP volunteers provide hundreds of community services. As an RSVP volunteer, you can tutor children in reading and math, help to build houses, help get children immunized, model parenting skills to teen parents, participate in neighborhood watch programs, plan community gardens, deliver meals, offer disaster relief to victims of natural disasters, and help community organizations operate more efficiently.

To find out more about how to volunteer for Senior Corps programs, go to www.seniorcorps.org and click on the link "I'm ready to serve" in the

Individuals section. You can also contact the Senior Corps by calling 1-800-424-8867 or e-mailing help@joinseniorservice.org.

Volunteers in Parks

If you enjoy hanging out in the national parks, an ideal volunteer opportunity for you is the Volunteers in Parks program (http://www.nps.gov/volunteer/), which was authorized by Congress in 1970. In Fiscal Year 2005, 137,000 volunteers donated 5.2 million hours to national parks at a value of $91.2 million.

Volunteers of all ages give of their time and expertise to help achieve the National Park Service mission. Many seniors help to manage the gift shops or serve as tour guides or teachers.

You can search for volunteer opportunities by either park or state by going to http://www.nps.gov/gettinginvolved/volunteer/opportunities.htm.

Volunteering Internationally

You can mix your volunteering choices with your travel plans. If living outside the U.S. for a period of time would enhance your retirement years, then consider volunteering internationally. In this section, I explore some of the best ways to find international volunteer opportunities.

Earthwatch Institute

Earthwatch (www.earthwatch.org) recruits close to 4,000 volunteers every year to collect field data in the areas of rainforest ecology, wildlife conservation, marine science, archaeology, and more.

Earthwatch's key activities in which volunteers can become involved include

- ✔ Scientists who can work on proposed research projects, analyze recent findings, and research results
- ✔ Teachers who can develop expedition-based curricula and lesson plans
- ✔ Communicators who can help keep Earthwatch members informed about program results and upcoming events

Since 1971, Earthwatch, which is a nonprofit organization, has placed more than 76,000 field researchers in scientific and social research projects around the globe. Forty percent of these volunteers were people over the age of 50, and many of the volunteers return for additional projects once they have completed one. All projects emphasize sustainability. Today, Earthwatch runs about 140 projects in 48 countries.

You can find out more about how to get involved in Earthwatch by going to www.earthwatch.org and clicking on the tab "Get Involved."

Global Citizens Network

Global Citizens Network (www.globalcitizens.org) seeks to create a network of people who are committed to the shared values of peace, justice, tolerance, cross-cultural understanding, and global cooperation, and who want to help preserve indigenous cultures, traditions, and ecologies, and to enhance the quality of life around the world. Fifty percent of Global Citizens's volunteers are older adults.

As a Global Citizens Network volunteer, you will learn from and work with people in other cultures. Each team visits a developing community where local people are involved in grassroots efforts to meet their human and community needs while preserving their culture and traditions.

You will have the opportunity to experience life in another culture by living with local people, eating local foods, and experiencing local hardships and triumphs. Volunteers receive instructions in language, social structure and issues, agriculture, industry, and arts. You could also visit a community that provides insight into specific issues or trends such as environmental protection, women in development, and traditional medicine. Global Citizens Network volunteers assist community people working on locally initiated projects, providing the human resources of mental and physical labor while working under the leadership of community people.

Each volunteer team member receives training materials and participates in an orientation session, generally on the first or second day of the trip. The team spends one to three weeks in the community (depending on the site), and is led by a trained and experienced team leader from Global Citizens Network. A local individual acts as cultural consultant, and when necessary, as translator and language tutor.

Each day as a volunteer, you'll both work and learn. Accommodations do vary, but often the team will live with local host families. At least one meal each day will be communal, with the team and community members eating together.

Global Citizens teams usually consist of six to people. You aren't required to have specific skills and there no upper age restrictions. When you return from volunteering outside the U.S., you can stay involved by working with a Global Citizens Network chapter, participating in advisory committees, or hosting seminars and community outreach events.

You can find out more about what is expected from volunteers and how to volunteer at `http://www.globalcitizens.org/faq.htm`. You can also call 800-644-9292 or e-mail `info@globalcitizens.org`.

Global Volunteers

Volunteers for Global Volunteers (`www.globalvolunteers.org`) work abroad on international service programs or serve on USA volunteer programs. Live and work with local people while working on life-affirming community development projects 1 to 43 weeks. Year-round volunteer teams support 100 host communities on six continents.

This nonprofit international development organization facilitates peace and mutual understanding among people of diverse cultures. You can work on projects in five primary categories:

- ✔ **Teach English language conversation skills:** Volunteers work in China, Ghana, Greece, Hungary, India, Italy, Mexico, Peru, Poland, Romania, and Tanzania, and in the U.S., in Minnesota.

- ✔ **Care for the disabled or orphaned children:** Volunteers work in Ecuador, Greece, India, Peru, Poland, and Romania.

- ✔ **Build and repair homes and community facilities:** Volunteers work in Australia, Costa Rica, Ecuador, Ghana, Greece, Ireland, Jamaica, Peru, and Tanzania, and in the U.S., in Minnesota, Mississippi, Montana, South Dakota, and West Virginia.

- ✔ **Tutoring and advance literacy:** Volunteers work in The Cook Islands, Ghana, Greece, India, Poland, and Tanzania, and in the U.S., in Minnesota, Mississippi, Montana, and West Virginia.

- ✔ **Improve basic healthcare services:** Volunteers work in The Cook Islands, Ecuador, Ghana, Jamaica, Romania, and Tanzania.

A majority of the volunteers are older adults from the U.S. and Canada. Most projects are from one to three weeks. You can find out more information about how to volunteer at `http://www.globalvolunteers.org/1main/volunteer_work.htm`.

Globe Aware

You can work as a volunteer for short-term volunteer programs with Globe Aware (www.globeaware.org). With its programs, Globe Aware seeks to promote cultural awareness and/or promote sustainability.

Globe Aware believes the concept of cultural awareness means to recognize and appreciate the real beauties and real challenges of a culture, but not to change it. The concept of sustainability is to help others stand on their own two feet; to teach skills rather than reliance.

Projects meet these key criteria: safe, culturally interesting, genuinely beneficial to a needy community, and involve significant interaction with the host community. When you volunteer for Globe Aware, you'll also have optional chances for cultural excursions that are designed to highlight local culture in a way the typical tourist can rarely experience. The organization has no political or religious affiliation.

Volunteers are discouraged from trying to change host communities and encouraged to help communities meet the needs that have been identified by members of the host communities as important. You must start your volunteer experience with an open mind and willingness to help in order to enjoy the experience. You'll find that the natural, healthy exchange of ideas and opinions fostered by Globe Aware leads to a mutual understanding of cultures.

Globe Aware's founders have been organizing volunteer missions since 2000. The first programs were run in Peru and Costa Rica, with several in Asia to follow. Locations are chosen based on a huge number of factors, but generally are communities that are safe, genuinely needy with significant cultural differences from the typical North American lifestyle, and willing to accept our involvement. Globe Aware was recognized as a nonprofit organization in 2003.

You can find out more about volunteering through Globe Aware at www.globe aware.org or by calling toll free at 877-588-4562.

Landscope Expeditions

If you think you'd like to travel and volunteer in Australia, you may want to consider Landscope Expeditions (http://www.extension.uwa.edu.au/tours/landscape.shtml), which are nonprofit, self-supported, study and research projects. These expeditions started in 1992, and are a joint project of the Australian government's Department of Conservation and Land Management (CALM) and the University of Western Australia.

Expeditions have been offered through CALM's publication *LANDSCOPE,* which is a quarterly magazine devoted to wildlife, conservation, and environmental issues in Western Australia. They are offered in association with UWA Extension. You can subscribe to *LANDSCOPE* at http://www.calm. wa.gov.au/landscope/index.html. An overseas subscription that includes four issues and a year's access to Australia's national parks is $90 is Australian currency, which was about $68 in U.S. currency at the time this was written, but currency exchange values do fluctuate. You'll find information about current and future projects.

Volunteers get an opportunity to work alongside scientists and promote wider cooperation in addressing conservation and land management challenges in Western Australia. Any member of the general public can be involved subject to fitness. You must be 13 years of age or over to be registered as a CALM volunteer. Seventy-five percent of Landscope volunteers are older adults.

As a volunteer, you'll be given the opportunity to

- ✔ Visit and gain understanding of remote or inaccessible places in Australia
- ✔ Contribute to Australia's knowledge of threatened environments and endangered species
- ✔ Enjoy unique photo opportunities
- ✔ See and handle unusual animals

Landscope Expeditions help to perpetuate cultural and biological diversity. As a volunteer, you'll help to identify and preserve natural and cultural resources. You can find out more about volunteer projects organized by CALM at http:// www.naturebase.net/vacancies/volunteer_programs.html.

LiFeline

If cats are your thing and you'd like to live in Belize for a while, you might want to consider volunteering at LiFeline (http://www.rtec.strayduck. com/index.html), which is a wild cat research and rehabilitation center that offers working vacations and conservation courses at its base in the foothills of the Maya Mountains in Belize.

You'll live and work on a 4,000-acre working ranch that is 4½ miles from the LiFeline centre. The centre is a 60-acre private jungle reserve that is home to a host of wildlife, including toucan, kinkajou, ocelot, puma, deer, paca, agoutis parrots, and hummingbirds.

You will be working with jaguars, pumas, ocelots, margays, and jaguarundis in their natural habitat. The LiFeline centre is on the edge of a National Park, which, with other protected areas, covers over 600 square miles. The centre is a government-approved facility, the first of its kind, concentrating solely on cats.

LiFeline seeks to conserve the wild cat species, not only in their native habitat through LiFeline's scientific field work, but also by advising on wild cat welfare issues and providing a safe haven for cats that would otherwise face a death penalty because of conflict with humans. LiFeline is a registered non-profit organization working in close collaboration with the Belize Conservation and Forestry Department. It is a project of The Ridgeway Trust for Endangered Cats, a UK-based registered wildlife charity.

Some of the centre's cats are awaiting release to the wild. Others are perma-nent residents and the subject of ongoing behavioral research. Most of the cats have found their way to LiFeline after a history of abuse, having been captured from the wild as kittens to be kept as pets. Others are problem cats that have taken to raiding livestock.

If you choose to be a volunteer, you'll be able to take part in many of the centre's areas of work. Each program is individually tailored to a small group of participants. After getting picked up at the airport and taken to the ranch, you'll be greeted by a LiFeline staff member who will advise you on your schedule for the next eight days. Following a short orientation course on your first day, your typical tasks may include radio-tracking a newly released cat, digging out a jaguar pond, helping to maintain cat enclosures, habitat vegetation analysis, setting camera traps, and assisting with behavioral stud-ies. During your free time, you will have the opportunity to swim under a 150-foot waterfall, to visit Belize Zoo, or tour Mayan archaeological sites.

You do pay for this working vacation/volunteer opportunity, but the costs cover airport transfers, accommodations for nine nights, all meals, transfers to and from the site each day, waterfall excursion, laundry service, and all activities at the LiFeline site. Trip costs are $1,790 plus $160 if you want to go to the Belize Zoo and Mayan archaeological sites.

You can book a trip by filling out the booking form at `http://www.rtec.strayduck.com/bookingform.htm` or you can e-mail `pm@li-feline.com` for more information. Because communications can sometimes be difficult, LiFeline recommends you copy e-mails to `lifelinebelize@yahoo.co.uk`.

Orphanage Outreach

Volunteers with Orphanage Outreach (www.orphanage-outreach.org) seek to provide opportunities to orphaned, abandoned, and disadvantaged children in the Dominican Republic. They help to provide the basic necessities and a quality education. Orphanage Outreach, which is a Christian-based interdenominational nonprofit organization, was incorporated in 1995.

Volunteers and donors have worked on its mission since the organization was founded. Nearly 4,000 short-term volunteers have worked with Orphanage Outreach since its founding. Thirty-five percent of the volunteers are older adults.

As a volunteer, you focus both on the orphanage children and the many disadvantaged children of the Monte Cristi community. The volunteer program during the school year is primarily focused on involving high school and college students and teams in teaching English in the local schools. During the summer, Orphanage Outreach focuses on involving church groups to partner with the local Monte Cristi churches.

As a volunteer, your basic logistical needs are taken care of. You don't have to worry about where your next shower, meal, or bus ride will come from. Those basic necessities are taken care of by the organization.

You can find out more about volunteering for Orphanage Outreach by going to http://www.orphanage-outreach.org/volunteer_overview. html or calling 602-375-2900.

Volunteering Virtually

If you want to work only from home, you might consider become a virtual volunteer, for which you can complete most of your work at home or via the Internet. You can find out more about Virtual volunteering at www.service leader.org/new/virtual/index.php.

Virtual volunteering gives nonprofit agencies a way to tap the expertise of people who want to volunteer their time, but can't come to an office. This helps the agencies to expand the benefits they offer by enabling more volunteers to participate and by using volunteers in new areas. Virtual volunteering allows anyone to contribute time and expertise to nonprofit organizations, schools, government offices, and other agencies that utilize volunteer services, from his or her home or office.

Part VI
The Part of Tens

The 5th Wave   By Rich Tennant

"I've been working over 80 hours a week for the past two years preparing for retirement, and it hasn't bothered me OR my wife, what's-her-name."

In this part . . .

The part of tens is a tradition of all Dummies books. In this part, I explore the top ten companies to work for in retirement, ten great volunteering opportunities, and the top ten skills you need to start a business.

Chapter 21

Top Ten Companies to Work for in Retirement

. . . .

In This Chapter

▶ Browsing the best companies

▶ Checking out companies with the top benefits

▶ Seeing who offers alternative work arrangements

. . . .

Some companies not only seek to hire retirees, they also offer an array of benefits that make them stand out as the best companies to work for after retirement. Each year, AARP honors the best companies for retirees.

In this chapter, I give you a sampling of ten of the companies named the best for retirees. You can find out more about these companies, as well as find others that might suit you better, at www.aarp.org/money/careers/employerresourcecenter/bestemployers.

Business Services

Adecco (www.adeccousa.com) provides employment and human resources services through its network of more than 6,000 offices in 71 countries and territories around the world, providing career growth and lifestyle benefits for its temporary employees. Adecco targets placement opportunities for older workers in its Renaissance program, which recruits mature workers for temporary positions.

Cars

Volkswagen of America, Inc. (www.vm.com) actively recruits older workers and provides benefits to attract them, including, one of the most popular, flexible spending accounts for dependent eldercare. One of its key sources for recruiting older workers is the Outplacement Career Transition Company's nationwide resume data base of individuals who have been laid off.

Popular benefits offered by Volkswagen for retirees include annual wellness physicals and health fairs, mentoring by older workers, a benefits newsletter providing guidance on health-wellness, retirement and investment planning, eldercare referrals, and pre-paid legal services. Employees can decide to move to part-time employment to phase into retirement. Others who are close to retirement may apply for a lower-level position to increase work-life balance. Full-time employees are eligible to move to part-time work on a permanent or temporary basis.

Consulting Services

Stanley Consultants (www.stanleyconsultants.com) provides engineering and related services worldwide. For more than 40 years, Stanley Consultants has shown it values its retirees through its mentor program that enables employees to pass on their invaluable knowledge. It regularly holds retirement training workshops that are open to employees 55+ and their spouses.

Health benefits for retirees before the age of 65 and 65+ include individual as well as spousal medical and drug coverage. Also included are vision and dental insurance, as well as individual life insurance or other death benefit coverage. Retirees 65+ also receive retiree and spousal life insurance or other death benefit coverage. New hires are eligible for all of these too.

The company offers its full- and part-time employees various work alternatives including flex time, compressed work schedules, telecommuting, and a formal phased retirement program. Full-time employees are eligible to move to part-time work on a permanent or temporary basis. The company's phased retirement program allows great flexibility in arranging reduced work schedules. Retirees are offered temporary work assignments, consulting or contract work, telecommuting, as well as full- and part-time work.

Education

Massachusetts Institute of Technology (MIT; www.mit.edu), which is a premiere science and technology university located in Cambridge, Massachusetts, encourages lifelong learning among all its employees. Special programs for retirees include Lincoln Laboratory Retiree Associations, MIT Quarter Century Club, MIT Campus Partners, and MIT Senior Focus. Retirees may remain engaged with the Institute through many activities such as special seminars, luncheons and dinners, and planned trips. Since 1998, the William Dickson Tuition Scholarship has awarded eligible retirees with grants up to $1,000 per year for study at accredited institutions.

MIT uses Operation ABLE, a senior placement agency, as well as employee and retiree referrals, to target mature workers. Available health benefits for retirees pre-age 65 and age 65+ include medical and drug coverage for individuals as well as spousal/domestic partners and dependents. Some plans include vision coverage. Other retiree benefits include life insurance, long-term care insurance, and Employee Assistance Programs. Alternative work arrangements include flex time, compressed work schedules, job sharing, and telecommuting. Full-time employees are eligible to move to part-time work on a permanent or temporary basis.

Employees who wish to phase into retirement have the opportunity to reduce schedules in current roles and apply for part-time positions as they become available. The Institute fosters a flexible work environment and has written guidelines to assist managers in accommodating workers' needs. Retirees are offered work arrangements such as temporary work assignments, consulting or contract work, telecommuting, as well as full- and part-time work.

Entertainment

The Anheuser-Busch Adventure Parks (Busch Entertainment Corporation; www.anheuser-busch.com), which runs the popular Busch Gardens amusement parks, actively recruits retirees through its "Legends Ambassadors" team, which is made up of employees aged 55+, who are committed to helping SeaWorld/Busch Gardens provide quality employment and job satisfaction to the 55+ population. The Ambassadors are selected annually to provide leadership, guidance, advice, and help in "learning the ropes" to employees. The company also uses senior placement agencies to target mature workers and retirees for employment.

One of the most popular benefits for older workers is the employee assistance offered to help find eldercare services and advice on nursing homes. In addition to this assistance, the company extends its long-term care policy to the parents and grandparents of employees.

Health benefits for retirees pre-65 and 65+ include individual as well as spouse medical and drug coverage. For the pre-65 age group category, new hires are eligible for all of the retiree benefits upon retirement. They are also eligible for the individual and spousal medical and prescription drug coverage benefits upon retirement.

The company offers alternative work arrangements such as flex time and job sharing to full- and part-time employees. Part-time employees must work eight hours a week to be eligible for the flex-time benefit and 24 hours per week to be eligible for the job-sharing benefit. Full-time employees are eligible to move to part-time work on a permanent or temporary basis. Retirees are offered temporary work assignments, consulting/contract work, as well as part-time work.

Financial Services

Principal Financial Group (www.principal.com), a financial services company, is famous for its "Happy Returns," which helps retirees return to work with the assistance of Manpower Staffing Service. Manpower enables retirees to work in a temporary position at the company while still receiving pension benefits.

The Principal Financial Group uses senior placement agencies to recruit mature workers. Health benefits for retirees pre-65 and 65+ include individual as well as spousal medical and drug coverage, vision, dental and long-term care insurance, as well as individual and spousal life insurance or other death benefit coverage. New hires are eligible for retiree benefits upon retirement.

Alternative work arrangements include flex time, compressed work schedules, job sharing, and telecommuting. Full-time employees are eligible to move to part-time work on a permanent or temporary basis. Although the company does not have a formal phased retirement program, employees are allowed to transition into part-time work with leader approval. The company offers paid time off that is specifically designated for caregiving. Retirees are offered temporary work assignments, consulting or contract work, telecommuting, part-time work, and full-time work.

Healthcare

Mercy Health System (www.mercyhealthsystem.org), a hospital system in Wisconsin, won top honors in 2006 for its Senior Connection, which includes free health insurance and financial counseling for its employees over 50. It also offers a free prescription discount card and sponsors senior activities such as brown bag lunches and trips.

Seniors can work using numerous flexible work options including the Weekender Program (work only on weekends), Traveler Option (work 6- to 13-week assignments), Nursing Float Option (nurses are guaranteed benefits while floating departments), Registry Pool Option (work 48 to 96 hours per month with benefits), 8-10-12 Hour Shift Options, Work at Home Option, and Work-To-Retire Program (work reduced hours — seasonally).

Mercy recruits retirees using e-cards and direct mailings to target mature workers and retirees. They also recruit via personal recommendations, sponsor booths, and attend job and product fairs targeted at the senior population. Retirees are offered the following work arrangements: temporary work assignments, consulting/contract work, telecommuting, and part- and full-time work.

Industrial Equipment

John Deere (www.johndeere.com), known worldwide for its industrial and commercial equipment, actively recruits older workers through senior placement agencies. It offers comprehensive health benefits to any employee working at least one hour per week. Health benefits for retirees pre-65 and 65+ include individual as well as spousal medical and drug coverage, vision, dental, long-term care, Employee Assistance Program services, as well as life insurance or other death benefit coverage. The company offers referral services to assist with child care and elder care.

In addition, the company offers alternative work arrangements such as flex time, compressed work schedules, telecommuting, and a formal phased retirement program to full- and part-time employees (working at least one hour per week). The phased retirement program allows a full-time employee to move to part-time work. Full-time employees are eligible to move to part-time work on a permanent or temporary basis. Retirees are offered the following work arrangements: temporary work assignments, consulting or contract work, telecommuting, as well as part- and full-time work.

Pharmaceuticals

Hoffmann-LaRoche, Inc. (www.rocheusa.com), a major pharmaceutical company, sponsors an Intergenerational Care program which pays grandparents to come to the on-site child care center weekly and play nostalgic games with the children. The company uses senior placement agencies to target mature workers.

Health benefits for both retirees pre-65 and 65+ include individual as well as spousal medical insurance, drug coverage, individual long-term care insurance, EAP services, and individual and spousal life insurance or other death benefit. New hires are eligible for these benefits.

Alternative work arrangements include flex time, compressed work schedules, job sharing, telecommuting, and a formal phased retirement program. Full-time employees are eligible to move to part-time work on a permanent or temporary basis. The phased retirement plan allows the retiree to work for the company through an on-site employment agency or via private contracts which in turn allows the retiree to continue collecting pension benefits while working. The company offers paid time off that is specifically designated for caregiving. Retirees are offered the following work arrangements: temporary work assignments, consulting or contract work, telecommuting, as well as part- and full-time work.

Retailing/Direct Selling

L.L. Bean, Inc. (www.llbean.com), which sells most of its products through its nationally recognized catalog, manages its flexible work schedules via its "Swap Book," which allows employees at any Customer Contact Center to trade, pick up, or give away shifts, or volunteer to stay late, leave early, or swap time with another employee. Its "Attendance Bank" provides a bank of time to be used without disciplinary action for time needed away from work for sickness, accident, or personal reasons.

Health benefits for retirees pre-65 and 65+ include individual as well as spousal medical and drug coverage, as well as individual life insurance or other death benefit coverage. Retiree health benefits are available to new hires upon retirement. In addition, dependent care reimbursement accounts are available to employees with up to $5,000 pre-tax contribution which is subject to income limits.

Alternative work arrangements include flex time, compressed work schedules, job sharing, and telecommuting to full- and part-time employees (working at least 20 hours per week). Full-time employees are eligible to move to part-time work on a permanent or temporary basis.

Retirees can participate in the on-site retiree exercise program, receive 50 percent discounts in the company cafeterias, access company recreational facilities, and receive special retiree hours for the employee store. Retirees can be offered temporary work assignments, consulting or contract work, part-time work, full-time work, and on-call work.

Chapter 22

Top Ten Skills for Running Your Own Business

In This Chapter

▶ Running the business

▶ Growing the business

▶ Managing yourself and others

*R*unning a business requires a great variety of skills, and you probably don't have them all. In this chapter, I pick the top ten skills you need. If you don't have them, or are weak in any of them, be sure to find a partner or top manager who can help fill the gaps.

Administrative Skills

You may be able to afford to hire a good assistant who can organize your office for you, but if you're just starting a business, that's not likely the case. If you haven't already done this in previous jobs, you need to get very good at preparing correspondence with your customers and vendors, invoicing and billing, collecting and tracking customer payments, and all the other tasks that an office manager, secretary, and bookkeeper might do in a large business.

You also need to keep your filing up to date so you know which bills you've paid, which customers have paid you, as well as all the details you'll need to file all the federal, state, and local government reports, including tax returns. Administrative skills are not the glamorous part of owning your own business, but they're certainly critical ones.

Decision Making

All small-business owners will need to make decisions every day, probably numerous times per day. You need to be able to make sound decisions quickly, constantly, and under pressure. You're the boss, so you need to be able to act correctly and independently. There won't be anyone else you can lean on for their opinion. While you can seek advice from employees or business advisors, such as accountants and lawyers, ultimately you're the one that must be able to make the right decisions for your business.

Financial Skills

Unless you're professionally trained as an accountant, you will most likely hire someone to do the financial statements for you, but that person won't take on the daily responsibilities of keeping your business's books. You could hire a bookkeeper when you can afford one to take care of the daily tasks, but you always want to keep on top of those books to avoid potential fraud or theft. As a business owner, you never want to turn your books over to someone else, unless it's a close family member or partner, without maintaining strong controls.

You also need to be good at managing cash flow and making sure you'll have enough money on hand to meet your bills. Vendors will quickly cut you off if they don't get paid, which can shut your business down.

Before you spend any money, you should know how to analyze the benefits of that expense to your business and whether that expense will ultimately add to your ability to make a profit. If you're not sure, take the time to analyze the expense further, and don't rush to make a financial decision until you are certain you know its ramifications for your business.

Industry-Specific Skills

I can't list specific skills here, but I do want to remind you that you should know and be sure you have the specific skills for the industry in which you plan to run your business. For example, if you're planning to buy or start a restaurant, you need to have many different industry-specific skills. You must know how to cook everything on your menu even if you plan to hire a chef. Remember that your chef could get sick or quit abruptly and you'll have to do the cooking to keep the business open.

You must know how to hire and manage servers to be sure your customers are getting the service you expect them to get. You must understand the technical aspects of buying your food for the restaurant, so you get the quality of food you want, when you want it, and at the best price.

For whatever business you're thinking of starting or buying, write down all the specific knowledge and skills you might need and either learn to do them yourself or find a partner who can fill any gaps. Only a partner will put in the time, effort, and dedication that you'll need to get a business off the ground and keep it going.

People Management

Can you work with all different types of people and manage what they do? A business owner must be good at developing working relationships with all kinds of people, including employees, customers, vendors, bankers, and professionals.

You must be good at recognizing an individual's idiosyncrasies and learn to use them to get what you want. Just about every day your business is open you will be faced with a demanding customer or a cranky employee. Frequently, you need to deal with an unreliable vendor. Can you handle the pressure and get even difficult people to work for you and do what you want?

Physical and Emotional Stamina

Running your own business can be very demanding both physically and emotionally. Do you have the stamina to handle the pressure? You will likely face 12-hour days (or more), six or seven days a week, as a business owner. Be sure you are ready to handle that both emotionally and physically.

Problem Solving

You must be a good problem solver. As a business owner, that will be one of your primary jobs. Everyone, including employees, vendors, and customers, will be bringing their problems to you. You need to be able to work with them to develop a solution quickly and move on.

You can't afford to tie yourself down to researching one solution and implementing it, while the rest of your business goes down the toilet. You must be able to either come up with a solution quickly, or know how, and to whom, you can designate responsibility to solve that problem.

If you are running the business all by yourself, you need to carefully manage your time and be sure you don't spend too much time solving one problem while ten others sit there waiting for a solution.

Self-Motivation

Every business owner must be good at self-motivation. You won't have anyone telling you what to do next. You must be good at developing your own to-do list and working through that list to get things done as quickly as possible.

Everything that needs to get done for your business must be done by you, from finding funding and developing your product, to developing a marketing plan and making sales. You will be the only one creating plans and altering those plans as you test various business theories. You need to know when something is working and when it's not, so you can quickly make adjustments and get the business back on track.

You must have a great deal of self-confidence in your abilities and you must know where you want the business to be in the next year or the next five years.

Sales and Marketing

The two most important skills for any business owner are sales and marketing. If you're not good at these two things, don't even try to start a business unless you find a partner who is. You could develop the greatest product or service in the world, but if you don't know how to attract and keep customers, your business will fail.

You must spend time developing your marketing plan, including identifying your target audience and how you will reach them. You must know who your competition is and how you will sell against that competition to convince people that your product or service is the best to buy. If you're opening a retail store, you must come up with a marketing plan that will differentiate your store from other similar stores.

Time Management

As you review all the skills you need, you'll probably think to yourself, "How can I possibly do all that in one day?" Well you can't. Good time management is knowing what you need to do yourself and what you can ask someone else to do for you.

In some cases, you may be able to pass the task on to an employee or ask a vendor's representative to do the task for you. You may decide you need to hire a professional — accountant, lawyer, consultant, or other specialist — to take care of some tasks for you, so you can spend time doing the other things you must do yourself.

If you're running a one-person business, you must put together a to-do list in the morning of all the things that must get done that day; prioritize that list and realize that some things just won't get done because of other problems or emergencies that will come your way. You must be able to multitask and keep a bunch of balls bouncing in the air at all times. As you find a few quiet minutes here and there throughout the day, get something else done on your list.

You also must be good at separating your work life from your home life, even if your business is in your home. You can't spend 100 percent of your time and effort on your business and ignore the needs of your family and friends. Not only will it be bad for you emotionally and physically, it can also destroy your relations with your family and friends, support that you'll need to keep yourself going.

Chapter 23

Ten (Almost) Great Volunteering Experiences to Take Advantage Of

In This Chapter
▶ Matching your skills to needs
▶ Finding the right spot
▶ Helping others

*Y*ou've worked all your life and you're ready to give back to others. In this chapter, I introduce you to ten great volunteering experiences, based on skills or interests you've developed throughout your life or career.

Advocate

If you've enjoyed advocating for various causes all your life, what better cause could you find now than to advocate for things that will most help you and other people in your age group. AARP (http://www.aarp.org/about_aarp/community_service) provides a wide variety of volunteer opportunities from which you can choose. Whether you enjoy political activism, helping those in need, working with children, or advising on monetary and tax matters, you'll find a volunteer opportunity that matches your desire to help.

Here are some of the programs you can volunteer for at AARP:

- **AARP Benefits Outreach Program:** Help older people with low or moderate incomes find public and private benefit programs for which they may be eligible to help pay for prescription drugs, groceries, doctor bills, heating bills, property taxes, and more.

- **AARP Chapters:** Get involved in local volunteer efforts including mentoring activities, food and clothing drives, friendly visits, state advocacy, and much more.

- ✔ **AARP Driver Safety Program:** Teach driver safety and help others qualify for reduced car insurance premiums.

- ✔ **AARP Money Management Program:** Help older or disabled people who have difficulty budgeting, paying bills, and keeping track of their finances, but have no family or friends able to help them out.

- ✔ **NRTA:** AARP's Educator Community: Volunteer with local retired educators' associations to tutor, provide school supplies and books, and help to run food and clothing drives. If you're a retired educator, you can help new teachers and administrators.

- ✔ **AARP Tax-Aide:** Provide free tax preparation services to millions of low- and moderate-income taxpayers, with special attention to those age 60 and older.

This is just a brief sample of what you can do. You can find more details about this and other volunteer opportunities mentioned in this chapter in Chapter 20.

Business Executive

If you're a successful former business executive and you'd like to share your knowledge and skills with small-business owners that need your help, you may find volunteering through SCORE (www.score.org) an excellent venue for passing on your knowledge. You can help a small-business owner develop a business plan, improve his marketing, increase his cash flow, or any number of other critical aspects needed to keep a business alive.

If you prefer to work from home by computer or phone, you can become part of SCORE's virtual advice network, where business people are helped online, primarily through e-mail requests.

Caregiver

If you enjoy aiding others one-on-one, you may want to become a mentor, coach, or companion through Senior Corps (www.seniorcorps.org), which connects people who are age 55 and over with people and organizations that need them most.

Here are three programs run by Senior Corps that you may like:

- ✔ **Foster Grandparent Program:** Help children and young people with exceptional needs who are among the most vulnerable children in the United States.

- ✔ **Senior Companion Program:** Help other seniors who have difficulty with the simplest tasks of day-to-day living, including shopping and light chores, interacting with doctors, or visiting them and keeping them company.

- ✔ **RSVP Program:** You can do a variety of things depending on what you enjoy, such as tutoring children in reading and math, helping to build houses, helping get children immunized, modeling parenting skills to teen parents, participating in neighborhood watch programs, planning community gardens, delivering meals, offering disaster relief to victims of natural disasters, and helping community organizations operate more efficiently.

Environmentalist

If you want to work on projects to protect the environment, consider joining the Environmental Alliance for Senior Involvement (EASI; www.easi.org).

Three programs that might interest you include

- ✔ **Local Senior Environment Corps Initiatives:** Focus on energy conservation, environmental education, environmental health, environmental monitoring, environmental restoration, and pollution prevention.

- ✔ **Senior Leadership Corps:** Provide leadership for local Bureau of Land Management volunteer projects and help manage various projects involving hundreds of volunteers.

- ✔ **Volunteer Senior Ranger Corps:** Help meet priority needs at eight of America's national parks through partnerships between the Park Service and its surrounding communities.

Home-Based

If you're stuck at home, but still want to volunteer your skills and experience, consider volunteering using your computer through Virtual Volunteering (www.serviceleader.org/new/virtual/index.php). You can contribute time and expertise to nonprofit organizations, schools, government offices, and other agencies that utilize volunteer services, from your home or office.

Internationalist

If you prefer to travel and work on a global scale, you may want to volunteer through one of two international agencies: Global Citizens or Global Volunteers.

Both agencies give you opportunities to live and work with the people you are helping, but with slightly different focuses.

Global Citizens Network (www.globalcitizens.org) seeks to create a network of people who are committed to the shared values of peace, justice, tolerance, cross-cultural understanding, and global cooperation, and who want to help preserve indigenous cultures, traditions, and ecologies, and to enhance the quality of life around the world. You will have the opportunity to experience life in another culture by living with local people, eating local foods, and experiencing local hardships and triumphs.

Global Volunteers (www.globalvolunteers.org) seeks to facilitate peace and mutual understanding among people of diverse cultures. You can work on projects in six primary categories: teaching English, caring for disabled or orphaned children, building and repairing homes and community facilities, tutoring, and improving.

Medical Professional

If you're a trained medical professional, you might enjoy helping people with limited resources find good medical care through Volunteers in Medicine (VIM) Clinic (http://www.vimi.org/volunteer.shtml). VIM clinics serve in areas where healthcare is most needed. The amount of time you decide to give to a clinic is up to you. VIM does recommend that retired physicians volunteer at least a half-day per week.

Park Enthusiast

If you enjoy visiting the national parks, you may enjoy volunteering for them even more. You can volunteer for the parks through the Volunteers in Parks program. Volunteers of all ages give their time and expertise to help achieve the National Park Service mission. Many seniors help to manage the gift shops or serve as tour guides or teachers. You can search for volunteer opportunities by either park or state by going to http://www.nps.gov/gettinginvolved/volunteer/opportunities.htm.

Index

• *Numerics* •

401(k)
  automatic enrollment, 113
  borrowing against, 22
  catch-up contribution, 118
  company match, 62
  contribution limits, 118
  loss of retirement nest egg, 21–22
  portability, 63
  rolling into IRA, 117
  rolling out of, 62, 63
  vesting, 62–63
  withdrawal rules, 66–67
403(b)
  description, 21
  portability, 63
  vesting, 62–63
  withdrawal rules, 66–67

• *A* •

AARP
  Best Employers for Workers Over 50
    Program, 203, 206, 226
  health insurance plan, 132–133
  Web site, 176, 185, 226, 307–310, 337
AARP volunteer opportunities
  Benefits Outreach Program, 307–308, 337
  chapter activities, 308
  Day of Service, 307
  Driver Safety Program, 308
  Money Management Program, 308–309
  Tax-Aide, 309
Abandoned Plan Program (U.S.
    Department of Labor), 22
Abruzzi Mountain Art Workshop, 298
accident costs, for older workers, 200
acinet.org (Web site), 39, 48
active phase, retirement, 78
activity log, 244
ADAP (AIDS Drug Assistance Programs), 154

adaptability, advertising your, 196–197
ADEA (Age Discrimination in Employment
    Act), 110–111, 186, 230–231
Adecco (business services company), 325
administrative skills, 331
Adult Residential Colleges Association
    (ARCA), 296
advisorteam.com (Web site), 47
ACEP (Annual Coordinated Election
    Period), Medicare, 156
Age Discrimination in Employment Act
    (ADEA), 110–111, 186, 230–231
AIDS Drug Assistance Programs (ADAP), 154
allocation. *See* asset allocation
A.M. Best (Web site), 161
American Self-Help Clearinghouse, 54
American Society of Appraisers
    (Web site), 272
America's Career InfoNet, 39
AmeriSpan (Web site), 298
Andrus, Dr. Ethel Percy
    (AARP founder), 307
Anheuser-Busch (entertainment company),
    205, 327
Annual Coordinated Election Period
    (ACEP), Medicare, 156
annuity
  pension, 23
  withdrawal options, 84–85
ARCA (Adult Residential Colleges
    Association), 296
Archaeology Abroad, 296–297
Artistic (creators) worker type, 35
Artist-in-Residence program, 292
artworkshopitaly.com (Web site), 298
assessment
  interest inventories, 46–47
  last job, 32
  personality tests, 47–48
  skills, 48
  talents, 11, 31–32
  values inventories, 45–46
  worker type, uncovering your, 33–37

asset allocation
  aggressive, 20
  conservative, 20
  financial resources, 74
  home in, 74
  investment goal, 72
  investment mix, 74
  mistakes, 71–72
  risk tolerance, 73–74
  time horizon, 72–73
  withdrawal strategies, 87–90
assignment, Medicare, 147
association health plans, 130, 132
attorney, finding for consulting business,
    251–252
autonomy, 38

● *B* ●

Ballpark E$timate (Internet worksheet), 25
bank teller, 212
banks, loan from, 268
benefit factor, 59
benefit periods, 143, 144
Benefits Outreach Program, AARP,
    307–308, 337
Bernstein, Dick and Carolyn (business
    owners), 262–263, 265
Best Employers for Workers Over 50
    Program, AARP, 203, 206, 226
BetterInvesting, 301–302
BLAZE (writing classes), 295
BNI (Business Network International), 247
body language, during interview, 182
bonds, asset allocation, 71–75, 88
bone mass measurements, Medicare
    coverage for, 145
book club, forming, 300–301
Book-Club-Resources.com (Web site),
    300, 301
Boston University's Center for Work and
    Family Balance (Web site), 226
brain drain, 15
breathing, relaxation techniques, 181
Brecher, Howie and Sandy (business
    owners), 270, 273
Brevard Public Schools, 205
britarch.ac.uk, 296
brokers, business, 272

budgeting
  for active phase of retirement, 78
  for debt obligations, 81
  for dependent phase of retirement, 78
  developing a budget, 82
  for donations, 81
  for entertainment, 80
  for food, 27, 79
  funding your business, 267–268
  for health care, 27–28
  healthcare costs, 79
  for hobbies, 80
  for home maintenance, 27
  insurance costs, 80
  leisure and travel costs, 80
  for passive phase of retirement, 78
  for pets and plants, 80
  Phase 1 of retirement, 25
  Phase 2 of retirement, 26
  Phase 3 of retirement, 26
  Phase 4 of retirement, 26
  for professional services, 81
  for reading materials, 80
  for savings and investments, 81
  for shelter, 79
  for taxes, 81
  transportation costs, 79
  for travel and entertainment, 26–27
Bureau of Labor Statistics, U.S., 195
business, buying existing. *See also*
    franchise
  description, 269–270
  finding a business for sale, 271–272
  funding purchase, 278
  Letter of Intent to Purchase, 278
  type of business, 270–271
  value assessment, 272–277
business format franchise, 279–281
Business Network International (BNI), 247
business plan
  consulting business, 257
  developing, 265–266
business skills
  administrative, 331
  decision making, 332
  financial, 332
  industry-specific, 332–333
  people management, 333
  problem solving, 333–334

sales and marketing, 334
self-motivation, 334
stamina, physical and emotional, 333
time management, 335
business, starting your own. *See also*
    franchise
    business plan, 265–266
    competition, 266–267
    consulting business, 257–259
    to fund retirement, 263–265
    funding, 267–269
    goals for, 261
    location, choosing, 269
    marketing, 266–267
    resources for, 264–265
    to supplement retirement, 262–263
business value, assessing
    accounting reports, 275–276
    balance sheets, 273
    building ownership, 274
    description, 272–273
    employee benefits, 276
    lease agreements, 274
    legal problems, 275
    loan documents, 273
    neighbors and customers, talking with, 277
    non-compete agreement, 272–273
    patents, trademarks, copyrights, and
        licenses, 274–275
    profit and loss statements, 273
    tax returns, 273
    title and title insurance, 276
    toxic waste, 277
    trade secrets, 276–277
    unemployment claims, 276
    worker's compensation, 276
    zoning, 277
business-planning course, online, 266
buying an existing business. *See* business,
    buying existing

• C •

calculator
    life-expectancy, 88, 122
    Social Security, 94, 121
Campbell, David (career expert), 46
Campbell Interest and Skill Survey, 46
car dealerships, 281

cardiovascular screenings, Medicare
    coverage for, 145
Career Builder (Web site), 168, 174, 211
career change, 172
career counselor
    activities of, 44
    choosing, 43–44
    credentials, 43
    finding, 42
    need for, 41–42
    questions to ask, 43–44
    scope, 44
Career InfoNet Skills Profiler, 48
Career Key (test), 46
Career-Intelligence.com
    Myers-Briggs Type Indicator, 47
    skills assessment, 48
    Strong Interest Inventory, 47
    values assessment, 46
caregiving, impact on life, 43
Carolyn-E's Dry Cleaning Valet Service,
    262–263
Cash Pensions (Web site), 24
cash-balance plan
    annuity, 61
    description, 24, 61
    lump-sum cash payout, 62
catch-up contributions
    Health Savings Account, 129
    IRA, 118
Centers for Medicare and Medicaid
    Services, 143
Centre for Lifelong Learning (Web site), 295
certified financial planner, 117
Certified Public Accountant (CPA), 275
Chamber of Commerce, 247, 250, 252
Charness, Neil (researcher), 196
checklist, interview, 190–191
choosetosave.org (Web site), 25
churches
    job listings at, 177
    support groups, 178
Citizen Advocate, AARP, 310
classified advertisements, 176
cliff vesting, 63
clubs, 29
COBRA (Consolidated Omnibus Budget
    Reconciliation Act), 28, 130–132, 154
Coca-Cola (beverage company), 22

co-insurance
  definition, 137
  Medicare, 142, 143–144
  PPO, 127
COLA (cost of living adjustment), 122
college, faculty position at, 213–214
colorectal cancer screening, Medicare
    coverage for, 145
communication, in job-share team, 223
community service, 29
company stock, 21
confidentiality agreement, 240
Consolidated Omnibus Budget
    Reconciliation Act (COBRA),
    28, 130–132, 154
consulting
  activity log, 244
  advantages of, 234
  attorney, help from, 251–252
  business plan, 257
  confidentiality, 240–243
  contacts, finding, 247–248
  contracts, negotiating, 240–244
  contracts, writing, 251–255
  cost of benefits, 238
  deadlines, 243–244, 253–254
  fee structure, researching, 237–238
  fees, setting, 238–239
  follow-ups, 258–259
  for former company, 233–244
  in former industry, 245–259
  how consultants work, 235–236
  interview questions concerning, 189–190
  invoices, 244
  known entity, becoming, 248–249
  listening skills, 236–237
  networking, 247–249, 257–258
  niche, finding yours, 247
  non-compete agreement, 241–242, 249
  pricing your services, 250–251, 254
  proposals, writing, 256
  roles of, 246
  skills required, 234–235, 246–247
  talking to employer about, 237
contacts
  building, 49
  for consulting work, 247–248
  professional, 28

contracts
  assigning work, 254–255
  attorney help with, 251–252
  confidentiality, 240–243
  consulting, 251–255
  deadlines, 243–244, 253–254
  designing, 255
  disputes, handling, 255
  expenses, 243
  negotiating, 240–244
  parts of, 252–255
  payment terms, 254
  price, setting, 254
  project summary, 252–253
  promises, 253
  reverse mortgage, 74
  termination, 254
  writing, 251–255
Conventional (organizers) worker type, 36
co-payment
  description, 136
  HMO, 126
  Medicare Advantage Plans, 150
  Medicare Part D, 152, 157
  paying with HSA account, 129
  PPO, 127
copyrights, 274
cost basis, asset, 83
cost of living adjustment (COLA), 122
costs
  franchise start-up, 286
  healthcare, 27–28, 79, 199
  hospitalization, 143–144
  insurance, 80
  leisure and travel, 80
  myths, coping with, 198–200
  prescription drugs, 156–157
  retirement benefits, 199
  transportation, 79
counselor. See career counselor
CPA (Certified Public Accountant), 275
creative talents, 40
creativity, capitalizing on your, 197
Creators worker type, 35
credit unions, loan from, 268
creditable plan, 153
customer greeters, 212–213

• D •

Day of Service, AARP, 307
deadlines, 243–244
debt obligation, budgeting for, 81
decision making, skills in, 332
deductibles
  description, 136
  High Deductible Health Plan (HDHP), 128
  Medicare, 142, 143–144
  Medicare Part D, 152, 156
  paying with HSA account, 129
deep breathing (relaxation technique), 181
defined-benefit plan. *See also* pension
  benefit factor, 59
  calculating payout, 59–60
  cash-balance plan, 10, 24, 61–62
  description, 23, 58
  disappearance of plans, 58–59
  payout method, 60–61
  Pension Benefit Guaranty Corporation,
    payment by, 23
  termination of, 24
  years of service, 59
defined-contribution plan. *See also specific*
    plan types
  description, 58, 62
  401(k), 21–22, 62–63, 66–67, 118
  403(b), 21, 62–63, 66–67
  Keoghs, 64
  profit-sharing plans, 64, 68
  SEP-IRA, 64, 67
  SIMPLE IRA, 21, 64, 67
  vesting, 62–63
Delphi Forums, 53
Department of Labor
  Abandoned Plan Program, 22
  state, 242
  Web site, 214, 215
dependent phase, retirement, 78
dexterity, declines in manual, 196
diabetes screenings, Medicare
    coverage for, 146
direction, working with, 38
discrimination, age, 186
discussion forum support groups, 53
Disney (entertainment company), 135
distribution factor, 69–70
dividends, 83

divorce, protecting retirement savings in, 22
Doers (worker type), 37
donations, budgeting for, 81
donut hole
  in coverage, 152, 157
  Medicare Part D, 10
Driver Safety Program, AARP, 308, 338
drug formulary, 155
drugs, coverage for. *See* Medicare Part D

• E •

early retirement
  delaying benefits, 119–124
  phased retirement program, 116, 230–231
  saving during, 117–119
  Social Security benefit reduction, 94–100
  taking pensions while still working,
    115–117
  withdrawing employer retirement
    savings, 117
Earthwatch Institute, 315–316
EASI (Environmental Alliance for Senior
    Involvement), 310–311, 339
e-cards, 204
EEOC (Equal Employment Opportunity
    Commission), 185, 186
Elderhostel, 290–291
Eli Lily and Company (pharmaceutical
    company), 50
Employee Retention (Web site), 226
Employee Retirement Income Security Act
    of 1974 (ERISA), 23, 110–111, 230–231
employee stock purchase plan, withdrawal
    options from, 86
employer, returning to work for former,
    109–112
employer savings plans. *See also specific*
    plan types
  cash-balance plan, 10, 24, 61–62
  description, 62
  401(k), 21–22, 62–63, 66–67, 118
  403(b), 21, 62–63, 66–67
  Keoghs, 64
  profit-sharing plans, 64, 68
  SEP-IRA, 64, 67
  SIMPLE IRA, 21, 64, 67
  types, 21
  vesting, 62–63

Employment Network for Retired
 Government Experts (ENRGE), 51, 174
employment, searching for. *See* job search
end-stage renal disease, 154
English instructor, 213
Enterprising (persuaders) worker type, 36
entertainment, budgeting for, 26–27, 80
Entrepreneur Source (Web site), 283
Environmental Alliance for Senior
 Involvement (EASI), 310–311, 339
Equal Employment Opportunity
 Commission (EEOC), 185, 186
ERISA (Employee Retirement Income
 Security Act of 1974), 23, 110–111,
 230–231
Excel For Dummies (Wiley
 Publishing, Inc.), 83
Excel 2007 For Dummies (Wiley
 Publishing, Inc.), 83
Excel (Microsoft), 83
exclusions, health coverage, 134–135
Executive Service Corps Affiliate Network
 (ESCAN), 306–307
expenses, of consulting, 243
Experience Works, 207–208
Extra Help program, Medicare, 157

• F •

Families and Work Institute (Web site), 226
Federal Employees Health Benefits
 (FEHB), 154
Federal Trade Commission (FTC), 280, 283
Fee-for-Service Plan, 128
fees, consulting, 237–239, 250–251
finances
 budgeting, 25–28
 failure to save, 24
 investing money in retirement accounts,
  71–76
 loss of nest egg, 20–22
 resources, 74
financial advisor, 90
Financial Planning Association (Web site),
 90, 117
financial skills, 332
floral assistant, 214
food, budgeting for, 27, 79
formularies, drug, 155

Forward Group, 51
401(k)
 automatic enrollment, 113
 borrowing against, 22
 catch-up contribution, 118
 company match, 62
 contribution limits, 118
 loss of retirement nest egg, 21–22
 portability, 63
 rolling into IRA, 117
 rolling out of, 62, 63
 vesting, 62–63
 withdrawal rules, 66–67
403(b)
 description, 21
 portability, 63
 vesting, 62–63
 withdrawal rules, 66–67
France, learning opportunities in, 297
franchise
 area development, 284
 business format, 279–281
 contract, 283–285
 finding opportunities, 282–283
 funding requirements, 285–286
 master, 285
 multiple single-unit, 284
 product distribution, 279, 281
 single-unit, 284
 start-up costs, 286
Franchising For Dummies (Seid and
 Thomas), 283
FranChoice (Web site), 283
FranNet (Web site), 283
FTC (Federal Trade Commission), 280, 283

• G •

Geezer Theater, 292
General Accountability Office (GAO), 151
Georgia Southwestern State University, 290
glaucoma screening, Medicare coverage
 for, 146
Global Citizens Network, 316–317, 339– 340
Global Volunteers, 317, 340
Globe Aware, 318
goal, investment, 72
Google (Web site), 175
government expert, jobs for, 210

graded vesting, 63
greeters, customer, 212–213
grocery stores, job listings at, 177
group health plans
  COBRA coverage, 130–132
  conversion to individual plan, 130
  Fee-for-Service Plan, 128
  HDHP (High Deductible Health Plan),
    128–129
  Health Maintenance Organization (HMO),
    126–127, 140
  Health Savings Account (HSA), 129
  Indemnity Plan, 128
  loss of, 129–133
  Point-of-Service (POS) plan, 127
  Preferred Provider Organization
    (PPO), 127
  professional or social association,
    coverage through, 130, 132
  types, 126–129

• H •

HDHP (High Deductible Health Plan),
  128–129
health centers, support groups, 178
health insurance. *See also* Medicare
  AARP, 132–133
  age limitation to coverage, 138
  agents, 136
  association health plans, 130, 132
  COBRA, 28, 130–132
  co-insurance, 127, 137, 142, 143–144
  converting group to individual, 130
  co-payments, 126, 129, 136, 150, 152
  cost of individual, 14
  costs, uncovering hidden, 136–137
  deductibles, 129, 136
  denial of coverage, 14
  discount plans compared, 131
  ending of coverage, 137–138
  exclusions, coverage, 134–135
  failure to pay premium, 137
  failure to qualify for, 27
  fee-for-service plan, 128
  finding coverage, 135–136
  fraudulent misstatements, 138
  Health Maintenance Organization (HMO),
    126–127
  Health Savings Account (HSA), 129

High Deductible Health Plan (HDHP),
  128–129
Indemnity Plan, 128
individual health plans, 133
long-term healthcare, 160–161
loss of group plan, 129–133
Medicare Advantage, 148–150, 158
Medigap, 158–159
paying with IRA funds, 68
Point-of-Service Plan (POS), 127
pre-existing conditions, 14, 130, 134
Preferred Provider Organizations
  (PPO), 127
as reason for return to work, 14, 135
rider, 130
state guaranteed issue health insurance
  pools, 133
state influence on plan rules, 131
supplemental coverage, 150
underwriter, 136
health insurance commissioner, state, 133
Health Maintenance Organization (HMO)
  common characteristics, 126–127
  description, 126
  Medicare, 148
  Point-of-Service (POS) plan, 127
Health Savings Account (HSA), 129
healthcare costs
  budgeting for, 27–28, 79
  of older workers, 199
HealthInsurance.org (Web site), 131
Helpers (worker type), 37
Herman Group (management-consulting
  firm), 226
High Deductible Health Plan (HDHP),
  128–129
HMO. *See* Health Maintenance
  Organization (HMO)
hobbies
  for Artistic worker type, 35
  budgeting for, 80
  for Conventional worker type, 36
  for Enterprising worker type, 36
  for Investigative worker type, 36–37
  networking, 29
  for Realistic worker type, 37
  for Social worker type, 37
Hoffmann-LaRoche, Inc. (pharmaceutical
  company), 329

home care aides, 214
Home Depot, 195
home equity, housing bubble, 10
home healthcare, Medicare coverage for, 142
home maintenance, budgeting for, 27
hospice, Medicare coverage for, 143
hospitalization, calculating cost of care, 143–144
HotGigs (Web site), 238
housing bubble, 10
HSA (Health Savings Account), 129

• *I* •

icons, used in text, 5
IFA (International Franchise Association), 282–283
illness, withdrawal rules exceptions, 68
income, calculating, 90–91
Indemnity Plan, 128
independent contractor
 IRS determination of status as, 227–229
 proposing arrangement, 226–229
 retired employees as, 111
 taxes paid as, 227
Individual Retirement Account (IRA)
 catch-up contributions, 118
 contribution limits, 118
 rolling employer retirement savings into, 117
 rolling pension funds into, 116
 rollovers, 86–87
 Roth, 65–66, 86–87, 92
 Saver's Credit for contributions, 118–119
 SEP, 64, 67
 SIMPLE, 21, 64, 67
 taxation issues, 92
 traditional non-tax-deductible, 65, 67
 traditional tax-deductible, 64, 67
 withdrawal options, 86–87
 withdrawal rules, 67–71
information interviews, 49
Institut Méditerranéen de Langues, 297
insurance commissioner, state health, 133
insurance costs, budgeting for, 80
insurance, medical. *See* health insurance
interest, asset, 83
interest inventories, 46–47
Internal Revenue Service. *See* IRS

International Franchise Association (IFA), 282–283
Internet. *See also* Web site
 business-planning course, online, 266
 for job searching, 174–176
 online job networks for seniors, 50–51
 resumé, posting online, 175
interview
 body language, 182
 checklist, 190–191
 enthusiasm, 183
 guidelines, 182–183
 information, 49
 longevity questions, 184–185, 188–190
 mental preparation for, 179–181
 practicing for, 183
 qualification questions, 186–187
 questions, answering basic, 183–185
 questions, asking, 182
 questions, dealing with tough, 185–190
 stress reduction prior to, 180–181
 testing your knowledge of the company, 184
inventory
 interests, 46–47
 personality, 47–48
 skills, 40
 values, 45–46
Investigative (thinkers) worker type, 36
investing
 asset allocation, 71, 72–74
 changing strategies with age, 75–76
 goal, 72
 mistakes to avoid, 71
 money in retirement accounts, 71–76
 time horizon, 72–73
investment club, 301–302
invoices, 244
IRA. *See* Individual Retirement Account (IRA)
IRS
 Form 1040, 119
 independent contractor status, 227–229
 mandatory distributions for retirement savings, 69–70
 Publication 590, 70
 Web site, 70, 104
 W-4V form, 105
Italy, learning opportunities in, 298

• J •

Jancyn (Web site), 215
job, previous
   assessment of, 32
   returning to work, effect on pensions,
      109–112
job search
   boards, job-posting, 177
   cost myths, coping with, 198–200
   electronic contact, 14
   Internet, 174–176
   interviews, 179–191
   networking, 15, 173–174
   newspapers, 176
   part-time work, 201–206
   productivity myths, dealing with, 195–197
   resumé, 165–173
   support groups, 177–178
   telecommuting, 15, 210–212
   temporary agencies, 206–210
   training myths, overcoming, 193–195
job sharing
   creating winning team, 223
   finding right fit, 222–223
   mentor/subordinate arrangement, 222
   popularity of, 221
   structuring, 222–223
John Deere (equipment manufacturer), 329
joint allowance, 60
joint and survivor (annuity withdrawal
      option), 85
Jung, Carl (psychologist), 47

• K •

Katepoo, Pat (Web site developer), 226
Keirsey Temperament Sorter, 47–48
Kelly Services (temporary agency), 206
Keogh Plan, 21, 64
Kiplinger's Finance (Web site), 85

• L •

Labor, Department of
   Abandoned Plan Program, 22
   state, 242
   Web site, 214, 215

Landscope Expeditions, 318–319
language, learning new, 298
lawsuits, 275
learning, emphasizing ability in, 194
learning opportunities
   abroad, 295–298
   Adult Residential Colleges Association
      (ARCA), 296
   Archaeology Abroad, 296–297
   book club, 300–301
   Elderhostel, 290–291
   in France, 297
   investment club, 301–302
   in Italy, 298
   language, 298
   learning group, starting, 300–302
   Osher Lifelong Learning Institute
      (OLLI), 292
   SeniorNet, 293–294
   teaching, 298–300
   travel group, 301
   TraveLearn, 291–292
   University of Strathclyde's Senior Studies
      Institute, 295
leisure costs, budgeting for, 80
Letter of Intent to Purchase, 278
licenses, 275
life-expectancy calculator, 88, 122
LiFeline, 319–320
Lifetime reserve days, 144
Lifework Transitions.com, 48
Lion's Club, 49
listening, developing skills of, 236–237
L.L. Bean, Inc. (retailer), 330
longevity
   interview questions, dealing with,
      184–185, 188–190
   leveraging your, 194–195
long-term care insurance
   finding and purchasing a policy, 160–161
   need for, 160
lump-sum cash payout, 62

• M •

MAGI (modified adjusted growth
      income), 65
Maid Brigade (franchise), 286

mammogram screening, Medicare
coverage for, 146
Manpower Services (temporary agency),
206, 238
MA-PD (Medicare Advantage Prescription
Drug Plan), 152
Maritz (Web site), 215
market value, asset, 83
marketing
business, 266–267
skills, 334
Markle Foundation, 294
Massachusetts Institute of Technology
(MIT), 326–327
May Department Stores Company, 242
MBTI (Myers-Briggs Type Indicator), 47
Medicaid, 145, 150, 160
medical insurance. *See* health insurance
Medical Savings Accounts (MSAs), 149
Medicare. *See also specific Medicare Parts*
Advantage Plans, 148–150
benefits periods, 143, 144
buying into, 162
card, 140
co-pays, 129
deadlines, missing, 140
delaying coverage, 141
eligibility, 14, 161–162
enrollment, 140
financial crisis in, 140
lifetime reserve days, 144
long-term healthcare, 160–161
Medigap supplemental policy, 158–159
penalties, 141
Personal Medical Plan Finder, 149
phased retirement arrangement, 231
retiring before eligibility, 25, 27
self-employment, 227
starting coverage, 140
terminology, 139
Web site, 149, 156
Medicare Advantage Plans, 158
Medicare Advantage Prescription Drug
Plan (MA-PD), 152
Medicare Part A
coinsurance, 142, 143–144
costs of inpatient care, 143–144
coverage, 142–143

deductible, 142, 143–144
working around rules for, 144–145
Medicare Part B
cost of premiums, 141, 147
coverage, 145–146
deadline, missing, 141
excluded services, 146
Medicare Part C
choosing best plan, 150
Health Maintenance Organizations
(HMOs), 148
Medical Savings Accounts (MSAs), 149
Preferred Provider Organizations
(PPOs), 148
Private Fee-for-Service Plans (PFFs), 149
Provider-Sponsored Organizations
(PSOs), 149
state variations, 149
Medicare Part D
basics of, 151–152
changing plans, 156
confusion concerning, 150–151
co-pay, 152, 157
costs, 141, 156–157
coverage from other sources, 153–154
creditable plans, 153
deadlines, missing, 141
deductible, 152, 156
donut hole, 10
Extra Help program, 157
finding the right plan, 156
formularies, 155
obtaining coverage, 152
paying for, 157–158
prior authorization requirement, 155
quantity limitations, 155
step therapy requirement, 155
Medicare Rights Center (Web site), 140
Medigap, 158–159
mentalhelp.net (Web site), 54
Mercy Health System (hospital system),
203–206, 328
Microsoft Excel, 83
Microsoft Outlook, 50
Military Health Care System, drug
coverage, 154
MIT (Massachusetts Institute of
Technology), 326–327

modified adjusted growth income (MAGI), 65

Money Management Program, AARP, 308–309, 338

moneycentral.msn.com (Web site), 78

mortgage
  budgeting for, 27
  reverse, 74

MSAs (Medical Savings Accounts), 149

MSN Life Expectancy Calculator (Web site), 122

MSN Money (Web site), 78, 88

Mutual Funds For Dummies (Wiley Publishing, Inc.), 75

Myers-Briggs Type Indicator (MBTI), 47

mystery shopper, 215

Mystery Shopping Providers Association (Web site), 215

myths, about older workers
  cost, 198–200
  productivity, 195–197
  training, 193–195

• *N* •

National Association for Alternative Certification, 298

National Association for Home Care and Hospice (NAHC), 214

National Association of Investors Corporation (NAIC), 301

National Board of Certified Counselors (NBCC), 42, 43

National Career Development Association, 43

National Council on Aging, 209

National Park Service, 314, 340

national wage index, 97

NCCCR (North Carolina Center for Creative Retirement), 312

NCS Pearson, 46

negotiation, of contracts, 240–244

nest egg
  loss of retirement, 20–22
  safe withdrawals from, 24

networks and networking
  building, 49
  consulting, 247–249, 257–258
  finding a new network of retired professionals, 29
  goals for, 49
  importance of, 48–49
  for job search, 15, 173–174
  keeping your professional network alive, 28–29
  online for seniors, 50–51
  organizing, 50
  planning, 49
  Seniors4Hire, 51
  YourEncore.com, 50–51

newsletter support groups, 52

newspapers
  businesses for sale in, 271
  employment section of, 176

NHC Group of Massachusetts (job bank), 51

non-compete agreement, 241–242, 249, 272–273

nondisclosure agreement, 241–242

nonprofit organization, volunteering at, 29

North Carolina Center for Creative Retirement (NCCCR), 312

Northwestern College Career Development Center, 46

NRTA *With Our Youth!* Program, 309, 338

nursing home
  long-term care insurance, 160–161
  Medicare Part A coverage, 142, 144

• *O* •

OASIS, 313

older workers, overcoming myths concerning, 193–200

online job networks for seniors, 50–51

Organizers (worker type), 36

Orphanage Outreach, 321

Osher Lifelong Learning Institute (OLLI), 292

Outlook (Microsoft), 50

• P •

PACE (Program of All Inclusive Care for the Elderly), drug coverage, 154
Pap test, Medicare coverage for, 146
part-time work
  bank teller, 212
  benefits, 202, 203, 204–205
  best employers, finding, 203–206
  college/university faculty member, 213–214
  convincing boss, 225–226
  customer greeters, 212–213
  English instructor, 213
  floral assistant, 214
  home care aides, 214
  independent contractor arrangement, 226–229
  job sharing, 221–224
  Mercy Health System, 203–206
  mystery shopping, 215
  needs and wants, consideration of, 202–203
  online resources, 226
  phased retirement arrangement, 230–231
  popular jobs, 212–216
  proposing change to, 221
  restructuring plan for, 220–221
  schedule flexibility, 202, 203
  seeking, 201–206
  switching to, 219–221
  teacher's assistant, 215–216
  telecommuting, 224
  temporary worker, 229–230
  time off, 202
  tour guide, 216
  training, 203, 207
passive phase, retirement, 78
patents, 274
payout
  annuity, 61
  calculating pension, 59–60
  joint allowance, 60
  lump-sum cash payout, 62
  method, choosing, 61
  pop-up joint allowance, 60
  single life allowance, 60
PBGC (Pension Benefit Guaranty Corporation), 23

PCP (primary care provider), 126, 127
PDP (Prescription Drug Plan), 152
Peace Corps, 313–314
pelvic examination, Medicare coverage for, 146
pension
  ADEA (Age Discrimination in Employment Act), 110–111
  benefit factor, 59
  calculating payout, 59–60
  cash-balance plan, 10, 61–62
  disappearance of plans, 58–59
  ERISA (Employee Retirement Income Security Act of 1974), 110–111
  fate of your funds, 113–114
  freezing plans, 112–113
  legislation, 109–114
  lump-sum distributions, 113–114, 116
  payout method, 60–61
  Pension Benefit Guaranty Corporation (PBGC), 23
  Pension Protection Act of 2006, 110–112, 230
  public service workers, 114
  reduced payments, 23–24
  taking while still working for your company, 115–117
  taxation, 91
  termination of, 24
  withdrawal options, 85
  years of service, 59
Pension Benefit Guaranty Corporation (PBGC), 23
Pension Protection Act of 2006, 110–112, 230
people management, 333
Personal Health Insurance Plan, AARP, 132–133
Personal Medical Plan Finder, 149
personal savings, to fund business, 268
personality tests, 47–48
personality types, 47
Persuaders (worker type), 36
pets, budgeting for, 80
PFFS (Private Fee-for-Service Plans), Medicare, 149
phased retirement, 116, 230–231
physical examination, Medicare coverage for, 146

plants, budgeting for, 80
Point-of-Service (POS) plan, 127
pop-up joint allowance, 60
portfolio balance, 75
pre-existing conditions, 14, 130, 132, 134
Preferred Provider Organization (PPO), 127, 148
Prescription Drug Plan (PDP), 152
prescription drugs, Medicare Part D coverage for
  basics of, 151–152
  changing plans, 156
  confusion concerning, 150–151
  co-pay, 152, 157
  costs, 141, 156–157
  coverage from other sources, 153–154
  creditable plans, 153
  deadlines, missing, 141
  deductible, 152, 156
  donut hole, 10
  Extra Help program, 157
  finding the right plan, 156
  formularies, 155
  obtaining coverage, 152
  paying for, 157–158
  prior authorization requirement, 155
  quantity limitations, 155
  step therapy requirement, 155
price, setting consulting, 250–251
primary care provider (PCP), 126, 127
Principal Financial Group (financial services company), 205, 328
Prioritizing Work Values Exercise, 46
Private Fee-for-Service Plans (PFFS), Medicare, 149
problem solving, 333–334
Proctor & Gamble (manufacturer), 50
product distribution franchise, 281
productivity myths, dealing with, 195–197
professional services, budgeting for, 81
profit-sharing plan
  description, 64
  withdrawal rules, 68
Program of All Inclusive Care for the Elderly (PACE), drug coverage, 154
property taxes, 27
proposals, writing, 256

prostate cancer screening, Medicare coverage for, 146
Provider-Sponsored Organizations (PSOs), Medicare, 149
public safety workers, 114
public service workers, 114

• *Q* •

qualifications, interview questions on, 186–187
Qualified Domestic Order, 22

• *R* •

reading materials, budgeting for, 80
Realistic (doers) worker type, 37
references, on resumé, 166
referral, to specialist, 126, 127
reimbursement, health insurance, 126–127
relaxation techniques, 180–181
Remember icon, 5
restaurant, franchise, 280
resumé
  accomplishments, emphasizing, 170
  active words, use of, 170
  dating yourself, avoiding, 170
  employer's needs, matching, 168–169
  formatting, 171–172
  highlighting skills, 169
  job history, 166
  keywords, 166, 168, 169
  length, 166, 171
  posting online, 175
  preparing as Word document, 167–168
  references, 166
  rules for, 166
  sample, 173
  screening of, 165–166
  snail mail, avoiding, 167
  spelling and grammar, 171
  submission method, 167
  tailoring, 167
  writing tips, 171
RET (Retirement Earnings Test), 96–97, 99–100
retainer fee, 251

retirement account. *See also specific plans*
  defined-benefit plans, 58–59
  defined-contribution plans, 58, 62–68
  employer savings plans, 62–64
  finding lost, 22
  investing money in, 71–76
  IRAs, 64–66
  pensions, 58–62
  taxation of savings, 92
  tracking holdings, 83–84
  withdrawal rules, 66–71
retirement benefits costs, of older
    workers, 199
Retirement Earnings Test (RET), 96–97,
    99–100
Retirement Living Information Center
    (Web site), 81
returning to work, reasons for, 10–11
reverse mortgage, 74
Reverse Mortgages For Dummies (Wiley
    Publishing, Inc.), 74
rider, 130
risk tolerance, 73
Rizzuto, Dr. Tracey (researcher), 196
Road Scholar, 291
rollovers, 86–87
Roth IRA
  description, 65–66
  rollovers, 86–87
  taxation issues, 92
  withdrawal rules, 68
Russell, Martha (career counselor), 43

• S •

salary, 198
San Francisco State University, 292
Saver's Credit, 118–119
Savings Incentive Match Plan for
    Employees (SIMPLE)
  description, 21, 64
  withdrawal rules, 67
savings, lack of, 24
SBA (Small Business Administration),
    263–264, 268, 273–278
SBDCs (Small Business Development
    Centers), 264
SCORE (Service Corps of Retired
    Executives), 264, 304–305, 338

SCSEP (Senior Community Service
    Employment Program), 208
Seid, Michael *(Franchising For
    Dummies)*, 283
Self-Directed Search (assessment), 48
self-employment. *See also* business, buying
    existing; business, starting your own;
    franchise
  independent contractor arrangement,
    226–229
  Social Security benefits, effect on, 101–102
self-motivation, 334
senior centers
  job listings at, 177
  support groups, 178
Senior Community Service Employment
    Program (SCSEP), 208
Senior Corps, 314–315, 338–339
Senior Employment Resources, 209
Senior Job Bank (Web site), 51, 174, 209
SeniorNet, 293–294
Seniors4Hire (Web site), 51, 174, 209
SEP (Simplified Employee Pension), 21
SEP-IRA, withdrawal rules, 67
Service Corps of Retired Executives
    (SCORE), 264, 304–305, 338
Service Intelligence (Web site), 215
serviceleader.org (Web site), 321
sharing a job
  creating winning team, 223
  finding right fit, 222–223
  mentor/subordinate arrangement, 222
  popularity of, 221
  structuring, 222–223
shelter costs, budgeting for, 79
SIMPLE (Savings Incentive Match Plan for
    Employees)
  description, 21, 64
  withdrawal rules, 67
Simplified Employee Pension (SEP), 21, 64
single life allowance, 60
single life (annuity withdrawal option), 85
skilled-nursing facility. *See* nursing home
skills. *See also* skills, business
  applying skill set, 39–40
  for Artistic worker type, 35
  assessments, 48
  consulting, required for, 234–235, 246–247
  for Conventional worker type, 36

for Enterprising worker type, 36
inventory, 40
for Investigative worker type, 36–37
for Realistic worker type, 37
researching skill set, 39
for Social worker type, 37
transfer of, 187
skills, business
administrative, 331
decision making, 332
financial, 332
industry-specific, 332–333
people management, 333
problem solving, 333–334
sales and marketing, 334
self-motivation, 334
stamina, physical and emotional, 333
time management, 335
Small Business Administration (SBA),
263–264, 268, 273, 278
Small Business Development Centers
(SBDCs), 264
Small Business Notes (Web site), 306
small-business incubators, 305–306
Smart Money.com (Web site), 87
snowbirds, 195
Social (helpers) worker type, 37
Social Security
at age 62, 95, 122
at age 66, 123
at age 70, 123
benefit calculation, 13, 120, 121
benefit taxation, 102–107
calculators, 94, 121
collecting and working, 96–102
cost of living adjustment (COLA), 122
delaying benefits, 13, 119–124
earnings threshold, 97
full retirement age, 94
increased benefits from return to work,
100–101
national wage index, 97
reduction in benefits, 13
Retirement Earnings Test (RET), 96–97,
99–100
self-employment, effect of, 101–102, 227

starting collection of benefits, best time
for, 122–123
tax issues, 13, 102–107
Web site, 94
Sologig (Web site), 211
Soul Survival (assessment), 46
space, redefining, 43
SSA-1099 form, 103
stamina, physical and emotional, 333
Standard & Poor's (Web site), 161
Stanley Consultants, 326
starting a business. *See* business, starting
your own
State Department (Web site), 297
state guaranteed issue health insurance
pools, 133
State Pharmacy Assistance Program
(SPAP), 153
statehealthfacts.org (Web site), 153
step therapy, 155
stocks
asset allocation, 71–75, 88
employee stock purchase plan, 86
loss of nest eggs, 20–21
strengths, determining, 31–32
stress-reduction techniques
deep breathing, 181
thought blocking, 181
visualization, 180
Strong Interest Inventory, 47
supervision
need for direction, 38
working autonomously, 38
supplemental coverage, 150
suppliers, business, 271
support group
benefits of joining, 52
choosing best type, 54
discussion forum, 53
finding near you, 54
job searching, 177–178
meeting, 53
newsletter, 52
synagogues
job listings at, 177
support groups, 178

• T •

talents
  assessing, 11, 31–32
  creative, 40
  strengths and weaknesses, 31–32
tax credit, 118–119
Tax-Aide, AARP, 309, 338
taxes
  budgeting for, 81
  estimated, 105
  filing status, 102–103
  paying estimated, 91
  of pension payout, 91
  property, 27
  rates, 104–105
  of retirement savings, 92
  on Social Security benefits, 102–107
  SSA-1099 form, 103
teacher's assistant, 215–216
teaching, 30, 298–300
teams, working in, 39
Technical Stuff icon, 5
telecommuting
  description, 211
  finding a job, 211–212
  office space, 224
  personal traits needed for, 224
  popularity of, 210
  proposing to boss, 224
telework center, 211
temporary agencies
  Experience Works, 207–208
  for government experts, 210
  Kelly Services, 206
  Manpower Services, 206, 238
  online resources, 208–209
  for scientists and engineers, 210
temporary worker, going back to work as,
    229–230
term certain (annuity withdrawal
    option), 85
tests
  interests, 46–47
  personality, 47–48
  values, 45–46
Thinkers (worker type), 36–37
Thomas, Dave *(Franchising For
    Dummies)*, 283

thought blocking (relaxation
    technique), 181
time horizon, investment, 72–73
time management, 335
Tip icon, 5
title and title insurance, 276
tour guide, 216
toxic waste, 277
trade associations, 271
trade secrets, 276–277
trademarks, 267, 274–275
training myths, overcoming, 193–195
Transitions Abroad (Web site), 213
transportation costs, budgeting for, 79
travel costs, budgeting for, 26–27, 80
travel group, 301
TraveLearn, 291
TRICARE, drug coverage, 154
True Stories icon, 5

• U •

underwriter, health insurance, 136
unemployment claims, 276
unemployment, withdrawal rules
    exceptions, 68
Uniform Franchise Offering Circular
    (UFOC), 283
United HealthCare Insurance Company, 132
university, faculty position at, 213–214
University of London, 296
University of Minnesota
  Prioritizing Work Values Exercise, 46
  Value Questionnaire, 45
University of Phoenix, 214
University of Strathclyde's Senior Studies
    Institute, 295
U.S. Bureau of Labor Statistics, 195
U.S. Department Labor, Abandoned Plan
    Program, 22
U.S. News and World Report (Web site), 46
U.S. State Department (Web site), 297

• V •

vaccinations, Medicare coverage for, 146
value inventories, 45–46
Value Questionnaire, 45

venture capital firms, 269
vesting, 62–63
Veterans Affairs (VA), drug coverage, 154
Victoria's Secret (lingerie store), 242
VIM (Volunteers in Medicine), 305, 340
visualization (relaxation technique), 180
Volkswagen of America, Inc. (car manufacturer), 325–326
volunteering
  AARP, 307–310, 337–338
  in business world, 304–306
  in community, 306–315
  Earthwatch Institute, 315–316
  Environmental Alliance for Senior Involvement (EASI), 310–311, 339
  Executive Service Corps Affiliate Network (ESCAN), 306–307
  Experience Corps, 311
  Generations United, 311
  Global Citizens Network, 316–317, 339–340
  Global Volunteers, 317, 339–340
  Globe Aware, 318
  internationally, 315–321
  Landscape Expeditions, 318–319
  LiFeline, 319–320
  networking, 29
  North Carolina Center for Creative Retirement (NCCCR), 312
  OASIS, 313
  Orphanage Outreach, 321
  Peace Corps, 313–314
  SCORE, 304–305, 338
  Senior Corps, 314–315, 338–339
  skills to offer, 303–304
  small-business incubators, 305–306
  virtually, 321, 339
  Volunteers in Medicine, 305, 340
  Volunteers in Parks, 315, 340

• W •

Wal-Mart (retailer), 212–213
Warning! icon, 5
WBCs (Women's Business Centers), 265
weaknesses, determining, 31–32
Web site
  AARP, 176, 185, 226, 307–310, 337
  acinet.org, 39, 48
  Adecco, 325

Adult Residential Colleges Association (ARCA), 296
advisorteam.com, 47
alternative teacher certification, 299
A.M. Best, 161
American Self-Help Clearinghouse, 54
American Society of Appraisers, 272
America's Career InfoNet, 39
AmeriSpan, 298
Anheuser-Busch, 327
artworkshopitaly.com, 298
Ballpark E$timate, 25
BetterInvesting, 301, 302
Book-Club-Resources.com, 300, 301
Boston University's Center for Work and Family Balance, 226
britarc.ac.uk, 296
Business Network International (BNI), 247
Campbell Interest and Skill Survey, 46
Career Builder, 168, 174, 211
Career Key, 46
Career-Intelligence, 46, 47, 48
Cash Pensions, 24
Centre for Lifelong Learning, 295
choosetosave.org, 25
company, 175–176
Delphi Forums, 53
Department of Labor, 214, 215
Earthwatch Institute, 315, 316
Elderhostel, 290
Employee Retention, 226
Employment Network for Retired Government Experts (ENRGE), 51, 174, 210
Entrepreneur Source, 283
Environmental Alliance for Senior Involvement (EASI), 311, 339
Executive Service Corps Affiliate Network (ESCAN), 306–307
Experience Corps, 311
Experience Works, 207
Families and Work Institute, 226
Federal Trade Commission (FTC), 280
Financial Planning Association, 90, 117
FranChoice, 283
FranNet, 283
Generations United (GU), 311
Global Citizens Network, 316, 317, 340
Global Volunteers, 317, 340

Web site *(continued)*
Globe Aware, 318
Google, 175
HealthInsurance.org, 131
Hoffmann-LaRoche, Inc., 329
HotGigs, 238
Institut Méditerranéen de Langues, 297
International Franchise Association (IFA), 282
IRS, 70, 104
Jancyn, 215
job-listing sites, 174–175
John Deere, 329
Keirsey Temperament Sorter, 47
Kiplinger's Finance, 85
Landscope Expeditions, 318, 319
LiFeline, 319, 320
lifeworktransitions.com, 48
L.L. Bean, Inc., 330
Maritz, 215
Massachusetts Institute of Technology, 326
Medicare, 149, 156
Medicare Rights Center, 140
mentalhelp.net, 54
Mercy Health System, 328
moneycentral.msn.com, 78
MSN Life Expectancy Calculator, 122
MSN Money, 78, 88
Mystery Shopping Providers Association, 215
National Association for Home Care and Hospice (NAHC), 214
National Board of Certified Counselors (NBCC), 42
National Council on Aging, 209
North Carolina Center for Creative Retirement (NCCCR), 312
Northwestern College Career Development Center, 46
OASIS, 313
Orphanage Outreach, 321
Osher Lifelong Learning Institute (OLLI), 292
Peace Corps, 313, 314
Pension Benefit Guaranty Corporation (PBGC), 23
Principal Financial Group, 328
Prioritizing Work Values Exercise, 46
Retirement Living Information Center, 81
Road Scholar, 291
SCORE, 264, 304–305, 338
Self-Directed Search, 47
Senior Corps, 314, 338
Senior Employment Resources, 209
Senior Job Bank, 51, 174, 209
SeniorNet, 293–294
Seniors4Hire, 51, 174, 209
Service Intelligence, 215
serviceleader.org, 321
Small Business Administration (SBA), 263, 264, 268, 278
Small Business Notes, 306
Smart Money.com, 87
Social Security, 94
Social Security benefits calculator, 121
Sologig, 211
Standard & Poor's, 161
Stanley Consultants, 326
statehealthfacts.org, 153
Transitions Abroad, 213
TraveLearn, 291
U.S. News and World Report, 46
U.S. State Department, 297
Value Questionnaire, 45
Volkswagen of America, Inc., 325
Volunteers in Medicine, 305, 340
Volunteers in Parks, 314, 340
Women's Business Centers (WBCs), 265
Work Options, 226
workingafterretirement.info, 45
Yahoo! Finance, 80
YourEncore.com, 50–51, 174, 210
W-4V form, 105

Wiley Publishing, Inc.
  Excel 2007 For Dummies, 83
  Excel For Dummies, 83
  Mutual Funds For Dummies, 75
  Reverse Mortgages For Dummies, 74
With Our Youth! Program (NRTA), 309, 338
withdrawal strategies
  from annuities, 84–85
  asset allocation, 87–90
  employee stock purchase plan, 86
  IRAs, 86–87
  pension, 85
  planning, 82–87
  safety, 87–90
withdrawals, from retirement accounts
  amount to withdraw, 68–71
  exceptions for illness and
    unemployment, 68
  mandatory distributions, table of, 69–70
  rules for, 66–71
Women's Business Centers (WBCs), 265
Work Options (Web site), 226
Work Related Values Assessment, 46
worker type
  Artistic (creators), 35
  Conventional (organizers), 36
  Enterprising (persuaders), 36

Investigate (thinkers), 36–37
Realistic (doers), 37
Social (helpers), 37
workers' compensation, 276
working style
  autonomously, 38
  needing direction, 38
  team, 39
working type
  determining, 33–34
  understanding, 35
  worksheet, 33–34
workingafterretirement.info (Web site),
  20, 45

• Y •

Yahoo! Finance (Web site), 80
years of service, 59
YourEncore.com, 50–51, 174, 210

• Z •

Zavala, Jay (online network founder), 51
zoning, 277

BUSINESS, CAREERS & PERSONAL FINANCE

Fundraising FOR DUMMIES
0-7645-9847-3

Investing FOR DUMMIES
0-7645-2431-3

Also available:

- Business Plans Kit For Dummies
  0-7645-9794-9
- Economics For Dummies
  0-7645-5726-2
- Grant Writing For Dummies
  0-7645-8416-2
- Home Buying For Dummies
  0-7645-5331-3
- Managing For Dummies
  0-7645-1771-6
- Marketing For Dummies
  0-7645-5600-2

- Personal Finance For Dummies
  0-7645-2590-5*
- Resumes For Dummies
  0-7645-5471-9
- Selling For Dummies
  0-7645-5363-1
- Six Sigma For Dummies
  0-7645-6798-5
- Small Business Kit For Dummies
  0-7645-5984-2
- Starting an eBay Business For Dummies
  0-7645-6924-4
- Your Dream Career For Dummies
  0-7645-9795-7

HOME & BUSINESS COMPUTER BASICS

Laptops FOR DUMMIES
0-470-05432-8

Windows Vista FOR DUMMIES
0-471-75421-8

Also available:

- Cleaning Windows Vista For Dummies
  0-471-78293-9
- Excel 2007 For Dummies
  0-470-03737-7
- Mac OS X Tiger For Dummies
  0-7645-7675-5
- MacBook For Dummies
  0-470-04859-X
- Macs For Dummies
  0-470-04849-2
- Office 2007 For Dummies
  0-470-00923-3

- Outlook 2007 For Dummies
  0-470-03830-6
- PCs For Dummies
  0-7645-8958-X
- Salesforce.com For Dummies
  0-470-04893-X
- Upgrading & Fixing Laptops For Dummies
  0-7645-8959-8
- Word 2007 For Dummies
  0-470-03658-3
- Quicken 2007 For Dummies
  0-470-04600-7

FOOD, HOME, GARDEN, HOBBIES, MUSIC & PETS

Chess FOR DUMMIES
0-7645-8404-9

Guitar FOR DUMMIES
0-7645-9904-6

Also available:

- Candy Making For Dummies
  0-7645-9734-5
- Card Games For Dummies
  0-7645-9910-0
- Crocheting For Dummies
  0-7645-4151-X
- Dog Training For Dummies
  0-7645-8418-9
- Healthy Carb Cookbook For Dummies
  0-7645-8476-6
- Home Maintenance For Dummies
  0-7645-5215-5

- Horses For Dummies
  0-7645-9797-3
- Jewelry Making & Beading For Dummies
  0-7645-2571-9
- Orchids For Dummies
  0-7645-6759-4
- Puppies For Dummies
  0-7645-5255-4
- Rock Guitar For Dummies
  0-7645-5356-9
- Sewing For Dummies
  0-7645-6847-7
- Singing For Dummies
  0-7645-2475-5

INTERNET & DIGITAL MEDIA

eBay FOR DUMMIES
0-470-04529-9

iPod & iTunes FOR DUMMIES
0-470-04894-8

Also available:

- Blogging For Dummies
  0-471-77084-1
- Digital Photography For Dummies
  0-7645-9802-3
- Digital Photography All-in-One Desk Reference For Dummies
  0-470-03743-X
- Digital SLR Cameras and Photography For Dummies
  0-7645-9803-1
- eBay Business All-in-One Desk Reference For Dummies
  0-7645-8438-3
- HDTV For Dummies
  0-470-09673-X

- Home Entertainment PCs For Dummies
  0-470-05523-5
- MySpace For Dummies
  0-470-09529-6
- Search Engine Optimization For Dummies
  0-471-97998-8
- Skype For Dummies
  0-470-04891-3
- The Internet For Dummies
  0-7645-8996-2
- Wiring Your Digital Home For Dummies
  0-471-91830-X

* Separate Canadian edition also available
† Separate U.K. edition also available

Available wherever books are sold. For more information or to order direct: U.S. customers visit www.dummies.com or call 1-877-762-2974.
U.K. customers visit www.wileyeurope.com or call 0800 243407. Canadian customers visit www.wiley.ca or call 1-800-567-4797.

WILEY

SPORTS, FITNESS, PARENTING, RELIGION & SPIRITUALITY

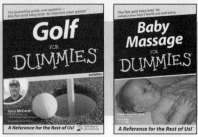

0-471-76871-5   0-7645-7841-3

Also available:
- Catholicism For Dummies
  0-7645-5391-7
- Exercise Balls For Dummies
  0-7645-5623-1
- Fitness For Dummies
  0-7645-7851-0
- Football For Dummies
  0-7645-3936-1
- Judaism For Dummies
  0-7645-5299-6
- Potty Training For Dummies
  0-7645-5417-4
- Buddhism For Dummies
  0-7645-5359-3

- Pregnancy For Dummies
  0-7645-4483-7 †
- Ten Minute Tone-Ups For Dummies
  0-7645-7207-5
- NASCAR For Dummies
  0-7645-7681-X
- Religion For Dummies
  0-7645-5264-3
- Soccer For Dummies
  0-7645-5229-5
- Women in the Bible For Dummies
  0-7645-8475-8

TRAVEL

0-7645-7749-2   0-7645-6945-7

Also available:
- Alaska For Dummies
  0-7645-7746-8
- Cruise Vacations For Dummies
  0-7645-6941-4
- England For Dummies
  0-7645-4276-1
- Europe For Dummies
  0-7645-7529-5
- Germany For Dummies
  0-7645-7823-5
- Hawaii For Dummies
  0-7645-7402-7

- Italy For Dummies
  0-7645-7386-1
- Las Vegas For Dummies
  0-7645-7382-9
- London For Dummies
  0-7645-4277-X
- Paris For Dummies
  0-7645-7630-5
- RV Vacations For Dummies
  0-7645-4442-X
- Walt Disney World & Orlando
  For Dummies
  0-7645-9660-8

GRAPHICS, DESIGN & WEB DEVELOPMENT

0-7645-8815-X   0-7645-9571-7

Also available:
- 3D Game Animation For Dummies
  0-7645-8789-7
- AutoCAD 2006 For Dummies
  0-7645-8925-3
- Building a Web Site For Dummies
  0-7645-7144-3
- Creating Web Pages For Dummies
  0-470-08030-2
- Creating Web Pages All-in-One Desk
  Reference For Dummies
  0-7645-4345-8
- Dreamweaver 8 For Dummies
  0-7645-9649-7

- InDesign CS2 For Dummies
  0-7645-9572-5
- Macromedia Flash 8 For Dummies
  0-7645-9691-8
- Photoshop CS2 and Digital
  Photography For Dummies
  0-7645-9580-6
- Photoshop Elements 4 For Dummies
  0-471-77483-9
- Syndicating Web Sites with RSS Feeds
  For Dummies
  0-7645-8848-6
- Yahoo! SiteBuilder For Dummies
  0-7645-9800-7

NETWORKING, SECURITY, PROGRAMMING & DATABASES

0-7645-7728-X   0-471-74940-0

Also available:
- Access 2007 For Dummies
  0-470-04612-0
- ASP.NET 2 For Dummies
  0-7645-7907-X
- C# 2005 For Dummies
  0-7645-9704-3
- Hacking For Dummies
  0-470-05235-X
- Hacking Wireless Networks
  For Dummies
  0-7645-9730-2
- Java For Dummies
  0-470-08716-1

- Microsoft SQL Server 2005 For Dummies
  0-7645-7755-7
- Networking All-in-One Desk Reference
  For Dummies
  0-7645-9939-9
- Preventing Identity Theft For Dummies
  0-7645-7336-5
- Telecom For Dummies
  0-471-77085-X
- Visual Studio 2005 All-in-One Desk
  Reference For Dummies
  0-7645-9775-2
- XML For Dummies
  0-7645-8845-1